W9-BUE-799

FIFTH EDITION

Focus on
Grammar 3

Marjorie Fuchs
Margaret Bonner
Miriam Westheimer

Focus on Grammar 3: An Integrated Skills Approach, Fifth Edition

Copyright © 2017, 2012, 2006, 2000 by Pearson Education, Inc.
All rights reserved.

No part of this publication may be reproduced, stored in a retrieval system, or transmitted in any form or by any means, electronic, mechanical, photocopying, recording, or otherwise, without the prior permission of the publisher.

Pearson Education, 221 River Street, Hoboken, NJ 07030

Staff credits: The people who made up the *Focus on Grammar 3, Fifth Edition* team, representing content creation, design, manufacturing, marketing, multimedia, project management, publishing, rights management, and testing, are Pietro Alongi, Rhea Banker, Elizabeth Barker, Stephanie Bullard, Jennifer Castro, Tracey Cataldo, Aerin Csigay, Mindy DePalma, Dave Dickey, Warren Fischbach, Pam Fishman, Nancy Flaggman, Lester Holmes, Gosia Jaros-White, Leslie Johnson, Barry Katzen, Amy McCormick, Julie Molnar, Brian Panker, Stuart Radcliffe, Jennifer Raspiller, Lindsay Richman, Robert Ruvo, Alexandra Suarez, Paula Van Ells, and Joseph Vella.

Text design and layout: Don Williams
Composition: Page Designs International
Project supervision: Bernard Seal
Contributing editors: Françoise Leffler and Bernard Seal

Cover image: Andy Roberts / Getty Images

Library of Congress Cataloging-in-Publication Data

A catalog record for the print edition is available from the Library of Congress.

Printed in the United States of America

ISBN 10: 0-13-458329-9
ISBN 13: 978-0-13-458329-7

23 2022

Contents

Contents (continued)

KD 12.05 2022 1635

WELCOME TO
FOCUS ON GRAMMAR
FIFTH EDITION

BUILDING ON THE SUCCESS of previous editions, *Focus on Grammar* continues to provide an integrated-skills approach to engage students and help them understand, practice, and use English grammar. Centered on thematic instruction, *Focus on Grammar* combines comprehensive grammar coverage with abundant practice, critical thinking skills, and ongoing assessment, helping students accomplish their goals of communicating confidently, accurately, and fluently in everyday situations.

New in the Fifth Edition

New and Updated Content
Focus on Grammar continues to offer engaging and motivating content that appeals to learners from various cultural backgrounds. Many readings and activities have been replaced or updated to include topics that are of high interest to today's learners.

Updated Charts and Redesigned Notes
Clear, corpus-informed grammar presentations reflect real and natural language usage and allow students to grasp the most important aspects of the grammar. Clear signposting draws attention to common usage, the difference between written and spoken registers, and common errors.

Additional Communicative Activities
The new edition of *Focus on Grammar* has been expanded with additional communicative activities that encourage collaboration and the application of the target grammar in a variety of settings.

Expanded Writing Practice
Each unit in *Focus on Grammar* now ends with a structured "From Grammar to Writing" section. Supported by pre-writing and editing tasks, students engage in activities that allow them to apply the target grammar in writing.

New Assessment Program
The new edition of *Focus on Grammar* features a variety of new assessment tools, including course diagnostic tests, formative and summative assessments, and a flexible gradebook. The assessments are closely aligned with unit learning outcomes to inform instruction and measure student progress.

Revised MyEnglishLab
The updated MyEnglishLab offers students engaging practice and video grammar presentations anywhere, anytime. Immediate feedback and remediation tasks offer additional opportunities for successful mastery of content and help promote accuracy. Instructors receive instant access to digital content and diagnostic tools that allow them to customize the learning environment to meet the needs of their students.

The *Focus on Grammar* Approach

At the heart of the *Focus on Grammar* series is its unique and successful four-step approach that lets learners move from comprehension to communication within a clear and consistent structure. The books provide an abundance of scaffolded exercises to bridge the gap between identifying grammatical structures and using them with confidence and accuracy. The integration of the four skills allows students to learn grammar holistically, which in turn prepares them to understand and use English more effectively.

STEP 1: Grammar in Context integrates grammar and vocabulary in natural contexts such as articles, stories, dialogues, and blog posts. Students engage with the unit reading and theme and get exposure to grammar as it is used in real life.

STEP 2: Grammar Presentation presents the structures in clear and accessible grammar charts and notes with multiple examples of form and meaning. Corpus-informed explanations and examples reflect natural usage of the target forms, differentiate between written and conversational registers whenever appropriate, and highlight common errors to help students avoid typical pitfalls in both speaking and writing.

STEP 3: Focused Practice provides numerous and varied contextualized exercises for both the form and meaning of the new structures. Controlled practice ensures students' understanding of the target grammar and leads to mastery of form, meaning, and use.

STEP 4: Communication Practice provides practice with the structures in listening exercises as well as in communicative, open-ended speaking activities. These engaging activities provide ample opportunities for personalization and build students' confidence in using English. Students also develop their critical thinking skills through problem-solving activities and discussions.

Each unit now culminates with the **From Grammar to Writing** section. Students learn about common errors in writing and how to recognize them in their own work. Engaging and motivating writing activities encourage students to apply grammar in writing through structured tasks from pre-writing to editing.

Recycling

Underpinning the scope and sequence of the *Focus on Grammar* series is practice that allows students to use target structures and vocabulary many times, in different contexts. New grammar and vocabulary are recycled throughout the book. Students have maximum exposure, leading them to become confident in using the language in speech and in writing.

Assessment

Extensive testing informs instruction and allows teachers and students to measure progress.

- **Unit Reviews** at the end of every unit assess students' understanding of the grammar and allow students to monitor their own progress.

- **Diagnostic Tests** provide teachers with a valid and reliable means to determine how well students know the material they are going to study and to target instruction based on students' needs.

- **Unit Review Tests, Mid- and End-of-Term Review Tests, and Final Exams** measure students' ability to demonstrate mastery of skills taught in the course.

- The **Placement Test** is designed to help teachers place students into one of the five levels of the *Focus on Grammar* course.

The Importance of Context

A key element of *Focus on Grammar* is presenting important grammatical structures in context. The contexts selected are most relevant to the grammatical forms being introduced. Contextualized grammar practice also plays a key role in improving fluent use of grammar in communicative contexts. It helps learners to develop consistent and correct usage of target structures during all productive practice.

The Role of Corpus

The most important goal of *Focus on Grammar* has always been to present grammar structures using natural language. To that end, *Focus on Grammar* has incorporated the findings of corpus linguistics,* while never losing sight of what is pedagogically sound and useful. By taking this approach, *Focus on Grammar* ensures that:

- the language presented reflects real, natural usage

- themes and topics provide a good fit with the grammar point and elicit the target grammar naturally

- findings of the corpus research are reflected in the syllabus, readings, charts, grammar notes, and practice activities

- examples illustrate differences between spoken and written registers, and formal and informal language

- students are exposed to common errors in usage and learn how to recognize and avoid errors in their own speech and writing

Focus on Grammar Efficacy

The fifth edition of *Focus on Grammar* reflects an important efficacy initiative for Pearson courses—to be able to demonstrate that all teaching materials have a positive impact on student learning. To support this, *Focus on Grammar* has been updated and aligned to the **Global Scale of English** and the **Common European Framework** (CEFR) to provide granular insight into the objectives of the course, the progression of learning, and the expected outcomes a learner will be able to demonstrate upon successful completion.

To learn more about the Global Scale of English, visit www.English.com.

Components

Student Books with Essential Online Resources include access codes to the course audio, video, and self-assessment.

Student Books with MyEnglishLab offer a blended approach with integration of print and online content.

Workbooks contain additional contextualized practice in print format.

Digital Teacher's Resources include printable teaching notes, GSE mapping documents, answer keys, audio scripts, and downloadable tests. Access to the digital copy of the student books allows teachers to project the pages for whole-class instruction.

***FOG Go* app** allows users to access the student book audio on their mobile devices.

---

* A principal resource has been Douglas Biber et al, *Longman Grammar of Spoken and Written English*, Harlow: Pearson Education Ltd., 1999.

The *Focus on Grammar* Unit

Focus on Grammar introduces grammar structures in the context of unified themes. All units follow a four-step approach, taking learners from grammar in context to communicative practice. Thematic units add a layer to learning so that by the end of the unit students will be able to discuss the content using the grammar points they have just studied.

STEP 1 GRAMMAR IN CONTEXT

Before You Read activities create interest and elicit students' knowledge about the topic.

Vocabulary exercises help students improve their command of English.

Engaging, high-interest **readings** in a variety of genres present the target structures in natural and realistic contexts. As students read, they encounter the form, meaning, and use of the grammar.

Comprehension and **Discussion** activities focus on the meaning of the text and draw students' attention to the target structures.

NEW!

Grammar Charts present the structures in a clear, easy-to-read format.

NEW!

The newly designed **Grammar Notes** highlight the main point of each note, making navigation and review easier. Simple corpus-informed **explanations** and **examples** ensure students' understanding.

STEP 2   GRAMMAR PRESENTATION

PRESENT PROGRESSIVE

Affirmative Statements

Subject	Be	Base Form of Verb + -ing	
I	am		
You	are		
He She It	is	traveling	now.
We You They	are		

Negative Statements

Subject	Be	Not	Base Form of Verb + -ing	
I	am			
He	is	not	traveling	now.
We	are			

Yes/No Questions

Be	Subject	Base Form of Verb + -ing	
Is	he	traveling	now?

Short Answers

Yes,	he	is.
No,		isn't.

Wh- Questions

Wh- Word	Be	Subject	Base Form of Verb + -ing	
Where	are	you	traveling	now?

SIMPLE PRESENT

Affirmative Statements

Subject		Verb
I		travel.
You		
He She It	often	travels.
We You They		travel.

Negative Statements

Subject	Do	Not	Base Form of Verb	
I	do			
He	does	not	travel	often.
We	do			

Yes/No Questions

Do	Subject	Base Form of Verb	
Does	he	travel	often?

Short Answers

Yes,	he	does.
No,		doesn't.

Wh- Questions

Wh- Word	Do	Subject		Base Form of Verb
Where	do	you	usually	travel?

GRAMMAR NOTES

1 Referring to Future Events

There are **several ways to refer to future events**. Sometimes only one form is appropriate, but in many cases more than one form is possible.

• *be going to*	They're **going to have** a meeting.
• *will*	I think I'll **go. Will** you **be** there?
• present progressive	It's **taking** place next week.
• simple present	It **starts** at 9:00 a.m. on Monday.

Past —— Now —— meeting —— Future

2 Future Facts

For facts or events that you are **certain** will happen in the future, you can use *be going to* or *will*.

• *be going to*	The sun **is going to rise** at 6:43 tomorrow.
• *will*	The sun **will rise** at 6:43 tomorrow.

3 Predictions

For predictions about things you are **quite sure** will happen in the future, you can also use *be going to* or *will*.

• *be going to*	I think a lot of people **are going to travel** to space.
• *will*	I think a lot of people **will travel** to space.

USAGE NOTE We often use *I think* before a prediction.	*I think* tickets **are going to get** cheaper.
IN WRITING We use *will* more in **formal writing** and *be going to* more in **conversation**.	Prices **will drop** in time. *(formal writing)* Prices **are going to drop** in time. *(conversation)*
BE CAREFUL! Do not use *will* when something you notice right now makes you almost certain that an event is going to happen. Use *be going to*.	A: Look at that car! B: Oh, no. It's **going to crash!** NOT It'll crash.

4 Future Plans

For plans or things that are **already decided**, use *be going to* or the **present progressive**.

• *be going to*	I'm **going to fly** to Chicago next week.
• present progressive	I'm **flying** to Chicago next week. NOT I'll fly to Chicago next week.

USAGE NOTE We often use the **present progressive** for plans that are already arranged.	I'm **flying** to Chicago next week. I already have a ticket.
USAGE NOTE When the main verb is *go*, it is more common to use the **present progressive** (*be going*) than *be going to go*.	I'm **going** to Paris tomorrow. *(more common)* I'm **going to go** to Paris tomorrow. *(less common)*

NEW!

Clear signposting provides corpus-informed notes about common usage, differences between spoken and written registers, and common errors.

PRONUNCIATION NOTE

Pronunciation of *Going to*

In **informal conversation**, we often pronounce *going to* as "gonna."	A: What time are you **going to** be home? *(gonna)* B: I'm **going to** get home late. *(gonna)*
IN WRITING Sometimes people use *gonna* in **informal notes**, **text messages**, and **email** to friends.	Hi Lyn, I'm **gonna** be late. *(email)*
BE CAREFUL! Do not use *gonna* when you write to people you have a formal relationship with. Also do not use *gonna* in formal writing.	Professor, I'm **going to** be late. *(email)* NOT Professor, I'm gonna be late. According to scientists, Mars is **going to** become a tourist destination. *(paper)* NOT According to scientists, Mars is gonna become a tourist destination.

Pronunciation Notes are now included with the grammar presentation to highlight relevant pronunciation aspects of the target structures and to help students understand authentic spoken English.

NEW!

Discover the Grammar activities develop students' recognition and understanding of the target structures before they are asked to produce them.

Controlled practice activities lead students to master form, meaning, and use of the target grammar.

EXERCISE 2 COMPARISONS WITH *AS . . . AS*

GRAMMAR NOTE 1 Look at the consumer magazine chart comparing three brands of pizza cheese. Complete the sentences. Use *(just) as . . . as* or *not as . . . as* and the correct form of the words in parentheses.

PIZZA CHEESE		Better ⟷ Worse	
Brand	**Price** (per serving)	**Taste**	**Smell**
X	45¢	◐	●
Y	30¢	◐	◐
Z	30¢	○	◐

1. Brand Z ___is as expensive as or is just as expensive as___ Brand Y.
   (be / expensive)
2. Brand Y _____ Brand X.
   (be / expensive)
3. Brand X _____ Brand Y.
   (taste / good)
4. Brand Z _____ Brand Y.
   (taste / good)
5. Brand Y _____ Brand X.
   (smell / delicious)
6. Brand Y _____ Brand Z.
   (smell / delicious)

EXERCISE 3 COMPARISONS WITH *THAN*

GRAMMAR NOTES 2–3 Look at the menu on the next page. Then complete these sentences comparing items on the menu. Use the appropriate comparative form of the adjectives in parentheses and *than* where necessary.

1. The sweet-and-sour shrimp is ___more expensive than___ the steamed scallops.
   (expensive)
2. The beef with red pepper is _____ the beef with broccoli.
   (hot)
3. The pork with scallions is _____ the sweet-and-sour shrimp.
   (expensive)
4. The chicken with orange sauce is _____ the steamed scallops.
   (spicy)
5. The steamed vegetables are _____ the pork with scallions.
   (salty)
6. The steamed vegetables are _____ the beef with red pepper.
   (healthy)
7. The broccoli with garlic is _____ the chicken with broccoli.
   (cheap)
8. The shrimp dish is _____ the scallop dish.
   (sweet)

282 Unit 20

Discover the Grammar activities develop students' recognition and understanding of the target structures before they are asked to produce them.

EXERCISE 1 DISCOVER THE GRAMMAR

GRAMMAR NOTES 1–7 Read this notice from a university bulletin board. Underline the adjectives and circle the adverbs. Then draw an arrow from the adjective or adverb to the word it is describing.

APARTMENT FOR RENT
140 Grant Street, Apt. 4B

Are you looking for a place to live? This amazing apartment is in a new building and has two large comfortable bedrooms and a small sunny kitchen. The building is very quiet—absolutely perfect for two serious students. It's near the campus on a peaceful street. There's convenient transportation. The bus stop is an easy, pleasant walk, and the express bus goes directly into town. You can run or ride your bike safely in nearby parks. The rent is very affordable. Small pets are welcome. The apartment is available on June 1. Interested students should call Megan at 555-5050. We're sure you'll be satisfied. Don't wait! This beautiful new apartment will rent fast. Nonsmokers, please.

EXERCISE 2 ADJECTIVE OR ADVERB

GRAMMAR NOTES 1–4 Circle the correct words to complete Maggie's email to her brother.

Hi Roger!

I wasn't sure I'd like living in a large / largely city, but I real / really love it! Maybe that's
                          1.   2.
because my new / newly neighborhood is located in such a beautiful / beautifully residential
            3.   4.
area with lots of nice old trees.

Last Saturday, I worked hard / hardly and unpacked all my stuff. Then I spent Sunday
                         5.
happy / happily exploring my new neighborhood. I couldn't believe the gorgeous / gorgeously
   6.   7.
houses on these streets. I feel very lucky / luckily to live in one of them.
                                        8.

266 Unit 19

A variety of exercise types engage students and guide them from recognition and understanding to accurate production of the grammar structures.

Editing exercises allow students to identify and correct typical mistakes.

EXERCISE 8 EDITING

GRAMMAR NOTES 1–6 Read this student's report on space travel. There are eleven mistakes in the use of the future. The first mistake is already corrected. Find and correct ten more.

>   travel
> Both astronauts and space tourists will ~~traveling~~ in space, but tourists are gonna have a
> much different experience. Space tourists is going to travel for fun, not for work. So, they
> will no have to worry about many of the technical problems that astronauts worry about. For
> example, space tourists will need not to figure out how to use tools without gravity. And they
> isn't going to go outside the spaceship to make repairs. For the most part, space tourists will
> just going to see the sights and have a good time.
>
>   Still, there will be similarities. Regular activities be the same for astronauts and space
> tourists. For example, eating, washing, and sleeping will turned into exciting challenges for
> everyone in space. And on long trips, everyone is going to doing exercises to stay fit in zero
> gravity. And both astronauts and space tourists will going to have many new adventures!

Listenings in a variety of genres allow students to hear the grammar in natural contexts.

STEP 4   COMMUNICATION PRACTICE

EXERCISE 6 LISTENING

▶21:02 **A** A couple is trying to choose a hotel for their trip to Toronto. Listen to their conversation. Look at the list below. Then listen again and check (✓) the correct hotel for each item.

	Westin Harbour Castle	Hôtel Le Germain	Eaton Chelsea
the best view	✓		
the most convenient			
the least convenient			
the most comfortable			
the most expensive			
the least expensive			
the biggest			
the smallest			

▶21:02 **B** Listen to the conversation again. Then work with a partner. Compare your answers. Give reasons.

EXAMPLE: A: I'd like to stay at the Hôtel Le Germain.
B: Yes. You can see the lake from a lot of the rooms.
A: And their restaurant has a good view, too.

C Work in a group. Which hotel would *you* like to stay at? Why?

EXAMPLE: A: I'd like to stay at the Hôtel Le Germain.
B: Oh. Why is that?
A: Because it's the smallest of the three. I don't like big hotels. What about you?
B: I'd prefer . . .

298   Unit 21

In the **listening activities**, students practice a range of listening skills. A **new step** has been added in which partners complete an activity that relates to the listening and uses the target grammar.   NEW!

Engaging **communicative activities** (conversations, discussions, presentations, surveys, and games) help students synthesize the grammar, develop fluency, and build their problem-solving skills.

EXERCISE 6 ON THE WITNESS STAND

ROLE PLAY Work with a partner. Look at the excerpt from a court transcript on page 61 again. Read it aloud. Then continue the lawyer's questioning of the witness. Ask at least six more questions.

EXAMPLE: LAWYER: When did the woman leave?
WITNESS: She was still there when we heard his car speed away.
LAWYER: What happened next?
WITNESS: I saw . . .

EXERCISE 7 TO TELL THE TRUTH

A GAME Work in a group of three. Each student tells the group an interesting fact about his or her life. The fact can *only* be true for this student.

EXAMPLE: A: I play three musical instruments.
B: I speak four languages.
C: I have five pets.

B The group chooses a fact and goes to the front of the class. Each student states the same fact, but remember: Only one student is telling the truth.

EXAMPLE:

C The class asks the three students *wh-* questions to find out who is telling the truth.

EXAMPLE: THEA: Cezar, which four languages do you speak?
CEZAR: I speak Russian, French, Spanish, and English.
LEV: Cezar, where did you learn Russian?
CEZAR: I was born in Russia.
MEI: Cezar, who taught you French?
CEZAR: My grandmother is French. I learned it from her.
JOSÉ: Cezar, how do you say "witness" in Spanish?
CEZAR: . . .

Go to MyEnglishLab for more communication practice.

Wh- Questions   69

FROM GRAMMAR TO WRITING

A **From Grammar to Writing** section, now in every unit, helps students confidently apply the unit's grammar to their own writing. **NEW!**

FROM GRAMMAR TO WRITING

Ⓐ BEFORE YOU WRITE Think about a new experience you are having (for example, living in a new country, taking a new class, working at a new job). Complete the outline.

_____ (New Experience) _____

Usually   Now

_____   _____

_____   _____

_____   _____

Ⓑ WRITE Use your outline to write a paragraph about your new experience. How is it different from what you usually do? How do you feel in the new situation? Use *but* or *however* to contrast your usual experience with your new experience. Try to avoid the common mistakes in the chart.

EXAMPLE: I usually live at home with my parents, but this month I'm living with my aunt and uncle. Everything seems different. My aunt always makes dinner at 6:00. However, at home we never eat before 8:00 p.m. . . .

Common Mistakes in Using the Present Progressive and Simple Present

Use the **simple present** with most **non-action verbs**. Do not use the present progressive.	I **think** my aunt's dinners are great. NOT I ~~am thinking~~ my aunt's dinners are great.
Put an **adverb of frequency before** the simple present verb. Do not put it after the verb.	We **always eat** at 6:00. NOT We ~~eat always~~ at 6:00.
Put an **adverb of frequency after** the verb *be*. Do not put it before *be*.	She is **always** on time. NOT She ~~always is~~ on time.

Ⓒ CHECK YOUR WORK Read your paragraph. Underline once the present progressive and underline twice the simple present forms. Circle the adverbs of frequency. Use the Editing Checklist to check your work.

Editing Checklist

Did you use . . . ?
- [ ] the present progressive to describe something that is happening right now
- [ ] the simple present to describe what regularly happens
- [ ] the simple present with non-action verbs such as *be, like, seem,* and *want*
- [ ] adverbs of frequency in the correct position

Ⓓ REVISE YOUR WORK Read your paragraph again. Can you improve your writing? Make changes if necessary. Give your paragraph a title.

Go to MyEnglishLab for more writing practice.

The **Before You Write** task helps students generate ideas for their writing assignment.

In the **Write** task, students are given a writing assignment and guided to use the target grammar and avoid common mistakes.

Check Your Work includes an Editing Checklist that allows students to proofread and edit their compositions.

In **Revise Your Work**, students are given a final opportunity to improve their writing.

UNIT **REVIEW**

Unit Reviews give students the opportunity to check their understanding of the target structures. Students can check their answers against the Answer Key at the end of the book. They can also complete the Review on MyEnglishLab.

UNIT 22 **REVIEW**

Test yourself on the grammar of the unit.

Ⓐ Circle the correct words to complete the sentences.

1. Chen plays just as good / well as Sanchez.
2. Maya is a slow runner. She runs / doesn't run as fast as her teammates.
3. Dan always shoots the ball more accurately / the most accurately than Will.
4. Inez plays the most aggressively of / than all the other players.
5. Our team didn't play the worst / as well as I expected. I was disappointed.
6. The faster Tranh runs, the more tired he gets / he gets more tired.
7. We need to practice harder / hardly if we want to win.
8. You're playing well / better and better!

Ⓑ Complete the sentences with the correct form of the words in parentheses.

1. You play just as _____ as Tomás.
   (good)
2. Olga runs _____ than any of her teammates.
   (fast)
3. Diego shoots the ball _____ of all the players.
   (accurate)
4. He practices _____ of all.
   (hard)
5. Their team played _____ of all the teams.
   (bad)

Ⓒ Find and correct seven mistakes.

   Last night's game was a very exciting one. The Globes played the best they've played all season. But they still didn't play as good as the Stars. The Stars hit the ball more frequent and ran more fast than the Globes, and their pitcher, Kevin Rodriguez, threw the ball more

MyEnglishLab delivers rich online content to engage and motivate **students**.

Grammar Coach videos give additional grammar presentations.

NEW!

MyEnglishLab provides students with:

- rich interactive practice in grammar, reading, listening, speaking, and writing
- immediate and meaningful feedback on wrong answers

  NEW!
- remediation activities
- grade reports that display performance and time on task

MyEnglishLab delivers innovative teaching tools and useful resources to **teachers**.

With **MyEnglishLab**, teachers can:

- view student scores by unit and activity
- monitor student progress on any activity or test
- analyze class data to determine steps for remediation and support

MyEnglishLab also provides teachers with:

- a digital copy of the student book for whole-class instruction
- downloadable assessments, including the placement test, that can be administered on MyEnglishLab or in print format
- printable resources including teaching notes, suggestions for teaching grammar, GSE mapping documents, answer keys, and audio scripts

Scope and Sequence

LISTENING	SPEAKING	WRITING	VOCABULARY
Interviews with foreign students ■ Can distinguish a present action from a habitual activity in short interviews	■ Can express beliefs and opinions about cultural topics and identify the opinions of others	■ Can write a basic description of a new experience, using a model for support if needed	abroad culture AWL distance (n) event misunderstanding native (adj)
An interview with a poet ■ Can recognize the main points of an interview that addresses familiar topics	■ Can convey simple biographical information to others, emphasizing the most important point	■ Can write a basic description of some important life events, using a model for support if needed	admirer emotion journey (n) restless topic AWL
A witness's description of a traffic accident ■ Can identify the main points of a description of an unfamiliar event	■ Can ask or answer questions about an unfamiliar event	■ Can write a basic description of an unfamiliar past event	alarmed area AWL calm (adj) disaster sink (v) AWL survivor AWL
A conversation about the changes in a small town ■ Can distinguish present events from past events in a conversation on familiar topics	■ Can describe one's past and present physical appearance and habits	■ Can write a description of a place and how it has changed	destination major (adj) AWL popular revenue AWL traditional AWL transformation AWL
A conversation about a court trial ■ Can identify the main point of a conversation	■ Can ask and answer basic interview questions	■ Can write a series of interview questions that elicit information about a past event	defendant frightened in a hurry indicate AWL record (n)
Conversations about current situations and future plans ■ Can recognize main points of conversations on familiar topics ■ Can distinguish between actions happening now and future plans	■ Can ask and answer questions about plans and intentions ■ Can make future arrangements and plans with reference to a diary or schedule	■ Can write a paragraph about a prediction	edge (n) experience (v) incredible purchase (v) AWL sold out takeoff (n)

AWL = Academic Word List item

LISTENING	SPEAKING	WRITING	VOCABULARY
A conversation about future plans ■ Can follow chronological sequences in extended informal speech at natural speed	■ Can describe future plans and intentions ■ Can discuss the order of future events using future time clauses	■ Can write a description of future plans and goals ■ Can show the time order of future events	achieve AWL catalog (n) goal AWL interview (n) path
A job interview ■ Can determine the length of time of events mentioned in an interview	■ Can carry out a prepared, structured interview with some spontaneous follow-up questions	■ Can write a paragraph about a person's experience and accomplishments	consider oneself dramatically AWL opportunity positive AWL residence AWL support oneself
A conversation about plans for a party ■ Can recognize and discuss tasks on a to-do list or plan	■ Can discuss what has or hasn't happened in everyday plans	■ Can write a paragraph about a goal and the steps needed to reach it	available AWL organized (adj) professional (adj) AWL specific AWL successful
A conversation with a travel agent ■ Can identify the main points of a conversation about travel plans	■ Can briefly give explanations and reasons for opinions ■ Can ask and answer questions about past activities	■ Can write a paragraph in response to a quote from literature	adventure affordable ancient annual AWL survey (n) AWL transportation AWL
An interview with two college professors ■ Can establish the time frame of important details in an interview	■ Can discuss past events and experiences and provide necessary details about them	■ Can write a paragraph about a personal experience of failure and success	attitude AWL award (n) create AWL discouraged (adj) reject (v) AWL
Conversations about recent finished and unfinished activities ■ Can determine the time frame of main events in short conversations	■ Can express opinions and attitudes and give reasons and explanations for them	■ Can write an email or letter that describes one's recent activities, both finished and unfinished	climate design (v) AWL develop energy AWL expert AWL trend AWL

AWL = Academic Word List item

LISTENING	SPEAKING	WRITING	VOCABULARY
A job interview ■ Can identify important details in a job interview	■ Can compare and contrast alternatives about plans and activities ■ Can effectively participate in a classroom discussion about an academic topic	■ Can write a paragraph in response to a question about progress and aspirations	adult AWL advantage field (n) majority AWL research (n) AWL retired
Short conversations asking and giving permission ■ Can distinguish between whether permission was granted or refused in a short conversation	■ Can come to a resolution with others by asking for permission to do something	■ Can write a short note or email that explains a day-to-day situation and asks or responds to a request for permission to do something	annoyed assume AWL establish AWL gain (v) guidelines AWL presentation
Short conversations making and answering requests ■ Can identify details related to a schedule in a short conversation	■ Can create and discuss a daily schedule that involves making requests of others	■ Can write and respond to a request in a text or email message	appreciate AWL deliver distribute AWL respond AWL urgent
An excerpt from a radio call-in show ■ Can evaluate statements of advice from radio and television shows	■ Can express opinions in regard to possible solutions and provide brief reasons and explanations for them	■ Can write a basic email or letter of complaint and request the recipient to take action	avoid behavior communication AWL identity AWL normal AWL protect

LISTENING	SPEAKING	WRITING	VOCABULARY
A discussion about a list of items ■ Can identify details in a conversation about day-to-day topics	■ Can use turn-taking to maintain a discussion, while emphasizing one's own points	■ Can write a note or letter that lists and describes quantities of items	civilization impressed intentional interpret AWL occasion (n) purpose
Short conversations about books and video games ■ Can understand and interpret important details in basic conversations about day-to-day activities	■ Can summarize and give opinions on the moral of a fable	■ Can write a paragraph about a personal experience that illustrates the meaning of a moral	enormous AWL famous honest immediately wonderful

AWL = Academic Word List item

LISTENING	SPEAKING	WRITING	VOCABULARY
A conversation about online apartment ads ■ Can identify speakers' opinions in a short conversation about day-to-day topics	■ Can use a range of adjectives and adverbs to compare and describe different options for an ideal home	■ Can write a description of one's ideal home	absolutely convenient ideal located in **AWL** peaceful satisfied
A conversation about opinions on food ■ Can recognize speakers' preferences and opinions in a short conversation	■ Can make simple, direct comparisons between two things using common adjectives ■ Can briefly give reasons and explanations for opinions	■ Can write a paragraph that compares and contrasts foods from different cities or countries	crowded delicious evident **AWL** relaxed **AWL** varied **AWL**
A conversation about travel plans ■ Can identify places and locations by their descriptions	■ Can give opinions and answer questions about cities	■ Can write a detailed description of one's hometown or city	continent (n) dynamic **AWL** feature (n) **AWL** financial **AWL** multicultural public (adj)
A debate ■ Can recognize the main ideas of and opinions in a debate about familiar topics	■ Can express and respond to opinions about controversial topics	■ Can write arguments for and against a statement about an everyday topic	compete debate (n) **AWL** insult (n) require **AWL** source (n) **AWL** value (n)
A conversation about health advice ■ Can determine whether an action is recommended or not recommended	■ Can discuss one's health and exercise habits ■ Can conduct a survey and discuss results ■ Can discuss and give one's opinion on a controversial topic	■ Can write a short opinion essay about a controversial topic	approve of ban (v) illegal **AWL** in favor of permit (v) prohibit **AWL**

AWL = Academic Word List item

LISTENING	SPEAKING	WRITING	VOCABULARY
A casual conversation between two friends ■ Can recognize who is being asked to do an action in a conversation on an everyday topic	■ Can give an opinion in response to a literary quote ■ Can start and maintain a discussion about an abstract topic	■ Can write a paragraph on a personal topic using transition words to establish a time frame	appropriate (adj) AWL focus (v) AWL interact AWL participate in AWL significant (adj) AWL tend to
A TV ad ■ Can identify key details about products and recognize whether they are important or not	■ Can express and comment on ideas and suggestions in informal discussions about everyday objects	■ Can write a paragraph that weighs the pros and cons of a smart device	benefit (n) AWL combine (v) device AWL function (n) AWL multipurpose old-fashioned
An interview with a student about her study habits ■ Can identify key details in a recorded interview	■ Can give an opinion in response to a literary quote ■ Can express and comment on how to solve problems in an informal discussion	■ Can write several paragraphs that outline how to achieve one's goals	anxious discouraging (adj) project (n) AWL tactic task AWL universal

LISTENING	SPEAKING	WRITING	VOCABULARY
Workplace conversations ■ Can identify important information in everyday conversations	■ Can complete a questionnaire and discuss results ■ Can discuss illustrations using phrasal verbs	■ Can write an email or letter giving advice	fault (n) impact (v) AWL maintain AWL reaction AWL realize temporary AWL
Classroom conversations about a science class ■ Can recognize the main points of conversations and confirm their validity	■ Can express and comment on ideas and suggestions in informal discussions ■ Can discuss illustrations using phrasal verbs	■ Can write a paragraph in response to a specific question and support opinions with examples and observations	get by go on grow up pick out pick up take off

AWL = Academic Word List item

LISTENING	SPEAKING	WRITING	VOCABULARY
Conversations about driving ■ Can identify the main points of conversations about a familiar topic spoken in standard speech	■ Can recognize common signs and discuss their meaning ■ Can express personal obligations ■ Can discuss the rules and regulations of a public or private institution	■ Can write a paragraph describing rules or procedures for obtaining an official document	equipment AWL hassle (n) inspect AWL regulation AWL strict valid AWL
A radio show about etiquette and manners ■ Can identify details in recorded conversations	■ Can initiate and maintain a discussion about cultural customs	■ Can write a paragraph about a life event in a specific culture	definite AWL familiar issue (n) AWL norm AWL rude sense (v)
A weather forecast ■ Can understand the probability of a situation in a report about a familiar topic	■ Can give a short, rehearsed talk or presentation on a familiar topic ■ Can describe future plans and intentions in detail and give degrees of probability that something will happen	■ Can write short emails or letters that express the probability of future plans	affect (v) AWL exceed AWL forecast (n) local (adj) region AWL
A conversation about a mystery ■ Can recognize the key events in a short conversation and identify the certainty of each speaker about the events	■ Can draw conclusions about everyday objects and situations	■ Can write a paragraph about a short story and draw possible conclusions	advertisement amazed method AWL position (n) salary

AWL = Academic Word List item

About the Authors

Marjorie Fuchs has taught ESL at New York City Technical College and LaGuardia Community College of the City University of New York and EFL at Sprachstudio Lingua Nova in Munich, Germany. She has a master's degree in Applied English Linguistics and a certificate in TESOL from the University of Wisconsin-Madison. She has authored and co-authored many widely used books and multimedia materials, notably *Crossroads 4*; *Top Twenty ESL Word Games: Beginning Vocabulary Development*; *Families: Ten Card Games for Language Learners*; *Focus on Grammar 3* and *4* (editions 1–5); *Focus on Grammar 3* and *4, CD-ROM*; *Longman English Interactive 3* and *4*; *Grammar Express Basic*; *Grammar Express Basic CD-ROM*; *Grammar Express Intermediate*; *Future 1: English for Results*; *OPD Workplace Skills Builder*; and workbooks for *Crossroads 1–4*; *The Oxford Picture Dictionary High Beginning* and *Low Intermediate*, (editions 1–3); *Focus on Grammar 3* and *4* (editions 1–5); and *Grammar Express Basic*.

Margaret Bonner has taught ESL at Hunter College and the Borough of Manhattan Community College of the City University of New York, at Taiwan National University in Taipei, and at Virginia Commonwealth University in Richmond. She holds a master's degree in library science from Columbia University, and she has done work toward a PhD in English literature at the Graduate Center of the City University of New York. She has authored and co-authored numerous ESL and EFL print and multimedia materials, including textbooks for the national school system of Oman, *Step into Writing: A Basic Writing Text*; *Focus on Grammar 3* and *4* (editions 1–5); *Focus on Grammar 4 Workbook* (editions 1–5); *Grammar Express Basic*; *Grammar Express Basic CD-ROM*; *Grammar Express Basic Workbook*; *Grammar Express Intermediate*; *Focus on Grammar 3* and *4, CD-ROM*; *Longman English Interactive 4*; and *The Oxford Picture Dictionary Low Intermediate Workbook* (editions 1–3).

Miriam Westheimer taught EFL at all levels of instruction in Haifa, Israel, for a period of six years. She has also taught ESL at Queens College, at LaGuardia Community College, and in the American Language Program of Columbia University. She holds a master's degree in TESOL and a doctorate in Curriculum and Teaching from Teachers College of Columbia University. She is the co-author of a communicative grammar program developed and widely used in Israel.

Acknowledgments

Before acknowledging the many people who have contributed to the fifth edition of *Focus on Grammar*, we wish to express our gratitude to the following people who worked on the previous editions and whose influence is still present in the new work: **Joanne Dresner**, who initiated the project and helped conceptualize the general approach of *Focus on Grammar*; our editors for the first four editions: **Nancy Perry**, **Penny Laporte**, **Louisa Hellegers**, **Joan Saslow**, **Laura LeDrean**, **Debbie Sistino**, and **Françoise Leffler**; and **Sharon Hilles**, our grammar consultant for the first edition.

In the fifth edition, *Focus on Grammar* has continued to evolve as we update materials and respond to valuable feedback from teachers and students who use the series. We are grateful to the following editors and colleagues:

- **Gosia Jaros-White** for overseeing with skill and sensitivity a complex series while never losing sight of the individual components or people involved in the project. She offered concrete and practical advice and was always mindful of learners' needs.

- **Bernard Seal**, of Page Designs International, who joined the *Focus on Grammar* team with a great deal of experience, expertise, energy, and enthusiasm. With his hands-on approach, he was involved in every aspect of the project. He read all manuscript, raising pertinent questions and offering sage advice.

- **Don Williams**, also of Page Designs International, for creating a fresh, new look, which is as user-friendly as it is attractive.

- **Françoise Leffler**, our editor *extraordinaire*, with whom we had the great fortune and pleasure of being able to continue our long collaboration. She provided both continuity and a fresh eye as she delved into another edition of the series advising us on all things—from the small details to the big picture.

- Series co-authors **Irene Schoenberg** and **Jay Maurer** for their suggestions and support, and Irene for sharing her experience in teaching with earlier editions of this book.

- **Jane Curtis** for her advice founded in many years of teaching with the series.

- **Julie Schmidt** for her helpful presentation of information that was easy to understand and use.

- **Sharon Goldstein** for her insightful and practical suggestions, delivered with wisdom and wit.

- **Cindy Davis** for her classroom-based recommendations at the very beginning of this edition.

Special thanks to **Dr. Eloy Rodriguez** of Cornell University for generously providing us with photos to accompany the unit which features his research on zoopharmacognosy.

Finally, as always, Marjorie thanks **Rick Smith** for his unswerving support and excellent suggestions. He was a steadfast beacon of light as we navigated our way through our fifth *FOG*.

MF and MB

To the memory of my parents, Edith and Joseph Fuchs—MF
To my parents, Marie and Joseph Maus, and to my son, Luke Frances—MB

Reviewers

We are grateful to the following reviewers for their many helpful comments.

Susanna Aramyan, Glendale Community College, Glendale, CA; **Homeretta Ayala**, Baltimore Co. Schools, Baltimore, MD; **Barbara Barrett**, University of Miami, Miami, FL; **Rebecca Beck**, Irvine Valley College, Irvine, CA; **Crystal Bock Thiessen**, University of Nebraska-PIESL, Lincoln, NE; **Janna Brink**, Mt. San Antonio College, Walnut, CA; **Erin Butler**, University of California, Riverside, CA; **Joice Cain**, Fullerton College, Fullerton, CA; **Shannonine M. Caruana**, Hudson County Community College, Jersey City, NJ; **Tonya Cobb**, Cypress College, Cypress, CA; **David Cooke**, Mt. San Antonio College, Walnut, CA; **Lindsay Donigan**, Fullerton College, Fullerton, CA; **Mila Dragushanskya**, ASA College, New York, NY; **Jill Fox**, University of Nebraska, Lincoln, NE; **Katalin Gyurindak**, Mt. San Antonio College, Walnut, CA; **Karen Hamilton**, Glendale Community College, Glendale, CA; **Electra Jablons**, International English Language Institute, Hunter College, New York, NY; **Eva Kozlenko**, Hudson County Community College, Jersey City, NJ; **Esther Lee**, American Language Program, California State University, Fullerton, CA; **Yenlan Li**, American Language Program, California State University, Fullerton, CA; **Shirley Lundblade**, Mt. San Antonio College, Walnut, CA; **Thi Thi Ma**, Los Angeles City College, Los Angeles, CA; **Marilyn Martin**, Mt. San Antonio College, Walnut, CA; **Eve Mazereeuw**, University of Guelph English Language Programs, Guelph, Ontario, Canada; **Robert Mott**, Glendale Community College, Glendale, CA; **Wanda Murtha**, Glendale Community College, Glendale, CA; **Susan Niemeyer**, Los Angeles City College, Los Angeles, CA; **Wayne Pate**, Tarrant County College, Fort Worth, TX; **Genevieve Patthey-Chavez**, Los Angeles City College, Los Angeles, CA; **Robin Persiani**, Sierra College, Rocklin, CA; **Denise Phillips**, Hudson County Community College, Jersey City, NJ; **Anna Powell**, American Language Program, California State University, Fullerton, CA; **JoAnna Prado**, Sacramento City Community College, Sacramento, CA; **Mark Rau**, American River College, Sacramento, CA; **Madeleine Schamehorn**, University of California, Riverside, CA; **Richard Skinner**, Hudson County Community College, Jersey City, NJ; **Heather Snavely**, American Language Program, California State University, Fullerton, CA; **Gordana Sokic**, Douglas College, Westminster, British Columbia, Canada; **Lee Spencer**, International English Language Institute, Hunter College, New York, NY; **Heather Stern**, Irvine Valley College, Irvine, CA; **Susan Stern**, Irvine Valley College, Irvine, CA; **Andrea Sunnaa**, Mt. San Antonio College, Walnut, CA; **Margaret Teske**, Mt. San Antonio College, Walnut, CA; **Johanna Van Gendt**, Hudson County Community College, Jersey City, NJ; **Daniela C. Wagner-Loera**, University of Maryland, College Park, MD; **Tamara Williams**, University of Guelph, English Language Programs, Guelph, Ontario, Canada; **Saliha Yagoubi**, Hudson County Community College, Jersey City, NJ; **Pat Zayas**, Glendale Community College, Glendale, CA

Credits

PHOTO CREDITS

2–3: Peshkov/Fotolia, (background) Pixelrobot/Fotolia; **9:** Gold36/Fotolia; **10:** (bottom) Elnur/Fotolia, (center) Ake1150/Fotolia, (top) Jolopes/Fotolia; **11:** (bottom) Sumire8/Fotolia, (top) Sanjagrujic/Fotolia; **12:** Jasminko Ibrakovic/123RF; **15:** (center left) Kantver/Fotolia, (center right) Jedi Master/Fotolia, (left) Pathdoc/Fotolia, (right) Slasnyi/Fotolia; **18:** Picsfive/123RF; **18–19:** John Stevenson/Asian Art & Archaeology, Inc/Corbis Historical/Getty Images; **24:** Mary Evans Picture Library/Alamy Stock Photo; **26:** Betty Udesen/KRT/Newscom; **27:** Becker/Fotolia; **29:** (center left) Pictures From History/akg-images, (left) Adrian Sherratt/Alamy Stock Photo, (center right) Sueddeutsche Zeitung Photo/Alamy Stock Photo, (right) Eric Harlow/Keystone/Hulton Archive/Getty Images, (top) Picsfive/Fotolia; **30:** Warner Bros/Everett Collection; **33:** (left) Milosluz/Fotolia, (right) SZ Photo/Knorr + Hirth/Sueddeutsche Zeitung Photo/Alamy Stock Photo; **34:** Isonphoto/Fotolia; **38:** (right) Roman Samokhin/Fotolia, (left) Glopphy/Fotolia; **44:** AF Archive/Alamy Stock Photo; **47:** (bottom) Xavier Arnau/E+/Getty Images, (center) Bottleneck Studios/Alamy Stock Photo; **51:** Konstantin Stepanenko/123RF; **53:** MARKA/Mezzabarba/Alamy Stock Photo; **54:** Ritu Jethani/123RF; **55:** Yossarian6/Fotolia; **56:** Michael Shake/Shutterstock; **58:** (left) Tammie Arroyo/Hulton Archive/Getty Images, (right) Splash News/Newscom; **61:** Bikeriderlondon/Shutterstock; **66:** Stockbyte/Getty Images; **68:** Goodween123/Fotolia; **69:** Michaeljung/Shutterstock; **72–73:** Maciek905/Fotolia; **74–75:** (bottom) Tsuneomp/Fotolia, (top) DM7/Fotolia; **80:** Tsuneo/123RF; **84:** Yossarian6/Fotolia; **85:** Arnau2098/Fotolia; **86:** Jakub Krechowicz/Fotolia; **88:** Syda Productions/Fotolia; **91:** Michaeljung/Fotolia; **95:** Salexander2/Fotolia; **96:** Archipoch/Fotolia; **99:** Africa Studio/Fotolia; **102–103:** Jan Will/123RF; **104:** Travis Rowan/Alamy Stock Photo; **109:** Lzf/Fotolia; **111:** (center) Zuzabax/Fotolia, (top) Rob/Fotolia; **112:** Lzf/Fotolia; **113:** Siraphol/Fotolia; **114:** (left) Suna/Fotolia, (right) David Gilder/123RF; **115:** Vlad_g/Fotolia; **118:** Shutterstock; **122:** Baibaz/Fotolia; **124:** (bottom) Chris Baker/123RF, (top) Donfiore/Fotolia; **125:** Sasajo/Fotolia; **129:** Anderm/Fotolia; **130:** (left) Cobalt/Fotolia, (right) Vetal1983/Fotolia; **134–135:** Pichugin Dmitry/Shutterstock; **136:** Onizu3d/Fotolia; **138:** JRB/Fotolia; **140–141:** Xbrchx/Fotolia; **144:** Superstock/Glow Images; **145:** Ray Mickshaw/WireImage/Getty Images; **148:** Tobias Hase/dpa/picture-alliance/Newscom; **149:** Katusha161107/Fotolia; **150:** Maksym Yemelyanov/Fotolia; **151:** Giuseppe Porzani/Fotolia; **152:** DragonImages/Fotolia; **154:** (bottom left) Robert Kaufman/Alamy Stock Photo, (bottom center) Susanna Saez/EFE/Newscom, (bottom right) Dennis Van Tine/LFI/Photoshot/Newscom, (top left) Adrian Sherratt/Alamy Stock Photo, (top center) Dennis Van Tine/UPI/Newscom, (top right) Richard Young/Ian Mcilgorm/REX/Newscom; **157:** Andrea Danti/Shutterstock; **164:** Bertrand Guay/AFP/Getty Images; **165:** Jesadaphorn/Fotolia; **166:** Markos86/Fotolia; **167:** (bottom left) Karmaknight/Fotolia, (bottom right) Tinx/Fotolia, (center left) Federico Rostagno/Fotolia, (center right) Alexey Stiop/Fotolia, (top left) Zigzagmtart/Fotolia, (top right) David_franklin/Fotolia; **168:** Jeffong/Fotolia; **169:** Jan Will/123RF; **172–173:** Angela Waye/Shutterstock; **174:** WENN Ltd/Alamy Stock Photo; **179:** Dpa picture alliance/Alamy Stock Photo; **179–180:** Flas100/Fotolia; **180:** PG/Splash News/Newscom; **182:** Sumire8/Fotolia; **185:** (bottom) Sumire8/Fotolia, (top) Stillfx/Fotolia; **194:** Roywylam/123RF; **197:** Roman Samokhin/Fotolia; **199:** Blaj Gabriel/123RF; **202:** Goodween123/Fotolia; **202–203:** (background) Denis_333/Fotolia, Vvoe/Fotolia; **203:** Alex/Fotolia; **211:** Aopsan/Fotolia; **214:** Elenarts/Fotolia; **214–215:** DigiClack/Fotolia; **215:** LuneWind/Fotolia; **219:** Digi Clack/Fotolia; **222:** Flashon Studio/123RF; **223:** Komi$ar/Fotolia; **224:** Phanuwatnandee/Fotolia; **228–229:** Reinhold Leitner/Shutterstock; **230:** Everett Collection/Newscom; **230–231:** C.E. Mitchell/BlackStar Photos/Newscom; **235:** (bottom) Alexzaitsev/Fotolia, (top) Tavarman/Fotolia; **236:** Sorincolac/Fotolia; **239:** (left) Tolgatezcan/Fotolia, (right) Picsfive/Fotolia; **240:** Okinawakasawa/Fotolia; **243:** 123dartist/Fotolia; **244:** 123dartist/Fotolia; **247:** Nexusseven/Fotolia; **248:** Shutterstock; **249:** (bottom) Olga Labusova/Fotolia, (top) Vladimir Tyutin/Fotolia; **250:** (bottom) Antiqueimages/Fotolia, (top) Dimashiper/Fotolia; **252:** Juan Carlos Rojas/Notimex/Newscom; **254:** Vladimir Prusakov/Fotolia; **258–259:** Quang Ho/Shutterstock; **260:** (bottom) Yossarian6/Fotolia, (background): rSnapshotPhotos/Shutterstock; **261:** (top) Yossarian6/Fotolia, (left) Pressmaster/Shutterstock, (center) AVAVA/Shutterstock, (right) S_l/Fotolia; **266:** Dragonstock/Fotolia; **267:** rSnapshotPhotos/Shutterstock; **269:** Ravennka/Fotolia; **270:** Jodie Johnson/Fotolia; **271:** Andy Dean/Fotolia; **272:** Ivonne Wierink/Shutterstock; **273:** Roman Bodnarchuk/Fotolia; **276:** (bottom) F9photos/Fotolia, (background) ki33/Fotolia; **277:** (left) Ki33/Fotolia, (right) Seamartini Graphics/Fotolia; **283:** (background) Peangdao/Fotolia, (bottom right) Raven/Fotolia, (center left) Volkovslava/Fotolia, (top) Gstudio Group/Fotolia; **284:** Rene Pi/Shutterstock; **285:** Alex/Fotolia; **287:** (bottom) Oly5/Fotolia, (top) Radoma/Fotolia; **290–291:** Stephanie Barbary/Shutterstock; **291:** Sumkinn/Fotolia; **294:** Earl Robbins/Fotolia; **295:** (top) Jacartoon/Fotolia, (top left) Pandavector/Fotolia, (center top) Pandavector/Fotolia, (center bottom) Skarin/Fotolia, (bottom left) Alek_maneewan/Fotolia, (bottom) Tackgalichstudio/Fotolia; **296:** Lisa Charbonneau/Shutterstock; **299:** Balaph/Fotolia; **302:** (background) Ki33/Fotolia, (bottom) Derek Shook/Splash News/Newscom; **303:** Ki33/Fotolia; **309:** Mezzotint/Shutterstock; **310:** Ron Sachs/UPI/Newscom; **311:** (left) Pathdoc/Shutterstock, (right) Wong Yu Liang/Fotolia; **312:** (bottom) Goir/Fotolia, (top) David Eulitt/MCT/Newscom; **313:** Nyul/Fotolia; **316–317:** Korn/Shutterstock; **318:** cartoonstock.com/Edgar Argo; **319:** Rob Epco/Fotolia; **322:** Ambassador806/Fotolia; **324:** Arek Malang/Shutterstock; **325:** Weedezign/Fotolia; **326:** Tyron Molteni/Fotolia; **330:** (background) Juri/Fotolia, (center) JHershPhoto/Shutterstock; **331:** Juri/Fotolia; **334:** Locotearts/Fotolia; **337:** Kaspars Grinvalds/Fotolia; **339:** Blaj Gabriel/Shutterstock; **342:** (bottom right) HektoR/Shutterstock, (top right) WavebreakMediaMicro/Fotolia, (top right) Pisit Santikulluk/123RF; **346:** Marc Dietrich/Shutterstock; **347:** (bottom) Antonio Diaz/Fotolia, (top left) Big-label/Fotolia, (top center) Vladimir Mucibabic/Fotolia, (center top) Alice_photo/Fotolia, (center bottom) Mario Beauregard/Fotolia, (bottom center) Adisa/Fotolia, (bottom left) Pavlo Burdyak/Fotolia, (top) Asierromero/Fotolia; **351:** Marisa Acocella Marchetto The New Yorker Collection/The Cartoon Bank; **352:** (bottom) Yeamake/Fotolia, (right) Alen Kadr/Fotolia, (left) Senkinv/Fotolia, (center left) Maxal Tamor/Fotolia, (right) Coprid/Fotolia, (top center right) Ilya Akinshin/Fotolia, (top center left) Vrisphuket/Fotolia, (top left) Vadidak/Fotolia, (top right) Coprid/Fotolia; **359:** Picsfive/Fotolia; **360:** Picsfive/Fotolia; **362:** Denchik/Fotolia; **364:** Joseph Helfenberger/Fotolia; **368–369:** Fikmik/123RF; **370:** Bikeriderlondon/Shutterstock; **370–371:** Weedezign/Fotolia; **371:** Andres Rodriguez/Fotolia; **374:** (bottom) Sari Gustafsson/REX/Newscom, (background) Siro46/Fotolia; **379:** Tortoon/Fotolia; **381:** (top right) Matthew Benoit/Fotolia, (background) Tolga Tezcan/Fotolia; **384:** Dr. Eloy Rodriguez; **385:** Dr. Eloy Rodriguez; **388:** Denchik/Fotolia; **389:** (bottom) Negoi Cristian/Fotolia, (background) Tanawatpontchour/Fotolia; **390:** TUNS/Picture Alliance/Arco Images G/Newscom; **396–397:** Aruba2000/Fotolia; **398:** (bottom) Eldad Carin/Fotolia, (top) Michael Jung/Fotolia; **404:** Sborisov/Fotolia; **405:** Elnur/Fotolia; **407:** Adimas/Fotolia; **411:** Andrey Kuzmin/Fotolia; **418:** (background) Paladin1212/Fotolia, (top) Patrisyu/Fotolia; **421:** Pathdoc/Fotolia; **424:** B Studio/Shutterstock; **427:** Semion/Fotolia; **432:** Picsfive/Fotolia; **434:** Mokee81/Fotolia; **435:** (background) Juri/Fotolia, (left) Leung Cho Pan/Fotolia, (right) Duckman76/Fotolia; **438:** (background) Pakhnyushchyy/Fotolia, (bottom) Franck Camhi/123RF; **439:** (bottom) Pakhnyushchyy/Fotolia, (top) Stillfx/Fotolia; **443:** (bottom) Aruba2000/Fotolia, (top) Pakhnyushchyy/Fotolia; **449:** (bottom center) Aleksandr Ugorenkov/Fotolia, (bottom left) Mercedes Fittipaldi/Fotolia, (bottom right) Mashe/Fotolia, (center top) Swisshippo/Fotolia, (right) Rob/Fotolia, (top center) My Portfolio/Shutterstock, (top left) Evgenia Tiplyashina/Fotolia; **450:** Scisetti Alfio/Fotolia

ILLUSTRATION CREDITS

Steve Attoe – pages 4, 5, 82, 83, 189, 225, 355, 423
Ron Chironna – page 25
Chi Chung – page 243
Jock MacRae – pages 43, 380, 414
Tom Newsom – pages 42, 137, 138, 376, 377
Dusan Petricic – page 251
Steve Schulman – pages 163, 365, 445 (left)
Gary Torrisi – pages 57, 126, 207, 255, 298, 445 (right)
Meryl Treatner – page 393

Present and Past

OUTCOMES
- Describe actions that are happening now
- Describe actions, states, and situations that happen regularly, and unchanging facts
- Recognize the use of the present progressive and the simple present in reading and listening
- Express opinions about topics related to cross-cultural differences
- Write a description of a new experience

OUTCOMES
- Use the simple past with regular and irregular verbs
- Describe events, states, and situations in the past
- Identify the order of events in a reading and listening
- Discuss past events and situations
- Write about some important life events

OUTCOMES
- Describe past events or situations
- Use *when* or *while* to link clauses in the simple past and the past progressive
- Identify the order of events in a description of an accident
- Report on events that were interrupted by other events
- Write a description of a past event

OUTCOMES
- Describe past habits and situations, using *used to* and *would*
- Evaluate events and situations described in a reading and a listening
- Describe and discuss one's past and present physical appearance and habits
- Write a description of a place and how it has changed

OUTCOMES
- Ask questions about the past, using *wh-* words
- Identify important information in an interview transcript
- Identify the main point of a conversation
- Write a series of interview questions to get information about a past event

Present Progressive and Simple Present

DIFFERENT CULTURES

OUTCOMES
- Describe actions that are happening now
- Describe actions, states, and situations that happen regularly, and unchanging facts
- Recognize the use of the present progressive and the simple present in reading and listening
- Express opinions about topics related to cross-cultural differences
- Write a description of a new experience

STEP 1   GRAMMAR IN CONTEXT

BEFORE YOU READ

Look at the cartoons. Discuss the questions.

1. What are the people doing?
2. How do they feel?

READ

01|01   Read this article about cross-cultural communication.

What's Your Cross-Cultural IQ?[1]

Are you living in your native country or in another country? Do you ever travel abroad? Do you understand the misunderstandings in these two situations?

Situation 1

Jason is standing at Dan's door. He thinks he's on time for the party, but he doesn't see any guests, and Dan is wearing shorts and a T-shirt! Dan looks surprised. In his culture, people never arrive at the exact start of a social event. They often come at least 30 minutes later.

---

1 *What's your cross-cultural IQ?:* How much do you know about other people's cultures?

What's the matter?² Why is Ina moving away from me? Maybe she doesn't like my perfume!³

Why is she standing so close to me? I feel like I have no room to breathe!

Situation 2

Ina and Marty are talking. They are both feeling very uncomfortable. In Marty's culture, people usually stand quite close. This seems friendly to them. In Ina's culture, people prefer to have more distance between them. This doesn't mean they are unfriendly.

2 *What's the matter?:* What's wrong?
3 *perfume:* a liquid with a strong pleasant smell that you put on your skin

AFTER YOU READ

A VOCABULARY Choose the word or phrase that is closest in meaning to the word in **bold**.

1. Are you living in your **native** country?
   a. first   **b.** new   **c.** favorite

2. Do you ever travel **abroad**?
   a. by boat   **b.** to foreign countries   **c.** on expensive trips

3. What was the **misunderstanding** about?
   a. fight   **b.** argument   **c.** confusion

4. They come from different **cultures**.
   a. schools   **b.** climates   **c.** ways of life

5. They prefer to have more **distance** between them.
   a. streets   **b.** space   **c.** time

6. There are a lot of parties and other **events** at the Students' Club.
   a. members   **b.** languages   **c.** activities

B COMPREHENSION Complete each statement with the correct name.

1. _____ doesn't have shoes on.

2. _____ isn't expecting people to arrive at 8:00.

3. _____ thinks he's on time.

4. _____ is wearing perfume.

5. _____ wants to stand farther away.

6. _____ probably thinks the other person is a little unfriendly.

C DISCUSSION Work with a partner. Compare your answers in B. Why did you choose each answer?

Present Progressive and Simple Present   **5**

PRESENT PROGRESSIVE

Affirmative Statements

Subject	*Be*	Base Form of Verb + *-ing*	
I	am		
You	are		
He She It	is	traveling	now.
We You They	are		

Negative Statements

Subject	*Be*	*Not*	Base Form of Verb + *-ing*	
I	am			
He	is	not	traveling	now.
We	are			

Yes/No Questions

Be	Subject	Base Form of Verb + *-ing*	
Is	he	traveling	now?

Short Answers

Yes,	he	is.
No,		isn't.

Wh- Questions

Wh-Word	*Be*	Subject	Base Form of Verb + *-ing*	
Where	are	you	traveling	now?

SIMPLE PRESENT

Affirmative Statements

Subject		Verb
I You		travel.
He She It	often	travels.
We You They		travel.

Negative Statements

Subject	*Do*	*Not*	Base Form of Verb	
I	do			
He	does	not	travel	often.
We	do			

Yes/No Questions

Do	Subject	Base Form of Verb	
Does	he	travel	often?

Short Answers

Yes,	he	does.
No,		doesn't.

Wh- Questions

Wh-Word	*Do*	Subject		Base Form of Verb
Where	do	you	usually	travel?

GRAMMAR NOTES

1 Present Progressive

Use the present progressive to show that something is **happening now** or **in a longer present time.**

- **happening now**
  (*right now, at the moment*)

Diego **is speaking** English *now*.
He**'s wearing** shorts *at the moment*.

- **happening in a longer present time**
  (*this month, this year, these days, nowadays*),
  even if it's not happening now

We**'re studying** U.S. history *this month*.
  (*But we aren't studying it now.*)
Laura**'s studying** in France *this year*.
Are you **studying** hard *these days*?

2 Simple Present

Use the simple present to show that something **happens regularly** or for **unchanging facts.**

- **happens regularly**
  (*usually, often, every day, always*)

Diego *usually* **speaks** Spanish.
He **wears** jeans *every day*.

- **unchanging facts**

Miguel **comes** from Oaxaca. Oaxaca **is** in Mexico.

BE CAREFUL! Remember to add *-s* or *-es* to third-person-singular (*he, she, it*) verbs. Also, remember to use *does* in questions and *doesn't* in negatives for third-person-singular verbs.

He **wears** jeans. He **doesn't wear** shorts.
NOT He ~~wear~~ jeans. He ~~don't~~ wear shorts.

3 Simple Present + Adverbs of Frequency

Use the simple present with adverbs of frequency to show **how often something happens.**

100%	*always*
	usually
	often/frequently
	sometimes
	rarely/seldom
	hardly ever
0%	*never*

In Spain, women *always* **kiss** on both cheeks.

In France, women *often* **kiss** on both cheeks.

We *rarely* **stand** very close to each other.

In China, children *never* **call** adults by their first names.

Adverbs of frequency usually go **before the verb.** However, *sometimes* and *usually* can also go at the **beginning of the sentence.**

I *sometimes* **wear** shorts at home.
or
Sometimes I **wear** shorts at home.

BE CAREFUL! Adverbs of frequency usually go **after** the verb *be*.

They **are** *never* late.
NOT They ~~never are~~ late.

4 Non-Action Verbs

Use non-action verbs to describe **states** or **situations**, but not actions.

Non-action verbs describe:

- **emotions**
  (*like, love, hate, want, feel, fear, trust*)

  We **like** Claude a lot.
  We **love** the stories he tells.

- **mental states**
  (*know, remember, believe, think, mean, understand, wonder*)

  I **know** a lot of U.S. customs now.
  We **think** they're from Spain.
  What **do** you **mean**? I **don't understand**.

- **possession**
  (*have, own, possess, belong*)

  Cesar **has** two brothers.
  Some students **own** cars.

- **senses** and **perceptions**
  (*hear, see, smell, taste, feel, notice, seem, look, be, appear, sound*)

  I **hear** the telephone.
  Dina **looks** tired.
  They both **sound** sick.

BE CAREFUL! Use the **simple present** with most **non-action verbs**. Do not use the present progressive—even when the verb describes a situation that exists at the moment of speaking.

Jane **wants** to go home now.
NOT Jane ~~is wanting~~ to go home now.

USAGE NOTE In **informal conversation**, some people use the **present progressive** with verbs of emotion (especially with *like* and *love*) and with verbs of mental state. This often describes a **temporary feeling** or a change of feelings.

I**'m loving** this book!
She**'s liking** him more and more.
He**'s understanding** a lot better these days.

5 Non-Action and Action Verbs

Some verbs can have both a **non-action** and an **action** meaning.

	NON-ACTION	ACTION
sense and perception verbs (*taste, smell, feel,* and *look*)	The soup **tastes** good. (*It's good.*)	He**'s tasting** the soup. (*He's trying it.*)
	His car **looks** great. (*It's beautiful.*)	I**'m looking** at his car. (*I'm examining it.*)
have and *think*	I **have** a new watch. (*I own a new watch.*)	I**'m having** fun. (*I'm experiencing fun.*)
	I **think** he's right. (*My opinion: He's right.*)	I**'m thinking** of going. (*I'm considering going.*)

USAGE NOTE We often use *feel* in the progressive form when it expresses an **emotion**. The **meaning is the same** as when we use the simple present form.

I **feel** very happy about this.
or
I**'m feeling** very happy about this.

PRONUNCIATION NOTE

01|02

Pronunciation of *What do you* and *What are you*

In informal American English conversation, people often pronounce *What do you . . . ?* and *What are you . . . ?* the same way: "whaddaya."	**A: What do you** do? *(whaddaya)* **B: What are you** doing? *(whaddaya)*

REFERENCE NOTES

For **spelling rules** on forming the **present progressive**, see Appendix 21 on page 462.

For **spelling rules** on forming the third-person singular of the **simple present**, see Appendix 20 on page 461.

For **pronunciation rules** for the **simple present**, see Appendix 29 on page 466.

For **contractions** of *I am, you are*, etc., see Appendix 26 on page 464.

For a list of **non-action verbs**, see Appendix 2 on page 454.

For the **present progressive** and the **simple present** to talk about the **future**, see Unit 6 on page 76.

STEP 3   FOCUSED PRACTICE

EXERCISE 1 DISCOVER THE GRAMMAR

GRAMMAR NOTES 1–5 Read the postings by Brian, a Canadian student studying in Argentina. Underline all the verbs that describe **what is happening now**. Circle the verbs that describe **what regularly happens.**

JUNE 30: 7:30 p.m. My host parents are still working. Carlos, my "father," works at home. My "little brother," Ricardo, is cute. He looks (and acts) a lot like Bobby. Right now, he's looking over my shoulder and trying to read my journal.

JULY 4: The weather is cold here in the summer. I usually spend the first weekend of July at the beach. Today, I'm walking around in a heavy sweater.

JULY 10: I'm sitting in the school cafeteria with some of my classmates. In Canada, I only drink tea, but at the moment I'm having a cup of strong coffee. It tastes great! The students here come from all over the world. Most of them don't speak English, so we're all speaking Spanish. It's a great way to learn!

AUGUST 6: I usually feel great in the evening, but tonight I feel really tired.

AUGUST 25: I'm feeling very comfortable here now—but it's almost time to go home! My host parents usually cook a light dinner, but tonight is a special event. They're preparing a big party for me to say goodbye. I miss them already!

EXERCISE 2 PRESENT PROGRESSIVE OR SIMPLE PRESENT

Ⓐ GRAMMAR NOTES 1–5 Some students are talking outside of a classroom. Circle the correct words to complete their conversations.

Conversation 1

TARO: There's Miguel. He talks / (He's talking) to Luisa.
1.

MARISA: Yes. They take / They're taking a class together this semester.
2.

TARO: They stand / They're standing very close to each other.
3.
Do you think / Are you thinking that they date / they're dating?
4.   5.

MARISA: No. I don't think / I'm not thinking that it means / it's meaning
6.   7.
anything special. I come / I'm coming from Costa Rica, and people
8.
usually stand / are standing that close to each other there.
9.

Conversation 2

LI-WU: Hi, Paulo. What do you do / are you doing?
1.

PAULO: Oh, I wait / I'm waiting for class to begin.
2.

LI-WU: What's the matter? You seem / You're seeming a little down.
3.

PAULO: I'm just tired. I work / I'm working evenings this semester. Hey, is
4.
that your teacher over there?

LI-WU: Yes. She talks / She's talking to a classmate.
5.

PAULO: What's wrong? He doesn't look / He's not looking at her.
6.
He seems / He's seeming uncomfortable.
7.

LI-WU: Oh. That doesn't mean / isn't meaning anything. In some countries,
8.
it's not polite to look directly at your teacher.

▶01│03 Ⓑ LISTEN AND CHECK Listen to the conversations and check your answers in A.

EXERCISE 3 QUESTIONS AND STATEMENTS

Ⓐ GRAMMAR NOTES 1–5 Other students are talking outside of a classroom. Complete the conversations. Use the present progressive or the simple present form of the verbs in parentheses.

Conversation 1

RASHA: There's Hans. Why _____is_____ he _____walking_____ so fast?
1. (walk)

Class _____ at 9:00. He still _____ 10 minutes!
2. (start)   3. (have)

CLAUDE: He always _____ fast. I _____ Swiss people
4. (walk)   5. (think)

often _____ to be in a hurry.
6. (appear)

Conversation 2

IZUMI: Isn't that Sergio and Luis? Why

_____ they _____ they
                  1. (shake)

hands? They already _____ each other!
                2. (know)

LI-JING: In Brazil, men _____ hands every time they
                   3. (shake)

_____ . It's normal in their culture.
    4. (meet)

IZUMI: _____ women _____ hands, too?
                    5. (shake)

▶ 01|04   **B** LISTEN AND CHECK   **Listen to the conversations and check your answers in A.**

EXERCISE 4   AFFIRMATIVE AND NEGATIVE STATEMENTS

GRAMMAR NOTES 1–2, 5   **Look at Brian's schedule in Argentina. He usually has a regular schedule, but today some things are different. Complete the sentences. Use the present progressive or the simple present. Choose between affirmative and negative.**

7:00–8:00	~~run in the park~~	*get ready for a field trip*
8:30–12:30	~~attend class~~	*go on a field trip to the museum*
1:00–2:00	eat lunch	
2:00–3:00	~~study with my classmates~~	*work on the family web page*
3:00–5:00	work in the cafeteria	
5:00–6:30	~~do homework~~	*play tennis*
6:30–8:30	~~play tennis~~	*watch a DVD with Eva*
8:30–9:30	have dinner	
9:30–10:00	~~send emails~~	*take a walk with the family*
10:00–10:30	~~take a shower~~	*do homework*

1. Brian always <u>*runs in the park*</u> _____ early in the morning,

    but today he <u>*is getting ready for a field trip*</u> _____ .

2. Brian usually _____ between 8:30 and 12:30,

    but today he _____ .

3. He always _____ between 1:00 and 2:00.

4. It's 1:30. He _____ .

5. He normally _____ after lunch,

    but today he _____ .

6. Every day from 3:00 to 5:00, he _____ .

7. It's 5:15, but he _____ now.

He _____ instead.

8. It's 6:45, but he _____ .

He _____ .

9. It's 8:30. Brian _____ .

10. He always _____ at 8:30.

11. After dinner, Brian usually _____ ,

but tonight he _____ .

12. It's 10:15, but he _____ .

He _____ .

EXERCISE 5 *WHAT DO YOU, WHAT ARE YOU,* OR *WHADDAYA*

01|05 PRONUNCIATION NOTE **Listen to the questions and answers. Check (✓)** *Formal* **if you hear** *What do you* **or** *What are you* **in the question. Check (✓)** *Informal* **if you hear** *Whaddaya.*

	Formal	Informal
1. What are you doing?	☐	☑
2. What do you do after school?	☐	☐
3. What do you usually eat for lunch?	☐	☐
4. What are you reading these days?	☐	☐
5. What do you like to read?	☐	☐
6. What do you like to read?	☐	☐

EXERCISE 6 EDITING

GRAMMAR NOTES 1–5 **Read this student's blog entry. There are eleven mistakes in the use of the present progressive or simple present. The first mistake is already corrected. Find and correct ten more.**

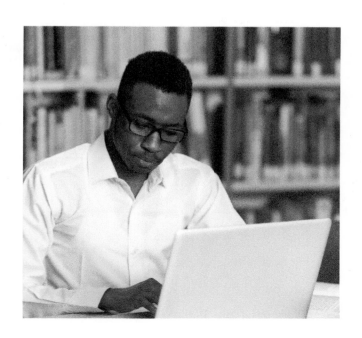

       I'm sitting
It's 12:30 and ~~I sit~~ in the library right now.

My classmates are eating lunch together,

but I don't feel hungry yet. At home, we eat

never this early. Today, our journal topic is

culture shock (the strange feelings you have

when you visit a foreign country for the first

time). It's a good topic for me right now because I'm being pretty homesick. I miss speaking my native language with my friends. And I miss my old routine. At home, we always are eating a big meal at 2:00 in the afternoon. Then we rest. But here in Toronto, I'm having a 3:00 conversation class. Every day, I almost fall asleep in class, and my teacher ask me, "Are you bored?" Of course I'm not bored. I just need my afternoon nap! This class always is fun. This semester, we work on a project with videos. My team is filming groups of people from different cultures at social events. We are analyze "personal space." That is meaning how close to each other these people stand. According to my new watch, it's 12:55, and I have a 1:00 class. That's all for now. Teachers here really aren't liking lateness!

STEP 4   COMMUNICATION PRACTICE

EXERCISE 7 LISTENING

01|06 **A** You are going to listen to five short interviews of foreign students studying at a summer language program in the United States. Listen and check (✓) the things the students *Usually* do and the things they are doing *Now or These Days*. Then listen again and check your answers.

	Usually	Now or These Days
1. Ana		
a. speak English	☐	☑
b. speak Spanish	☐	☐
2. Mehmet		
a. live in a small town	☐	☐
b. live in a big city	☐	☐
3. Eva		
a. walk slowly	☐	☐
b. move quickly	☐	☐
4. Paulo		
a. wear a watch	☐	☐
b. ask other people for the time	☐	☐
5. Olga		
a. study grammar and pronunciation	☐	☐
b. study English literature	☐	☐

B Work with a partner. Listen to each interview again. Discuss the questions.

Interview 1

How does Ana feel? Why?

What does she find most difficult? Why?

EXAMPLE: A: Ana feels good.

B: Yes. Things are going well for her. She . . .

Interview 2

Does Mehmet like living in New York? Why or why not?

Interview 3

Is Eva experiencing culture shock?

What does she think about the "pace of life" in the United States?

Interview 4

What does Paulo do at home without a watch?

Why is Paulo upset?

Do *you* wear a watch? Why or why not?

Interview 5

How does Olga feel about her classes? Why?

What is she studying now?

EXERCISE 8 FIND SOMEONE WHO . . .

A GAME Walk around your classroom. Ask your classmates questions and fill out the chart. The first person to finish wins.

EXAMPLE: A: Tania, are you living in a dormitory?

B: No, I'm not. I'm living with a family.

Find someone who . . .	Name
isn't living in a dormitory	_____
likes visiting foreign countries	_____
speaks more than two languages	_____
is studying something in addition to English	_____
doesn't watch sports on TV	_____
is planning to travel abroad this year	_____
_____ (add your own)	_____

B Report back to the class.

EXAMPLE: Tania isn't living in a dormitory.

EXERCISE 9 WHAT'S HAPPENING?

PICTURE DISCUSSION **Work with a partner. Look at the photos. Describe them. What's happening? How do the people feel? Discuss possible explanations for each situation. Compare your answers with those of your classmates.**

EXAMPLE: A: She's pointing and she looks . . .
B: She also has a finger in front of her . . . Maybe she . . .

EXERCISE 10 IS IT OK IN YOUR CULTURE?

Ⓐ CROSS-CULTURAL COMPARISON **Look at the questions. In your culture, which questions are appropriate to ask someone you just met? Check (✓) OK. Which questions are not appropriate? Check (✓) NOT OK.**

Questions	OK	NOT OK
1. Are you married?	☐	☐
2. How much rent do you pay?	☐	☐
3. How old are you?	☐	☐
4. What are you studying?	☐	☐
5. What do you do?	☐	☐
6. Where do you live?	☐	☐

Ⓑ **Work in a group. Compare your choices with those of your classmates.**

EXAMPLE: A: In my culture, it's OK to ask someone the question "Are you married?" What about in your culture?
B: It depends. It's OK for an older person to ask a young person this question. But, it's *not* OK for a man to ask a strange woman the question. What about in your culture?

Ⓒ **What are other examples of inappropriate questions in your culture?**

EXAMPLE: A: In my culture, it's not OK to ask someone the questions "How tall are you?" or "What do you weigh?" What about in your culture?
B: . . .

A BEFORE YOU WRITE Think about a new experience you are having (for example, living in a new country, taking a new class, working at a new job). Complete the outline.

_____
(New Experience)

Usually   **Now**

_____   _____

_____   _____

_____   _____

B WRITE Use your outline to write a paragraph about your new experience. How is it different from what you usually do? How do you feel in the new situation? Use *but* or *however* to contrast your usual experience with your new experience. Try to avoid the common mistakes in the chart.

EXAMPLE: I usually live at home with my parents, but this month I'm living with my aunt and uncle. Everything seems different. My aunt always makes dinner at 6:00. However, at home we never eat before 8:00 p.m. . . .

Common Mistakes in Using the Present Progressive and Simple Present

Use the **simple present** with most **non-action verbs**. Do not use the present progressive.	I **think** my aunt's dinners are great. NOT I ~~am thinking~~ my aunt's dinners are great.
Put an **adverb of frequency before** the simple present verb. Do not put it after the verb.	We *always* **eat** at 6:00. NOT We ~~eat always~~ at 6:00.
Put an **adverb of frequency after** the verb *be*. Do not put it before *be*.	She **is** *always* on time. NOT She ~~always is~~ on time.

C CHECK YOUR WORK Read your paragraph. Underline once the present progressive and underline twice the simple present forms. Circle the adverbs of frequency. Use the Editing Checklist to check your work.

Editing Checklist

Did you use . . . ?

☐ the present progressive to describe something that is happening right now

☐ the simple present to describe what regularly happens

☐ the simple present with non-action verbs such as *be, like, seem,* and *want*

☐ adverbs of frequency in the correct position

D REVISE YOUR WORK Read your paragraph again. Can you improve your writing? Make changes if necessary. Give your paragraph a title.

UNIT 1 REVIEW

Test yourself on the grammar of the unit.

(A) Circle the correct words to complete the sentences.

1. What courses <u>are you taking</u> / <u>do you take</u> this semester?

2. <u>I don't</u> / <u>I'm not</u> understand this phrase. What's *culture shock*?

3. At home, we <u>often speak</u> / <u>speak often</u> Spanish.

4. Look! That's my teacher. <u>He's talking</u> / <u>He talks</u> to Andrea, one of my classmates.

5. <u>Are</u> / <u>Do</u> you feel better today?

(B) Complete the conversation with the present progressive or simple present form of the verbs in parentheses.

A: What _____ you _____ right now?
   1. (do)

B: Not much. I _____ just _____ a video game. Why?
   2. (play)

A: _____ you _____ to get some lunch?
   3. (want)

B: Sure. I usually _____ this early, but I _____ pretty hungry right now.
   4. (not eat)   **5.** (feel)

A: Mmm, mushroom soup. It _____ good.
   6. (look)

B: It _____ good, though. I had it yesterday.
   7. (not taste)

A: Hey, there's Costa and Libby. Why _____ they _____ like that?
   8. (shout)

   _____ they angry?
   9. (be)

B: I don't think so. They always _____ like that. Let's go sit with them. They're fun.
   10. (talk)

(C) Find and correct five mistakes.

I live in Qatar, but right now I stay in Wisconsin. I'm studying English here. I have

a good time this summer, but in some ways it's a pretty strange experience. Summer

in Wisconsin feel like winter in Qatar! Every weekend, I go to the beach with some

classmates, but I go never into the water—it's too cold! I'm enjoy my time here

though, and my culture shock is going away fast.

Now check your answers on page 475.

Simple Past

POETS

OUTCOMES
• Use the simple past with regular and
  irregular verbs
• Describe events, states, and situations in the past
• Identify the order of events in a reading
  and listening
• Discuss past events and situations
• Write about some important life events

STEP 1   GRAMMAR IN CONTEXT

BEFORE YOU READ

Look at the title of the reading and the handwritten text. Discuss the questions.

1. How long did Matsuo Basho live?

2. What did he do?

READ

02|01   Read this short biography of Basho.

Matsuo Basho, 1644–1694

Matsuo Basho wrote more than 1,000 *haiku* (three-line poems). He chose topics from nature, daily life, and human emotions. He became one of Japan's most famous poets, and his work established haiku as an important art form.

> The old pond
> A frog jumped in~
> The sound of water
> ~Matsuo Basho

Basho was born Matsuo Munefusa near Kyoto in 1644. ("Basho" is the name he later used as a poet.) He did not want to become a samurai[1] like his father. Instead, he moved to Edo (present-day Tokyo) and studied poetry. Then he became a teacher, and by 1681 he had many students and admirers.

Basho, however, was restless. Starting in 1684, he traveled on foot and on horseback all over Japan. Sometimes his friends joined him, and they wrote poetry together. Travel was difficult in the seventeenth century, and Basho often got sick. He died in 1694 during a journey to Osaka. At that time, he had 2,000 students.

---

1 *samurai*: a member of the soldier class in Japan in past times

AFTER YOU READ

A VOCABULARY Complete the sentences with the words from the box.

| admirers | emotions | journey | restless | topic |

1. Basho wrote about everyday things. A frog is the _____ of one of his most famous poems.

2. Basho's students and _____ loved him and called him a great poet.

3. On his first _____, Basho traveled a long way and visited his native village.

4. Basho became _____ and did not want to stay in one place for very long.

5. Basho felt all kinds of strong _____ in his travels, such as fear and happiness.

B COMPREHENSION Check (✓) the boxes to complete the statements. Each statement has two correct answers.

1. Basho lived _____.
   - ☐ from 1644 to 1694
   - ☐ in the sixteenth century
   - ☐ in the seventeenth century

2. Basho became a _____.
   - ☐ samurai
   - ☐ poet
   - ☐ traveler

3. In Edo, Basho _____.
   - ☐ studied poetry
   - ☐ became a teacher
   - ☐ became a samurai

4. On his journeys, he _____.
   - ☐ traveled in boats
   - ☐ walked
   - ☐ rode horses

5. At the end of his life, Basho _____.
   - ☐ had only a few students
   - ☐ traveled to Osaka
   - ☐ was famous

C DISCUSSION Work with a partner. Compare your answers in B. Why did or didn't you check each answer?

SIMPLE PAST: *BE*

Affirmative Statements

Subject	*Be*	
I	was	
You	were	
He She It	was	famous.
We You They	were	

Negative Statements

Subject	*Be + Not*	
I	wasn't	
You	weren't	
He She It	wasn't	famous.
We You They	weren't	

Yes/No Questions

Be	Subject	
Was	I	
Were	you	
Was	he she it	famous?
Were	we you they	

Short Answers

Affirmative		
Yes,	you	were.
	I	was.
	he she it	was.
	you we they	were.

Negative		
No,	you	weren't.
	I	wasn't.
	he she it	wasn't.
	you we they	weren't.

Wh- Questions

Wh- Word	*Be*	Subject	
Where When Why	was	I	
	were	you	
	was	he she it	famous?
	were	we you they	

SIMPLE PAST: REGULAR AND IRREGULAR VERBS

Affirmative Statements

Subject	Verb	
I You He She It We You They	**moved traveled**	to Japan.
	came left	in 2012.

Negative Statements

Subject	*Did not*	Base Form of Verb	
I You He She It We You They	**didn't**	**move travel**	to Japan.
		come leave	in 2012.

Yes/No Questions

Did	Subject	Base Form of Verb	
Did	I you he she it we you they	**move travel**	to Japan?
		come leave	in 2012?

Short Answers

Affirmative		
Yes,	you I he she it you we they	**did.**

Negative		
No,	you I he she it you we they	**didn't.**

Wh- Questions

Wh- Word	*Did*	Subject	Base Form of Verb	
When Why	**did**	I you he she it we you they	**move travel**	to Japan?
			come? leave?	

GRAMMAR NOTES

1 Simple Past

Use the simple past to show that an action, state, or situation is **finished**.

Basho **lived** in the 17th century.
He **was** a poet. He **wrote** haiku.
He **didn't stay** in one place.
Where **did** he **travel**?

2 Simple Past + Past Time Expressions

We often use the simple past with past time expressions.

Some examples of **past time expressions** are:

- *yesterday*
- *last week*
- *300 years ago*
- *in the 17th century*
- *by 1681*

Yesterday, I **wrote** my first poem.
Last week, I **read** a poem by Basho.
He **died** more than *300 years ago*.
He **lived** *in the 17th century*.
By 1681, he **had** many students.

3 Regular Verbs

Form the simple past of regular verbs by **adding** *-d* or *-ed* to the base form of the verb.

	BASE FORM	SIMPLE PAST
• adding *-d*	live →	live**d**
• adding *-ed*	want →	want**ed**

IN WRITING There are often **spelling changes** when you add *-ed* to the verb.

study →	stud**ied**
plan →	plan**ned**

4 Irregular Verbs

Many common verbs are irregular. Do not form their simple past by adding *-d* or *-ed* to the base form of the verb.

The list to the right includes the **most common irregular verbs**. They are especially common in conversation.

BASE FORM	SIMPLE PAST	BASE FORM	SIMPLE PAST
be →	**was/were**	know →	**knew**
come →	**came**	make →	**made**
get →	**got**	mean →	**meant**
give →	**gave**	say →	**said**
go →	**went**	see →	**saw**
have →	**had**	think →	**thought**

USAGE NOTE Some verbs have **two simple past forms**—one **regular** and one **irregular**. In conversation, the irregular past form is more common. There is one exception: for *dream*, the regular form is more common.

kneel →	kneel**ed**/kne**lt**
light →	light**ed**/l**it**
dream →	dream**ed**/drea**mt**

USAGE NOTE A few verbs have **two irregular simple past forms**.

forbid →	**forbade/forbid**
sink →	**sank/sunk**

REFERENCE NOTES

For **spelling rules** for the **simple past of regular verbs**, see Appendix 22 on page 462.
For **pronunciation rules** for the **simple past of regular verbs**, see Appendix 30 on page 467.
For a list of **irregular verbs**, see Appendix 1 on page 453.

STEP 3 FOCUSED PRACTICE

EXERCISE 1 DISCOVER THE GRAMMAR

GRAMMAR NOTES 1–4 Read more about Basho. Underline all the regular simple past verbs. Circle all the irregular simple past verbs. Then complete the timeline on the right.

As the son of a samurai, Basho (grew up) in the household of Todo Yoshitada, a young lord. After his father's death in 1656, Basho stayed in the Yoshitada household. He and Todo wrote poetry together, and in 1664, they published some poems. Two years later, Todo died suddenly. Basho left the area.

Basho was a restless young man, and he moved around for several years. In the 1670s, he went to Edo and stayed there. He found friendship and success once again. Basho judged poetry contests, published his own poetry, and taught students. His students built him a home outside the city in 1681. They planted a banana tree (*basho* in Japanese) in front and called his home "Basho Hut." That is how the poet got his name: Basho.

In spite of this success, Basho became unhappy. He often wrote about loneliness. He dreamed of traveling. His mother died in 1683, and he began his travels a year later. His trip to the northern part of Honshu in 1689 was difficult, but his travel diary about this journey, *Narrow Road to the Deep North*, became one of Japan's greatest works of literature.

As a famous poet, Basho had many visitors—too many, in fact. In 1693 he locked his gate for a month, stayed alone, and wrote. The following year, he took his final journey, to Osaka. He died there among his friends and admirers.

Year	Event
1644	Basho was born.
1656	Basho's father died.
1664	Basho (and Todo) published some poems.
1666	_____ _____
_____	Students built the Basho Hut.
1683	_____ _____
1684	_____ _____
_____	Basho traveled to northern Honshu.
_____	Basho locked his gate to visitors.
1694	_____ _____

EXERCISE 2 AFFIRMATIVE STATEMENTS

GRAMMAR NOTES 1–4 Complete this biography of American poet Emily Dickinson. Use the simple past form of the verbs in parentheses. See Appendix 1 on page 453 for help with the irregular verbs.

Emily Dickinson, one of the most famous American poets,

_____lived_____ from 1830 to 1886. Her favorite topics
    1. (live)

_____ nature, time, and human emotions.
    2. (be)

Dickinson _____ an unusual life. During the
           3. (lead)

1860s, she _____ a recluse[1]—she almost never
          4. (become)

_____ her house in Amherst, Massachusetts, and she
   5. (leave)

only _____ white. Dickinson _____
      6. (wear)   **7.** (allow)

very few people to visit her, but she _____ a lot of
                 8. (have)

friends, and she _____ them many letters.
         9. (write)

---

1 *recluse:* someone who stays away from other people

EXERCISE 3 AFFIRMATIVE AND NEGATIVE STATEMENTS

GRAMMAR NOTES 1–4 Complete this list of facts about Emily Dickinson. Use the simple past form of the verbs in parentheses. See Appendix 1 on page 453 for help with the irregular verbs.

1. Dickinson _____wasn't_____ only interested in poetry.
           (not be)

2. She also _____ science.
        (like)

3. She _____ topics from science in many of her poems.
      (use)

4. She never _____ far from home, but she _____ many people.
        (go)   (know)

5. Dickinson _____ only poetry.
       (not write)

6. She _____ her friends and admirers hundreds of letters.
      (send)

7. Her letters _____ full of jokes, recipes, cartoons, and poems.
      (be)

8. But she _____ the envelopes—other people _____ that for her.
    (not address)   (do)

9. Dickinson _____ a typewriter.
      (not own)

10. She _____ the first drafts[1] of her poems on the back of old grocery lists.
    (write)

11. During her lifetime, 7 of her 1,700 poems _____ in print.
             (appear)

12. She _____ about this, and no one _____ her permission.
  (not know)   (ask)

---

1 *first drafts:* first copies of a piece of writing, with no corrections

EXERCISE 4 REGULAR AND IRREGULAR VERBS

A GRAMMAR NOTES 1–4 Complete the lines from a poem by Emily Dickinson. Use the simple past form of the verbs from the box. See Appendix 1 on page 453 for help with the irregular verbs.

bite	~~come~~	drink	eat	hop	not know

A bird _____came_____ down the walk:
1.

He _____ I saw;
2.

He _____ an angle-worm in halves
3.

And _____ the fellow raw.
4.

And then he _____ a dew
5.

from a convenient grass,

And then _____ sidewise to the wall
6.

To let a beetle pass.

⏵02|02 **B** LISTEN AND CHECK Listen to the poem and check your answers in A.

EXERCISE 5 QUESTIONS AND ANSWERS

A GRAMMAR NOTES 1–4 Read the statements about Basho. Write questions about Emily Dickinson using the words in parentheses. Then answer your questions using the information from Exercises 2 and 3. Use short answers for *yes/no* questions and long answers for *wh-* questions.

1. Basho was a poet. (Dickinson / a poet)

   Q: _Was Dickinson a poet?_

   A: _Yes, she was._

2. He was born in 1644. (when / she / born)

   Q: _When was she born?_

   A: _She was born in 1830._

3. He lived in Japan. (where / she / live)

   Q: _____

   A: _____

4. He became famous during his lifetime. (she / become / famous during her lifetime)

   Q: _____

   A: _____

5. Basho's admirers often visited him. (Dickinson's admirers / often / visit her)

Q: _____

A: _____

6. He traveled a lot. (she / travel / a lot)

Q: _____

A: _____

7. Basho wrote more than 1,000 poems. (how many poems / Dickinson / write)

Q: _____

A: _____

8. He wrote about nature. (what / she / write about)

Q: _____

A: _____

9. He died in 1694. (when / she / die)

Q: _____

A: _____

02|03 **B** LISTEN AND CHECK **Listen to the Questions and Answers about Emily Dickinson and check your answers in A.**

EXERCISE 6 AFFIRMATIVE AND NEGATIVE STATEMENTS

A GRAMMAR NOTES 2–4 **Read this article about a modern writer.**

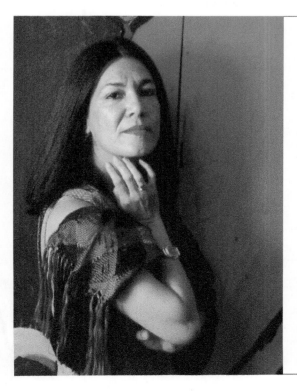

ANA CASTILLO is a modern poet, novelist, short story writer, and teacher. She was born in Chicago in 1953, and she lived there for 32 years. *Otro Canto*, her first book of poetry, appeared in 1977.

In her work, Castillo uses humor and a lively mixture of Spanish and English (Spanglish). She got her special writer's "voice" by living in a neighborhood with many different ethnic groups. She also thanks her father for her writing style. "He had an outgoing and easy personality, and this . . . sense of humor. I got a lot from him."

Castillo attended high school, college, and graduate school in Chicago. In the 1970s, she taught English and Mexican history. She received a PhD in American Studies from Bremen University in Germany in 1992. Her latest novel, *Give It to Me*, appeared in 2014.

B Read the statements. Write *That's right* or *That's wrong*. Correct the incorrect statements.

1. Ana Castillo was born in Mexico City.

   That's wrong. She wasn't born in Mexico City. She was born in Chicago.

2. She lived in Chicago until 1977.

   _____

3. Her father was very shy.

   _____

4. She grew up among people of different cultures.

   _____

5. Castillo got most of her education in Chicago.

   _____

6. She taught Spanish in the 1970s.

   _____

7. She went to France for her PhD.

   _____

8. Her latest novel appeared in 2004.

   _____

EXERCISE 7 EDITING

GRAMMAR NOTES 1–4 **Read this student's journal. There are ten mistakes in the use of the simple past. The first mistake is already corrected. Find and correct nine more.**

Today in class, we read a poem by the American poet Robert Frost.
I really ~~enjoy~~ *enjoyed* it. It was about a person who choosed between two roads in a forest. Many people believed the person were Frost. He thinked about his choice for a long time. The two roads didn't looked very different. Finally, he didn't took the road most people take. He took the one less traveled on. At that time, he didn't thought it was an important decision, but his choice change his life.

Sometimes I feel a little like Frost. As a child, I dreamed of traveling. Two years ago, I decide to move to a new country. It was a long journey and a big change. Did I made the right decision? I hope so.

EXERCISE 8   LISTENING

▶02|04   **A**   Read the statements. Then listen to the interview with a poet. Listen again and circle the correct information.

1. Murat came to the United States before / (after) his parents.

2. He had a wonderful life with his grandparents in Baltimore / Turkey.

3. In Baltimore, he had no friends, so he wrote poems / read books.

4. He wrote his first poem in English / Turkish.

5. In college, Murat studied farming / poetry.

▶02|04   **B**   Read the information in the timeline. Then listen again to the interview and write the year for each event.

was born	parents left Turkey	moved to the U.S.	began to write poetry	graduated from college	won a poetry award	became a teacher
1970						

▶02|04   **C**   Work with a partner. Listen again to the interview. Discuss these questions.

1. Why did Murat's parents go to the United States before Murat?

     EXAMPLE: A: They needed to find jobs.
                B: They also found a house.

2. Who did Murat live with when his parents left Turkey? How did he feel?

3. How did Murat feel when he first moved to the United States?

4. Why did he hate the city at first?

5. When did he write his first poem?

6. How did he learn to write poetry?

EXERCISE 9   BASHO AND DICKINSON

DISCUSSION   Work in a group. Reread the information about Matsuo Basho (see pages 18 and 23) and Emily Dickinson (see page 24). In what ways were the two poets similar? How were they different? With your group, write as many ideas as you can. Compare your ideas with those of your classmates.

EXAMPLE: A: Both Basho and Dickinson were poets.
                B: Basho lived in the seventeenth century. Dickinson lived in the nineteenth century.
                C: Dickinson stayed at home, but Basho was restless and traveled a lot.

EXERCISE 10 RHYME TIME

▶ 02|05 **A** WORD PLAY In a poem, the last word in a line often rhymes[1] with the last word in another line. For example, read and listen to these lines of a famous poem called "Trees" by Joyce Kilmer. Notice that *see* rhymes with *tree* and *wear* rhymes with *hair*.

> *I think that I shall never see*
> *A poem lovely as a tree*
>
> *A tree that may in Summer wear*
> *A nest of robins in her hair*

B Work with a partner. See Appendix 1 on page 453. How many irregular past tense verbs rhyme with the verbs in the list? Write them. You have five minutes.

led _____ *fed,* _____

bought _____

meant _____

drew _____

C Compare your answers with those of your classmates'. Who found the most pairs that rhyme?

---

1 *rhymes:* ends with the same sound as another word

EXERCISE 11 A TWENTIETH-CENTURY POET

A GROUP PROJECT Work in a group. Look at the photos of four twentieth-century poets. Choose one poet to research. Answer some of the questions below.

EXAMPLE: **A:** Maya Angelou was born in the United States in 1928. She grew up in Missouri and Arkansas.
B: She also spent time in California.
C: She became a poet. . . .
D: In addition to a poet, she . . .

Maya Angelou

Xu Zhimo

Yehuda Amichai

Gabriela Mistral

Possible questions:

- When and where was he/she born?
- Where did he/she grow up?
- When did he/she write his/her first poem?
- What did he/she write about?
- Where did he/she attend school?

- When did he/she win a poetry prize?
- When and where did he/she travel?
- When and where did he/she die?
- What interesting fact(s) did you learn about this poet?

B Report back to your class. If your group chose the same poet as another group, do you have the same information about that poet? Compare answers.

EXAMPLE: A: Maya Angelou was born in the United States.
 B: Right.
 A: She grew up in Missouri.
 B: She also grew up in Arkansas.
 A: . . .

EXERCISE 12 CELEBRITY PROFILE

A INFORMATION GAP Work with a partner. Student A will follow the instructions below. Student B will follow the instructions on page 485.

STUDENT A

- Read the profile of an actor who is also a poet, painter, and musician. Ask your partner questions to complete the missing information.

  EXAMPLE: A: When was Viggo born?
   B: He was born on October 20, 1958.

- Answer your partner's questions.

  EXAMPLE: B: Where was Viggo born?
   A: He was born in New York.

- If you don't know how to spell something, ask your partner.

  EXAMPLE: A: How do you spell October?
   B: Capital *O, c, t, o, b, e, r.*

SCREEN-TIME PROFILE

Viggo Mortensen
actor, poet, painter, musician

Date of Birth: *October 20, 1958*

Place of Birth: New York

Mini Bio:
- lived in Argentina, Venezuela, and _____ as a child

- attended school in Argentina

- learned to speak _____

- returned to the United States in 19_____

- became a movie actor in 1985

- first movie was *Witness*

- played the part of _____ in *Lord of the Rings* (This movie made him famous.)

- finished his first _____ in 1993 (The title was *Ten Last Night.*)

- created the paintings for the movie *A Perfect Murder* (He played the part of the artist.)

- wrote music for *Lord of the Rings*

B When you are finished, compare the profiles. Are they the same?

FROM GRAMMAR TO WRITING

A BEFORE YOU WRITE Create a timeline like the one on page 28. Choose five important events in your life. Write the year of each event in the timeline and give a short description of the event above the year.

Events: _____ _____ _____ _____ _____

_____ _____ _____ _____ _____

Years: [ ]   [ ]   [ ]   [ ]   [ ]

B WRITE Use your timeline to write a paragraph about some important events in your life. Include your feelings about the events. Try to avoid the common mistakes in the chart.

EXAMPLE: I was born in the Dominican Republic in 1990. In 1999, I moved to Canada with my family. At first, I felt lonely and missed my country. My mother got a job as a cook in a restaurant. I loved to eat there. My father was an electrician and he found a job at a large school. That's where I met my future wife, Lidia. We didn't get married until 2015 and we had our first child a year later. It was the happiest time in my life.

Common Mistakes in Using the Simple Past

Use the **base form** of the verb **after *did* or *didn't***. Do not use the past form after *did* or *didn't*.	We didn't **get** married until 2015. NOT We didn't ~~get~~ married until 2015.
Use the **correct spelling** of **regular** simple past verbs. Do not forget that the spelling often changes when you add *-ed* to the base form.	I **studied** English. NOT I ~~studyed~~ English.
Use the **correct form** of **irregular** simple past verbs. Do not add *-d* or *-ed* to the base form.	He **found** a job at a school. NOT He ~~finded~~ a job at a school.

C CHECK YOUR WORK Read your paragraph. Underline the regular simple past verbs and circle the irregular simple past verbs. Use the Editing Checklist to check your work.

Editing Checklist

Did you use . . . ?

☐ the simple past for actions, states, or situations that are finished

☐ the correct spelling of regular simple past verbs

☐ the correct form of irregular simple past verbs

D REVISE YOUR WORK Read your paragraph again. Can you improve your writing? Make changes if necessary. Give your paragraph a title.

UNIT 2 REVIEW

Test yourself on the grammar of the unit.

Ⓐ Choose the correct answer to complete each sentence.

1. Last night, I _____ a poem for my English class.
    a. write   **b.** wrote   **c.** written

2. It _____ about my childhood.
    a. be   **b.** were   **c.** was

3. At first, I didn't _____ what to write about.
    a. know   **b.** knowing   **c.** knew

4. My roommate _____ a good suggestion.
    a. makes   **b.** did make   **c.** made

5. Did you _____ a poem for your class?
    a. write   **b.** writing   **c.** wrote

6. I really _____ the experience.
    a. enjoy   **b.** enjoys   **c.** enjoyed

Ⓑ Complete the conversation with the simple past form of the verbs in parentheses and a short answer.

A: I _____ you last night, but you _____. _____ you
           1. (call)   **2.** (not answer)

_____ out?
  3. (go)

B: _____, I _____. I _____ to the movies.
                 4.   **5.** (go)

A: What _____ you _____?
                       6. (see)

B: I _____ *Dead Poets Society*. I _____ it very much, though.
    7. (see)   **8.** (not like)

Ⓒ Find and correct six mistakes.

The poet Elizabeth Alexander was born in New York City, but she didn't grew up there. Her father taked a job with the government, and her family moved to Washington, D.C. As a child, she have a loving family. Her parents were active in the civil rights movement, and Alexander gots interested in African-American history. In her first book, she wrote about important African leaders. She met Barack Obama at the University of Chicago. They both teached there in the 1990s. On January 20, 2009, she reads a poem at President Obama's inauguration.

Now check your answers on page 475.

Past Progressive and Simple Past

REPORTING EVENTS

OUTCOMES
- Describe past events or situations
- Use *when* or *while* to link clauses in the simple past and the past progressive
- Identify the order of events in a description of an accident
- Report on events that were interrupted by other events
- Write a description of a past event

STEP 1   GRAMMAR IN CONTEXT

BEFORE YOU READ

Look at the picture. Discuss the questions.

1. What do you know about the *Titanic*?
2. What happened to the ship?

READ

03|01   Read this newspaper article about a terrible event.

VOL CCXII, NO 875   Monday, April 15, 1912   Price One Cent

DISASTER AT SEA

NEW YORK, April 15—It was a clear night. The sea was calm. The *Titanic*, the largest luxury ship[1] in the world, was sailing from Southhampton, England, to New York City. This was its first voyage,[2] and it was carrying more than 2,200 passengers and crew.[3] At around 11:30 p.m. crew member Frederick Fleet was looking at the sea when, suddenly, he saw a huge white

---

1 *luxury ship:* a boat that has many great things (beautiful rooms, swimming pools, restaurants, etc.)
2 *voyage:* a long trip, usually on a ship
3 *crew:* the people who work on a ship or airplane

form in front of the ship. When he saw it, Fleet immediately rang the ship's bell three times and shouted, "Iceberg ahead!" But it was too late. The great ship crashed into the mountain of ice.

When the *Titanic* hit the iceberg, people were sleeping, reading, and playing cards. Some passengers heard a loud noise, but they were not alarmed. They believed the ship was unsinkable.[4] But soon it became clear that the *Titanic* was in danger. There was a hole in the side of the ship. Water was entering fast, and it was starting to sink. There were lifeboats, but only 1,178 spaces for 2,224 people. In an attempt to keep everyone calm, the ship's band played a lively tune while people were getting into the boats.

The *Titanic* was not the only ship on the sea that night. There were several other ships in the area. The *Californian* was nearby, but it did not hear the *Titanic's* calls for help. And then there was the *Carpathia*. While the *Titanic* was sailing toward New York, the *Carpathia* was traveling from New York to the Mediterranean.

When it heard the *Titanic's* distress signals,[5] the *Carpathia* turned around and headed back toward the sinking ship. By the time the *Carpathia* arrived, the *Titanic* was already at the bottom of the sea, but there were 18 lifeboats full of cold and frightened survivors. Thanks to the *Carpathia*, more than 700 people lived to tell the story of that terrible night.

---

4 *unsinkable:* cannot go underwater
5 *distress signals:* calls for help

AFTER YOU READ

A VOCABULARY **Match the words with their definitions.**

_____ **1. disaster**   **a.** afraid

_____ **2. calm**   **b.** someone who continues to live after an accident

_____ **3. area**   **c.** to go underwater

_____ **4. survivor**   **d.** one part of a larger place

_____ **5. alarmed**   **e.** a terrible event

_____ **6. sink**   **f.** quiet

B COMPREHENSION **Number the events in order (1–7).**

_____ Water entered the *Titanic*.

_____ Frederick Fleet rang the ship's bell.

_____ The *Titanic* hit an iceberg.

_____ The *Carpathia* arrived and saved the survivors.

_____ The *Titanic* was sailing to New York.

_____ The *Titanic* sank.

_____ Frederick Fleet saw an iceberg.

C DISCUSSION **Work with a partner. Compare your answers in B. Are they the same? Explain your choices.**

PAST PROGRESSIVE

Statements

Subject	Was/Were	(Not)	Base Form of Verb + -ing	
I	was			
You	were			
He She	was	(not)	reading eating sleeping	yesterday at 11:30 p.m. when Anton called. while Mia was talking.
We You They	were			

Yes/No Questions

Was/Were	Subject	Base Form of Verb + -ing	
Was	I		
Were	you		
Was	he she	reading eating sleeping	yesterday at 11:30 p.m.? when Anton called? while Mia was talking?
Were	we you they		

Short Answers

Affirmative				Negative		
	you	were.			you	weren't.
	I	was.			I	wasn't.
Yes,	he she	was.		No,	he she	wasn't.
	you we they	were.			you we they	weren't.

Wh- Questions

Wh-Word	Was/Were	Subject	Base Form of Verb + -ing	
	was	I		
	were	you		
Why	was	he she	reading eating sleeping	yesterday at 11:30 p.m.? when Anton called? while Mia was talking?
	were	we you they		

GRAMMAR NOTES

1 Past Progressive

Use the past progressive to focus on the **duration of a past action**, not its completion.

Paul **was reading** a book last night. *(We don't know if he finished it.)*	

USAGE NOTE We often use the past progressive with a **specific time in the past**.

He **was reading** a book *at 11:30 p.m.*

2 Simple Past

Use the simple past to focus on the **completion of a past action**.

Paul **read** a book last night.
(He finished it.)

BE CAREFUL! Use the **simple past** with most **non-action verbs**. Do not use the past progressive.

She **heard** about the disaster.
NOT She ~~was hearing~~ about the disaster.

3 Past Progressive + Simple Past

Use the past progressive with the simple past to show that **one action interrupted another action in progress in the past**. Use the simple past for the interrupting action.

I **was exercising** when he **called**.
(I was exercising. The phone rang and interrupted my exercises.)

Use *when* or *while* to introduce one of the actions:

- *when* for the action in the **simple past**
- *while* for the action in the **past progressive**

He was running *when* he **fell**.
While he **was running**, he fell.

USAGE NOTE We can also use *when* to introduce the action in the past progressive.

When he **was running**, he fell.

4 Past Progressive + *While* or *When*

Use the past progressive with *while* or *when* to show **two actions in progress at the same time in the past**. Use the past progressive in both clauses.

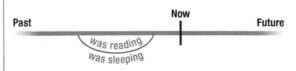

While I **was reading**, Amy **was sleeping**.
When I **was reading**, Amy **was sleeping**.
(I was reading. At the same time, Amy was sleeping.)

5 **Simple Past + Simple Past or Simple Past + Past Progressive**

A sentence with both clauses in the simple past has a very **different meaning** from a sentence with one clause in the simple past and one clause in the past progressive.

• both clauses in the **simple past**	When she **heard** the news, she **drove** home. *(First she heard the news; then she drove home.)*

Past   heard   drove   **Now**   Future
✕——✕

• one clause is in the **simple past**, the other clause in the **past progressive**	When she **heard** the news, she **was driving** home. *(First she was driving home; then she heard the news.)*

Past   heard   **Now**   Future
✕
was driving

6 **Position of the Time Clause**

The **time clause** (the part of the sentence with *when* or *while*) can come at **the beginning or the end** of the sentence. The meaning is the same.

• at the **beginning**	*When* you called, I was eating.
• at the **end**	I was eating *when* you called.

IN WRITING Use a **comma after the time clause** when it comes at the **beginning** of the sentence. Do not use a comma after the main clause when the main clause comes first.	*While* she was sleeping, I was reading. I was reading *while* she was sleeping. **NOT** I was reading, while she was sleeping.

REFERENCE NOTES

For **spelling rules** on forming the **past progressive**, see Appendix 21 on page 462.
For a list of **non-action verbs**, see Appendix 2 on page 454.

STEP 3   **FOCUSED PRACTICE**

EXERCISE 1   DISCOVER THE GRAMMAR

GRAMMAR NOTES 1–6 **Read each question. Then choose the correct sentence (*a* or *b*). In one item, both answers are correct.**

1. In which sentence did the passengers arrive before the ship left?
   a. When the passengers arrived, the ship was leaving.
   (b.) When the passengers arrived, the ship left.

2. Which sentence tells us that the ship reached New York?
   a. It was sailing to New York.
   b. It sailed to New York.

3. In which sentence do we know that the ship went completely underwater?

  a. It was sinking.

  b. It sank.

4. In which sentence did the man fall asleep during the movie *Titanic*?

  a. He fell asleep while he was watching *Titanic*.

  b. While he was watching *Titanic*, he fell asleep.

5. Which sentence talks about two actions that were in progress at the same time?

  a. While the ship was sinking, passengers were getting into lifeboats.

  b. When the ship sank, passengers got into lifeboats.

6. In which sentence was the phone call interrupted?

  a. When he heard the news, he called me.

  b. When he heard the news, he was calling me.

7. In which sentence did the woman leave after the phone call?

  a. When he called her, she left the house.

  b. When he called her, she was leaving the house.

EXERCISE 2
PAST PROGRESSIVE STATEMENTS

GRAMMAR NOTE 1 Douglas is sailing to Europe on the SS *Atlantic*. Look at his schedule for yesterday. Complete the sentences. Use the past progressive form of the verbs in parentheses. Choose between affirmative and negative.

SS ATLANTIC

10:00 breakfast – Sea Breezes – Donna
11:00 exercise – gym – Michel
12:00 swimming contest – Olympic pool
1:00 lunch – Oceania – Raul
2:30 lecture on Italian art – library
4:00 coffee – Café Rose – Natasha
5:00 haircut – Suave Salon – Alain
7:00 dinner – Thalassa – Kim and Jason
9:00 card game – Casino Royal – Massimo

1. At 10:15, Douglas _____*wasn't sleeping*_____ in his cabin.
  a. (sleep)

  He _____*was having*_____ breakfast at Sea Breezes with Donna.
  b. (have)

2. At 11:05, he _____ in the ship's gym with Michel.
  a. (exercise)

  He _____ in the pool.
  b. (swim)

3. At 1:10, he _____ coffee at Café Rose.
  a. (drink)

  He _____ lunch at Oceania with Raul.
  b. (eat)

4. At 2:40, he _____ for a book in the ship's library.
  a. (look)

  He _____ to a lecture on Italian art.
  b. (listen)

5. At 4:05, he _____ a haircut at the Suave Salon.
            a. (get)

He _____ coffee at Café Rose with Natasha.
     b. (have)

6. At 7:10, he _____ in his room.
            a. (rest)

He _____ dinner at Thalassa with Kim and Jason.
     b. (enjoy)

7. At 9:15, he _____ cards at the Casino Royal with Massimo.
            a. (play)

He _____ with Donna at the Discothèque.
     b. (dance)

EXERCISE 3 PAST PROGRESSIVE OR SIMPLE PAST

GRAMMAR NOTES 1–5 Complete the information about the *Titanic* disaster. Use the past progressive or simple past form of the verbs in parentheses. See Appendix 1 on page 453 for help with irregular verbs.

Eyewitness Accounts[1]

According to eyewitness Lawrence Beesley, when the ship _____*hit*_____ the iceberg, the
                                                       1. (hit)

engines _____. Minutes later, when Professor Beesley _____ on deck,
         2. (stop)   **3. (go)**

he _____ only a few other passengers there. Everyone was calm. A few people
    4. (find)

_____ cards in the smoking room. When he _____ out the window,
 5. (play)   **6. (look)**

he _____ an iceberg at the side of the ship.
    7. (see)

Another survivor, Washington Dodge, said that it _____ 11:30 p.m. when the
                                                  8. (be)

crash _____. He _____ to go on deck. While the ship
       9. (happen)   **10. (decide)**

_____, the band _____ a lively tune. At 1:55 a.m., the ship
 11. (sink)   **12. (play)**

_____ completely into the sea.
 13. (sink)

While passenger Elizabeth Shutes _____ a chicken sandwich in her cabin, she
                                  14. (eat)

"_____ a shudder[2] travel through the ship." Shortly after, she _____ in
 15. (feel)   **16. (sit)**

a lifeboat in the middle of the ocean with thirty-four other people. Hours later, someone shouted

"A light, a ship!" When Shutes _____, she _____ a ship with bright
                                17. (look)   **18. (see)**

lights coming toward them. It was the *Carpathia*—the only ship in the area that came to help.

When Harold Bride, one of the ship's two radio operators, _____ some lights in
                                                           19. (notice)

the distance, he _____ it was a steamship. It _____ to rescue them.
                  20. (know)   **21. (come)**

When the *Carpathia* _____, it _____ all of the survivors—including
                      22. (arrive)   **23. (pick up)**

Mr. Bride.

---

1 *eyewitness accounts:* reports by people who saw an accident or crime
2 *shudder:* a quick shaking movement

EXERCISE 4 *YES/NO* AND *WH-* QUESTIONS

A GRAMMAR NOTES 1–5 A newspaper is interviewing a *Titanic* passenger. Read the passenger's answers. Write the interviewer's questions. Use the words in parentheses and the past progressive or simple past.

1. INTERVIEWER: _What were you doing Sunday night?_
   (what / you / do / Sunday night)

   PASSENGER: As I was saying, I was playing cards with some other passengers.

2. INTERVIEWER: _____
   (your wife / play / with you)

   PASSENGER: No, she wasn't. My wife wasn't with me at the time.

3. INTERVIEWER: _____
   (what / she / do / while you / play cards)

   PASSENGER: She was reading in our room.

4. INTERVIEWER: _____
   (you / feel / the crash)

   PASSENGER: Not really. But I heard a very loud noise.

5. INTERVIEWER: _____
   (what / you / do / when you / hear the noise)

   PASSENGER: At first, we all continued to play. We weren't alarmed. Everyone stayed calm.

6. INTERVIEWER: _____
   (what / you / do / when the lights / go out)

   PASSENGER: I tried to find my wife.

7. INTERVIEWER: _____
   (what / she / do / while you / look for her)

   PASSENGER: She was looking for *me*. Thank goodness we found each other!

8. INTERVIEWER: _____
   (what / you / do / when you / find her)

   PASSENGER: We tried to get into a lifeboat.

▶03|02 **B** LISTEN AND CHECK Listen to the interview and check your answers in A.

EXERCISE 5 STATEMENTS WITH *WHEN* AND *WHILE*

GRAMMAR NOTES 1–6 Combine the pairs of sentences. Use the past progressive or the simple past form of the verb. Keep the order of the two sentences. Remember to use commas when necessary.

1. The storm started. Mr. Taylor attended a party.

   When _the storm started, Mr. Taylor was attending a party._

2. The electricity went out. The wind began to blow.

   _____ when _____

3. He drove home. He listened to his car radio.

   While _____

4. He pulled over to the side of the road. He couldn't see anything.

_____ when _____

5. He listened to the news. He heard about a car crash near his home.

While _____

6. It stopped raining. Mr. Taylor drove home in a hurry.

When _____

EXERCISE 6 EDITING

GRAMMAR NOTES 1–6 Read this blog post. There are ten mistakes in the use of the past progressive and the simple past. The first mistake is already corrected. Find and correct nine more. Remember to look at punctuation!

● ● ●

Julio Delgado   6:15 p.m.   April 15

This afternoon I ~~was going~~ *went* to a movie at school. It was *Titanic*. They were showing it because it was the anniversary of the 1912 disaster. What a beautiful and sad film! Jack (Leonardo DiCaprio) was meeting Rose (Kate Winslet) while they both sailed on the huge ship. It was the *Titanic*'s first voyage.

Rose was from a very rich family; Jack was from a poor family. They fell in love, but Rose's mother wasn't happy about it. When the ship was hitting the iceberg, the two lovers were together, but then they got separated. Rose was finding Jack while the ship was sinking. Seconds before the ship went under, they held hands and were jumping into the water. Rose survived, but Jack didn't. It was so sad. When I left the theater, I still was having tears in my eyes.

That wasn't my only adventure of the day. When the movie was over I left the school auditorium. While I walked home, I saw an accident between two pedestrians and a car. I was the only one in the area, so while I saw the accident, I immediately called the police. When the police got there, they asked me a lot of questions—there were no other witnesses. I'm glad to say that the accident had a happier ending than the movie!

EXERCISE 7   LISTENING

A You're going to hear a witness describe a traffic accident. Before you listen, look at the pictures. The pictures show three versions of what happened. Work with a partner and describe what happened in each of the three stories.

1.

2.

3.

03|03 **B** Listen to the witness describe the traffic accident. According to the witness, which set of pictures is the most accurate? Circle the number.

03|03 **C** Work with a partner. Listen to the conversation again. Discuss the questions.

1. What was the witness doing when the accident happened?

   EXAMPLE: A: What was the witness doing when the accident happened?
   B: She was walking down the street.
   A: That's right. She was walking down the street when she heard a car honking its horn.

2. How was the man driving?

3. What were the two friends doing?

4. When did the driver honk his horn?

5. Who was responsible for the accident? Why?

EXERCISE 8 ARE YOU A GOOD WITNESS?

A GAME Look at the picture for 30 seconds. Then close your book and write down what was happening. Make a list of all the details you can remember: What were the people doing? What were they wearing? Was anything unusual going on?

EXAMPLE: *A man and a woman were standing by the fireplace.*
The woman was wearing . . .

B When you are finished, compare your list with those of your classmates. Who remembered the most?

EXERCISE 9 ALIBI[1]

A ROLE PLAY There was a bank robbery yesterday at 2:15 p.m. Work in a group of three to six. Some students are police officers; some are witnesses; and some are suspects.[2] The police are questioning the witnesses and the suspects. Use your imagination to ask and answer questions.

EXAMPLE: OFFICER: What were you doing when the robbery took place?
WITNESS 1: I was standing in line at the bank.
WITNESS 2: I was crossing the street in front of the bank. I saw everything.
OFFICER: What was happening in the bank? . . .

EXAMPLE: OFFICER: Where were you yesterday at 2:15 p.m.?
SUSPECT 1: At 2:15? I was sitting in class.
SUSPECT 2: I was at home. I was watching TV.
OFFICER: Were there other people with you?

B Discuss these questions with your group.

EXAMPLE: A: So, what happened at the bank?
B: There was a robbery.
C: What were the witnesses doing?
D: Well, one woman . . .

1. What happened at the bank?

2. What were the witnesses doing?

3. Do the suspects have good alibis?

4. What were they doing when the robbery occurred?

5. Do you believe their alibis?

---

1 *alibi:* the proof that someone was not at the location of a crime at the time of the crime
2 *suspects:* people who may be guilty of a crime

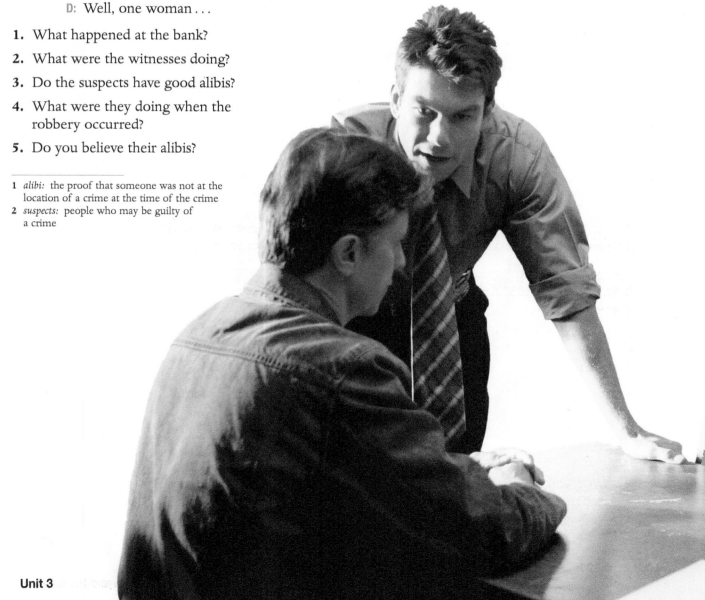

FROM GRAMMAR TO WRITING

A BEFORE YOU WRITE Think about a past event you witnessed. Answer these questions.

1. What was the event? _____

2. When and where did it happen? _____

3. What happened? _____

4. What were you doing when it happened? _____

5. What did you do while it was happening? _____

6. How did you feel after it happened? _____

B WRITE Use your answers to write a paragraph about the event. Use the past progressive and simple past to describe what was happening and what happened during the event. Use *when* and *while*. Try to avoid the common mistakes in the chart.

EXAMPLE: While I was going to lunch today, I saw a wedding party. People were waiting for the bride and groom outside City Hall. When they saw the couple, they . . .

Common Mistakes in Using the Past Progressive and Simple Past

Use the **past progressive** when an action was **interrupted**. Do not use the simple past.	While I **was driving** home, I saw an accident. NOT While I ~~drove~~ home, I saw an accident.
Use the **simple past** with most **non-action verbs**. Do not use the past progressive.	I **saw** an accident. NOT I ~~was seeing~~ an accident.
Use a **comma after the time clause** when it comes **first**. Do not use a comma after the main clause when the main clause comes first.	***When* I saw the accident,** I called the police. NOT I called the police_x when I saw the accident.

C CHECK YOUR WORK Read your paragraph. Underline the past progressive verbs and circle the simple past verbs. Use the Editing Checklist to check your work.

Editing Checklist

Did you use . . . ?

☐ the past progressive to show the duration of a past action

☐ the simple past to show the completion of a past action

☐ the simple past with non-action verbs

☐ *while* with a past progressive action

☐ *when* with a simple past action

☐ commas after time clauses at the beginning of a sentence

D REVISE YOUR WORK Read your paragraph again. Can you improve your writing? Make changes if necessary. Give your paragraph a title.

UNIT 3 REVIEW

Test yourself on the grammar of the unit.

Ⓐ Complete the conversation with the past progressive or simple past form of the verbs in parentheses.

A: _____ you _____ about the big storm last night?
                    1. (hear)

B: Yes, I _____ the pictures when I _____ on the news.
         2. (see)   **3.** (turn)

   _____ you _____ home during the storm?
                        4. (drive)

A: No. At 6:00, I _____ in my office. So while it _____ really hard,
           5. (work)   **6.** (rain)

   I _____ a report. And just when I _____ work, the rain
      7. (finish)   **8.** (leave)

   _____!
     9. (stop)

B: I'm glad. Those pictures on the news _____ pretty bad. There were a lot of
                     10. (look)

accidents because of the storm.

Ⓑ Combine the sentences. Use the past progressive or simple past form of the verbs.

1. While _____.
                     (Danielle watched TV. At the same time, I studied.)

2. _____ when _____.
         (I closed my book. The show *Dr. Davis* came on.)

3. _____ when _____.
         (Dr. Davis talked to his patient. The electricity went off.)

4. When _____.
            (The electricity went off. We lit some candles.)

5. _____ while _____.
         (We talked about a lot of things. We waited for the lights to come on.)

Ⓒ Find and correct five mistakes.

     When I turned on the TV for the first episode of *Dr. Davis*, I unpacked boxes in my freshman dorm room. I stopped and watched for an hour. After that, I wasn't missing a single show while I was attending school. While I was solving math problems, Dr. Davis was solving medical mysteries. And *just* while my dumb boyfriend broke up with me, the beautiful Dr. Grace left Davis for the third time. I even watched the show from the hospital when I was breaking my leg. The show just ended. I was sad when I was seeing the last episode, but I think it's time for some real life!

Now check your answers on page 475.

4

Used to and *Would*

CHANGES

OUTCOMES
- Describe past habits and situations, using *used to* and *would*
- Evaluate events and situations described in a reading and a listening
- Describe and discuss one's past and present physical appearance and habits
- Write a description of a place and how it has changed

STEP 1 GRAMMAR IN CONTEXT

BEFORE YOU READ

Look at the photos. Discuss the questions.

1. What part of the world is Dubai in?

2. What was Dubai like before 1966? What is it like now?

READ

04|01 Read this article about an amazing change.

Dubai: Then and Now

Cities change, but usually not as much or as fast as Dubai. This exciting city in the United Arab Emirates used to be a small town in the desert. Today, it is a large international center with towering[1] skyscrapers. Not very long ago, people used to ride camels to get from place to place, and they would do most of their shopping at outdoor markets. Today, they drive expensive foreign sports cars and shop at huge indoor malls filled with luxury stores.[2]

Before 1966

Now

How did this amazing transformation happen? The answer is oil. After its discovery in 1966, oil provided 60 percent of the city's revenue. The government used the money to build roads, ports,[3] and

1 *towering:* very tall
2 *luxury stores:* stores selling expensive, high-quality items
3 *ports:* places where ships can load and unload people or things

skyscrapers. Today, a large part of the city's money comes from tourism. Tourism? People never used to think of Dubai as a popular vacation destination. But today, tourists come from around the world to view the sights from the Burj Khalifa, the tallest building in the world. They also come to ski indoors when it's 120°F (49°C) outside and to dance under the stars on artificial[4] islands in the shape of palm trees.

The city planners did an amazing job in changing Dubai from a sleepy town to a major international city. Not everyone, however, believes that all the changes are good. For example, because of heavy traffic, a trip that used to take only 10 minutes now takes much longer. And some people believe that Dubai lost a lot of its charm[5] when the skyscrapers went up. They miss the small, traditional houses and markets. But love the changes or not, one thing everyone agrees on: Dubai is not the same city it used to be.

---

4 *artificial*: not natural, made by people
5 *charm*: the special quality that makes people like something or someone

AFTER YOU READ

Ⓐ VOCABULARY Choose the word or phrase that best completes each sentence.

1. If a city is **popular**, _____ .
   a. it's very large   b. it's poor   c. many people like it

2. A **destination** is a place people _____ .
   a. live in   b. travel to   c. don't like

3. A **transformation** is a _____ .
   a. way to travel   b. city   c. change

4. A **traditional** house has a(n) _____ style.
   a. old   b. modern   c. amazing

5. A **major** city is usually _____ .
   a. important   b. small   c. not very big

6. **Revenue** is _____ that a government gets.
   a. a review   b. information   c. money

Ⓑ COMPREHENSION Read the statements. Check (✓) *True* or *False*.

	True	False
1. Dubai is a small town in the desert.	☐	☐
2. In the past, camels were a common form of transportation.	☐	☐
3. Today, most people shop at outdoor markets.	☐	☐
4. In the past, Dubai was a popular tourist destination.	☐	☐
5. Today, traffic is a problem in Dubai.	☐	☐
6. Dubai today is very different from Dubai in the past.	☐	☐

Ⓒ DISCUSSION Work with a partner. Compare your answers in B. Why did you check *True* or *False*?

USED TO

Statements

Subject	Used to / Did not use to	Base Form of Verb	
I You He She It We You They	**used to** **didn't use to**	**be**	popular.

Yes/No Questions

Did	Subject	Use to	Base Form of Verb	
Did	you it they	**use to**	**be**	popular?

Short Answers

Affirmative			Negative		
Yes,	I it they	**did.**	**No,**	I it they	**didn't.**

Wh- Questions

Wh- Word	Did	Subject	Use to	Base Form of Verb	
When	**did**	you it they	**use to**	be	popular?

WOULD

Statements

Subject	Would	Base Form of Verb	
I He They	**would**	**shop**	all day.

Contractions*

I would	=	I**'d**
He would	=	He**'d**
They would	=	They**'d**

*The contraction for *would* is the same for all subjects.

GRAMMAR NOTES

1 *Used to* for Past Habits and Situations

Use *used to* + **base form** of the verb for past habits (repeated activities) and situations that are no longer happening or true in the present.

• **past habits**	When my father was a teenager, he **used to ride** a camel. *(He rode a camel many times in the past, but he doesn't ride one now.)*
• **past situations**	We **used to live** in Dubai. *(We lived in Dubai for a period of time, but we don't live there any longer.)*

USAGE NOTE We often use *used to* in order to contrast the past and the present. **Time expressions** such as *now*, *no longer*, and *not anymore* emphasize the contrast.	He **used to ride** his camel every day, but *now* he drives a car. They **used to shop** at an outdoor market, but they do**n't** shop there **anymore**.
BE CAREFUL! Use the **simple past** for a one-time past activity. Do not use *used to*.	He **drove** to the mall *yesterday*. NOT He ~~used to drive~~ to the mall yesterday.
BE CAREFUL! Use the **simple past** in a time clause with *when*. Do not use *used to*.	*When* I **lived** in Dubai, I used to ride a camel. NOT When I ~~used to live~~ in Dubai, . . .

2 Forms of *Used to*

Used to always refers to the **past**. There is no present or future forms.	She **used to** ski when she was younger. NOT She ~~uses~~ to ski every winter. NOT She ~~will use~~ to ski next month.
IN WRITING The form *use to* often comes after *did* in **negative statements** or **questions**, but people sometimes write *used to*. Some people, including many English teachers, think this is not correct in American English. However, other people think it is correct. In conversation, *use to* and *used to* sound the same: /ˈyustə/	He *didn't* **use to** live there. or He *didn't* **used to** live there. *Did* you **use to** have long hair? or *Did* you **used to** have long hair?
USAGE NOTE In **negative statements**, *never + used to* is much more common than *didn't use(d) to*.	He *never* **used to** study. *(more common)* He *didn't* **use(d) to** study. *(less common)*
USAGE NOTE In **questions**, the **simple past** is more common than *did + use(d) to*.	*Did* you **have** long hair then? *(more common)* *Did* you **use(d) to** have long hair then? *(less common)*

3 *Would* for Past Habits

You can also use *would* + **base form** of the verb for past habits (repeated activities) that no longer happen in the present.

• past habits Past ──×──×──×──│──── Future would go Now	When I was a teenager, I **would go** to the mall every Saturday afternoon. *(I went to the mall every Saturday afternoon, but I no longer do that.)*

BE CAREFUL! Do not use *would* for past situations. Use *used to*. → I **used to live** in Dubai.
 NOT I ~~would live~~ in Dubai.

USAGE NOTE When we reminisce (tell stories) about the past, we often begin with *used to* and then continue with *would* to give more details or examples. → When I was a kid, I **used to ride** my bike everywhere. I **would ride** it to school during the week, and I **would take** it to the park on weekends.

BE CAREFUL! When we use *would*, it must already be clear that we are talking about the past. Do not begin a story with *would*. → I hear you got a new bike! I **used to** ride my bike everywhere. I would ride it to school . . .
 NOT I hear you got a new bike! I ~~would~~ ride my bike everywhere. I would ride it to school . . .

STEP 3   FOCUSED PRACTICE

EXERCISE 1   DISCOVER THE GRAMMAR

GRAMMAR NOTES 1–3   Read this tourist's email. Underline the expressions that refer to past habits and situations that are no longer true.

Greetings from Dubai!

Every time I return here, I'm absolutely amazed at all the changes! Today, I did some typical tourist things. First, I went to the top of the Burj Khalifa—the tallest building in the world. (As I'm sure you know, our CN Tower back home in Canada <u>used to be</u> the tallest. Oh, well. Things change.) Today, from the observation deck, I had a bird's-eye view of the city. It's hard to believe that Dubai used to be just a small town! The transformation is really amazing.

This afternoon, I walked around for hours. I also visited one of the Palm Islands. They're islands built in the early 2000s in the Persian Gulf. They are artificial, but the builders used only natural sand and rock. Amazing—as you can see from the photo. By the way, I used that new travel app on my smartphone. Thanks for telling me about it! It was really helpful—especially the maps. I used to get lost a lot!

After all my sightseeing, I was tired, so right now I'm sitting in an Internet café. There used to be a small hotel right across the street on the corner. I would sometimes stay there when I came here on business. Now there's another huge skyscraper in its place. So many changes! Prices have changed, too. This cup of tea didn't use to cost so much!

Wish you were here. I think you would like it.

Dania

EXERCISE 2 FORMS OF *USED TO*

GRAMMAR NOTE 2 Complete the Questions and Answers (Q & A) about Dubai. Use the correct form of *used to* and the words in parentheses.

Q: What are some of the major tourist attractions in Dubai?

A: Well, there are many, of course, but the Burj Khalifa is probably the most famous one. It's the tallest building in the world. That title _____*used to belong*_____ to the CN Tower in Canada.
               1. (belong)

Q: What's the population of Dubai?

A: It _____ just about 60,000. And that was only fifty years ago! Today, it's over
     2. (be)
two million.

Q: Do many foreigners live in Dubai?

A: Yes. Very few foreigners _____ here, but now a large percentage of Dubai's
              3. (live)
population is foreign born. Many of them are workers from other countries.

Q: _____ there always _____ so much traffic?
              4. (be)

A: No, not at all. Traffic is much worse these days. Remember, not too long ago many people
_____ camels.
  5. (ride)

Q: How are the roads?

A: Dubai _____ many roads. In fact, there was only one major road. Today, of
      6. (not have)
course, there are many more and they are very good. The famous Sheikh Zayed Road, for
example, _____ just one lane. Today, it has twelve.
     7. (have)

Q: Where _____ people _____ before all the big malls?
            8. (shop)

A: They _____ to outdoor marketplaces. These traditional *souks* still exist, but
       9. (go)
there are fewer of them.

Q: Do a lot of tourists visit Dubai?

A: Yes! Dubai never _____ a tourist destination, but today it is very, very popular.
                       10. (be)

EXERCISE 3 *USED TO* OR *WOULD*

GRAMMAR NOTES 1–3 Just like cities, people's lives can change a lot. Read this online newsletter. Circle *used to* or *would* to complete the article. Sometimes only *used to* is possible. Sometimes both *used to* and *would* are possible.

David Beckham (used to) / would live in London, England. Today, he owns homes around the world,
                        1.
including on one of the Palm Islands in Dubai. Born in 1975, Beckham grew up in a family that loved
football,[1] and he used to / would often play in London's Ridgeway Park. His family used to / would
                         2.   3.
frequently travel to see their team, Manchester United, compete. Beckham
used to / would love those trips, and he knew even then that he wanted to play
      4.
football professionally. When his teachers used to / would ask the young Beckham the
                                             5.
typical "What do you want to be when you grow up?" question, his answer was
always the same: "I want to be a footballer." Beckham, who is now retired,
went on to become one of the greatest football players in the world.

BECKHAM BIO BYTES ● He used to / would be a famous football
                                  6.
player, but now he's retired. ● When he was a child, Beckham and his
father used to / would play football together for hours. ● They also
        7.
used to / would watch Manchester United compete. ● Later, Beckham joined
      8.
the team. ● He didn't use to / wouldn't be rich, but he became the richest athlete
                       9.
in England. ● He used to / would be single, but now he's married to famous
                 10.
Spice Girls singer Victoria Adams. ● In the past, the couple used to / would
                                                                11.
spend most of their time in the United States, but now they live in England
again. ● They used to / would have all boys, but now they also have
              12.
a daughter.

_____
1 *football:* the sport called "soccer" in the United States

EXERCISE 4 *USED TO* OR *WOULD*

GRAMMAR NOTES 1–3 **Complete the conversation between two travelers at Dubai International airport. Use *used to* or *would* and the correct verb from the box. Use *would* when possible. You will use one verb more than once.**

| be | buy | eat | live | make | take | watch |

A: This is a beautiful airport. And it's huge!

B: Yes. I remember when it _____*used to be*_____ just a small airport with only a few flights a
1.

week and there were often delays. It really _____ a long time to get anywhere.
2.

A: I remember that, too, of course. And there

_____ so many stores
3. (negative)

or restaurants.

B: That's right. We _____
4.

cheese sandwiches at home and then we

_____ them right here
5.

in the terminal.

A: Flying from here _____
6. (negative)

much fun. Now, there are more than eighty

places to get something to eat or drink.

B: Oh, look. Isn't that David and Victoria

Beckham over there?

A: Yes! I read that they own a house on one of

the Palm Islands.

B: But don't they live in California?

A: No. They _____ there, but they moved back to England. And now they come
7.

here sometimes, too.

B: I'm a big football fan. When I was younger, I _____ all Beckham's games on
8.

TV. And I _____ tickets every time he played in England.
9.

A: Oh, wait. There's an announcement. . . . Our flight is delayed.

B: Well, you know that old saying: "The more things change, the more they remain the same!"

A: But not in Dubai! Things are *always* changing here, and life seems very different from the

way it _____.
10.

EXERCISE 5 EDITING

GRAMMAR NOTES 1–3 **Read these online posts from foreigners visiting or living in Dubai. There are seven mistakes in the use of *used to* and *would*. The first mistake is already corrected. Find and correct six more.**

Jason Smith, USA: I come here often for business. It's a great city, but driving in Dubai is
difficult. The traffic is really heavy. It used to ~~took~~ *take* me just 20 minutes to drive from the airport
to my hotel. Now, it sometimes takes me almost an hour. Also, the police are very strict. I was
only going a little over the speed limit, but I got a ticket last week on the way to my hotel. I
was upset at first, but at least these days you can pay the ticket online. You used to have to pay
in person. It would took forever!

Lynda Davis, Australia: I love Dubai. It's so international. The population never would be
so diverse. Now, more than 85 percent of the people living here are foreign born (including
me)! It's all very exciting. And there is so much to do. Today, I used to visit the Burj Khalifa.
Afterwards, I walked around for hours. I love all the malls and theaters. When I first came here,
there didn't use to be that many things to do in the evening. After work, I would just go home.
Now, I can choose from many different activities and events.

Wolfgang Meyer, Germany: There are still these wonderful traditional *souks* (marketplaces),
but there used to be many more of them. When I lived here twenty years ago, I would stop at
one or more of them on my way home from work. I would buy some fresh fish and vegetables
and maybe some interesting spices. Then I would went home and cook a great meal for
my family.

Graham Scott, UK: This is my first time back in fifteen years. People look really different
from before. For one thing, you used to saw more people wearing traditional clothing. Men
would wearing *kanduras* (long white robes). Women would wear the *abaya* (a full-length black
piece of clothing they wear over other clothes). Today, you see more Western-style clothing.

EXERCISE 6 LISTENING

○ 04|02 **A** Listen to the conversation between two friends. Decide if the woman is talking about something that was true in the past or that is true now. Then listen again and check (✓) *Past* or *Now*.

	Past	Now
1. a lot of small family-owned stores	✓	☐
2. a lot of banks	☐	☐
3. big shopping malls outside of town	☐	☐
4. people hanging out on the street	☐	☐
5. some break-ins[1]	☐	☐
6. clean streets	☐	☐
7. garbage on the street	☐	☐
8. free parking	☐	☐
9. pay parking	☐	☐
10. large movie theaters outside of town	☐	☐
11. small neighborhood movie theaters	☐	☐
12. a lot of restaurants	☐	☐

1 *break-ins:* crimes in which criminals enter buildings in order to steal things

○ 04|02 **B** Listen to the conversation again. Then work with a partner. Do you think the changes in the woman's town are good or bad? Would *you* like to live there? Why or why not? Discuss your answers.

EXAMPLE: A: There used to be a lot of small stores. Now, there are a lot of banks. I don't think that's a good thing.

B: I agree. It's nicer to shop in your neighborhood. And how many banks does a town need? But, . . .

EXERCISE 7 THINGS CHANGE

A PICTURE COMPARISON **Work with a partner. Look at the pictures. What changes do you notice? Discuss them with your partner.**

EXAMPLE: A: The street used to be called First Avenue. Now it's called Park Avenue.
            B: Right. And there didn't use to be many trees. Now there are a lot of trees.

B **Compare your answers with those of your classmates. Who noticed the most changes?**

EXERCISE 8 A PLACE YOU KNOW WELL

CONVERSATION **Work in a group. Talk about changes in a place you know well. Don't forget to use** *used to* **and** *would***.**

EXAMPLE: A: Last month, I went back to the town I grew up in. It was very different. I used to know a lot of people there. I would see them every day.
            B: Oh. What happened to them? Did they move?
            A: Yes. Many of them used to have jobs in the local factory, but the factory closed and they left town to look for work.

EXERCISE 9 PEOPLE CHANGE

PICTURE COMPARISON Work with a partner. Look at the photos of Jennifer Lopez and read the information about her. Discuss the changes in her appearance and in her life. Use *used to* to describe her past and the simple present to describe her present.

EXAMPLE: A: She used to be very pretty.
B: What do you mean "used to be"? She still is!

Then

Now

- was called Jennifer Lopez
- lived in New York City
- shared a small apartment with her family
- didn't have a lot of money
- took singing and dancing lessons
- dreamed of becoming a movie star
- was single
- wasn't a star

- people call her J. Lo
- divides her time between Los Angeles and New York
- owns several mansions[1]
- earns millions of dollars a year
- sings and dances professionally
- is a world-famous actress
- is divorced from singer Marc Anthony
- performs all over the world (including Dubai!)

1 *mansions:* very large houses

EXERCISE 10 WHAT ABOUT YOU?

CONVERSATION Work in a group. Talk about how you used to be and how you are now. Answer the questions below. Use *used to* and *would*. If you have a picture of yourself from that time, you can bring it to class and show it to your group.

EXAMPLE: A: I used to have very long hair. Now I wear my hair short.
B: Anton, did you use to have long hair?
C: Everybody used to have long hair back then. I wouldn't get a haircut for months and months!

1. How did you use to look?

2. What type of things would you do?

3. How did you use to dress?

FROM GRAMMAR TO WRITING

A BEFORE YOU WRITE Think of a place you know that has changed. You can choose, for example, a country, city, neighborhood, school, or workplace. Complete the outline. List four changes.

_____: Then and Now
(Name of Place)

Then   **Now**

1. _____   _____

2. _____   _____

3. _____   _____

4. _____   _____

B WRITE Use your outline to write a paragraph about the changes. Contrast how the place was in the past and how it is now. Use *used to* and *would*. You can use *Today, however,* or *Now, however,* to introduce the contrasts. Try to avoid the common mistakes in the chart.

EXAMPLE: Greenville is very different from the way it used to be. People used to shop in local stores. They would buy their vegetables at the corner grocery store and their clothes at a neighborhood shop. Today, however, they drive to big shopping malls in the suburbs . . .

Common Mistakes in Using *Used to* and *Would*

Use the **base form** of the verb after *used to* or *would*. Do not use the verb + *-ing* and do not add *-s* to the base form after *he, she,* or *it*.	She **used to shop** every day. NOT She used to ~~shopping~~ every day. She **would buy** fresh fruit and vegetables. NOT She would ~~buys~~ fresh fruit and vegetables.
Use *used to* to describe **past situations**. Do not use *would*.	I **used to** live in Dubai. NOT I ~~would~~ live in Dubai.
Use *used to* to show that you are writing about the past. Then, you can change to *would* for **past habits**. Do not begin your writing with *would*.	I **used to** ride my bike every day. I **would** spend hours in the park. NOT I ~~would~~ ride my bike every day . . .

C CHECK YOUR WORK Read your paragraph. Underline *used to* and circle *would*. Use the Editing Checklist to check your work.

Editing Checklist

Did you use . . . ?

☐ *used to* + base form of the verb to write about past situations or habits

☐ *would* + base form of the verb to write about past habits (but not situations)

☐ *used to* and then change to *would* to write about past habits

D REVISE YOUR WORK Read your paragraph again. Can you improve your writing? Make changes if necessary. Give your paragraph a title.

UNIT 4 REVIEW

Test yourself on the grammar of the unit.

A Circle the correct words to complete the sentences.

1. What <u>did</u> / <u>would</u> you use to like to do when you were a kid?

2. I <u>used to</u> / would love hanging out at the mall.

3. <u>Do</u> / <u>Did</u> you use to go to concerts?

4. My sister would <u>plays</u> / <u>play</u> video games for hours.

5. I never <u>used to</u> / <u>would</u> like video games before, but now I love them.

6. My life <u>used to</u> / <u>would</u> be so different back then.

B Complete the conversations with *used to* or *would* and the verb in parentheses. Use *would* when possible.

1. IAN: Hey, is that Jorge? He _____ very different. I almost didn't recognize him!
   a. (look)

   BEN: Yes. He _____ long hair, but he cut it last month.
   b. (have)

   IAN: I _____ my hair very long, too, especially in the summer.
   c. (wear)

   BEN: Me too. Sometimes I _____ a haircut for a whole year!
   d. (not get)

2. MIA: I _____ the guitar. I'm sorry I quit.
   a. (play)

   LEE: I had a guitar, too. I _____ for hours.
   b. (practice)

   MIA: _____ you _____ to concerts when you were a student?
   c. (go)

   LEE: Yes. I _____ the free concerts in the park. Once, I even heard J. Lo!
   d. (love)

C Find and correct six mistakes.

1. As a little girl, Yi Ling would live in Singapore.

2. In 1998, her family used to move to England.

3. Singapore used to being a part of Malaysia. Today, it is a separate country.

4. The Singapore River used to had hundreds of small boats on it.

5. The water would be very dirty.

6. In the past, flights from England to Singapore would took several days. Planes used to make many stops to refuel.

Now check your answers on page 475.

UNIT

5

Wh- **Questions**

IN COURT

OUTCOMES
• Ask questions about the past, using *wh-* words
• Identify important information in an interview transcript
• Identify the main point of a conversation
• Write a series of interview questions to get information about a past event

BEFORE YOU READ

A lawyer is questioning a crime witness in court. Look at the photo. Discuss the questions.

1. Who is the lawyer? The judge? The witness?

2. What do you think the lawyer is asking?

READ

05|01   Read this excerpt from a court transcript.

State of Illinois vs.[1] Harry M. Adams

March 30, 2015

LAWYER: What happened on the night of May 12, 2014? Please tell the court.[2]

WITNESS: I went to Al's Grill.

LAWYER: Who did you see there?

WITNESS: I saw one of the defendants.

LAWYER: Which one did you see?

WITNESS: It was that man. *[The witness is pointing to Mr. Adams.]*

---

1   *vs.:* against (*vs.* is the written abbreviation of *versus*)
2   *court:* the people (judge, lawyers, jury) who decide if someone is guilty of a crime

LAWYER:	Let the record show that the witness is indicating the defendant, Harry Adams. OK, you saw Mr. Adams. Did he see you?
WITNESS:	No, no, he didn't see me.
LAWYER:	But somebody saw you. Who saw you?
WITNESS:	A woman. He was talking to a woman. She saw me.
LAWYER:	OK. What happened next?
WITNESS:	The woman gave him a box.
LAWYER:	A box! What did it look like?
WITNESS:	It was about this long...
LAWYER:	So, about a foot and a half. What did Mr. Adams do then?
WITNESS:	He took the box. He looked frightened.
LAWYER:	Why did he look frightened? What was in the box?
WITNESS:	I don't know. He didn't open it. He just took it and left in a hurry.
LAWYER:	Where did he go?
WITNESS:	Toward the parking lot.
LAWYER:	When did the woman leave?
WITNESS:	I don't know. She was still there when we heard his car speed away.

AFTER YOU READ

A VOCABULARY **Choose the word or phrase that best completes each sentence.**

1. A **defendant** is someone that _____.

   a. saw a crime   **b.** possibly broke a law   **c.** works in the court

2. If something is for the **record**, you can find it in a _____.

   a. music CD   **b.** box   **c.** written report

3. If you are **frightened**, you are _____.

   a. dangerous   **b.** afraid   **c.** unhappy

4. If you leave **in a hurry**, you leave _____.

   a. quickly   **b.** in a storm   **c.** by bus

5. The witness **indicated** Harry Adams by _____ him.

   a. laughing at   **b.** speaking about   **c.** pointing to

B COMPREHENSION **Match the questions and answers.**

_____	**1.** Where does the reading take place?	**a.**	Harry Adams.
_____	**2.** When did the events take place?	**b.**	In court.
_____	**3.** Where did the witness go that night?	**c.**	A box.
_____	**4.** Who did the witness see there?	**d.**	Toward the parking lot.
_____	**5.** Who saw the witness?	**e.**	May 12, 2014.
_____	**6.** What did the woman give Mr. Adams?	**f.**	Al's Grill.
_____	**7.** Where did Mr. Adams go?	**g.**	A woman.

C DISCUSSION **Work with a partner. Compare your answers in B. Why did you choose each answer?**

WH- QUESTIONS: WHO, WHAT

Questions About the Subject		
Wh- Word Subject	Verb	Object
Who	saw	Harry?
		the box?

Answers		
Subject	Verb	Object
Marta	saw	him.
		it.

Questions About the Object			
Wh- Word Object	Auxiliary Verb	Subject	Main Verb
Who	did	Marta	see?
What			

Answers		
Subject	Verb	Object
She	saw	Harry.
		the box.

WH- QUESTIONS: WHICH, WHOSE, HOW MANY

Questions About the Subject		
Wh- Word + Noun	Verb	Object
Which witness	saw	you?
Whose lawyer		
How many people		

Answers		
Subject	Verb	Object
Mr. Ho	saw	me.
Harry's lawyer		
Five people		

Questions About the Object			
Wh- Word + Noun	Auxiliary Verb	Subject	Main Verb
Which witness	did	you	see?
Whose lawyer			
How many people			

Answers		
Subject	Verb	Object
I	saw	the first witness.
		Harry's lawyer.
		five people.

WH- QUESTIONS: WHEN, WHERE, WHY

Questions			
Wh- Word	Auxiliary Verb	Subject	Main Verb
When	did	Marta	go?
Where			
Why			

Answers		
Subject	Verb	Time/Place/Reason
She	went	yesterday.
		to the police.
		because she was frightened.

GRAMMAR NOTES

1 Wh- Questions and Wh- Words

Use **wh- questions** (also called **information questions**) to ask for specific information.

Wh- questions begin with **wh- words** such as: *who, what, when, where, why, which, whose, how, how many, how much,* and *how long.*

A: **Who** did you see at Al's Grill?
B: Harry Adams.

A: **When** did you go there?
B: On May 12, 2014.

A: **How many** people saw you?
B: Two.

USAGE NOTE In conversation, **answers** to wh- questions are usually **short**. They just give the requested information.

A: How long did you stay there?
B: **Three hours.** *(more common)*
I stayed there three hours. *(less common)*

2 Wh- Questions with Who and What

Use *who* to ask for information about **people**. Use *what* to ask for information about **things**.

For **questions about the subject**, use *who* or *what* in place of the subject, and use statement word order: *wh- word (= subject) + verb*

SUBJECT
Someone saw you.
Who saw you?

SUBJECT
Something happened.
What happened?

For **questions about the object**, use *who* or *what* and question word order: *wh- word + auxiliary + subject + verb*

OBJECT
You saw someone.
Who did you see?

OBJECT
He said something.
What did he say?

Remember that an **auxiliary verb** is a verb such as *do* (does, did), **have** (has, had), **can**, or **will**. *Be* can be an auxiliary too.

What *does* he **do**?
Who *will* she **defend**?
What *is* he **doing**?

BE CAREFUL! Do not use an auxiliary verb in questions about the **subject**.

Who **saw** you there?
NOT Who ~~did see~~ you there?

USAGE NOTE In very formal English, we sometimes use *whom* instead of *who* in questions about the **object**.

Whom did you see? *(very formal)*
Who did you see? *(more common)*

3 Wh- Questions with Which, Whose, and How many

You can also use *which, whose,* and *how many* to ask for information about **people** and **things**.

- *which* + **noun** (to ask about a choice)
- *whose* + **noun** (to ask about possessions)
- *how many* + **noun** (to ask about quantities)

Which **witness** told the truth?
Whose **lawyer** do you believe?
How many **questions** did the lawyer ask?

For **questions about the subject**, use the word order: *wh- word + noun + verb*

Which **defendant answered** best?

For **questions about the object**, use the word order: *wh- word + noun + auxiliary + subject + verb*

Which **defendant did you trust** more?

4 Wh- Questions with *Where*, *Why*, and *When*

Use *where*, *why*, and *when* to ask about **place**, **reason**, and **time**.

• *where* (to ask about place)	**Where** will she go?
• *why* (to ask about reason)	**Why** does she want to defend him?
• *when* (to ask about time)	**When** did she arrive?
Use the word order: *wh-* word + auxiliary + subject + verb	*Where* **did they travel?**

5 Wh- Questions with *Be*

When the **main verb** is a form of *be* (*am, is, are, was, were*), it goes directly after the *wh-* question word or *wh-* question word + noun combination.

• *wh-* word + *be*	*Who* **is** the witness?
	What **was** the best answer?
	Where **are** the lawyers?
• *wh-* word + noun + *be*	*Which* **witnesses are** in court?
	How many **people were** in the room?

STEP 3   FOCUSED PRACTICE

EXERCISE 1 DISCOVER THE GRAMMAR

GRAMMAR NOTES 1–5 Match the questions and answers.

_h_ **1.** Where were you?

_____ **2.** Who did you see?

_____ **3.** Who saw you?

_____ **4.** What hit her?

_____ **5.** Why did he leave?

_____ **6.** What did she hit?

_____ **7.** Which man did you give the money to?

_____ **8.** Which man gave you the money?

_____ **9.** How many witnesses were there?

a. His wife saw me.

b. She hit a car.

c. I gave the money to Harry.

d. A car hit her.

e. Six.

f. Harry gave me the money.

g. I saw the defendant.

~~**h.**~~ At Al's Grill.

i. Because he wanted to meet Harry.

EXERCISE 2 *WH-* QUESTIONS

Ⓐ GRAMMAR NOTES 1–5 Complete the cross-examination. Write the lawyer's questions.
Use the words in parentheses and make any necessary changes.

1. LAWYER: *What time did you return home?*
      (what time / you / return home)
   WITNESS: I returned home just before midnight.

2. LAWYER: _____
      (how / you / get home)
   WITNESS: Someone gave me a ride. I was in a hurry.

3. LAWYER: _____
      (who / give you / a ride)
   WITNESS: A friend from work.

4. LAWYER: _____
      (what / happen / next)
   WITNESS: I opened my door and saw someone on my living room floor.

5. LAWYER: _____
      (who / you / see)
   WITNESS: Deborah Collins.

6. LAWYER: For the record, _____
      (who / be / Deborah Collins)
   WITNESS: She's my wife's boss. I mean, she *was* my wife's boss. She's dead now.

7. LAWYER: _____
      (what / you / do)
   WITNESS: I called the police.

8. LAWYER: _____
      (when / the police / arrive)
   WITNESS: In about 10 minutes.

9. LAWYER: _____
      (what / they / ask you)
   WITNESS: They asked me to describe the crime scene.

10. LAWYER: _____
(how many police officers / come)

     WITNESS: I don't remember. Why?

     LAWYER: I'm asking the questions here. Please just answer.

⏵05|02 **Ⓑ LISTEN AND CHECK** Listen to the cross-examination and check your answers in A.

EXERCISE 3 *WH-* QUESTIONS

GRAMMAR NOTES 1–5 **Read the answers. Then ask questions about the underlined words or phrases.**

1. Court begins at 9:00 a.m.

   When does court begin? _____

2. Something horrible happened.

_____

3. Five witnesses described the crime.

_____

4. The witness indicated Harry Adams.

_____

5. The witness indicated Harry Adams.

_____

6. The lawyer questioned the restaurant manager.

_____

7. The manager looked frightened.

_____

8. The judge spoke to the jury.

_____

9. The verdict was "guilty."

_____

10. The jury found Adams guilty because he didn't have an alibi.

_____

11. The trial[1] lasted two weeks.

_____

12. Adams paid his lawyer $2,000.

_____

---

1 *trial:* a legal process in a court of law that decides if someone is guilty of a crime

QUESTIONS

did Jones go
Where ~~Jones went~~ on January 15?

Who went with him?

What time he return home?

Who he called?

How much money he had with him?

Whom saw him at the station the next day?

How did he look?

Why he was in a hurry?

How many suitcases did he have?

When the witness call the police?

What did happen next?

What his alibi was?

EXERCISE 4
EDITING

GRAMMAR NOTES 1–5

Read a reporter's notes. There are nine mistakes in the use of *wh-* questions. The first mistake is already corrected. Find and correct eight more.

STEP 4 | **COMMUNICATION PRACTICE**

EXERCISE 5 LISTENING

⏵ 05|03 **A** Listen to the conversation between two reporters who are covering a trial. Check (✓) the questions you hear.

☑ **1.** Where were you?

☐ **2.** What happened to you?

☐ **3.** What did they say?

☐ **4.** What did they do?

☐ **5.** Who did they see at the movies?

☐ **6.** Who saw them at the movies?

☐ **7.** What happened after the movie?

☐ **8.** Why did they go?

☐ **9.** What did her boss say?

☐ **10.** Who did you believe?

☐ **11.** Who believed you?

☐ **12.** Who did the jury believe?

⏵ 05|03 **B** Listen to the conversation again. Then work with a partner. Discuss your answers. Did you check the same questions? Explain why you didn't check a question.

EXAMPLE: **A:** Well, number 1 is already checked. What about number 2? I checked it. Did you?
B: No. I didn't because the woman didn't ask, "What happened to you?" She asked, "What happened here?"
A: You're right. What about question 3 . . . ?

EXERCISE 6 ON THE WITNESS STAND

ROLE PLAY Work with a partner. Look at the excerpt from a court transcript on page 61 again. Read it aloud. Then continue the lawyer's questioning of the witness. Ask at least six more questions.

EXAMPLE: LAWYER: When did the woman leave?
WITNESS: She was still there when we heard his car speed away.
LAWYER: What happened next?
WITNESS: I saw . . .

EXERCISE 7 TO TELL THE TRUTH

Ⓐ GAME Work in a group of three. Each student tells the group an interesting fact about his or her life. The fact can *only* be true for this student.

EXAMPLE: A: I play three musical instruments.
B: I speak four languages.
C: I have five pets.

Ⓑ The group chooses a fact and goes to the front of the class. Each student states the same fact, but remember: Only one student is telling the truth.

EXAMPLE:

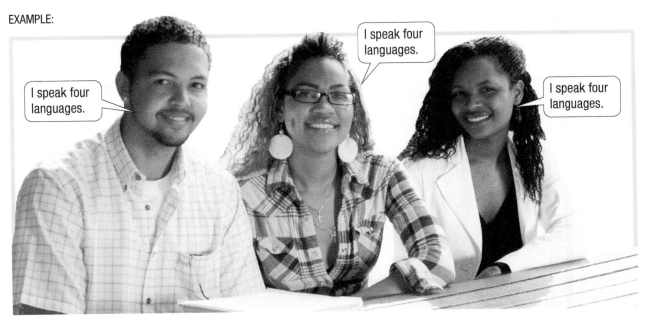

Ⓒ The class asks the three students *wh-* questions to find out who is telling the truth.

EXAMPLE: THEA: Cezar, which four languages do you speak?
CEZAR: I speak Russian, French, Spanish, and English.

LEV: Cezar, where did you learn Russian?
CEZAR: I was born in Russia.

MEI: Cezar, who taught you French?
CEZAR: My grandmother is French. I learned it from her.

JOSÉ: Cezar, how do you say "witness" in Spanish?
CEZAR: . . .

FROM GRAMMAR TO WRITING

Ⓐ BEFORE YOU WRITE Work with a partner. Your partner will tell you about something exciting he or she once saw. Write a list of questions to ask your partner in order to get more information. Then interview your partner and take notes on the answers.

EXAMPLE: A: I once saw a bad car accident.
B: When did the accident happen?
A: About two years ago.
B: Where . . . ?

Questions to Ask

When _____   How much/How many _____

Where _____   Why _____

Who _____   *Other:* _____

What _____   _____

Ⓑ WRITE Use your notes to write up the interview. Try to avoid the common mistakes in the chart.

EXAMPLE: TANIA: I once saw a bad car accident.
OMARI: When did the accident happen?
TANIA: About two years ago.
OMARI: Where . . . ?

Common Mistakes in Using *Wh-* Questions

Use the **auxiliary** *do* in questions about the **object**. Do not leave it out.	What **did** he say? NOT What he say?
Use **question word order** with an auxiliary verb. Do not use statement word order.	Who **did you see**? NOT Who you saw?

Ⓒ CHECK YOUR WORK Read your interview. Circle the *wh-* words and underline the *wh-* questions. Use the Editing Checklist to check your work.

Editing Checklist

Did you use . . . ?

☐ the correct *wh-* words

☐ the correct word order

☐ auxiliary verbs in questions about the object

☐ auxiliary verbs in questions beginning with *when, where,* and *why*

Ⓓ REVISE YOUR WORK Read your interview again. Can you improve your writing? Make changes if necessary.

UNIT 5 REVIEW

Test yourself on the grammar of the unit.

A Match the questions and answers.

_____ 1. Where did Feng go Wednesday night?

_____ 2. When was the movie over?

_____ 3. How long was it?

_____ 4. Which movie did he see?

_____ 5. How many people went?

_____ 6. Who went with him?

_____ 7. Whose car did they use?

_____ 8. Why did they choose that movie?

a. *Night Court 2*

b. It got great reviews.

c. Feng's.

d. At 11:00.

e. Laurel and Xavier.

f. Two and a half hours.

g. Three.

h. To the movies.

B Circle the correct words to complete the sentences.

1. Which court does Shari work / works at now?

2. How did she / she did find that job?

3. Who did tell / told Shari about it?

4. Why she left / did she leave her old job?

5. When did she start / started to work there?

6. Who is her boss / her boss is?

7. What did / does she do at her new job?

C Find and correct five mistakes.

A: What did you did with my law book? I can't find it.

B: Nothing. Where you saw it last?

A: In the living room. I was watching *Judge Judy* on TV. What Zack's phone number?

B: I'm not sure. Why you want to know?

A: He took the course last year. I'll call him. Maybe he still has his book.

B: Good idea. What time does he gets out of work?

Now check your answers on page 476.

The Future

PART 2

OUTCOMES

- Discuss future facts, predictions, plans, and scheduled events
- Express quick decisions, offers, and promises
- Identify important information in an interview transcript
- Identify actions happening now and future plans in a conversation
- Write a paragraph about a prediction

OUTCOMES

- Describe the order between future events, using a future time clause
- Follow the sequence of two future events in a reading
- Follow the time order of events in a conversation
- Discuss future plans and goals
- Write a description of future plans and goals

OUTCOMES
- Discuss future facts, predictions, plans, and scheduled events
- Express quick decisions, offers, and promises
- Identify important information in an interview transcript
- Identify actions happening now and future plans in a conversation
- Write a paragraph about a prediction

STEP 1 GRAMMAR IN CONTEXT

BEFORE YOU READ

Look at the photo. Discuss the questions.

1. Where do you think the first space tourists will travel?

2. Why do people want to travel into space? Would *you* like to?

READ

 Read this transcript of a radio program about space tourism.

Space Tourism: Not Just Science Fiction[1]

ROHAN: Good evening, and welcome to *The Future Today*. I'm Enid Rohan, and tonight Dr. Richard Starr, president of YourSpace, Inc., is going to talk to us about space tourism. Dr. Starr, is space really going to become a popular tourist destination?

STARR: Yes, it is, Enid. We're already building the space planes. And we're selling tickets and planning our first trips now. In fact, our training program for passengers is starting next January.

ROHAN: Where will these tours go? Will they travel to the Moon? Mars?

STARR: No, they won't. The first space tourists aren't going to go that far. They're only going to travel about 110 kilometers, or 68 miles above the Earth. That's the edge of space. A trip will last about two and a half hours.

ROHAN: Tickets cost $250,000. Who's going to pay that much for just a few hours?

STARR: Hundreds of people are purchasing tickets and are waiting for takeoff. It's going to be an incredible trip. And tickets won't always be so expensive. Costs are going to fall a lot.

ROHAN: What will a trip be like?

---

1 *science fiction:* stories about the future, often about space travel and scientific discoveries

STARR: First of all, you'll experience zero gravity.[2] That means you will float freely in the cabin. And you'll get a bird's-eye view[3] of the Earth from space. You won't believe your eyes! You're going to think about the Earth in a whole new way.

ROHAN: Sounds great. I think I'll ask my boss to send me on a trip. When does the next flight leave?

STARR: January 1, two years from now. But you won't be on that one—our next three flights are already sold out!

---

2 *gravity:* the force that makes things fall to the ground. (In zero gravity, things do not stay on the ground.)

3 *bird's-eye view:* a view from a very high place

AFTER YOU READ

Ⓐ VOCABULARY Complete the sentences with the words from the box.

edge	experience	incredible	purchase	sold out	takeoff

1. I want to go on this trip. How can I _____ a ticket?

2. There are no more tickets for the space tour. It's _____.

3. I was so excited watching *Gravity 3* that I was at the _____ of my seat!

4. I was only scared at _____—when the space plane left the ground.

5. Sy took _____ photos from the spacecraft. He saw some amazing sights.

6. In space, people _____ a lot of feelings—amazement, excitement, fear, and much more.

Ⓑ COMPREHENSION Read the statements. Which of the statements are true right now? Which will be true only in the future? Check (✓) *Now* or *Future*.

	Now	Future
1. Tourists are buying tickets.	☐	☐
2. A training program for passengers is starting.	☐	☐
3. Space tours travel about 110 km (68 miles) above the Earth.	☐	☐
4. Tickets are very expensive.	☐	☐
5. The next flight is ready to leave.	☐	☐
6. A trip lasts about two and a half hours.	☐	☐

Ⓒ DISCUSSION Work with a partner. Compare your answers in B. Why did you check *Now* or *Future*?

BE GOING TO FOR THE FUTURE

Statements

Subject	*Be*	*(Not) Going to*	Base Form of Verb	
I	am			
You	are			
He She It	is	(not) going to	leave	soon.
We You They	are			

Yes/No Questions

Be	Subject	*Going to*	Base Form of Verb	
Am	I			
Are	you			
Is	he she it	going to	leave	soon?
Are	we you they			

Short Answers

	Affirmative				Negative		
Yes,	you	are.		No,	you're		
	I	am.			I'm		
	he she it	is.			he's she's it's	not.	
	you we they	are.			you're we're they're		

Wh- Questions

Wh- Word	*Be*	Subject	*Going to*	Base Form of Verb
When Why	are	you	going to	leave?

WILL FOR THE FUTURE

Statements

Subject	*Will (not)*	Base Form of Verb	
I You He She It We You They	**will (not)**	**leave**	soon.

Yes/No Questions

Will	Subject	Base Form of Verb	
Will	I you he she it we you they	**leave**	soon?

Short Answers

Affirmative		
Yes,	you I he she it you we they	**will.**

Negative		
No,	you I he she it you we they	**won't.**

Wh- Questions

Wh- Word	*Will*	Subject	Base Form of Verb
When	**will**	you	**leave?**

PRESENT PROGRESSIVE FOR THE FUTURE

Statements

Subject + *Be*	*(Not)* + Base Form + *-ing*	
We're	(not) leaving	soon.
It's		

SIMPLE PRESENT FOR THE FUTURE

Statements

Subject	Verb	
We	**leave**	Monday at 6:45 a.m.
It	**leaves**	

GRAMMAR NOTES

1 Referring to Future Events

There are **several ways to refer to future events**. Sometimes only one form is appropriate, but in many cases more than one form is possible.

- *be going to*
- *will*
- **present progressive**
- **simple present**

They**'re going to have** a meeting.
I think I**'ll go. Will** you **be** there?
It**'s taking** place next week.
It **starts** at 9:00 a.m. on Monday.

Past	Now	meeting	Future

2 Future Facts

For facts or events that you are **certain will happen in the future**, you can use *be going to* or *will*.

- *be going to*
- *will*

The sun **is going to rise** at 6:43 tomorrow.
The sun **will rise** at 6:43 tomorrow.

3 Predictions

For predictions about things you are **quite sure will happen in the future**, you can also use *be going to* or *will*.

- *be going to*
- *will*

I think a lot of people **are going to travel** to space.
I think a lot of people **will travel** to space.

USAGE NOTE We often use *I think* before a prediction. | *I think* tickets **are going to get** cheaper.

IN WRITING We use *will* more in **formal writing** and *be going to* more in **conversation**.

Prices **will drop** in time. *(formal writing)*
Prices **are going to drop** in time. *(conversation)*

BE CAREFUL! Do not use *will* when something you notice right now makes you almost certain that an event is going to happen. Use *be going to*.

A: Look at that car!
B: Oh, no. It**'s going to crash**!
NOT It'll crash.

4 Future Plans

For plans or things that are **already decided**, use *be going to* or the **present progressive**.

- *be going to*
- **present progressive**

I**'m going to fly** to Chicago next week.
I**'m flying** to Chicago next week.
NOT I'll fly to Chicago next week.

USAGE NOTE We often use the **present progressive** for plans that are already arranged.

I**'m flying** to Chicago next week. I already have a ticket.

USAGE NOTE When the main verb is *go*, it is more common to use the **present progressive** (*be going*) than *be going to go*.

I**'m going** to Paris tomorrow. *(more common)*
I**'m going to go** to Paris tomorrow. *(less common)*

5 Quick Decisions, Offers, and Promises

For decisions that you make quickly while you are speaking, or to make offers or promises, use **will**.

• quick decision • offer • promise	**A:** The Space Show is opening next week. **B:** Really? Sounds interesting. I think **I'll go**. **A:** I'd like to go too, but I don't have a ride. **B:** **I'll drive** you. But I'd like to leave by 7:00. **A:** No problem. **I'll be** ready.

6 Future Scheduled Events

For scheduled future events such as **timetables**, **programs**, and **schedules**, you can use the **simple present**.

• simple present	The shuttle **leaves** at 9:00 a.m. Dr. Starr **speaks** Tuesday afternoon.
USAGE NOTE We often use verbs such as *begin*, *start*, *leave*, *arrive*, *last*, and *end* for scheduled future events.	The conference **begins** May 11. Registration **lasts** until May 10.
USAGE NOTE You can also use *be going to* and *will* for scheduled future events.	Registration **is going to last** until May 10. Registration **will last** until May 10.

PRONUNCIATION NOTE

⏵06|02   **Pronunciation of *Going to***

In **informal conversation**, we often pronounce *going to* as "gonna."	**A:** What time are you **going to** be home?
	         (gonna)
	B: I'm **going to** get home late.
	      (gonna)

IN WRITING Sometimes people use *gonna* in **informal notes**, **text messages**, and **email** to friends.	Hi Lyn, I'm **gonna** be late. *(email)*
BE CAREFUL! Do not use *gonna* when you write to people you have a formal relationship with. Also do not use *gonna* in formal writing.	Professor, I'm **going to** be late. *(email)* NOT Professor, I'm ~~gonna~~ be late. According to scientists, Mars is **going to** become a tourist destination. *(paper)* NOT According to scientists, Mars is ~~gonna~~ become a tourist destination.

REFERENCE NOTES

For **contractions** of *I am, you are, I will, you will*, etc., see Appendix 26, page 464.

For the **present progressive** and **simple present** forms, see Unit 1, page 4.

For *will* for **making a request**, see Unit 15 on page 204.

EXERCISE 1   DISCOVER THE GRAMMAR

A GRAMMAR NOTES 1–6   **Read this transcript of an interview with a future space tourist. There are thirteen forms of the future. The first form is already underlined. Find and underline twelve more.**

Out of This World

ROHAN: This is Enid Rohan, reporting from Spaceport America. Lyn Filipov is in the training program here for a flight with YourSpace, Inc. She's <u>going to fly</u> to the edge of space very soon. So, Lyn, which flight are you taking?

FILIPOV: The one that leaves on March 30. By the time I purchased my ticket, the earlier flights were all sold out.

ROHAN: What's the training like?

FILIPOV: Well, at 110 kilometers—that's 68 miles—above the Earth, there won't be any gravity, so we're practicing moving around in zero-g. It's an incredible feeling—like floating in water, or flying. You feel really free.

ROHAN: Aren't you even a little scared?

FILIPOV: Right now, I can't wait to go. I'm pretty sure I'll be terrified on takeoff, but it'll be worth it. Totally.

ROHAN: How can you afford this? Are you an Internet millionaire?

FILIPOV: No, I'm not. Actually, I won a big lottery. When I saw my winning numbers, my first thought was, "I'll buy a ticket for a space tour."

ROHAN: What an amazing story! But you're very young. How does your family feel about this?

FILIPOV: I'm not that young. I'll be 23 next month. But my parents are nervous, of course. My mother is really afraid I'm going to love space travel and I'll want to keep doing it. And my younger brother is jealous.

ROHAN: What do you say to make them feel better?

FILIPOV: I tell my mother, "Listen, Mom, this is an incredible once-in-a-lifetime thing. I won't make a habit of space travel, I promise." My brother? He wants a career in space travel, so he's going to study a lot harder from now on. That's what he says, anyway.

ROHAN: Thanks for the interview, Lyn. And good luck!

FILIPOV: Thanks. I'll send you photos.

B Complete the chart. List the thirteen future verb forms. Then check (✓) the correct column for each form.

	Facts	Predictions	Plans	Quick Decisions	Promises	Schedules
1. 's going to fly			✓			
2.						
3.						
4.						
5.						
6.						
7.						
8.						
9.						
10.						
11.						
12.						
13.						

EXERCISE 2 *WILL* FOR FACTS AND PREDICTIONS

A GRAMMAR NOTES 1–2 It is the year 2020, and an international group of space tourists is getting ready for its space flight. Part of the training program includes a Question and Answer (Q & A) session. Complete the questions and answers. Use the verbs in parentheses with *will* or *won't*.

Q: _____ Will _____ it _____ take _____ a long time to get used to zero gravity?
  1. (take)

A: No, it _____ won't _____ . Every day you _____ more comfortable, and after
  2.   **3.** (feel)

three days you _____ used to being in space.
  4. (become)

Q: _____ I _____ sick?
            5. (feel)

A: Yes, you might feel sick for a little while. But it _____ long.
                                              6. (last)

Q: I'm a runner. How _____ I _____ in shape in space?

7. (stay)

A: Actually, all space tourists, or "spaceflight participants," as they prefer to be called,

_____ exercises during the flight. There _____ at least one stationary

8. (do)   9. (be)

bike on board, for example.

Q: _____ I _____ the same?

10. (look)

A: Actually, you _____ the same at all. Your face and eyes _____ puffy.

11. (look)   12. (get)

The first time you look in a mirror, you probably _____ yourself.

13. (recognize)

Q: _____ I _____ in my sleep?

14. (float)

A: Yes, if you are not tied down. And then you should be careful because you _____

15. (bump)

into things all night long. Trust me. You can get hurt!

Q: I like salt and pepper on my food. Can I still use them in zero gravity?

A: Yes, you _____ still _____ salt and pepper, but not like you do on

16. (have)

Earth. You _____ small, squeezable bottles with salt water and pepper water so the

17. (use)

grains don't float away. You just squeeze it on your food. Don't worry about it. It

_____ great!

18. (be)

▶06|03 **B** LISTEN AND CHECK **Listen to the Question and Answer session and check your answers in A.**

EXERCISE 3 *BE GOING TO* FOR PREDICTION

GRAMMAR NOTE 3 **Look at the pictures. They show future events in the life of Professor Starr. Write predictions or guesses. Use the words from the box and a form of *be going to* or *not be going to*. Choose between affirmative and negative.**

| answer the phone | get out of bed | give a speech | rain | ~~take a trip~~ |
| drive | get very wet | have dinner | sleep | watch TV |

1. _He's going to take a trip._ _____   2. _____

3. _____

4. _____

5. _____

6. _____

7. _____

8. _____

9. _____

10. _____

EXERCISE 4 PRESENT PROGRESSIVE FOR PLANS

GRAMMAR NOTE 4 Write about Professor Starr's plans for next week. Use the information from his calendar and the present progressive.

	MONDAY	TUESDAY	WEDNESDAY	THURSDAY	FRIDAY	SATURDAY
A.M.	Teach my science class	Take the train to Chicago	Do the interview for *The Space Show*	Work on the Space Future website	Go to an exercise class	Answer emails from the Space Future website
P.M.		Meet friends from England for dinner	Answer questions from the online chat		Fly to New York for the Space Transportation Conference	Write a speech for the next space travel conference

1. On Monday morning, *he's teaching his science class* .

2. On Tuesday morning, _____ .

3. On Tuesday evening, _____ .

4. On Wednesday morning, _____ .

5. On Wednesday afternoon, _____ .

6. All day Thursday, _____ .

7. On Friday morning, _____ .

8. On Friday evening, _____ .

9. On Saturday morning, _____ .

10. On Saturday afternoon, _____ .

EXERCISE 5 SIMPLE PRESENT FOR SCHEDULES

GRAMMAR NOTE 6 It is June 2050. You and a friend are planning a trip to the Moon. Your friend just got the schedule, and you are deciding which shuttle to take. Use the words in parentheses to ask questions and look at the schedule to write the answers. Use the simple present.

2050 SHUTTLE SERVICE TO THE MOON					
Fall Schedule • All times given in Earth's Eastern Standard Time					
SEPTEMBER		OCTOBER		NOVEMBER	
Leave Earth	Arrive Moon	Leave Earth	Arrive Moon	Leave Earth	Arrive Moon
9/4 7:00 a.m.	9/7 6:00 a.m.	10/15 4:00 a.m.	10/18 3:00 a.m.	11/4 1:00 a.m.	11/8 12:00 a.m.
9/20 10:00 a.m.	9/23 9:00 a.m.	10/27 11:00 a.m.	10/30 10:00 a.m.	11/19 6:00 a.m.	11/23 5:00 a.m.

1. (when / the shuttle / fly to the Moon this fall)

   A: _When does the shuttle fly to the Moon this fall?_

   B: _It flies to the Moon in September, October, and November._

2. (how many / shuttle flights / leave this fall)

   A: _____

   B: _____

3. (how often / the shuttle / depart for the Moon each month)

   A: _____

   B: _____

4. (when / the October 27 flight / arrive on the Moon)

   A: _____

   B: _____

5. (how long / the November 19 flight / last)

   A: _____

   B: _____

EXERCISE 6 FORMS OF THE FUTURE

Ⓐ GRAMMAR NOTES 1–6 Two people are having a cup of coffee and planning their trip to the Space Conference. Circle the correct words to complete their conversation.

JASON: I just heard the weather report. It's raining / (It's going to rain) tomorrow.
1.

ARIEL: Oh no. I hate driving in the rain. And it's a long drive to the conference.

JASON: Wait! I have an idea. We'll take / We're going to take the train instead!
2.

ARIEL: Good idea! Do you have a train schedule?

JASON: Yes. Here's one. There's a train that will leave / leaves at 7:00 a.m.
3.

ARIEL: What about lunch? Oh, I know. I'll make / I'm making some sandwiches for us.
4.

JASON: Good idea! You know, it's a long trip. What are we doing / are we going to do all those hours?
5.

ARIEL: Don't worry. We'll think / We're thinking of something.
6.

JASON: Maybe I'll bring / I'm bringing my laptop, and we can watch a movie.
7.

ARIEL: Great. Hey, Jason, your cup will fall / is going to fall! It's right at the edge of the table.
8.

JASON: Got it! You know, we have to get up really early. I think I'm going / I'll go home now.
9.

ARIEL: OK. In that case, I'm seeing / I'll see you tomorrow. Good night.
10.

⏵06|04 Ⓑ LISTEN AND CHECK Listen to the conversation and check your answers in A.

EXERCISE 7 *GOING TO* OR *GONNA*

⊙06|05 PRONUNCIATION NOTE Listen to the sentences. Check (✓) *More Formal* if you hear **be going to**. Check (✓) *Less Formal* if you hear **gonna**.

	More Formal	Less Formal
1. Takeoff is going to be soon.	☐	☑
2. It's going to be full.	☐	☐
3. Professor Starr is going to be on the flight.	☐	☐
4. He's going to speak at the space conference.	☐	☐
5. He believes that people are going to fly to the moon.	☐	☐
6. Are you going to be at the conference?	☐	☐
7. It's going to be very interesting.	☐	☐

EXERCISE 8 EDITING

GRAMMAR NOTES 1–6 Read this student's report on space travel. There are eleven mistakes in the use of the future. The first mistake is already corrected. Find and correct ten more.

> travel
> Both astronauts and space tourists will ~~traveling~~ in space, but tourists are gonna have a much different experience. Space tourists is going to travel for fun, not for work. So, they will no have to worry about many of the technical problems that astronauts worry about. For example, space tourists will need not to figure out how to use tools without gravity. And they isn't going to go outside the spaceship to make repairs. For the most part, space tourists will just going to see the sights and have a good time.
>
> Still, there will be similarities. Regular activities be the same for astronauts and space tourists. For example, eating, washing, and sleeping will turned into exciting challenges for everyone in space. And on long trips, everyone is going to doing exercises to stay fit in zero gravity. And both astronauts and space tourists will going to have many new adventures!

EXERCISE 9 LISTENING

▶06|06 **A** Listen to six short conversations. Decide if the people are talking about something happening now or in the future. Then listen again and check (✓) *Now* or *Future*.

	Now	Future			Now	Future			Now	Future
1.	☐	☑		3.	☐	☐		5.	☐	☐
2.	☐	☐		4.	☐	☐		6.	☐	☐

▶06|06 **B** Listen to each conversation again. Then work with a partner and decide if each statement below is *True* or *False*. If there isn't enough information to decide, check (✓) *Don't Know*. Discuss your answers. Give a reason for each answer.

EXAMPLE: **A:** Is the woman going out with friends tonight?
B: No she's not. That's false. She says she's staying home and watching TV.

		True	False	Don't Know
1.	The woman is going out with friends tonight.	☐	☑	☐
2.	The woman will probably watch the rest of the TV show.	☐	☐	☐
3.	Professor Starr won't take the call.	☐	☐	☐
4.	The lecture is about traveling to Mars.	☐	☐	☐
5.	The man is going to meet his parents at the airport.	☐	☐	☐
6.	The train to Chicago left five minutes ago.	☐	☐	☐

EXERCISE 10 DO YOU HAVE PLANS FOR THE WEEKEND?

A MAKING PLANS Before you make plans, complete your weekend schedule. If you have no plans, write *free*.

	SATURDAY	SUNDAY
12:00 p.m.		
1:00 p.m.		
2:00 p.m.		
3:00 p.m.		
4:00 p.m.		
5:00 p.m.		
6:00 p.m.		
7:00 p.m.		
8:00 p.m.		
9:00 p.m.		

B Work with a partner. Ask questions to decide on a time when you are both free to do something together.

EXAMPLE: A: What are you doing Saturday afternoon? Do you want to go to the movies?
B: I'm going to the library. How about Saturday night? Are you doing anything then?

EXERCISE 11 DO YOU WANT TO...?

REACHING AGREEMENT Work with a partner. Look at the weekend schedule of events. Then look at your schedules from Exercise 10. Decide which events to attend and when.

EXAMPLE: A: What are you doing Sunday? Do you want to see *Zero G* at 3:00 p.m.?
B: Hmm. I'd like to go, but I can't. I'm meeting my sister on Sunday afternoon.
A: There's also a show at 6:00 p.m. Could you make that show?
B: Yes! Great! Are you going to get the tickets?
A: Yes, I'll get them online. See you Sunday!

WEEKEND EVENTS IN RIVERSIDE
June 20 and 21

EVENTS	WHERE AND WHEN
Art in the Park Painting, photography, jewelry, and more! Support our local artists.	River Park, all day Saturday and Sunday
International Food Festival Moussaka, pad thai, spaetzle—you'll find plenty of interesting tastes here. International music and dance, too.	Conference Center, Saturday, 1:00 p.m.–7:00 p.m.
Walking Event 5 kilometers for Jay Street Clinic. Join us and help the city's only free clinic.	Start at River Park, Sunday, 11:00 a.m. End at the clinic, 10 W. Jay St.
Zero G Experience space travel in this new film. On the big IMAX screen, it'll feel like you're really there. Purchase tickets online.	Science Museum, starts Sunday Show times: 3:00 p.m. and 6:00 p.m.
Dancing with the Stars Free concert, with plenty of room for dancing. Bring a picnic and your own chairs.	Brown's Beach, Sunday 7:00 p.m.–Midnight

EXERCISE 12 WHAT DO YOU THINK?

DISCUSSION Work in a group. Discuss these questions.

1. Do you think space tourism will become really popular? Why or why not?

   EXAMPLE: A: I don't think space tourism will become really popular. Only very rich people will be able to afford a ticket.
   B: Oh, I don't know about that. In time, prices will come down.
   C: Yeah, but they're never going to be low enough for most people.

2. How will space tourism change the world? Think about positive and negative changes.

3. Do you think you will ever fly to the moon? What about your children?

A BEFORE YOU WRITE Choose one of the ideas below to write a paragraph about the future of space travel. Then list three reasons for your idea.

- Space travel is going to become very popular.
- Space travel will change the world.
- One day, I am going to travel to space.
- Space travel won't help people.

Reason 1: _____

Reason 2: _____

Reason 3: _____

B WRITE Use your list of reasons to write a paragraph about the future of space travel. Put your most important reason last. Connect your reasons with *To begin with*, *In addition*, and *Most importantly*. Try to avoid the common mistakes in the chart.

EXAMPLE: I don't think space travel is going to become very popular in the near future. To begin with, it is much too expensive. I don't believe prices will fall very much. Only extremely wealthy people will have enough money to purchase tickets. In addition, . . .

Common Mistakes in Using the Future

Use the **base form** of the verb after *will*. Do not add *-s* to the base form after *he*, *she*, or *it*.	My son **will travel** to space one day. NOT My son will ~~travels~~ to space one day.
Use *will* or *be going to* in formal writing. Do not use *gonna*.	I'm **going to** look for a job in space tourism. NOT I'm ~~gonna~~ look for a job . . . .

C CHECK YOUR WORK Read your paragraph. Underline *be going to* + base form of the verb and circle *will* + base form of the verb. Use the Editing Checklist to check your work.

Editing Checklist

Did you use . . . ?

☐ *will* or *be going to* for predictions and facts

☐ *be going to* or the present progressive for plans

☐ the base form of the verb after *will* and *be going to*

D REVISE YOUR WORK Read your paragraph again. Can you improve your writing? Make changes if necessary. Give your paragraph a title.

UNIT 6 REVIEW

Test yourself on the grammar of the unit.

Ⓐ Circle the correct words to complete the sentences.

1. We'll go / We're going to Dr. Starr's lecture tomorrow night. I already have the tickets.

2. Great! I'll meet / I'm going to meet you after school.

3. Take your umbrella. It'll rain / It's going to rain.

4. Sara gives / is giving a party after the lecture. Why don't we go?

5. Oh! Look out! That vase will fall / is going to fall off the shelf!

Ⓑ Complete the sentences about the future with the correct form of the verbs in parentheses. Sometimes there may be more than one correct answer.

1. It's almost 9:00. What time _____ our flight _____?
   (leave)

2. Don't eat so much. You _____ sick during the flight.
   (feel)

3. The plane _____ in a few minutes.
   (land)

4. Our taxi driver _____ a speeding ticket. The police are right behind us.
   (get)

5. Put your wallet away. I _____.
   (pay)

6. Look at those clouds. I think it _____.
   (rain)

7. What time _____ the lecture _____?
   (start)

8. _____ Dr. Starr _____ back this afternoon?
   (call)

9. Don't worry. He _____ to call you.
   (not forget)

10. Bye. I _____ to you next week.
    (speak)

Ⓒ Find and correct five mistakes.

1. When will Dr. Starr gets home tomorrow?

2. His lecture starts at 7:00, so I think I go.

3. Do you want to go with me, or are you study tonight?

4. What you are going to do next weekend?

5. I'm going be home all day.

Now check your answers on page 476.

Future Time Clauses
SETTING GOALS

OUTCOMES
- Describe the order between future events, using a future time clause
- Follow the sequence of two future events in a reading
- Follow the time order of events in a conversation
- Discuss future plans and goals
- Write a description of future plans and goals

STEP 1   GRAMMAR IN CONTEXT

BEFORE YOU READ

Look at the photo and at the title of the article. Discuss the questions.

1. The girl wants to become a businesswoman. What do you think she will do to reach her goal?

2. What are some other typical goals that people have?

3. What's one of *your* goals?

READ

07|01   Read this article.

From Dream to Reality

We all have dreams, but how can we make them a reality? We change them into goals and make an action plan. Read about how one student, Latoya Jones, turned *her* dreams into goals and made an action plan.

PUT YOUR DREAMS ON PAPER. After you write a dream down, it will start to become a goal. Your path will then be a lot clearer.

Latoya Jones wrote this:
- Before I turn 30, I'm going to be a successful businessperson.

LIST YOUR REASONS. When things get difficult, you can read this list to yourself and it will help you go on.

This is what Latoya put at the top of her list:
- My parents will be proud of me when I'm a successful businessperson.

WRITE AN ACTION PLAN. Once you know what your goal is and why you want to achieve it, you must write an action plan.

This is Latoya's action plan:
- I'm going to go to business school as soon as I save enough money to pay for it.
- When I graduate, I'll get a job with a big company.
- After I get some experience, I'll find a better job.

TAKE YOUR FIRST STEPS TODAY. Don't wait. As soon as you have an action plan, take steps to achieve it.

Here are the first steps Latoya is going to take:
- Before I apply to schools, I'm going to download some catalogs.
- After I apply, I'll prepare carefully for interviews.

You can do exactly what Latoya did to achieve your goals and turn them into reality. It's not always easy, but remember: The longest journey starts with the first step!

AFTER YOU READ

A VOCABULARY Choose the word or phrase that best completes each sentence.

1. When you **achieve** something, you get it _____.
   a. as a gift   **b.** after hard work   **c.** from your family

2. Sam got a college **catalog** because he wanted to _____.
   a. pay his bill   **b.** do his homework   **c.** learn about classes

3. A **goal** is something you _____.
   a. don't want very much   **b.** plan and work for   **c.** buy at a store

4. A **path** is a way to _____ your goals.
   a. reach   **b.** buy   **c.** choose

5. At a college **interview**, someone _____.
   a. asks you questions   **b.** shows you the school   **c.** gives you a job

B COMPREHENSION For each pair of statements about Latoya's action plan, choose the action (a or b) that comes first.

1. **a.** She will download school catalogs.
   b. She will apply to schools.

2. **a.** She will save money.
   b. She will go to business school.

3. **a.** She will get a job with a big company.
   b. She will graduate.

4. **a.** She will find a better job.
   b. She will get some experience.

5. **a.** She will turn 30.
   b. She will become a successful businesswoman.

C DISCUSSION Work with a partner. Compare your answers in B. Explain why you think your answers are correct.

FUTURE TIME CLAUSES

Statements

Main Clause			Time Clause	
I **will** I **am going to**				I **graduate**.
She **will** She **is going to**	**get** a job	**when**	she **graduates**.
They **will** They **are going to**				they **graduate**.

Yes/No Questions

Main Clause			Time Clause	
Will you	**get** a job	**when**	you **graduate**?
Are you **going to**			

Short Answers

Affirmative			Negative		
Yes,	I	**will**. **am**.	No,	I	**won't**. **'m not**.

Wh- Questions

Main Clause				Time Clause	
Where	**will** you **are** you **going to**	**get** a job	**when**	you **graduate**?

GRAMMAR NOTES

1 Function of a Future Time Clause

Use a future time clause to show the **time order between two future events**.

A future time clause begins with a **time expression** such as *when, after, as soon as, before, until,* or *while*.

MAIN CLAUSE   TIME CLAUSE
He**'s going to move** *after* he **graduates**.
    (First he'll graduate. Then he'll move.)

The time expression shows which of two future events **will** happen first.

MAIN CLAUSE   TIME CLAUSE
We**'ll visit** him *before* he **leaves**.
    (First we'll visit him. Then he'll leave.)

BE CAREFUL! A **future time clause** is about a **future event**, but its verb is in the **simple present**. Do not use *be going to* or *will* in a future time clause. Use the simple present.

He's going to move after he **graduates**.
NOT after he ~~is going to graduate~~
We'll miss him when he **leaves**.
NOT when ~~he'll leave~~

2 Position of the Future Time Clause

The **time clause** can come **at the beginning or the end** of the sentence. The meaning is the same.

• at the **beginning** • at the **end**	***Before* she applies,** she'll visit schools. She'll visit schools ***before* she applies.**
IN WRITING Use a **comma after the time clause** when it comes at the **beginning** of the sentence. Do not use a comma after the main clause when the main clause comes first.	***After* he graduates,** he'll look for a job. He'll look for a job ***after* he graduates.** NOT He'll look for a job_x after he graduates.
USAGE NOTE In **conversation**, we often answer a *when* question with **just the time clause.**	A: When will she visit schools? B: ***Before* she applies.**

3 Time Words for the First Event

When, *after*, and *as soon as* introduce the **first event**.

***When* I graduate,** I'll look for a job.
I'll look for a job ***after* I graduate.**
   (First I'll graduate. Then I'll look for a job.)

USAGE NOTE Use *as soon as* to emphasize that the second event will happen immediately after the first event.	***As soon as* I graduate,** I'll look for a job. *(First I'll graduate. Immediately after that, I'll look for a job.)*

4 Time Words for the Second Event

Before and *until* introduce the **second event**.

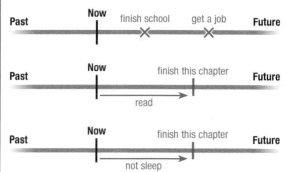

***Before* I get a job,** I'll finish school.
  (First I'll finish school. Then I'll get a job.)

I'll read ***until* I finish this chapter.**
  (I'll keep reading, but only up to the time that I finish this chapter. Then I'll stop.)

I won't sleep ***until* I finish this chapter.**
  (I'll stay awake, but only up to the time that I finish this chapter. Then I'll go to sleep.)

5 *While* for Same-Time Events

While introduces an event that will happen **at the same time** as another event.

***While* I look for a job,** I'll go on studying.
or
***While* I'm looking for a job,** I'll go on studying.
  (I'll look for a job and study at the same time.)

Notice that you can use the **simple present** or **present progressive** with an action verb after *while*.

EXERCISE 1 DISCOVER THE GRAMMAR

GRAMMAR NOTES 1–5 **Read the numbered sentence. Then choose the pair of sentences that has a similar meaning.**

1. Amber will open her own business when she finishes school.
   a. Amber will open her own business. Then she'll finish school.
   (b.) Amber will finish school. Then she'll open her own business.

2. Denzell won't quit until he finds another job.
   a. Denzell will find another job. Then he'll quit.
   b. Denzell will quit. Then he'll find another job.

3. Jake is going to retire as soon as he turns 60.
   a. Jake is going to retire. Then he'll turn 60.
   b. Jake is going to turn 60. Then he'll retire.

4. After the Morrisons sell their house, they'll move to Florida.
   a. The Morrisons will sell their house. Then they'll move to Florida.
   b. The Morrisons will move to Florida. Then they'll sell their house.

5. Marisa will call you when she gets home.
   a. Marisa will call you. Then she'll get home.
   b. Marisa will get home. Then she'll call you.

6. Dimitri is going to live with his parents until he gets married.
   a. Dimitri is going to get married. Then he'll live with his parents.
   b. Dimitri will live with his parents. Then he'll get married.

7. While Li-jing is in school, she's going to work part-time.
   a. Li-jing will finish school. Then she's going to get a part-time job.
   b. Li-jing will go to school. At the same time, she's going to have a part-time job.

8. Marta will have her degree before she turns twenty-one.
   a. Marta will get her degree. Then she'll turn twenty-one.
   b. Marta will turn twenty-one. Then she'll get her degree.

9. Adel and Farah won't buy a house until their son is two years old.
   a. They'll buy a house. Then their son will turn two.
   b. Their son will turn two. Then they'll buy a house.

10. Ina will live in Paris while she's studying French cooking.
    a. First she'll study French cooking. Then she's moving to Paris.
    b. She'll study French cooking. At the same time, she'll live in Paris.

EXERCISE 2 SIMPLE PRESENT OR FUTURE

GRAMMAR NOTES 1–3 Complete this student's worksheet. Use the correct form of the verbs in parentheses.

GOAL PLANNING WORKSHEET

A. What is your most important goal?

- To find a job after graduation.

B. List the reasons you want to achieve this goal.

- When I _____*get*_____ a job, I _____*'ll have*_____ more money.
  1. (get)   2. (have)
- When I _____ enough money, I _____ a used car.
  3. (save)   4. (buy)
- I _____ happier when I _____ employed.
  5. (feel)   6. (be)
- I _____ new skills while I _____ .
  7. (learn)   8. (work)

C. What is your action plan? What path will you take to reach your goal?

- Every morning when I _____ , I _____ online for
  9. (get up)   10. (check)
  employment ads.
- When I _____ to my friends, I _____ them if they know
  11. (talk)   12. (ask)
  of any jobs.
- I _____ information about résumé writing
  13. (download)
  before I _____ a new résumé.
  14. (write)
- While I _____ to find a job, I
  15. (try)
  _____ my computer skills.
  16. (improve)
- Before I _____ on an interview, I
  17. (go)
  _____ how to use Excel and PowerPoint.
  18. (know)

D. What are the steps you will take right away?

- Before I _____ anything else, I
  19. (do)
  _____ a list of people to contact
  20. (write)
  for help.
- As soon as I _____ all the
  21. (contact)
  people on my list, I _____
  22. (work)
  on fixing up my résumé.

EXERCISE 3 ORDER OF EVENTS

GRAMMAR NOTES 1–5 Combine each pair of sentences. Use the future or the simple present form of the verb. Decide which sentence goes first. Remember to use commas when necessary.

1. Sandy and Jeff will get married. Then Sandy will graduate.

   _Sandy and Jeff will get married_____ before _Sandy graduates_____.

2. Jeff is going to get a raise. Then they are going to move to a larger apartment.

   _____ as soon as _____.

3. They're going to move to a larger apartment. Then they're going to have a baby.

   After _____.

4. They'll have their first child. Then Sandy will get a part-time job.

   _____ after _____.

5. Sandy will work part-time. Then their child will be two years old.

   _____ until _____.

6. Jeff will go to school. At the same time, Sandy will work full-time.

   _____ while _____.

7. Sandy and Jeff will achieve their goals. Then they'll feel very proud.

   When _____.

EXERCISE 4 EDITING

GRAMMAR NOTES 1–5 Read this student's blog. There are eight mistakes in the use of future time clauses. The first mistake is already corrected. Find and correct seven more.

● ● ●

Graduation is next month! I need to make some plans now because when exams ~~will start~~,
  start

I don't have any free time. What am I going to do when I'll finish school? What path will

I take? My roommate is going to take a vacation before she'll look for a job. I can't do

that because I need to earn some money soon. I think that after I'll graduate, I'm going to

take a desktop publishing class. As soon as I learned the software, I look for a job with

a business publisher. It's hard to find full-time jobs, though. Part-time jobs are easier to

find. Maybe I'll take a part-time job until I'll find a good full-time one. Or maybe I'll take a

workshop in making decisions before I do anything!

EXERCISE 5 LISTENING

▶07|02 **A** Two classmates are discussing Ela's future plans. Listen to their conversation. Listen again and number the steps in order.

Ela is going to:

_____ **a.** go back to Turkey

_____ **b.** take a course in German

_____ **c.** take some more English classes

_____ **d.** return to the United States

_____ **e.** take a degree program in hotel management

__/__ **f.** get a part-time job

▶07|02 **B** Listen again to the conversation. Then work with a partner and discuss your answers to the questions.

1. Why is Ela going to get a part-time job after she finishes her English class?

   EXAMPLE: A: So, why is Ela going to get a part-time job after she finishes her class?
             B: She wants to save enough money to return to Turkey. She misses her family.

2. Will she return to Turkey before or after she takes another English course?

3. Why is she going to study German while she's back in Turkey?

4. What else will Ela do while she's in Turkey?

5. After she returns to the United States, what step will she take to reach her goal?

6. Why does Ela's friend say, "You'll need to check into a hotel for a vacation!"?

EXERCISE 6 WHAT ABOUT YOU?

A SURVEY Complete the notes with information about yourself.

1. I'm going to continue studying English until _____.

2. While I'm in this class, _____.

3. When I finish this class, _____.

4. I'll stay in this country until _____.

5. As soon as _____, I'll _____.

6. I'm not going to _____ until _____.

7. I'm going to feel a lot better after _____.

8. Before _____, _____.

B Work in a group. Compare your answers with those of your classmates. How many different answers are there?

EXAMPLE: **A:** I'm going to study English until I pass the TOEFL exam. What about you?

B: I'm going to continue studying until I get a job.

C: Me too!

EXERCISE 7 YOUR BUCKET LIST

A CONVERSATION People sometimes make a list of things they want to achieve or experience in their lives. They call it a "bucket list." What's on your bucket list? Before you talk about it, make a list of four to six items.

EXAMPLE: *visit Tahiti*

write a song and sing it on YouTube

buy a house

visit my hometown again

B Work with a partner. Talk about each other's lists. Choose one thing on your list. Why is it important to you? What will you need to do to achieve that goal?

EXAMPLE: **A:** So, what's on *your* bucket list?

B: Well, I want to visit Tahiti, write a song and sing it on YouTube, buy a house, and visit my hometown again. Most of all I *really* want to visit Tahiti. They say it's incredibly beautiful.

A: OK. And what will you do to make your dream come true?

B: First I'll save some money for the trip. As soon as I have enough money, I'll look for good flights and hotels on the Internet. After I find a good flight, I'll . . .

EXERCISE 8 WHAT'S NEXT?

GAME Work in a group and form a circle. One person says a sentence with a future time clause. The next person begins a new sentence using information from the main clause. Continue around the circle as long as you can. Use your imagination—your sentences don't have to be true!

EXAMPLE:

When class is over, I'm going to go to the student lounge.

As soon as I go to the student lounge, I'll buy a sandwich.

After I buy a sandwich, I'll find my friends.

As soon as I find my friends, . . .

FROM GRAMMAR TO WRITING

A BEFORE YOU WRITE Think about a goal you have. Then complete the worksheet. Use future time clauses in some of your answers.

Goal Planning Worksheet

What is your goal? _____

Why do you want to achieve this goal? _____

What are the first three steps of your action plan? Put them in order.

1. _____

2. _____

3. _____

B WRITE Use your worksheet to write a paragraph about your goal. Use future time clauses in your paragraph. Try to avoid the common mistakes in the chart.

EXAMPLE: My goal is to buy a used car so I can take some trips. As soon as I have a car, I'm going to drive to Montreal to visit my cousins. While I'm Montreal, I'll take a cooking course . . .

Common Mistakes in Using Future Time Clauses

Use the **simple present** in the future time clause. Do not use *be going to* or *will* in the time clause.	I'll take a course when I **finish** school. NOT I'll take a course when I'll finish school.
Use a **comma after the time clause** when the time clause comes first. Do not use a comma after the main clause when the main clause comes first.	**When I finish school,** I'll take a course. NOT I'll take a course, when I finish school.

C CHECK YOUR WORK Read your paragraph. Underline the future time clauses. Circle the verbs in the main clauses and in the time clauses. Use the Editing Checklist to check your work.

Editing Checklist

Did you use . . . ?

☐ sentences with future time clauses

☐ the simple present in the time clauses

☐ the future in the main clauses

☐ commas after time clauses at the beginning of a sentence

☐ *when, after,* or *as soon as* for the first event

☐ *after* or *until* for the second event

☐ *while* for same-time events

D REVISE YOUR WORK Read your paragraph again. Can you improve your writing? Make changes if necessary. Give your paragraph a title.

UNIT 7 REVIEW

Test yourself on the grammar of the unit.

A Circle the correct words to complete the sentences.

1. What are you going to do after you <u>will graduate / graduate</u>?

2. We won't start a new chapter until we <u>finished / finish</u> this one.

3. <u>When / Until</u> Jorge gets a raise, he's going to buy a new car.

4. <u>Is / Will</u> Andrea find a job by the time she graduates?

5. Where will you live while you're <u>learning / going to learn</u> English?

6. We won't start the test <u>until / when</u> the teacher arrives. She has the tests.

7. <u>Will you / Are you</u> going to take another class after you finish this one?

B Complete the sentences with the correct form of the verbs in parentheses.

1. Yuri is going to take night classes while he _____ full-time.

(work)

2. Until he buys a new computer, he _____ for online courses.

(not register)

3. When he takes online courses, he _____ more time at home.

(spend)

4. He'll help his daughter with her homework while he _____ for his own courses.

(study)

5. He _____ for a new job before he graduates.

(not look)

6. As soon as he _____, he's going to find a job.

(graduate)

7. Before he starts his new job, he _____ a vacation.

(take)

C Find and correct six mistakes. Remember to look at punctuation.

A: Are you going to call Phil when we'll finish dinner?

B: No, I'm too tired. I'm just going to watch TV after I go to sleep.

A: Before I wash the dishes, I'm going answer some emails.

B: I'll help you, as soon as I'll drink my coffee.

A: No rush. I have a lot of emails. I won't be ready to clean up until you'll finish.

Now check your answers on page 476.

Present Perfect

PART 3

OUTCOMES

- Describe events that began in the past and continue into the present
- Describe the duration of events, using the present perfect + *since/for*
- Identify key details in a short biography
- Identify the length of time of events in an interview
- Ask and answer questions about life events and experiences
- Write a paragraph about experiences and accomplishments

OUTCOMES

- Use *already*, *yet*, and *still* with the present perfect
- Discuss events that happened or did not happen at some time in the past
- Identify key details in an information article and a conversation
- Recognize and discuss tasks on a to-do list or plan
- Write a paragraph about a goal and the steps needed to reach it

OUTCOMES

- Describe events that happened at an indefinite time in the past
- Describe repeated actions and states in the past
- Identify main points of an article and a conversation about travel
- Discuss famous quotes, giving explanations and reasons for opinions
- Write a paragraph in response to a quote from literature

OUTCOMES

- Recognize when to use the present perfect and the simple past
- Identify key details in a short, factual text
- Understand the time frame of important details in an interview
- Discuss past events and experiences
- Research a famous person and present findings to the class
- Write a paragraph about a personal experience

OUTCOMES

- Describe actions that started in the past and are still in progress
- Describe actions that started at an indefinite time in the past and are finished
- Identify main points of a short text on a scientific topic
- Understand the time frame of main events in conversations
- Discuss climate change
- Write an email or letter about recent activities

Present Perfect:
Since and *For*
CAREERS

OUTCOMES
- Describe events that began in the past and continue into the present
- Describe the duration of events, using the present perfect + *since/for*
- Identify key details in a short biography
- Identify the length of time of events in an interview
- Ask and answer questions about life events and experiences
- Write a paragraph about experiences and accomplishments

STEP 1   GRAMMAR IN CONTEXT

BEFORE YOU READ

Look at Bob Burnquist's sports card. Discuss the questions.

1. What are his interests?
2. What are *your* interests?
3. What is Bob's motto?[1]
4. Do you have a motto? What is it?

READ

▶08|01   Read this article about a champion skateboarder.

King of Skate

When he was only 11 years old, Bob Burnquist's life changed dramatically. A skate park opened just three blocks from his house in São Paulo, Brazil. Bob got his very first skateboard and started skating. He's been a skater since then.

---

1 *motto:* a short statement of life goals or beliefs
2 *individuality:* the way people are different from each other

SPORTS CARD
Bob Burnquist

Date of Birth	October 10, 1976
Place of Birth	Rio de Janeiro, Brazil
Residence	California, U.S.
Citizenship	Brazil and U.S.
Started Skateboarding	1987
Turned Professional	1991
Other Interests	Reading, travel, photography, snowboarding, mountain biking, surfing, skydiving
Motto	"Be good, be positive, respect individuality[2] and nature."

At first, he did it just for fun, but soon he turned pro.[3] Before long, he made enough money to support himself while doing what he loved most. His first big international competition was in Canada in 1995. Bob won. Since then, he has won many more first-place prizes. And he is still winning. Since 2002, when he was voted "King of Skate" in a California contest, Bob has won twelve gold medals—three of them in 2013.

Bob has lived in California since 1995, but he frequently returns to Brazil. He's had dual citizenship (Brazil and the United States) for many years. Does he consider himself American? Bob says, "I'm American, South American.... A citizen of the world."

The skateboard isn't the only board Bob uses. He also enjoys snowboarding and surfing. Since he moved to California, he has been close to snow-topped mountains and the beach. His backyard and, of course, the streets provide opportunity for skating. As he once said, "If you snowboard, surf, and skate, you pretty much cover the whole earth."

---

3 *turned pro:* became a professional (did the sport for money)

AFTER YOU READ

A VOCABULARY **Choose the word or phrase that is closest in meaning to the word(s) in bold.**

1. Bob's life changed **dramatically**.
   a. slowly and a little   b. dangerously   c. quickly and a lot

2. He earned enough money to **support himself**.
   a. pay for lessons   b. pay for things he needs   c. buy a new skateboard

3. Does Bob **consider himself** American?
   a. want to be   b. like being   c. think he is

4. The streets provide **opportunity** for skating.
   a. some dangers   b. good chances   c. a lot of contests

5. Bob's **residence** is in California.
   a. home   b. office   c. family

6. Bob always says, "Be **positive**."
   a. 100 percent sure   b. hopeful   c. strong

B COMPREHENSION **Read the statements. Check (✓) *True* or *False*.**

	True	False
1. Bob Burnquist doesn't skate anymore.	☐	☐
2. He has won only one first-place prize since 1995.	☐	☐
3. Bob moved to California in 1995.	☐	☐
4. Bob is a citizen of many countries.	☐	☐
5. He lives close to the beach.	☐	☐

C DISCUSSION **Work with a partner. Compare your answers in B. Why did you check *True* or *False*?**

STEP 2 | GRAMMAR PRESENTATION

PRESENT PERFECT WITH *SINCE* AND *FOR*

Statements

Subject	*Have (not)*	Past Participle		*Since/For*
I You* We They	**have (not)**	**been**	here	**since** 2002. **for** a long time.
He She It	**has (not)**	**lived**		

You is both singular and plural.

Contractions

Affirmative	Negative
I have = **I've** you have = **you've** we have = **we've** they have = **they've** he has = **he's** she has = **she's** it has = **it's**	have not = **haven't** has not = **hasn't**

Yes/No Questions

Have	Subject	Past Participle		*Since/For*
Have	I you we they	**been**	here	**since** 2002? **for** a long time?
Has	he she it	**lived**		

Short Answers

Affirmative			Negative		
Yes,	you I/we you they	**have.**	**No,**	you I/we you they	**haven't.**
	he she it	**has.**		he she it	**hasn't.**

Wh- Questions

Wh- Word	*Have*	Subject	Past Participle	
How long	**have**	I you we they	**been**	here?
	has	he she it	**lived**	

Short Answers

Since 2002.
For many years.

GRAMMAR NOTES

1 Present Perfect + *Since* or *For*

Use the present perfect with *since* or *for* to show that something **began in the past and continues into the present** (and may continue into the future).

Past	1987	**Now**	Future

has been

Bob **has been** a skater *since* 1987.
> *(He became a skater in 1987, and he is still a skater.)*

He **has been** a skater *for* many years.
> *(He became a skater many years ago, and he is still a skater.)*

2 *Since* and *For*

Since shows **when** something started. *For* shows **how long** something has lasted.

Use *since* + **point in time** (*since yesterday, since 5:00, since Monday, since 1995, since then*) to show when something started.

He **has won** many contests *since 1995*.
He **has become** famous *since then*.

Since can also introduce a time clause.

He **has loved** sports *since he was a child*.

Use *for* + **length of time** (*for 10 minutes, for two weeks, for years, for a long time*) to show how long something has lasted.

Bob **has had** a restaurant *for years*.
He **hasn't broken** a board *for a long time*.

Expressions with *since* or *for* can go at the **end** or the **beginning** of the sentence.

He has become famous *since then*.
Since then, he has become famous.

USAGE NOTE It is **more common** to put the expression with *since* or *for* at the **end** of the sentence.

He has lived in L.A. *for many years*. *(more common)*
For many years, he has lived in L.A. *(less common)*

IN WRITING Use a **comma** when the expression with *since* or *for* comes at the **beginning** of the sentence.

Do not use a comma when the expression with *since* or *for* comes at the end of the sentence.

Since he turned pro, he hasn't taken a vacation.
For many years, he's had dual citizenship.

NOT He hasn't taken a vacation_x since he turned pro.
NOT He's had dual citizenship_x for many years.

Form the present perfect with *have* + **past participle**.	He **has lived** there for years. They **have been** partners since 1998.	

	BASE FORM	SIMPLE PAST	PAST PARTICIPLE
To form the **past participle** of **regular verbs** add *-d* or *-ed* to the base form of the verb. It is the same as the regular simple past form of the verb.	love want	lov**ed** want**ed**	lov**ed** want**ed**

	BASE FORM	SIMPLE PAST	PAST PARTICIPLE
IN WRITING There are often **spelling changes** when you add *-ed* to the verb.	marry stop	marr**ied** stop**ped**	marr**ied** stop**ped**

	BASE FORM	SIMPLE PAST	PAST PARTICIPLE
Many common verbs are **irregular**. They do not form the past participle by adding *-d* or *-ed* to the base form of the verb. Here is a list of some of the **irregular verbs used in this unit**. It shows both the simple past and the past participle of each verb. Notice that most irregular verbs have a past participle form that is different from the simple past form.	be become go have meet take wear win write	was/were became went had met took wore won wrote	**been** **become** **gone** **had** **met** **taken** **worn** **won** **written**

	BASE FORM	SIMPLE PAST	PAST PARTICIPLE
USAGE NOTE Some verbs have **two past participle forms**—one **regular** and one **irregular**. In conversation, the irregular past participle form is more common. There is one exception: For *dream*, the regular form is more common.	kneel light prove dream	knelt/kneeled lit/lighted proved dreamed/dreamt	**knelt/kneeled** **lit/lighted** **proven/proved** **dreamed/dreamt**

	BASE FORM	SIMPLE PAST	PAST PARTICIPLE
USAGE NOTE A few verbs have **two irregular past participles**. The form *have gotten* is very common in American English.	beat get	beat got	**beaten/beat** **gotten/got**

BE CAREFUL! Do not form the **past participle of irregular verbs** by adding *-d* or *-ed* to the base form of the verb.	He has **won** many contests. NOT He has ~~winned~~ many contests.	

REFERENCE NOTE

For a more complete list of **irregular verbs**, see Appendix 1 on page 453.

EXERCISE 1
DISCOVER THE GRAMMAR

GRAMMAR NOTES 1–3 **Read the information about a skater, Caterina. Then choose the sentence (*a* or *b*) that best describes the situation.**

1. Caterina has been a skater since 2008.
   a. She is still a skater.
   b. She is not a skater anymore.

2. She has lived in the same apartment for five years.
   a. She lived in a different apartment six years ago.
   b. She moved two years ago.

3. Caterina has been married for five years.
   a. She is not married now.
   b. She got married five years ago.

4. Catarina and her husband haven't been on a vacation since 2011.
   a. They are on a vacation now.
   b. They were on a vacation in 2011.

5. Caterina hasn't won a contest for two years.
   a. She won a contest two years ago.
   b. She didn't win a contest two years ago.

6. She has stayed positive about her career since she won her last contest.
   a. She expects to win more contests.
   b. She isn't hopeful anymore.

EXERCISE 2 *SINCE* OR *FOR*

GRAMMAR NOTE 2 **Complete the sentences about Brazilian sportswriter Mariana Andrade. Use *since* or *for*.**

1. Mariana Andrade has lived in São Paulo _____*since*_____ 2000.

2. She has supported herself as a sportswriter _____ four years.

3. _____ June, she has written several articles about skateboarding.

4. This sport has been very popular in Brazil _____ many years.

5. Mariana has met Burnquist twice _____ she started her job.

6. She loves to skate, but she hasn't had much opportunity _____ a long time.

7. She has been married to Alvaro, another skater, _____ 2008.

EXERCISE 3 FORMS OF THE PRESENT PERFECT

GRAMMAR NOTE 3 Complete this article about Lauren Jones. Use the correct form of the verbs in parentheses.

Lauren Jones ____*has loved*____ skating since she was a little girl. She began skating
                    1. (love)

when she was 10, and she _____ since then. She _____ a
                                2. (not stop)   **3. (be)**

professional skater now for several years. She and her husband _____ in San
                                                                4. (live)

Diego, California since the two got married. They _____ the same one-bedroom
                                                    5. (have)

apartment for three years. They _____ a vacation for many years, but they
                                 6. (not take)

_____ to several international skating contests since Lauren turned pro. Lauren
7. (go)

_____ in three contests since last year, and she _____ two
8. (skate)   **9. (win)**

second-place prizes since then. Lauren _____ to be a pro since she was a child.
                                         10. (want)

"There aren't many professional female skateboarders," she says. "Ever since my dream came true, I

_____ myself a lucky woman."
11. (consider)

EXERCISE 4 FORMS OF THE PRESENT PERFECT WITH *SINCE* OR *FOR*

GRAMMAR NOTES 2–3 Complete the sentences. Use the present perfect form of the verbs
in parentheses and *since* or *for*.

1. Skateboarding ____*has been*____ popular ____*for*____ more than 50 years.
                    a. (be)   **b.**

2. Skateboards _____ around _____ a long time. In the 1930s,
                 a. (be)   **b.**
   the first ones were simple wooden boxes on metal wheels. They _____
                                                                 c. (change)
   dramatically _____ then!
                 d.

3. The first skateboarding contest took place in California in 1963. _____ then,
                                                                      a.
   thousands of contests _____ place internationally.
                          b. (take)

4. In 1976, the first outdoor skate park opened in the United States. _____ then,
                                                                       a.
   hundreds of parks _____ in countries around the world such as Australia,
                      b. (open)
   China, England, France, Israel, Japan, and Kenya.

5. Skateboarding can be dangerous. _____ the 1960s, hundreds of thousands of
                                    a.
   people _____ to hospital emergency rooms because of injuries.
          b. (go)

6. When he was seven years old, Jon Comer lost his right foot as a result of a car accident. But that
   didn't stop him. _____ then, he _____ one of the best-known
                     a.   **b. (become)**
   professional skateboarders in the world, thanks to his great skill and very positive attitude.

7. Tony Hawk _____ professionally _____ many years, but he is
              a. (not compete)   **b.**
   still the most famous and successful skateboarder of all time.

110   Unit 8

EXERCISE 5 QUESTIONS, STATEMENTS, AND SHORT ANSWERS

A GRAMMAR NOTES 1–3 Amy Lu is applying for a job as a college sports instructor. Look at her résumé and the interviewer's notes. The year is 2016.

Amy Lu

525 Ahina St.
Honolulu, HI 96816

Interviewed
09/19/16

Education:
2008 Certificate (American College of Sports Medicine)
2005 M.A. Physical Education (University of Texas)

moved to Honolulu in 2006

Employment:
2007–present part-time physical education teacher (high school)
2005–present sports trainer (private)

teaches tennis, swimming

Skills:
speaks English, Portuguese, and Chinese
practices martial arts   *got black belt in tae kwon do*
2 mos. ago

Other Interests:
travel, sports photography, skateboarding, surfing

Awards:
2008 Teacher of the Year Award
2005 First Prize in Sunburn Classic Skate Contest

Memberships:
2008–present member of National Education Association (NEA)

B John Sakaino is interviewing Amy Lu for a job as a college sports instructor. Use the words in parentheses to complete the questions. Use the information in Amy's résumé to write her answers. Use contractions when possible.

1. (how long / live in Honolulu)

   JOHN: *How long have you lived in Honolulu?*

   AMY: *I've lived in Honolulu for 10 years.* **or** *I've lived in Honolulu since 2006.*

2. (how long / have your M.A. degree)

   JOHN: _____

   AMY: _____

3. (have any more training / since / you get your M.A.)

JOHN: _____

AMY: _____

4. (how long / be a physical education teacher)

JOHN: _____

AMY: _____

5. (how long / work as a sports trainer)

JOHN: _____

AMY: _____

6. (how long / have a black belt in tae kwon do)

JOHN: _____

AMY: _____

7. (win any awards since then)

JOHN: I see you won a medal in skateboarding. _____

AMY: _____ I won the Teacher of the Year Award in 2008.

8. (how long / be a member of NEA)

JOHN: _____

AMY: _____

EXERCISE 6 EDITING

GRAMMAR NOTES 1–3 **Read these posts to a skateboard message board. There are ten mistakes in the use of the present perfect with *since* and *for*. The first mistake is already corrected. Find and correct nine more.**

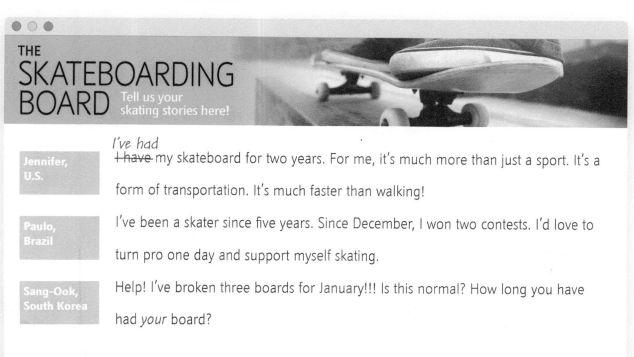

Jennifer, U.S.	*I've had* ~~I have~~ my skateboard for two years. For me, it's much more than just a sport. It's a form of transportation. It's much faster than walking!
Paulo, Brazil	I've been a skater since five years. Since December, I won two contests. I'd love to turn pro one day and support myself skating.
Sang-Ook, South Korea	Help! I've broken three boards for January!!! Is this normal? How long you have had *your* board?

Marta, Mexico	Broken boards?! That's nothing! Consider yourself lucky! I've break my wrist twice since I started skating!
Megan, Australia	Last year, my board hit a rock while I was skating in the street. I fell and hit my head and had to go to the emergency room. I always worn a helmet since then!
Ming, U.S.	I live in California since 2006. My first love is surfing, but when there aren't any waves, I jump on my skateboard and take to the streets! My motto is "Make the best of what you have!"
Todd, Canada	Wow! Yesterday, my friend gave me a copy of the video "OP King of Skate." I've watch it three times since then. The Burnquist part is awesome!
Sylvie, France	At last! A skate park opened near my home last week. Since then, I gone every day. It's a lot more fun than skating in the streets!

STEP 4   COMMUNICATION PRACTICE

EXERCISE 7   LISTENING

▶08|02   **A**   Listen to Eliana Serrano's job interview. Then listen again and complete the interviewer's notes. Use *since* and *for*.

— WSPR Radio —

Eliana Serrano   Interviewed Sept. 9

Eliana has been an athlete _for fifteen years_____.
                                                    1.

She's been an announcer _____.
                                        2.

She's lived in L.A. _____.
                                  3.

She hasn't worked full-time as an announcer _____.
                                                            4.

She's worked part-time at WABC _____.
                                              5.

She's written sports articles _____.
                                          6.

She's considered herself an announcer _____.
                                                    7.

B Listen to the interview again and read the interviewer's notes. Do you think Eliana should get the job? Why or why not? Discuss your opinion with a partner.

EXAMPLE: **A:** I think Eliana should get the job. She has had a lot of experience. She . . .
B: Yes, but she hasn't . . .

EXERCISE 8 WHO GETS THE JOB?

A ROLE PLAY Work with a partner. You are going to role-play two interviews for a job as a college music teacher. Look at the résumés. Write five or more interview questions. Begin your questions with *How long*, *How many*, and *Have you . . . since?*

EXAMPLE: *How long have you been a music teacher?*

CHIN HO CHO

EDUCATION:
2005 M.A. in Music Education
(Boston University)

TEACHING EXPERIENCE:
2005–present The Juilliard School

COURSES TAUGHT:
Voice and Piano
History of Music
Symphonies of Beethoven
Twentieth-century Jazz

PUBLICATIONS:
"Introducing Computers into Music Class"
(*The Journal of Music*, 2007)

AWARDS:
Teacher of the Year, 2007
Winner of University of Maryland Piano
Competition, 2014

CLARA RESTON

EDUCATION:
1991 M.A. in Music Education
(Boston University)

TEACHING EXPERIENCE:
2011–present Barnard College
2006–2010 Boston University
1997–2005 Yale University
1994–1996 Sarah Lawrence College
1991–1993 Boston University

COURSES TAUGHT:
Music Theory I
Music and Culture

PUBLICATIONS:
"Rachmaninoff Revisited" (*MJ*, 1996)
"Favorite Instruments of High School
Students" (*Music Education*, 1996)
"World Music in a Small World" (*Music
and Culture*, 1998)

B Work with your partner. Role-play two interviews (one for Chin Ho Cho and one for Clara Reston). Take turns being the interviewer.

EXAMPLE: A: How long have you been a music teacher, Chin Ho?
B: I've been a music teacher since 2005.

C Work in a group. Decide who to hire for the job and why. Remember to use *since* and *for*.

EXAMPLE: A: Chin Ho Cho has had the same job since he got his M.A. degree.
B: Clara Reston has a lot more experience. She's been a teacher since 1991.
C: But Chin has taught . . .

EXERCISE 9 WHAT ABOUT YOU?

A CONVERSATION Before you talk with your partner about your life, complete these notes.

1. I live in _____ .
   (a country, city)

2. I study _____ .
   (a language, another subject)

3. I am a(n) _____ .
   (an occupation)

4. I play _____ .
   (a sport, a game, a musical instrument)

5. I want to _____ .
   (a goal)

6. *Other:* _____

B Work with a partner. Show your partner your notes. Ask and answer questions with *How long* to learn more about your partner. Do you and your partner have anything in common?

EXAMPLE: A: How long have you lived in Canada?
B: For about five years. What about you?
A: Oh, since . . .

FROM GRAMMAR TO WRITING

A BEFORE YOU WRITE You are going to write about a person's experience and accomplishments. You can write about yourself, a famous person, a person you know, or one of the people in Exercise 8. You can also make up information. Choose a person and complete the outline.

Name: _____

Occupation: _____ From: _____ To: _____
                                                       (year)   (year)

Accomplishments: _____

_____

_____

B WRITE Use your outline to write a paragraph about that person's accomplishments. Remember to use the present perfect with *since* and *for*. Try to avoid the common mistakes in the chart.

EXAMPLE: Amy Lu has been a high school physical education teacher and a private sports trainer for many years. She has received two awards since 2005, one for teaching and the other for skateboarding. She has been a member of the National Education Association since 2008. Amy has many interests. She speaks three languages. She has also been . . .

Common Mistakes in Using the Present Perfect with *Since* and *For*

Use *for* with a **length of time**. Do not use *since*.	She's been a teacher **for five years**. NOT She's been a teacher ~~since~~ five years.
Use a **comma** after a time clause that begins with *since* when the **time clause comes first**. Do not use a comma when the time clause comes last.	**Since I moved here,** I've had two jobs. NOT I've had two jobs, since I moved here.
Be careful to make **spelling changes** in some regular past participles. Do not just add -*ed*.	They've **studied** English since May. NOT They've ~~studyed~~ English since May.

C CHECK YOUR WORK Read your paragraph. Underline the present perfect verbs. Circle *since* and *for* and the time expressions. Use the Editing Checklist to check your work.

Editing Checklist

Did you use . . . ?

☐ *since* with a point in time

☐ *for* with a length of time

☐ *have* + the correct past participle

☐ the correct spelling for the past participles

D REVISE YOUR WORK Read your paragraph again. Can you improve your writing? Make changes if necessary. Give your paragraph a title.

UNIT 8 REVIEW

Test yourself on the grammar of the unit.

Ⓐ Complete the sentences with _since_ or _for_.

1. Sara has lived in San Francisco _____ 10 years.

2. She has wanted to be a tennis player _____ she was a little girl.

3. She's been a professional player _____ several years.

4. Sara has had the same trainer _____ a long time.

5. _____ 2010, she has won several competitions.

6. _____ the past few weeks, she has had a wrist injury.

7. _____ then, she hasn't been able to practice.

Ⓑ Complete the sentences with the present perfect form of the verbs in parentheses. Use contractions when possible.

1. I _____ a skateboarder for many years.
   (be)

2. Since 2010, I _____ any skating accidents.
   (not have)

3. My brother _____ the sport since he was a little boy.
   (love)

4. Together we _____ in many competitions.
   (compete)

5. He _____ several competitions since last year.
   (win)

6. We _____ each other for a few months.
   (not see)

Ⓒ Find and correct seven mistakes.

1. Marta and Tomás lived here since they got married in 2013.

2. Tomás has been a professional tennis player since he has come to this country.

3. He has won several competitions for then.

4. Since I have known Tomás, he had three different coaches.

5. I haven't see Marta for several weeks.

6. She have been in Brazil since April 1.

7. I've wanted to visit Brazil since years, but I haven't had any vacation time since I got this new job.

Now check your answers on page 476.

Present Perfect:
Already, Yet, and *Still*
PARTY PLANNING

OUTCOMES
- Use *already, yet,* and *still* with the present perfect
- Discuss events that happened or did not happen at some time in the past
- Identify key details in an information article and a conversation
- Recognize and discuss tasks on a to-do list or plan
- Write a paragraph about a goal and the steps needed to reach it

---

STEP 1 **GRAMMAR IN CONTEXT**

BEFORE YOU READ

Look at the photo. Discuss the questions.

1. How do you feel about parties?
2. Which do you prefer: giving a party or going to one? Why?

READ

▶ 09|01 Read this article about how to plan a party.

It's Party Time!

It's almost the end of the year, and you've already been to several parties, but you haven't given a party of your own yet. You're a little nervous, but you decide it's time to take the plunge.¹

First things first: Have you chosen the date yet? What about the time?

OK. You've already chosen the date and the time and emailed the invitations. But you still haven't decided on the menu, and now your party is just one week away! Don't panic!

---

1 *take the plunge:* do an activity that seems difficult or frightening

We spoke to Patty Cake, a professional party planner. She says, "It *is* very important to be organized, but remember: You don't need a whole new set of skills. Think about your everyday life. You've already done many of the things you need to do for a party. You know how to shop for food, put it on plates, and introduce friends to one another. Now, all you need to do is just bring your many skills together."

Still need help? Party planners, like Patty Cake, can offer specific advice. She says, "We've already helped hundreds of people plan successful parties—big and small. If you haven't used a party-planning service yet, you should give it a try." And you don't have to spend a lot of money. Free advice is available on the Internet. There, you will also find handy[2] lists where you can check off things you've already done (and see the things you haven't done yet!). So, take a deep breath, relax, and enjoy the party!

2 *handy:* useful; easy to use

AFTER YOU READ

A VOCABULARY Complete the sentences with the words from the box.

| available | organized | professional | specific | successful |

1. OK. The drinks are on the table over there. Extra chairs are in the bedroom. The cake is in the refrigerator. I'll take it out at 8:00 p.m. That's it! I think I'm quite _organized_.

2. I can meet you for lunch any day this week to discuss plans for your party. You can also call me anytime—day or night. As you can see, I'm pretty _available_.

3. The party is for my friend Marta. She's a writer. Her latest book is on the bestseller list! She's really _successful_.

4. Please bring two large bags of Crispy Chips. The ones in the blue bag—they're low in fat, but not low in salt. You'll find them at Shopwise in aisle 6. I know I'm being very _specific_, but I want to be sure you get the right ones!

5. Jake offered to paint the apartment before the party, but I prefer to hire _professional_ painters. They have training, job experience—and insurance if something goes wrong!

B COMPREHENSION Reread the first three paragraphs in the article. Check (✓) the correct answers.

The party giver . . .

☒ 1. went to several parties

☐ 2. gave a party of her own

☒ 3. chose a date for the party

☒ 4. chose the time

☒ 5. sent invitations

☐ 6. decided on a menu

C DISCUSSION Work with a partner. Compare your answers in B. Why did you or didn't you check each item?

PRESENT PERFECT: *ALREADY*, *YET*, AND *STILL*

Affirmative Statements: *Already*

Subject	*Have*	*Already*	Past Participle		*Already*
They	have	*already*	emailed	the invitations.	
She	has		chosen	the menu.	
They	have		emailed	the invitations	*already*.
She	has		chosen	the menu	

Negative Statements: *Yet*

Subject	*Have not*	Past Participle		*Yet*
They	haven't	emailed	them	*yet*.
She	hasn't	chosen	it	

Negative Statements: *Still*

Subject	*Still*	*Have not*	Past Participle	
They	*still*	haven't	emailed	them.
She		hasn't	chosen	it.

Yes/No Questions: *Yet*

Have	Subject	Past Participle		*Yet*
Have	they	emailed	them	*yet*?
Has	she	chosen	it	

Short Answers

Affirmative		Negative	
Yes,	they **have**.	No,	they **haven't**.
	she **has**.		she **hasn't**.
			not *yet*.

GRAMMAR NOTES

1 Present Perfect + *Already*, *Yet*, or *Still*

Use the present perfect with *already*, *yet*, or *still* to show that something **happened or did not happen at an indefinite** (not exact) **time in the past**.

• *already*	I've *already* **emailed** the invitations.
• *yet*	We **haven't ordered** the cake *yet*.
• *still*	He *still* **hasn't replied**.

BE CAREFUL! Do not use *already*, *yet*, or *still* with past time expressions.

NOT I've *already* mailed the invitations ~~last week~~.

USAGE NOTE In American English, we sometimes use the **simple past** with *already* and *yet*.

Jenna **has** *already* **left**. or Jenna *already* **left**.
Ebo **hasn't left** *yet*. or Ebo **didn't leave** *yet*.

2 Statements

In **affirmative statements**, use *already*. In **negative statements**, use *yet* or *still*.

Use *already* in **affirmative statements** to show that something **has happened before now**.	Jenna **has** *already* **met** Carlos.
USAGE NOTE We often use the present perfect with *already* for something that happened sooner than expected.	You**'ve** *already* **set** the table. Great!
Use *yet* in **negative statements** to show that something **has not happened before now** (in the near past).	A: Jenna **has***n't* **called** *yet*. B: Oh, I'm sure we'll hear from her later.
USAGE NOTE We often use the present perfect with *not yet* for something we expected to happen earlier, but did not happen. It is possible that it will happen soon.	Where's Tom? I expected him at 8:00, but he **hasn't arrived** *yet*. I hope he gets here soon.
You can also use *still* in **negative statements**. *Still* has a similar meaning to *not yet*.	Jenna *still* **hasn't called**.
USAGE NOTE We often use the present perfect with *still* to show that we are surprised or unhappy with the situation.	I don't know if Jenna is coming or not. I've texted her several times, but she *still* **hasn't answered**. She promised to help me.

3 Questions

In questions, we usually use *yet*.

Use the present perfect with *yet* in **questions** to ask if something has happened before now.	A: **Have** you **bought** the soda *yet*?
Notice the different possible ways of giving **negative answers**.	B: **No, I haven't.** or **No, *not yet*.** or ***Not yet*.**
USAGE NOTE We sometimes use *already* in questions to express **surprise** that something has happened sooner than expected.	**Has** Carlos **arrived** *already*? What's he doing here? The party doesn't start until 8:00!

4 Word Order

Already usually goes **before the past participle**. It can also go at the **end of the clause**.	I**'ve** *already* **made** the cake. I**'ve made** the cake *already*.
Yet usually goes at the **end of the clause**.	They **haven't arrived** *yet*. She **hasn't invited** Mehmet *yet*.
Still goes **before** *have not*.	They *still* **haven't arrived**. She *still* **hasn't invited** Mehmet.

REFERENCE NOTES

For a list of **irregular past participles**, see Appendix 1 on page 453.

For more information on the **indefinite past**, see Unit 10 on page 131.

For a list of **irregular past participles**, see Appendix 1 on page 453.

For more information on the **indefinite past**, see Unit 10 on page 131.

STEP 3   **FOCUSED PRACTICE**

EXERCISE 1   DISCOVER THE GRAMMAR

GRAMMAR NOTES 1–3   Read the first statement. Then decide if the second statement is *True (T)* or *False (F)*.

1. I've already given many parties.

   _F_ This will be my first party.

2. I haven't made the cake yet.

   _T_ I plan to make a cake.

3. Has Bev arrived yet?

   _F_ I'm surprised that Bev is here.

4. Tom and Lisa still haven't arrived.

   _T_ I expect them to arrive.

5. Has Jenna left already?

   _F_ I'm surprised that Jenna left.

6. Have you had a cup of tea yet?

   _T_ I don't know if you had a cup of tea.

7. Carlos has already met my sister.

   _F_ I need to introduce Carlos to her.

8. I still haven't called Mehmet.

   _F_ I don't plan to call him.

9. Has Tom bought the chips yet?

   _T_ I think Tom is going to bring the chips.

10. I still haven't talked to the party planner.

    _T_ I should call her.

11. Have you taken any photos yet?

    _F_ I saw you take some photos.

12. We've already finished all the cake.

    _F_ There is more cake.

EXERCISE 2   QUESTIONS, STATEMENTS, SHORT ANSWERS

A   **GRAMMAR NOTES 1–3**   Complete these conversations that take place at Marta's party. Use the present perfect form of the verbs in parentheses with *already* or *yet* and short answers. Use contractions when possible. See Appendix 1 on page 453 for help with irregular verbs.

1. **A:** This is a great party. Marta made the cake. She's

   a professional baker. _____*Have*_____ you

   _____*tried*_____ it _____*yet*_____?
   (try)

   B: _____*No*_____, I _____*haven't*_____.

   But I'm going to have a piece now.

2. A: Jenna, I'd like you to meet my friend Carlos.

B: We *alredy* *have* *meet* (meet). Marta introduced us.

3. A: Would you like another cup of coffee?

B: No, thanks. I *have* *alredy* *had* (have) three cups!

4. A: *Has* Jenna *left* (leave) *alreadly*? It's still early!

B: *No*, she *hasn't*. She's in the kitchen.

5. A: *Have* you *seen* (see) Tarantino's new movie *alredy*?

B: *Yes*, I *have*. It's great. What about you?

A: I *haven't* *seen* (see) it *yet*, but I want to.

6. A: This was a great party. I'm giving my own party next week. I *have* *already* *planned* (plan) the whole thing, but I'm still nervous about it.

B: Don't worry. If you organize it well, the rest will take care of itself!

⏺ 09|02 **B** LISTEN AND CHECK **Listen to the conversations and check your answers in A.**

EXERCISE 3 WORD ORDER

GRAMMAR NOTE 4 **Unscramble the words to complete what some of the guests at Marta's party said.**

1. (tried / have / yet / the cake / you)

Have you tried the cake yet ?

2. (Jenna / yet / haven't / seen / I)

I haven't seen Jenna yet .

3. (already / met / I've / Carlos)

I've already met Carlos .

4. (yet / seen / Bruno / you / have)

have you seen Bruno yet? ?

5. (still / tried / I / the cake / haven't)

I still haven't tried the cake .

6. (some of the guests / left / already / have)

some of the guests have already left .

7. (Bruno / arrived / hasn't / still)

Bruno still hasn't arrived !

THINGS TO DO

- ☑ pick a date
- ☐ choose a time!!
- ☑ find a location
- ☑ write a guest list
- ☑ buy invitations
- ☐ send invitations!!
- ☐ plan the menu!!
- ☑ pick out music
- ☐ shop for food
- ☐ clean the house

EXERCISE 4 AFFIRMATIVE AND NEGATIVE STATEMENTS

GRAMMAR NOTES 1–4 Read Dante's party-planning checklist. Write statements about the things that he *has already done* and the things that he *hasn't done yet* (or the things that he *still hasn't done!*). See Appendix 1 on page 453 for help with irregular verbs.

1. *He's already picked a date.*

2. *He hasn't chosen a time yet.* or *He still hasn't chosen a time.*

3. He's already found a location.

4. He's already written a guest list.

5. He's already bought invitations

6. He hasn't sent invitations yet.

7. He hasn't planned the menu yet.

8. He's already picked out the music.

9. He hasn't shopped for food yet.

10. He still hasn't cleaned the house

EXERCISE 5 EDITING

GRAMMAR NOTES 1–4 Read this online bulletin board. There are nine mistakes in the use of the present perfect with *already*, *yet*, and *still*. The first mistake is already corrected. Find and correct eight more.

Ask the Party Planner!

Doug asked: Help! My party is next week, and I ~~already~~ _still_ haven't figured out the food! I'm not at all

organized. I've _already_ ~~yet~~ wasted three days worrying, and I still don't have any ideas. What should I do?

The Party Planner's Advice: Don't panic! Your guests haven't started arriving ~~already~~ _yet_, so there's

still time. Ask everyone to bring something! (You've already _invited_ ~~invite~~ people, right?) Or order pizza. I

haven't met anyone already who doesn't like pizza.

124 Unit 9

Rosa asked: I'd like to find a "theme" for my next birthday party. I've already have a pasta party (10 kinds of pasta!), and I've already gave a movie party (everyone dressed up as a movie character). Both were very successful, but I haven't still decided what to do this time. Any ideas?

The Party Planner's Advice: Sure. Has you tried this one yet? Ask each guest to bring a baby photo of himself or herself. Collect the photos. People try to match the photos with the guests! Your guests will love it!

<table>
<tr><td>STEP 4</td><td>COMMUNICATION PRACTICE</td></tr>
</table>

EXERCISE 6 LISTENING

▶09|03 **Ⓐ** A couple is planning a party. Look at their "To Do" list. Then listen to their conversation. Listen again and check (✓) the things they've already done.

▶09|03 **Ⓑ** Listen to the conversation again. Then work with a partner. Discuss your answers in A. Why did or didn't you check each item?

EXAMPLE: A: Did you check item 2?
B: Yes. They've already found a place.
A: Right. They're going to have the party at Jason's. What about item 3? Have they invited people yet?

Ⓒ Work with your partner. What are some additional things the couple may need to do? Brainstorm ideas. Ask questions with *yet*. Compare your questions with another pair.

EXAMPLE: A: Have they bought a gift yet?
B: If they bought a gift, have they wrapped it yet?

TO DO:
✓ 1. choose a date
2. find a place
3. invite people
4. borrow extra chairs
5. figure out food
6. buy soda
7. find someone to help set up
8. select music

EXERCISE 7 PARTY CHORES

A INFORMATION GAP Work with a partner. Student A will follow the instructions below. Student B will follow the instructions on page 486.

> **STUDENT A**
>
> - Look at the picture of the Stangers' dining room and at Gisela's "To Do" list. Check (✓) the chores that Gisela has already done. Then answer your partner's questions about Gisela's chores.
>
>   EXAMPLE: B: Has Gisela vacuumed the carpet yet?
>   A: No, she hasn't. **or** No, not yet.
>
> - Look at Karl's "To Do" list. Ask your partner questions to find out which chores Karl has already done. Check (✓) those chores.
>
>   EXAMPLE: A: Has Karl bought a memory card yet?
>   B: Yes, he has. **or** Yes, he's already gotten one.
>
>
>
> **To Do: Karl**
> - ☑ buy memory card for camera
> - ☐ bake the cake
> - ☐ put the turkey in the oven
> - ☐ mop the floor
> - ☐ wash the dishes
> - ☐ cut up the vegetables
>
> **To Do: Gisela**
> - ☐ vacuum the carpet
> - ☑ buy flowers
> - ☐ wash the windows
> - ☐ set the table
> - ☐ hang the balloons
> - ☐ wrap the gift

B Now compare lists with your partner. Are they the same?

EXERCISE 8 WHAT ABOUT YOU?

A CONVERSATION Before you talk with a partner about your plans, write a list of things that you planned or wanted to do by this time (for example, organize a big party for my parents, find a new job, paint the apartment, buy a new computer). Include things that you *have already done* and things that you *haven't done yet*.

B Work with a partner. Exchange lists and ask and answer questions about the items on the lists.

EXAMPLE: A: Have you organized the party for your parents yet?
B: No, not yet. I'm still trying to find a place to have it. **or** Yes, I have. What about you? Have you . . . ?

FROM GRAMMAR TO WRITING

A BEFORE YOU WRITE Think about a goal you are working on at the moment. Write a list of things people do to reach this goal. Then check (✓) the things you have already done to reach *your* goal.

My Goal: _Save money_

- [✓] 1. _Open a savings account_
- [ ] 2. _choose a target amount_
- [✓] 3. _track your goals_
- [✓] 4. _make adjustments_
- [ ] 5. _Be patience_

B WRITE Use your list to write a paragraph. Describe your goal. Then write about the things you *have already done* and things you *haven't done yet* or that you *still haven't done* to reach your goal. Try to avoid the common mistakes in the chart.

EXAMPLE: I would like to find a new apartment. I've already done a few things to reach my goal. For example, I've already chosen a neighborhood where I would like to live. However, I haven't been to see any apartments yet. And I still haven't spoken to . . .

Common Mistakes in Using the Present Perfect with *Already*, *Yet*, and *Still*

Put *already* between *have* and the past participle. Do not put *already* after the past participle.	I've *already* **chosen** a neighborhood. NOT I've chosen already a neighborhood.
Put *yet* at the end of the clause. Do not put *yet* after the past participle.	I **haven't seen** apartments *yet*. NOT I haven't seen yet apartments.
Put *still* before *haven't*. Do not put *still* between *haven't* and the past participle or at the end of the clause.	I *still* **haven't found** an apartment. NOT I haven't still found an apartment. NOT I haven't found an apartment still.

C CHECK YOUR WORK Read your paragraph. Underline the present perfect verbs and circle *already*, *yet*, and *still*. Use the Editing Checklist to check your work.

Editing Checklist

Did you use . . . ?

- [ ] the present perfect with *already* for things that have happened before now
- [ ] the present perfect with *yet* or *still* for things that haven't happened before now
- [ ] the correct word order

D REVISE YOUR WORK Read your paragraph again. Can you improve your writing? Make changes if necessary. Give your paragraph a title.

UNIT 9 REVIEW

Test yourself on the grammar of the unit.

A Circle the correct words to complete the sentences.

1. I've started planning your graduation party last night / ~~already~~.

2. We *still* / yet haven't chosen a restaurant for the party. I'm getting nervous.

3. I met Nita yesterday, but I haven't met her boyfriend already / *yet*.

4. Did / *Has* Marla left already? The party just started!

5. Have you *told* / tell your friends about the party yet?

6. No, not already / *yet*.

B Complete the conversations with the present perfect form of the verbs in parentheses and *already*, *still*, or *yet*.

1. ANN: Ed ___has___ ___already graduated___. Amazing!
   a. (graduate / already)

   BEN: I know, but don't relax yet. We ___still___ ___haven't had___ ___ the party.
   b. (have / still)

2. ANN: ___Have___ they ___delivered___ the food ___yet___? Should I begin to worry?
   a. (deliver / yet)

   BEN: It just arrived. But Ed ___still___ ___hasn't set___ the tables.
   b. (set / still)

   ANN: Well, he ___'s___ ___already started___. I'll help him finish.
   c. (start / already)

3. BEN: Some of Ed's friends ___still___ ___haven't arrived___.
   a. (arrive / still)

   ANN: I know . . . I don't think his new girlfriend ___has___ ___arrived___ ___yet___.
   b. (arrive / yet)

   ED: Mom and Dad, ___have___ you ___met___ Christy ___yet___?
   c. (meet / yet)

C Find and correct six mistakes.

A: I can't believe it's the 10th already. And we still didn't finished planning.

B: We haven't checked the guest list for a while. Who hasn't replies yet?

A: Sally hasn't called about the invitation already. I wonder if she's coming.

B: Maybe she just forgot. Have you called yet her?

A: I've already call her a couple of times. She hasn't called back still.

Now check your answers on page 477.

Present Perfect: Indefinite Past
ADVENTURE TRAVEL

OUTCOMES
- Describe events that happened at an indefinite time in the past
- Describe repeated actions and states in the past
- Identify main points of an article and a conversation about travel
- Discuss famous quotes, giving explanations and reasons for opinions
- Write a paragraph in response to a quote from literature

STEP 1   GRAMMAR IN CONTEXT

BEFORE YOU READ

Look at the photos and at the title of the article. Discuss the questions.

1. What do you think the article is about?

2. Would you like to do the things in the photos? Why or why not?

READ

▶10|01   Read this article about unusual vacations.

Been There? Done That?
Maybe it's time for something new . . .

Today's world is getting smaller. People are traveling the globe[1] in record numbers.[2] Our readers have been to Rome. They've visited Greece. They've seen the ancient pyramids of Egypt. They've gone skiing in the Swiss Alps. Now, they're looking for new places to see and new things to do. They want adventure. *Travel Today* has just come out with its annual survey. As part of the survey, the magazine asks its readers the following question: "What would you like to do that you've never done before?"

Here are some of their answers:

1 *the globe:* the world
2 *in record numbers:* much more than in the past

> *I've made **several trips to Egypt**, but I've never ridden **a camel**. I've always wanted **to do that.***

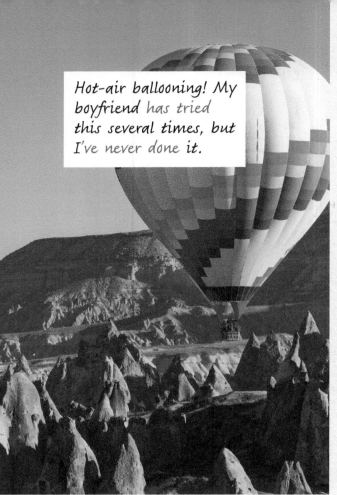

Hot-air ballooning! My boyfriend has tried this several times, but I've never done it.

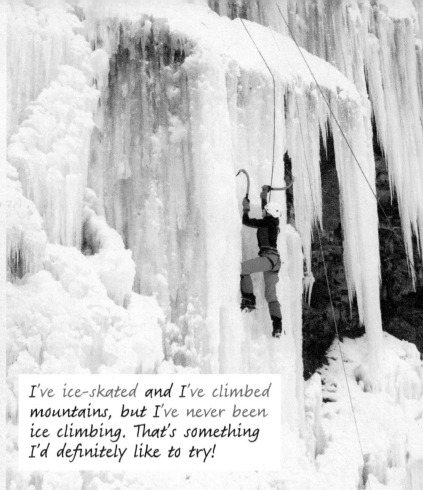

I've ice-skated and I've climbed mountains, but I've never been ice climbing. That's something I'd definitely like to try!

Riding a camel, hot-air ballooning, ice climbing . . . These are just a few activities that travelers can choose from today. All you need is time, money (a lot of it!), and a sense of adventure.[3] But you don't have to go to a faraway place in an unusual type of transportation to have a great vacation! Have you ever spent the day walking in the woods, heard the sound of the wind, or watched the sun set over the ocean? These can be wonderful adventures, too! And a lot more affordable!

---

3 *sense of adventure:* the ability to enjoy new things

AFTER YOU READ

A VOCABULARY Match the words with their definitions.

b **1. adventure**   a. very old
d **2. survey**   b. an exciting, unusual experience
f **3. affordable**   c. happening every year
e **4. transportation** d. a questionnaire
a **5. ancient**   e. a way of traveling someplace
c **6. annual**   f. not expensive

B COMPREHENSION Which activities have the readers of *Travel Today* tried? Check (✓) them.

- ✓ **1.** skiing in the Alps
- ☐ **2.** riding a camel
- ✓ **3.** hot-air ballooning
- ✓ **4.** ice-skating
- ✓ **5.** mountain climbing
- ☐ **6.** ice climbing

C DISCUSSION Work with a partner. Compare your answers in B. Why did you or didn't you check each activity?

STEP 2 GRAMMAR PRESENTATION

PRESENT PERFECT: INDEFINITE PAST

Statements

Subject	Have (not)	Past Participle	
They	**have (not)**	**visited**	Egypt.
She	**has (not)**	**been**	there.

Statements with Adverbs

Subject	Have (not)	Adverb	Past Participle		Adverb
They	**have**	*never* *just* *recently*	**visited**	Egypt.	
She	**has**		**been**	there.	

Subject	Have (not)		Past Participle		Adverb
They	**have (not)**		**visited**	Egypt	*twice.* *lately.* *recently.*
She	**has (not)**		**been**	there	

Yes/No Questions

Have	Subject	(Ever)	Past Participle	
Have	they	*(ever)*	**visited**	Egypt?
Has	she		**been**	there?

Short Answers

Affirmative		Negative	
Yes,	they **have**.	No,	they **haven't**.
	she **has**.		she **hasn't**.
			never.

Wh- Questions

Wh- Word	Have	Subject	Past Participle	
How often	**have**	they	**visited**	Egypt?
	has	she	**been**	there?

GRAMMAR NOTES

1 Present Perfect

Use the present perfect to show that something **happened at an indefinite** (not exact) **time in the past**.

Use the present perfect when you **don't know when** something happened or when the specific **time is not important**.	They**'ve traveled** to Egypt. *(You don't know the exact time.)* We**'ve been** to Rome. *(The exact time isn't important.)*

Past   ?   **Now**   Future

We've been to Rome.

Use the present perfect (not the simple past) to show a **connection to the present**: the result of the action or state is important in the present.	The hotel **has closed**. *(So we can't stay there now.)*
USAGE NOTE For many speakers *have been to* and *have gone to* have different meanings.	He**'s been to** France. *(At some point in the past, he visited France, but he's not necessarily there now.)* He**'s gone to** France. *(He's in France now.)*

2 Present Perfect + Adverbs of Time or Time Expressions

You can also use the present perfect with **adverbs of time** or **time expressions** to show that something happened at an **indefinite time in the past**.

For **repeated actions** at some indefinite time in the past, use adverbs of time or time expressions such as: • *twice* • *often* • *many times*	They**'ve seen** the Pyramids *twice*. We**'ve often stayed** at that hotel. We**'ve stayed** there *many times*.
For **repeated actions** or **states** that continue up to the present and may continue into the future, use: • *so far* ~~We don't have Homework so far~~	*So far*, I**'ve taken** more than 1000 photos. I'm sure I'll take many more before this trip is over! *So far*, the weather **has been** great.
USAGE NOTE We often use *so far* with numbers, adverbs like *twice*, and *only*.	*So far*, she's bought *four* souvenirs. *So far*, they've traveled to Egypt *twice*. *So far*, he's *only* been to Cairo.
For states or actions that **continue in the present**, use: • *always* • *never*	We**'ve always wanted** to go to Egypt. I**'ve never ridden** a camel.

CONTINUED ▶

To ask **questions** and give **negative answers**, use:	
• *ever* (= at any time before now)	A: **Have** you *ever* **been** to Rome?
• *never*	B: **No, I've** *never* **been** there. **or No,** *never*.

To stress that something happened in the very **recent past**, use:	
• *just* (= a very short time before now)	**I've** *just* **gotten** back from China.
• *lately/recently* (= in the near past)	They **haven't been** there *lately*.
	He**'s flown** a lot *recently*.

USAGE NOTE In American English, we often use *just* and *recently* with the **simple past**. You can't, however, use *lately* with the simple past.	**I've** *just* **returned** or I *just* **returned**.
	NOT I returned ~~lately~~.

BE CAREFUL! Do not use the present perfect with adverbs or expressions that refer to a **specific time in the past**. Use the simple past.	I **got** back *yesterday*.
	NOT ~~I've gotten~~ back *yesterday*.

3 Word Order

With the present perfect, most **adverbs of time** or **time expressions** can go at the **end of the clause** or **before the past participle**.

Some adverbs of time and time expressions go at the **end of the clause**:	
• *twice*	She**'s been** there *twice*.
• *many times*	**I've been** there *many times*.
• *lately*	I **haven't traveled** *lately* because it's too expensive.

Other adverbs go **before the past participle**:	
• *always*	**I've** *always* **wanted** to stay there.
• *often*	We**'ve** *often* **talked** about it.
• *ever*	**Have** you *ever* **seen** the pyramids?
• *never*	We**'ve** *never* **been** to Egypt.
• *just*	His plane **has** *just* **landed**.

Recently can go **at the end of the clause** or **before the past participle**.	They**'ve traveled** a lot *recently*.
	They**'ve** *recently* **traveled** a lot.

So far usually goes at the **beginning** or **end of the clause**.	*So far*, I've read 100 pages of my guide book.
	I've read 100 pages of my guide book *so far*.

REFERENCE NOTES

For a list of **irregular past participles**, see Appendix 1 on page 453.
For all **present perfect forms**, see Unit 8 on page 106.
For **present perfect with *already, yet,* and *still***, see Unit 9 on page 120.

EXERCISE 1   DISCOVER THE GRAMMAR

GRAMMAR NOTES 1–3   Read the first statement. Then decide if the second statement is *True (T)* or *False (F)*. If there isn't enough information in the first statement to know the answer, put a question mark *(?)* on the line.

1. Adventure vacations have become very popular.

    __T__ They are popular now.

2. I've been to Italy twice.

    __F__ I was there two years ago.

3. I have never been to the Himalayas.

    __F__ I went to the Himalayas a long time ago.

4. I've just returned from China.

    __T__ I was in China a short time ago.

5. Greg asks you, "Have you ever been to Costa Rica?"

    __F__ Greg wants to know when you were in Costa Rica.

6. Marta asks you, "Have you read any good travel books lately?"

    __F__ Marta wants to know about a travel book you read last year.

7. We have visited Egypt several times.

    __T__ This is not our first visit to Egypt.

8. He's recently been to Greece.

    __T__ He's been to Greece recently.

9. I've spent $100 so far.

    __T__ I've spent $100 up to now.

10. I've been on an African safari.[1]

    __F__ I'm on a safari now.

---

1 *safari:* a trip through the country areas of Africa in order to watch wild animals

EXERCISE 2 STATEMENTS AND QUESTIONS

A GRAMMAR NOTES 1–2 *Travel Today* (TT) interviewed travel writer Rosa García (RG). Complete this interview. Use the present perfect form of the verbs in parentheses. Use contractions when possible.

TT: As a travel writer, you ___'ve visited___ many places. Any favorites?
1. (visit)

RG: Thailand. It's a beautiful, amazing country. I ___have been___ there five times.
2. (be)

TT: What ___has been___ your most unusual travel experience?
3. (be)

RG: My *most* unusual? I ___had___ so many! I ___swam___ near sharks (in a cage,
4. (have)   **5.** (swim)
of course!), I ___'ve eaten___ dinner next to a very active volcano, I've ___slept___ in
6. (eat)   **7.** (sleep)
an ice hotel in Finland . . .

TT: The world ___has become___ a lot smaller. There are fewer and fewer "undiscovered" places.
8. (become)
___Have___ you ever ___found___ a really great place and decided not to tell
9. (find)
your readers about it?

RG: No, never. I ___'ve thought___ about doing that a few times, but so far, I ___'ve___
10. (think)
never actually ___done___ it. I ___have___ always ___written___
11. (do)   **12.** (write)
about it.

TT: Where ___have___ you ___been___ recently?
13. (be)

RG: I ___'ve___ just ___returned___ from a hot-air ballooning trip in Australia. It was
14. (return)
really fantastic. In fact, ballooning is my new favorite form of transportation!

TT: Where are you going next?

RG: On an African safari! I ___'ve___ never ___been___ on one, and I'm really
15. (be)
excited. I ___have alwa___ always ___wanted___ to do that.
16. (want)

TT: Good luck! And I look forward to your African safari article.

▶10|02 **B** LISTEN AND CHECK Listen to the interview and check your answers in A.

EXERCISE 3 AFFIRMATIVE AND NEGATIVE STATEMENTS

GRAMMAR NOTES 1–3 **Look at this survey. Then write sentences about things Andy *has done* and things he *hasn't done* (or *has never done*). Use contractions when possible.**

Travel Time Survey

Name: _Andy Cheng_

Have you ever done the following activities? Check (✔) the ones you have done.

1. rent a car ☐
2. rent a motorcycle ☑
3. ride a camel ☐
4. go up in a hot-air balloon ☑
5. have some really unusual food ☑
6. see ancient pyramids ☐
7. sail a boat on the Nile River ☑
8. swim with dolphins in the ocean ☑
9. be on a safari ☐
10. fly around the world ☐

1. _He hasn't rented a car._ **or** _He's never rented a car._
2. _He's rented a motorcycle._
3. _____
4. _____
5. _____
6. _____
7. _____
8. _____
9. _____
10. _____

EXERCISE 4 WORD ORDER

A GRAMMAR NOTE 3 **Complete this conversation. Put the words in parentheses in the correct order. Use the present perfect form of the verbs. Include short answers. Use contractions when possible.**

EVAN: Hot-air ballooning! What's it like? _I've never done this_____ before!
   1. (I / do this / never)

ANDY: You'll love it. _____ ,
   2. (I / a few times / go up)

   but _____ .
   3. (not do it / lately / I)

EVAN: _____ ?
   4. (you / a lot / travel)

ANDY: Yes, _____ . I'm a travel writer, so it's part of my job.
   5.

EVAN: That's great! _____ on a safari?
                                       6. (you / be / ever)

ANDY: No, _____, but _____.
          7.   **8.** (want / to go / always / I)

EVAN: Me too. _____.
                           9. (I / several times / to Africa / be)

    In fact, _____ back from a trip there.
                        10. (I / get / just)

    But _____ on a safari.
                     11. (so far / I / not be)

ANDY: Look. _____ getting the balloon ready. It's time to go up!
                12. (they / finish / just)

▶10|03 **B** LISTEN AND CHECK **Listen to the conversation and check your answers in A.**

EXERCISE 5 STATEMENTS

GRAMMAR NOTES 1–3 **Look at some of Rosa's things. Write sentences using the present perfect form of the verbs from the box. Use adverbs of time or time expressions when possible.**

~~be~~	ride	see	stay	travel	write

1. _She's been to Egypt twice._

2. _____

3. _____

4. _____

5. _____

6. _____

EXERCISE 6   EDITING

GRAMMAR NOTES 1–3   Read these comments found on a hot-air ballooning website. There are twelve mistakes in the use of the present perfect and adverbs. The first mistake is already corrected. Find and correct eleven more.

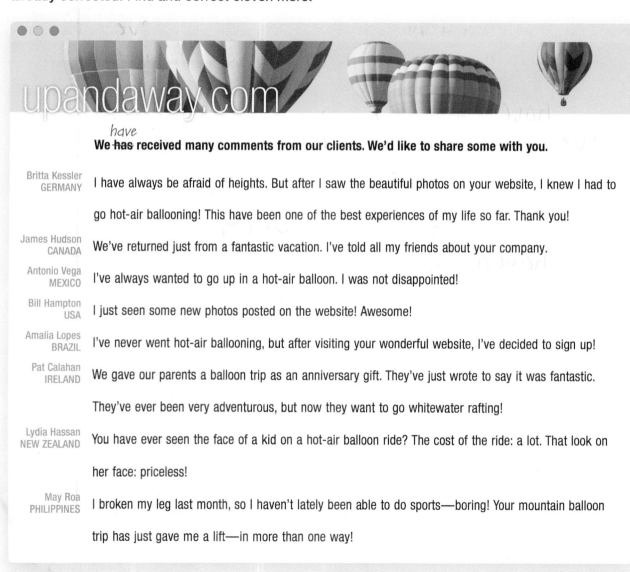

upandaway.com

　　　　　　　　　　have
We ~~has~~ received many comments from our clients. We'd like to share some with you.

Britta Kessler
GERMANY

I have always be afraid of heights. But after I saw the beautiful photos on your website, I knew I had to go hot-air ballooning! This have been one of the best experiences of my life so far. Thank you!

James Hudson
CANADA

We've returned just from a fantastic vacation. I've told all my friends about your company.

Antonio Vega
MEXICO

I've always wanted to go up in a hot-air balloon. I was not disappointed!

Bill Hampton
USA

I just seen some new photos posted on the website! Awesome!

Amalia Lopes
BRAZIL

I've never went hot-air ballooning, but after visiting your wonderful website, I've decided to sign up!

Pat Calahan
IRELAND

We gave our parents a balloon trip as an anniversary gift. They've just wrote to say it was fantastic. They've ever been very adventurous, but now they want to go whitewater rafting!

Lydia Hassan
NEW ZEALAND

You have ever seen the face of a kid on a hot-air balloon ride? The cost of the ride: a lot. That look on her face: priceless!

May Roa
PHILIPPINES

I broken my leg last month, so I haven't lately been able to do sports—boring! Your mountain balloon trip has just gave me a lift—in more than one way!

EXERCISE 7 LISTENING

▶10|04 **A** Read the statements. Then listen to the conversation and look at the brochures. Listen again and check (✓) *True* or *False*.

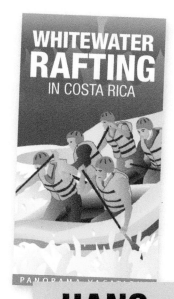

WHITEWATER **RAFTING** IN COSTA RICA

	True	False
1. The woman has gone to a travel agent.	✓	☐
2. She has just been on her annual vacation.	☐	☐
3. She has never done adventure traveling.	☐	☐
4. She wants to do something new.	☐	☐
5. She has been hang gliding a few times.	☐	☐
6. She has been skydiving several times.	☐	☐
7. She has never been shark diving.	☐	☐
8. She's never been snowmobiling in Canada.	☐	☐

SHARK **DIVING** IN SOUTH AFRICA

SNOWMOBILING IN CANADA

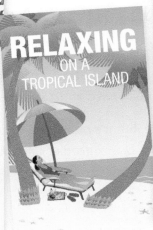

RELAXING ON A TROPICAL ISLAND

HANG GLIDING IN AUSTRALIA

PANORAMA VACATIONS

SKYDIVING IN CALIFORNIA

PANORAMA VACATIONS

▶10|04 **B** Listen to the conversation again. Then work with a partner. Look at the travel brochures. Together, decide on a good vacation choice for the woman. Give your reasons.

EXAMPLE: **A:** I think she would like whitewater rafting.
B: Oh, I don't know about that. She's done whitewater rafting. She says she wants to try something new. What about shark diving?
A: Shark diving? Well, she . . .

EXERCISE 8 QUOTABLE QUOTES

DISCUSSION Work with a partner. Read the quotes about travel. Choose three quotes and discuss them. What do they mean? Do you agree with them? Why or why not?

1. Once a year, go someplace you've never been before.

   —Dalai Lama *(1935–   , Tibetan Buddhist religious leader)*

   EXAMPLE: A: I think the quote means that it's important to go someplace new every year.
   B: I agree with you. I also agree with the idea of the quote.
   A: Me too. I think you learn a lot from traveling. I know I've always learned a lot from my trips.
   B: I'm going to Rome next summer. I've never been there, and I'm really looking forward to it.

2. Like all great travelers, I have seen more than I remember, and remember more than I have seen.

   —Benjamin Disraeli *(1804–1881, British politician and writer)*

3. Every dreamer knows that it is entirely possible to be homesick[1] for a place you've never been to, perhaps more homesick than for familiar ground.

   —Judith Thurman *(1946–   , U.S. writer)*

4. The traveler sees what he sees. The tourist sees what he has come to see.

   —G.K. Chesterton *(1874–1936, British writer and poet)*

5. Tourists don't know where they've been, travelers don't know where they're going.

   —Paul Theroux *(1941–   , U.S. travel writer and novelist)*

6. I haven't been everywhere, but it's on my list.

   —Susan Sontag *(1933–2004, U.S. writer and filmmaker)*

---

1 *homesick:* feeling sad because you are away from your home

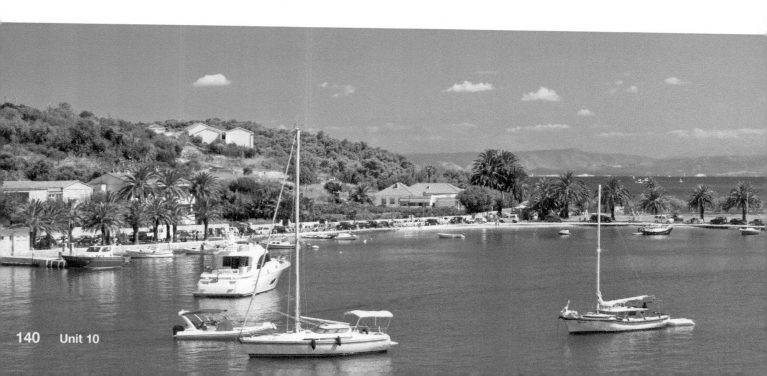

EXERCISE 9 FIND SOMEONE WHO...

A GAME Walk around your classroom. Try to find someone for each of the activities below. When you find someone, write the person's name next to the activity. You have 10 minutes. The student with the most names is the winner.

EXAMPLE: A: Ana, have you ever been on a boat?
          B: No, I haven't.
          A: Dimitris, have *you* ever been on a boat?
          C: Yes, I have. I used to go boating a lot when I lived in Greece.
          A: Olga, have you ever taken a long car trip?
          D: Yes, I have. Two years ago...

Activities	Names
be on a boat	
take a long car trip	
climb a mountain	
eat something unusual	
ride a horse	
go camping	
swim in a river	
see a beautiful sunset	
hear a mariachi band	
have dinner on the beach	

B Report back to the class.

EXAMPLE: I have six names on my list: Dimitris, Olga, Murat, Vania, Nai-Kwan, and Kunio.
        Dimitris has been on a boat. Olga has taken a long trip. Murat...

FROM GRAMMAR TO WRITING

A BEFORE YOU WRITE Read this quote by U.S. photographer Diane Arbus. Discuss it with a partner. Answer the questions.

My favorite thing is to go where I've never been.
—*Diane Arbus (1923–1971, U.S. photographer)*

1. What does Arbus mean?
2. Do you feel the same way?
3. What is your favorite thing about travel?
4. Where have you been so far?
5. Would you like to go there again?
6. Where have you never been that you would like to go?

B WRITE Use your answers to write a paragraph about the quote from Diane Arbus. Give reasons why you agree or disagree with Arbus. Use the present perfect and give examples. Try to avoid the common mistakes in the chart.

EXAMPLE: Diane Arbus said, "My favorite thing is to go where I've never been." This means that she . . . I don't feel the same way. I enjoy returning to places I have already been. For example, I've been to China several times, but I would like to go back there because . . .

Common Mistakes in Using the Present Perfect for the Indefinite Past

Use the present perfect with or without adverbs or time expressions to talk about the indefinite past. Do not use **adverbs or expressions** that refer to a **specific time in the past**.	**I've seen** a beautiful sunset. **I've seen** a beautiful sunset *many times*. NOT **I've seen** a beautiful sunset ~~yesterday~~.
Put adverbs of time such as *twice* and *lately* or time expressions such as *many times* at the **end of the clause**. Do not put them **before or after the past participle**.	I've been to Greece *twice*. NOT I've ~~been twice~~ to Greece. NOT I've ~~twice been~~ to Greece.

C CHECK YOUR WORK Read your paragraph. Underline all the verbs in the present perfect. Circle the adverbs of time and time expressions. Use the Editing Checklist to check your work.

Editing Checklist

Did you use . . . ?

☐ the present perfect without adverbs of time or time expressions

☐ the present perfect with adverbs of time or time expressions such as *twice, often, many times, always, never, just, lately, recently, so far*

☐ the correct word order

D REVISE YOUR WORK Read your paragraph again. Can you improve your writing? Make changes if necessary. Give your paragraph a title.

UNIT 10 REVIEW

Test yourself on the grammar of the unit.

A Circle the correct words to complete the sentences.

1. Have you twice / ever been to Egypt?

2. I've just / lately returned from Cairo.

3. I've was / been there twice, and I'm returning next summer.

4. Has / Have Jon ever ridden a camel?

5. I haven't read any good travel books lately / never.

6. One of my classmates is / has recommended a good book.

B Complete the sentences with the present perfect form of the correct verbs from the box. Use contractions when possible.

be	give	read	see	show	take	want

1. _____ you ever _____ the pyramids?

2. I _____ never _____ to Egypt.

3. Elena _____ just _____ an interesting book about ancient Egypt.

4. She _____ _____ it to me to read.

5. I _____ always _____ to ride a camel.

6. My brother _____ _____ several trips there.

7. He _____ recently _____ me his photos.

C Find and correct seven mistakes.

1. I've lately traveled a lot.

2. We've returned just from an African safari.

3. I've never have so much fun before.

4. Have you been ever on a safari?

5. No, but I've recently went hot-air ballooning.

6. My wife and I has decided to go next summer.

7. I've saw a lot of great photos on a hot-air ballooning website.

Now check your answers on page 477.

Present Perfect and Simple Past
FAILURE AND SUCCESS

OUTCOMES
- Recognize when to use the present perfect and the simple past
- Identify key details in a short, factual text
- Understand the time frame of important details in an interview
- Discuss past events and experiences
- Research a famous person and present findings to the class
- Write a paragraph about a personal experience

STEP 1   GRAMMAR IN CONTEXT

BEFORE YOU READ

Look at the photo of Thomas Edison. Discuss the questions.

1. What is Thomas Edison famous for?
2. Why do you think people call him a "first-time failure"?

READ

⊙11|01 Read this article about failure and success.

Famous First-Time Failures

Have you ever tried and failed, and then quit something really very important to you? Thomas Alva Edison failed thousands of times before he created the first successful electric light bulb. But the famous inventor had a great attitude. He never lost hope and never gave up. "I have not failed, not once. I've discovered ten thousand ways that don't work," he said after one of many tries.

Like Edison, author Melissa de la Cruz didn't have it easy at first. She wrote her first book at age 22 and sent it to many publishers.[1] They all rejected it. Nobody wanted her next few books either. Then, when she decided to take a writing course, every school rejected her. The young writer probably wanted to give up many times, but she didn't quit. Since her early failures, de la Cruz has written more than twenty-five

Thomas Alva Edison

---

1 *publishers:* people or companies that arrange the writing, printing, and sale of books

books—many of them best sellers. She has won several awards and has sold millions of copies of her books around the world.

Melissa de la Cruz

Have you ever quit too soon? Has your own failure really been a success that is waiting for a few more tries? Maybe you haven't failed enough times yet? Try again, and when you feel discouraged, remember Edison and de la Cruz and follow the advice in the famous saying: "If at first you don't succeed, try, try, try again."

AFTER YOU READ

A VOCABULARY **Choose the word or phrase that best completes each sentence.**

1. Edison **created** many things. This means that he _____ many new things.
   a. bought   **b.** made   **c.** wanted

2. The opposite of **failure** is _____.
   a. health   **b.** happiness   **c.** success

3. If you are **discouraged**, you don't feel _____.
   a. hopeful   **b.** nervous   **c.** tired

4. If people **reject** your ideas, they _____ them.
   a. say *yes* to   **b.** think about   **c.** say *no* to

5. Your **attitude** is how you _____ about something.
   a. act   **b.** feel or think   **c.** learn

6. You win an **award** for being _____ at something you do.
   a. pretty good   **b.** good   **c.** the best

B COMPREHENSION **Read the statements. Check (✓) *True* or *False*.**

	True	False
1. Thomas Edison was immediately successful.	☐	☐
2. Edison never quit.	☐	☐
3. Publishers immediately accepted Melissa de la Cruz's first book.	☐	☐
4. Publishers rejected de la Cruz's next books.	☐	☐
5. De la Cruz is still writing books.	☐	☐
6. De la Cruz is very successful.	☐	☐

C DISCUSSION **Work with a partner. Compare your answers in B. Why did you check *True* or *False*?**

PRESENT PERFECT AND SIMPLE PAST

Present Perfect
She **has been** here since 2014.
They**'ve lived** here for 20 years.
She**'s written** ten pages today.
He **hasn't flown** this month.
Has she **called** him today?

Simple Past
She **was** in the Philippines in 2013.
They **lived** there for 10 years.
She **wrote** twenty pages yesterday.
He **didn't fly** last month.
Did she **call** him yesterday?

GRAMMAR NOTES

1   Present Perfect or Simple Past + *For*

The present perfect with *for* has a **very different meaning** from the simple past with *for*.

Use the **present perfect** to show that something began in the past and **continues into the present** (and may continue into the future).

She **has lived** in the United States for more than thirty years.
> (She moved to the United States more than thirty years ago, and she is still living there.)

Use the **simple past** to show that something happened in the past and has **no connection to the present**.

She **lived** in the Philippines for fourteen years.
> (She lived there until 1985, but she no longer lives there.)

2   Indefinite Time or Specific Time in the Past

Use the **present perfect** to show that something happened at an **indefinite time** in the past. The exact time is not known or not important.

They **have decided** to write another book.
> (We don't know exactly when they made the decision, or the time of the decision is not important.)

Use the **simple past** to show that something happened at a **specific time** in the past. The exact time is known and often included.

She **wrote** her first book *in 2001*.
> (We know the exact time and it is important information.)

BE CAREFUL! Do not use the present perfect with a specific time in the past. The only exception is with *since*.

I **lived** in Manila *in 2007*.
NOT I've lived in Manila *in 2007*.
I**'ve lived** in Manila *since 2007*.

3 Unfinished Time or Finished Time

Use the **present perfect** to show that something happened in a time period that is **unfinished**, such as *today, this morning, this month, this year.*	Her publisher **has called** three times *today*. *(Today isn't finished, and it's possible that the publisher will call again.)*
Use the **simple past** to show that something happened in a time period that is **finished**, such as *yesterday, yesterday morning, last month, last year.*	Her publisher **called** three times *yesterday*. *(Yesterday is finished.)*
BE CAREFUL! Some time expressions such as *this morning, this month,* or *this year* can refer to an **unfinished** or a **finished** time period. Use the present perfect if the time period is unfinished. Use the simple past if the time period is finished.	It's 10:00 a.m. She**'s had** three cups of coffee *this morning*. *(The morning isn't finished.)* It's 1:00 p.m. She **had** three cups of coffee *this morning*. *(The morning is finished.)*

REFERENCE NOTES

For the **simple past**, see Unit 2 on page 20.
For the **present perfect** with *since* and *for*, see Unit 8 on page 106.
For the **present perfect** for **indefinite past**, see Unit 10 on page 131.
For a list of **irregular verbs**, see Appendix 1 on page 453.

STEP 3   FOCUSED PRACTICE

EXERCISE 1 DISCOVER THE GRAMMAR

GRAMMAR NOTES 1–3 Read the information about Melissa de la Cruz. Then choose the sentence (*a* or *b*) that best describes the situation.

1. Melissa de la Cruz was born in the Philippines in 1971. She lived there until she moved to the United States.
   a. She lived in the Philippines for fourteen years.
   b. She's lived in the Philippines for fourteen years.

2. She moved to the United States in 1985. She still lives there.
   a. She lived in the United States for more than thirty years.
   b. She's lived in the United States for more than thirty years.

3. She was a computer programmer for nine years.
   a. She has had a job as a computer programmer for nine years.
   b. She had a job as a computer programmer for nine years.

4. She has always loved to read.
   a. Her love of books started early.
   b. She didn't love books until she became an adult.

5. At first, many publishers rejected her books.
   a. She was not successful.
   b. She has not been successful.

6. In 2013, she returned to the Philippines for a book-signing tour.
   a. She has been there for a few weeks.
   b. She was there for a few weeks.

7. In 2002, she married architect Michael Johnston. The couple is still married.
   a. The couple has been married for many years.
   b. The couple was married for many years.

8. They write books together.
   a. They have written together for a while.
   b. They wrote together for a while.

9. Their books sell all over the world.
   a. Their books have been a great success.
   b. Their books were a great success.

10. It's April and they are on their third book-signing tour.
   a. They went on several trips this year.
   b. They've been on several trips this year.

EXERCISE 2 PRESENT PERFECT OR SIMPLE PAST

GRAMMAR NOTES 1–3 Complete this article about best-selling author Stephen King (1947–). Circle the correct verb forms.

Stephen King (has written) / wrote more than 60 novels and almost
                        1.
200 short stories. As a child in Portland, Maine, he has enjoyed / enjoyed
                                                                    2.
reading horror comics.[1] He has begun / began writing in school, where
                              3.
he has sold / sold his stories to his friends. But his early
    4.
success as a writer did not continue without problems.

In 1973, he has written / wrote his first novel, *Carrie*,
                         5.
about a teenage girl with frightening magical powers. It
has received / received thirty rejections. Discouraged, King
       6.
has thrown / threw the book away. Luckily for him and
      7.
his many future fans, his wife has removed / removed it
                                              8.
from the trash and encouraged him to submit it again.

This time the publishers have accepted / accepted it.
                                        9.

---
1 *horror comics:* magazines (often for children) that use pictures
  to tell very frightening stories

Stephen King

Since 1974, King has sold / sold more than 350 million books around the world.
   10.
In addition to his books, he has written / wrote scripts for movies and television.
   11.
He has received / received many awards including the World Fantasy Award for Life
   12.
Achievement, which he has won / won in 2004. In spite of his huge success, King lives a
   13.
simple life. He has continued / continued to live in Maine and he has remained / remained
   14.   15.
married to the same woman who has rescued / rescued *Carrie* from the trash can many
   16.
years ago. In a 2014 interview with *Rolling Stone Magazine*, the interviewer has asked / asked
   17.
King about his fear of failure. "I'm afraid of failing at whatever story I'm writing," King

has admitted / admitted. His fear, however, never stops him. King continues to be one of the
   18.
best-selling authors in the world.

EXERCISE 3 PRESENT PERFECT OR SIMPLE PAST STATEMENTS

GRAMMAR NOTES 1–3 Complete this entry in a writer's online journal. Use the present
perfect or simple past form of the verbs in parentheses.

Thursday, 4:00 p.m.

It _____has been_____ a very difficult day, and it's not over yet! I _____
        1. (be)   **2.** (begin)

working at 8:00 a.m. this morning. I _____ to finish the next chapter of my
                                          3. (want)

book, but I _____ only two pages all day! It's so frustrating. It's already
              4. (write)

Thursday, and I _____ a good idea all week. (Last week, I _____
                    5. (not have)   **6.** (write)

two whole chapters!) Yesterday, I _____ so discouraged that I almost
                                        7. (feel)

_____ . But then I _____ Thomas Edison and the trouble he
   8. (quit)   **9.** (remember)

_____ when he was trying to create the light bulb. He _____
   10. (experience)   **11.** (have)

such a great attitude about failure and success. It really _____ me to go on. I
                                                                12. (help)

guess I can look at today in a positive way and say "This morning, I _____
                                                                        13. (discover)

another way not to finish this chapter!"

EXERCISE 4 PRESENT PERFECT OR SIMPLE PAST QUESTIONS

A GRAMMAR NOTES 1–3 *Success Magazine* (SM) is interviewing a famous author, Emil Karlsson (EK). Complete the interview questions. Use the words in parentheses. Choose between the present perfect and simple past.

SM: *How long have you been an author?*
1. (how long / you / be an author)

EK: Oh, for about fifteen years.

SM: And _____
2. (when / you / write your first book)

EK: I wrote my first book when I was twenty-one.

SM: _____
3. (be / it / immediately successful)

EK: Yes. I was very lucky. And very surprised!

SM: _____
4. (how many copies / it / sell during its first year)

EK: More than a million.

SM: More than a million copies? That's a lot of copies! Now, tell me about your most recent book.

_____
5. (when / it / come out)

EK: It came out about a year ago.

SM: And _____ since then?
6. (it / win / any awards)

EK: Yes. It won *Mystery Mag's* Best Book of the Year Award.

SM: Congratulations! _____?
7. (how many copies / it / sell)

EK: I'm not sure. You'll have to ask my publisher!

▶11|02 **B** LISTEN AND CHECK Listen to the interview and check your answers in A.

EXERCISE 5 EDITING

GRAMMAR NOTES 1–3 Read these online comments about a book called *Failure and Success*. There are twelve mistakes in the use of the present perfect and simple past. The first mistake is already corrected. Find and correct eleven more.

Comments from Readers

November 4

I've just finished reading *Failure and Success* by Nila Sciretta. Actually, ~~I read~~ *I've read* several of her

books this year. The book is great! It's no surprise that it sold so many copies. —**Marta Lopez**

I was a big fan of this author for many years, so I was very happy to find her latest book

online. I've downloaded it last week and I finished it in two days. It's a great book—perhaps

the best book I read so far this year. I highly recommend it. —**Burak Mardin**

Have these other people read the same book as me? I haven't liked it at all. I thought it was

boring. I've finished it last night, but I'm sorry I bought it. Save your money! —**Felipe Casa**

For the last few months, I tried suggestions from *Failure and Success*. This book has changed

my attitude about failure. Everyone has failed at some time, but the author has not failed in

communicating her message: Failure can be a great teacher! —**Soon-Bok Park**

I only read two chapters so far, but I think it's a very interesting and helpful book. I've already

learned a lot from it. I especially like all the examples about famous people, like Edison, who

have failed at first before they became successful. —**Jason Morgen**

My husband and I are both college professors. Before we finally have found teaching jobs at

the same school, we had to live in different cities. It was a very difficult time for us. A friend

recommended one of Sciretta's earlier books and it really helped. We're also authors, but we

didn't find a publisher yet. But thanks to Sciretta's advice, we won't give up! —**Ann Braid**

EXERCISE 6 LISTENING

▶11|03 **A** A student is interviewing two college professors for the school newspaper. Read the list. Then listen to the interview. Listen again and check (✓) the items that are true now.

The professors _____.

- ☐ **1.** are married
- ☐ **2.** live in different cities
- ☐ **3.** live in Boston
- ☐ **4.** live in Los Angeles
- ☐ **5.** teach at the same university
- ☐ **6.** have a house
- ☐ **7.** teach creative writing 101
- ☐ **8.** write books together
- ☐ **9.** have best-selling books
- ☐ **10.** love teaching
- ☐ **11.** are happy in Los Angeles
- ☐ **12.** get positive reviews from their students

▶11|03 **B** Work with a partner. Listen again. In your opinion, what successes have the couple had? What failures have they had? Give reasons for your answers. Remember to use the present perfect and simple past.

EXAMPLE: A: Well, they seem to have a successful marriage.
B: Yes, they've been married for ten years.
A: And times haven't always been easy for them, but they've stayed together.

EXERCISE 7 A FAMOUS WRITER

ROLE PLAY Work with a partner. Take turns being a magazine interviewer (A) and a famous writer (B). The interviewer asks questions using the words in the box with the present perfect or simple past. The writer answers the interviewer's questions, using his or her imagination.

EXAMPLE: A: How long have you been a writer?
B: I've been a writer since I was twenty-one.

how long / be a writer?

when / write your first book?

you / successful right away?

how many books / write?

why / become a writer?

when / your new book / come out?

how many copies / it / sell?

how many copies / your first book / sell?

your books / win / awards?

how many awards / your books / win?

Other: _____?

EXERCISE 8 LAST YEAR AND THIS YEAR

COMPARISON Work with a partner. Sumni Wook is a successful musician. Look at her records from last year and this year. It is now the end of August. Compare what she did last year and what she has done this year. You can use the verbs from the box.

EXAMPLE: A: Last year, she performed in New York twice.
B: So far this year, she's only performed there once.

attend	give	go	have	perform	practice	study	win

LAST YEAR

January	February	March	April	May	June
• concert in N.Y. • L.A. – violin workshop	• L.A. – violin workshop • 1 seminar	• concert in N.Y.	• attend lecture	• 10 vacation days	• 2 concerts – Ottawa • 1 concert – Toronto

July	August	September	October	November	December
• receive Young Musician award	• music conference – Seoul	• Mom's visit • attend lecture	• concert in Toronto	• _Modern Day_ interview	• 10 vacation days

THIS YEAR

January	February	March	April	May	June
• concert in San Francisco	• concert in N.Y. • attend lecture	• Nan's wedding	• concert in Toronto	• concert in Paris	• 5 vacation days • 1 seminar

July	August	September	October	November	December
• visit Tania	• music conference • attend lecture				

EXERCISE 9 TRY, TRY, TRY

DISCUSSION Work with a partner. Think about the famous saying "If at first you don't succeed, try, try, try again." Do you agree with the saying? Give an example about a time when this worked, or didn't work, for you or someone you know who is still alive. Think about the questions below.

EXAMPLE: A: I think the saying is true. I remember when I wanted to learn to drive. I failed my road test three times! But I didn't give up. I took some more driving lessons and I finally passed. I've had my license now for three years and I've never even gotten a parking ticket!
B: That's great. I think it's good to try and not give up, but . . .

1. What did the person want to achieve?

2. What did the person do to try to reach his or her goal?

3. Did he or she succeed?

4. How has it changed the person's life?

5. How does the person feel now?

EXERCISE 10 FAMOUS FIRST-TIME FAILURES

A GROUP PROJECT Work in a group. Look at the photos of six famous first-time "failures." Choose one of them and research that person online. Discuss the person with your group.

EXAMPLE: A: So, what did we find out about James Dyson?

B: He's a British inventor.

C: What's he famous for?

B: He invented a vacuum cleaner that works without a bag.

C: Oh! That's right! I've seen TV ads for it!

B: And he wasn't successful right away. He . . .

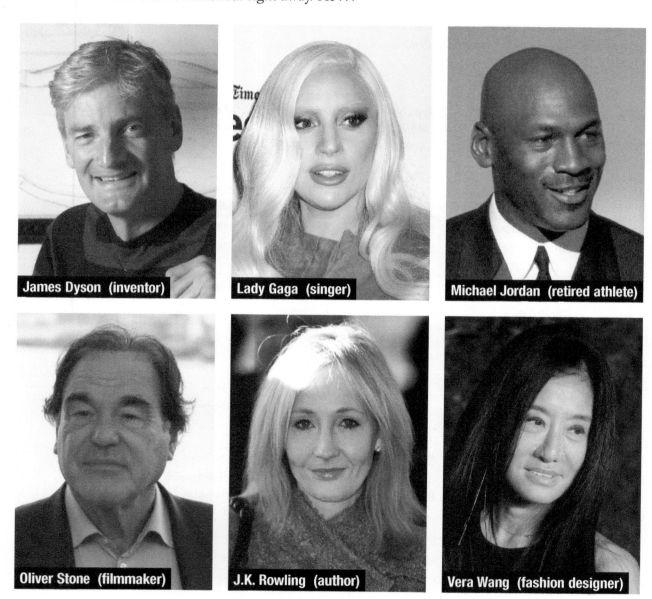

James Dyson (inventor)

Lady Gaga (singer)

Michael Jordan (retired athlete)

Oliver Stone (filmmaker)

J.K. Rowling (author)

Vera Wang (fashion designer)

B Report back to the class.

EXAMPLE: James Dyson is a British inventor. He created the first vacuum cleaner that worked without a bag. Before he succeeded, he failed more than 5,000 times and he went through all his savings. Today, his vacuum cleaner has become very popular and he has made billions of dollars with his invention.

A BEFORE YOU WRITE Choose one of the titles below for a paragraph about failure and success. You can also choose your own title. Give an example to support your title.

Failure Is a Good Teacher   Everyone Fails Some of the Time

From Failure to Success   There Is Nothing Good About Failure

You Can't Always Succeed   *Other:* _____

An example for _____
(the title you chose)

_____

_____

B WRITE Use your example to write a paragraph about failure and success. Remember to use the present perfect and simple past. Write your title above the paragraph. Try to avoid the common mistakes in the chart.

EXAMPLE:

Failure Is a Good Teacher

I believe that failure is a good teacher. For example, when I was younger, I tried to . . . Even though I failed several times, I still learned a lot. I . . . As a result of my experience, I have become . . .

Common Mistakes in Using the Present Perfect and Simple Past

Use the **past participle** form of the verb **after** *have*. Do not use the simple past form.	She **has written** many books. NOT She has ~~wrote~~ many books.
Use the **simple past** with a **specific time in the past**. Do not use the present perfect.	She **won** an award *last year*. NOT She ~~has won~~ an award *last year*.

C CHECK YOUR WORK Read your paragraph. Underline the verbs in the present perfect and circle the verbs in the simple past. Use the Editing Checklist to check your work.

Editing Checklist

Did you use . . . ?

☐ the present perfect for things that began in the past and continue into the present

☐ the simple past for things that happened in the past and have no connection to the present

☐ the present perfect for things that happened at an indefinite time in the past

☐ the simple past for things that happened at a specific time in the past

☐ the present perfect for things that have happened in a time period that is not finished

☐ the simple past for things that happened in a time period that is finished

D REVISE YOUR WORK Read your paragraph again. Can you improve your writing? Make changes if necessary.

UNIT 11 REVIEW

Test yourself on the grammar of the unit.

A Imagine you are interviewing Ken Sousa, an engineer. Write questions with the words in parentheses. Use the present perfect or the simple past.

Ken moves to Vancouver		gets engineering degree	starts first professional job	marries Tina	loses job	moves to Singapore to work	Tina joins him in Singapore
2010	2011	2012	2013	2014	2015	2016	July, this year

1. _____
   (when / move to Vancouver)
2. _____
   (how long / be an engineer)
3. _____
   (work / in Vancouver for a long time)
4. _____
   (when / get married)
5. _____
   (how many years / live in Singapore)
6. _____
   (your wife / live in Singapore long)

B Complete the paragraph from Tina's journal. Use the present perfect or the simple past form of the verbs in parentheses.

I _____ in Singapore for a month. It's great to be with Ken, but there's so
    1. (be)

much to do! We _____ five apartments last week, and so far this evening we
    2. (see)

_____ three places off our list. I still _____ very much of
3. (cross)   **4.** (not see)

the city, but this morning we _____ a boat tour. It _____
      5. (take)   **6.** (be)

great! Ken _____ some Chinese already, so he _____
    7. (learn)   **8.** (order)

lunch for us. I _____ much Chinese in Vancouver, but I'll learn fast here.
    9. (not learn)

C Find and correct five mistakes.

Tina and Ken lived apart for a while, but then Tina found a job in Singapore. She has moved

there last month. Here are some of their thoughts:

KEN: I'm so glad Tina is finally here. Last year has been the hardest time of my life.

TINA: Before I got here, I didn't understood Ken's experiences. But I was in culture shock since

    I arrive. Now I know what a difficult time Ken had at first. But he never gave up.

Now check your answers on page 477.

Present Perfect Progressive and Present Perfect

CLIMATE CHANGE

OUTCOMES
- Describe actions that started in the past and are still in progress
- Describe actions that started at an indefinite time in the past and are finished
- Identify main points of a short text on a scientific topic
- Understand the time frame of main events in conversations
- Discuss climate change
- Write an email or letter about recent activities

STEP 1 GRAMMAR IN CONTEXT

BEFORE YOU READ

Look at the photo and at the title of the article. Discuss the questions.

1. What is happening to the Earth?
2. Why does the Earth have a thermometer in it?
3. What is a hot topic?

READ

12|01   Read this article about climate change.

Global Warming:[1] A Hot Topic

The Earth's climate has changed many times. Warm oceans covered the Earth for millions of years. Then those oceans turned to ice for millions more. If the climate has been changing for five billion years, why is global warming such a hot topic today?

Almost everyone agrees that the Earth has been getting hotter. But not everyone agrees about the cause. Most climate experts think that human activities have added to global warming. The coal and oil we burn for energy have been sending more and more gases into the air around the Earth. The gases keep the

---

1 *global warming:* the continuing increase in the Earth's temperatures (including air and oceans) since the 1950s

heat in the atmosphere[2] and also cause air pollution.[3] These experts believe humans can slow global warming.

Others say global warming is mostly the result of natural causes, such as changes in the sun. They don't believe that human activities can make things better or worse.

Human or natural, the effects of global warming have been powerful. Here are just two examples:

- In the Arctic,[4] ice has been melting quickly. As a result, polar bears and other animals have become endangered species.[5] Arctic towns and villages are also in danger as sea levels rise.

- In parts of Africa, rainfall has decreased. Water and food have become very hard to find. Both people and animals have been suffering badly.

Recently, people have been taking steps to slow these dangerous trends. They have been developing ways to use clean solar energy. In addition, they have been designing homes and cars that use less energy.

Does it really matter what causes global warming? Environmentalists[6] believe that it does, and they say that if we have been part of the cause, then we can also be part of the solution.

---

2 *atmosphere:* the air that surrounds the Earth
3 *air pollution:* something dirty and unhealthy in the air
4 *the Arctic:* the most northern part of the Earth
5 *endangered species:* a type of animal or plant that may not continue to exist
6 *environmentalists:* people who want to protect the environment (land, water, and air)

AFTER YOU READ

A VOCABULARY **Match the words with their definitions.**

_____ 1. expert	**a.**	the power that makes machines work
_____ 2. climate	**b.**	to create a drawing that shows how to build something
_____ 3. develop	**c.**	someone with special knowledge of a subject
_____ 4. energy	**d.**	the typical weather in an area
_____ 5. design	**e.**	the way a situation is generally changing
_____ 6. trend	**f.**	to work on a new idea or product to make it successful

B COMPREHENSION **Read the statements. Check (✓) *True* or *False*.**

	True	False
1. Climate change is something new.	☐	☐
2. Almost everyone believes that the Earth used to be cooler.	☐	☐
3. Coal and oil are still sending gases into the air around the Earth.	☐	☐
4. Ice in the Arctic has stopped melting.	☐	☐
5. In parts of Africa, people and animals are still suffering.	☐	☐
6. People are no longer developing ways to use solar energy.	☐	☐

C DISCUSSION **Work with a partner. Compare your answers in B. Why did you check *True* or *False*?**

PRESENT PERFECT PROGRESSIVE AND PRESENT PERFECT

Present Perfect Progressive

Statements

Subject	Have (not)	Been	Base Form of Verb + -ing	(Since/For)
I You* We They	**have (not)**	**been**	**working**	(**since** 2009). (**for** years).
He She It	**has (not)**			

* *You* is both singular and plural.

Yes/No Questions

Have	Subject	Been	Base Form of Verb + -ing	(Since/For)
Have	you	**been**	**working**	(**since** 2009)?
Has	she			(**for** years)?

Short Answers

Affirmative			Negative		
Yes,	I/we	**have.**	**No,**	I/we	**haven't.**
	she	**has.**		she	**hasn't.**

Wh- Questions

Wh- Word	Have	Subject	Been	Base Form of Verb + -ing
How long	**have**	you	**been**	**working?**
	has	she		

Present Perfect Progressive and Present Perfect

Present Perfect Progressive
They **have been living** here for many years.
I**'ve been reading** this book since Monday.
Dr. Owen **has been writing** articles since 2000.
She**'s been working** in Kenya for a year.

Present Perfect
They **have lived** here for many years.
I**'ve read** two books about solar energy.
Dr. Owen **has written** many articles.
She**'s worked** in many countries.

GRAMMAR NOTES

1 Present Perfect Progressive or Present Perfect

The present perfect progressive and the present perfect usually have **different meanings**.

Use the **present perfect progressive** to show that something is **unfinished**. It started in the past and is still continuing. The focus is on the **continuation** of the action.	**I've been reading** a book about solar energy. *(I'm still reading it.)* **She's been writing** an article. *(She's still writing it.)*

Past —————————————— **Now** —————— **Future**

have been reading

Use the **present perfect** to show that something is **finished**. It happened at an indefinite time in the past. The focus is on the **result** of the action.	**I've read** a book about solar energy. *(I finished the book.)* **She's written** an article. *(She finished the article.)*

Past ——————×—————— **Now** —————— **Future**

have read

USAGE NOTE We also use the **present perfect progressive** for finished actions that **ended in the very recent past**. You can often still see the results of the action.	Look! The streets are wet. **It's been raining.** *(It stopped raining very recently.)* NOT It's rained.
BE CAREFUL! We usually do not use **non-action verbs**, such as *be*, *have*, and *know* in the progressive.	She's had the same job since 2000. NOT She's been having the same job since 2000.

2 With Time Expressions, Quantifiers, and Numbers

Use the **present perfect progressive** with *for +* **time expression** to show *how long* something has been happening.	**I've been reading** books about wind energy *for two months*.
Use the **present perfect** with a **quantifier or number** to show: • *how much* someone has done • *how many things* someone has done • *how many times* someone has done something	**I've read** *a lot* about it. She**'s written** *three* articles. **I've read** that book *twice*.
BE CAREFUL! Do not use the present perfect with a **specific time in the past**. The only exception is with *since*.	She**'s read** three articles. NOT She's read three articles *last week*. She**'s read** three articles *since last week*.

With verbs that show **duration** such as *live*, *study*, *teach*, and *work*, you can use the **present perfect progressive** or the **present perfect** with *for* or *since*. The meaning is the same: something is **unfinished**.

• **present perfect progressive**	He**'s been studying** global warming *for* ten years.
	or
• **present perfect**	He**'s studied** global warming *for* ten years.
	(In both examples, he is still studying it.)

USAGE NOTE We often use the **present perfect progressive** to show that something is **temporary**.	They**'ve been living** here *since* 1995, but they are moving next month.
USAGE NOTE We often use the **present perfect** to show that something is **permanent**.	They**'ve lived** here *since* they were children, and they're not planning on moving.

REFERENCE NOTES

For a list of **non-action verbs**, see Appendix 2 on page 454.

For the **present perfect with** *since* **and** *for*, see Unit 8 on page 106.

For the **present perfect for the indefinite past**, see Unit 10 on page 131.

For the **present perfect and simple past**, see Unit 11 on page 146.

EXERCISE 1 DISCOVER THE GRAMMAR

GRAMMAR NOTES 1–3 Read each statement. Decide if something is finished or unfinished. Check (✓) *Finished* or *Unfinished*.

	Finished	Unfinished
1. I've been reading a book about global warming.	☐	☑
2. I've read a book about global warming.	☐	☐
3. She's written two magazine articles about air pollution.	☐	☐
4. She's been waiting for some supplies.	☐	☐
5. They've lived in Ontario since 2002.	☐	☐
6. They've been living in Ontario since 2002.	☐	☐
7. We've been developing plans with the leaders of many countries.	☐	☐
8. We've developed these plans with many leaders.	☐	☐
9. Look out the window—it's been raining.	☐	☐
10. Look. Someone has watered the plants.	☐	☐

EXERCISE 2 PRESENT PERFECT PROGRESSIVE OR PRESENT PERFECT

GRAMMAR NOTES 1–3 Complete the statements about an expert on climate change, Professor Jane Owen, and her work. Circle the correct words. Sometimes both answers are correct.

1. *Green Earth* magazine has been publishing / (has published) Professor Owen's third annual report on environmental trends. It's an excellent report.

2. Professor Owen is working on two articles for the next issue of *Green Earth* magazine. She has been writing / has written these articles since Monday.

3. She has been writing / has written about global warming many times.

4. Professor Owen has been speaking / has spoken at our school several times about climate change.

5. She has been speaking / has spoken since 8:00 p.m., and she still has a lot more to tell us.

6. Professor Owen has a lot of work to do. Lately, she has been studying / has studied the use of solar energy for homes. She's learning about pollution from buildings.

7. She was late for a meeting with the members of her group. When she arrived they said, "At last, you're here. We've been waiting / We've waited for you."

8. Professor Owen has been living / has lived in Kenya for the last two years, but she will return to the United States in January.

9. She has been working / has worked with environmentalists in Kenya and Tanzania.

10. Kenyans have been planting / have planted 30 million trees since the 1970s.

EXERCISE 3 PRESENT PERFECT PROGRESSIVE

GRAMMAR NOTES 1–2 Look at the two pictures of Professor Owen. Complete the sentences describing what has been happening. Use the present perfect progressive form of the verbs in parentheses. Choose between affirmative and negative.

1. She _____'s been working_____ in her office.
   (work)

2. She _____ a book.
   (write)

3. She _____ TV.
   (watch)

4. She _____ her computer.
   (use)

5. She _____ coffee.
   (drink)

6. She _____ tea.
   (drink)

7. She _____ her sandwich.
   (eat)

8. She _____ her new black sweater.
   (wear)

9. She _____ hard.
   (work)

10. It _____ all day.
    (rain)

EXERCISE 4 STATEMENTS

GRAMMAR NOTES 1–3 Complete Professor Owen's blog about the European Solar Decathlon, a competition for the best solar houses (homes that get all their energy from the sun). Use the present perfect progressive or the present perfect form of the verbs in parentheses. Sometimes both forms are possible.

One of the solar houses in this year's competition

Green Mail

JUNE 28, 2014 VERSAILLES, FRANCE — A beautiful solar village _____has appeared_____ on
                                                                          1. (appear)

the grounds of the Versailles Palace. Twenty teams from universities in Europe, Asia, and North and

South America _____ these houses here for an international competition of
                    2. (bring)

solar houses. Universities _____ in this competition since 2007. For all the
                          3. (participate)

contests, talented students _____ the energy-efficient houses, and they
                            4. (design)

_____ them as well. Over the years, the homes _____
5. (build)   **6.** (get)

more energy efficient *and* more beautiful. This year, twenty houses _____ the
                                                                      7. (enter)

competition. I _____ the houses since I got here. I still have several more to
               8. (visit)

see, and I am looking forward to it. I _____ also _____ to many of the
                                                          9. (talk)

student designers. So far, what I hear most often is, "I could *totally* live in this house!" I agree.

Check back in about two weeks for the winners.

JULY 14 — Well, the contest is finally over and Team RhOME (RhOME = Rome home) from Italy

_____ this year's first prize. The teams from France and the Netherlands also
10. (win)

_____ prizes for their creative work. Tomorrow, it's back to Kenya for me. This
11. (receive)

_____ a really great event.
12. (be)

EXERCISE 5
QUESTIONS AND ANSWERS

GRAMMAR NOTE 2 Professor Owen is interviewing one of the student designers at Solar Decathlon Europe. Use the words in parentheses to write Professor Owen's questions. Use her notes to complete the student's answers. Choose between the present perfect progressive and the present perfect. Use contractions when possible.

> started project two years ago
> cost – $250,000
> house tours – all afternoon
> visitors this week – so far about 30,000
> interest in solar energy – started three
>   years ago
> total energy production today – more than
>   the house needs!
> the team's first competition – 2010
> one prize for lighting design

1. (how long / your team / work / on this project)

OWEN: _How long has your team been working on this project?_

STUDENT: _We've been working on this project for two years._

2. (how much money / the team / spend / on the house)

OWEN: _____

STUDENT: _____

3. (how long / you / lead tours / today)

OWEN: _____

STUDENT: _____

4. (how many people / visit / this week)

OWEN: _____

STUDENT: _____

5. (how long / you / be / interested in solar energy)

OWEN: _____

STUDENT: _____

6. (how much energy / the house / produce today)

OWEN: _____

STUDENT: _____

7. (how long / your team / compete)

OWEN: _____

STUDENT: _____

8. (how many prizes / your team / win)

OWEN: _____

STUDENT: _____

EXERCISE 6 EDITING

GRAMMAR NOTES 1–3 Read this student's email. There are eight mistakes in the use of the present perfect progressive and the present perfect. The first mistake is already corrected. Find and correct seven more.

Hi guys,

Sorry I haven't ~~wrote~~ *written* sooner. I haven't been having any free time since we arrived in Versailles for the solar house competition. (Our house got here before us!) I'm really excited and also really tired. Since we arrived, we've been lived on pizza and coffee. I haven't sleeping more than a few hours since . . . well, I can't remember when. Our team has been working day and night for the last two weeks, and today the house looks wonderful. I'm so proud—we've designed a home that's beautiful AND reduces pollution. We're finally ready for the judges, so I've spent most of the day looking at other teams' houses. I've been visiting ten houses today. They are so interesting and creative! I hope they help start a new trend in housing that is good for the environment. For the last hour, I've just been hanging out in a café with some people from the other teams. I've already been drinking three cups of coffee—it's delicious, but really strong! We been practicing our French. I still don't understand too much, but our teammate Jacques Renard is from Quebec, Canada, and he's been helped me out a lot. Wish us luck and check your text messages for photos of the house.

Katie

EXERCISE 7 LISTENING

▶12|02 **A** You're going to listen to six short conversations. Before you listen, look at the photos. Then listen. Do the photos match the conversations? Check (✓) *Matches* or *Doesn't Match*.

1. ☐ Matches ☑ Doesn't Match

2. ☐ Matches ☐ Doesn't Match

3. ☐ Matches ☐ Doesn't Match

4. ☐ Matches ☐ Doesn't Match

5. ☐ Matches ☐ Doesn't Match

6. ☐ Matches ☐ Doesn't Match

B Listen to each conversation again. Work with a partner. Compare your answers in A. Give reasons for your choices.

EXAMPLE: **A:** For Conversation 1, the answer is *Doesn't Match*.

B: Right. The photo doesn't match the conversation. The man said "They've planted some trees." But in the photo, they haven't planted any trees yet.

A: OK. What about the photo in Conversation 2?

EXERCISE 8 CLIMATE CHANGE

Ⓐ GROUP PROJECT Work in a group. Do an online search for "climate change." How have things been changing? What have some of the effects been? Consider some of the topics below.

EXAMPLE: **A:** The average air temperature around the world has increased by more than 1.53 degrees Fahrenheit (0.85 degrees Celsius) in the last 100 years.

B: There have been more . . .

- air temperature
- ocean temperature
- water level (how high the ocean is)
- amount and frequency of rain
- rain storms
- ice caps (large areas of thick ice that cover the North and South Poles)

Ⓑ Compare your results with those of your classmates. Did you find the same information online?

EXAMPLE: **A:** I read that the temperature *hasn't* been changing.

B: One report says that it hasn't changed since 1958.

C: But there has definitely been evidence of . . .

EXERCISE 9 A PICTURE IS WORTH A THOUSAND WORDS

Ⓐ PICTURE DISCUSSION Work with a partner.
Look at the photo and discuss the questions.

EXAMPLE: A: The photo shows a polar bear.
It's . . .
B: I think it means . . .

1. What does the photo show?

2. What does it mean?

3. Is it a strong message? Why or why not?

4. Do you agree with the message?

Ⓑ Compare your ideas with those of another pair of students.

EXAMPLE: A: We think it means . . .
B: We think it's a strong message because . . .

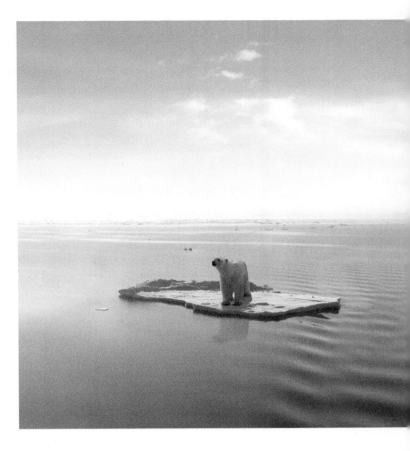

EXERCISE 10 WHAT ABOUT YOU?

DISCUSSION Work in a group. What changes have you made or experienced recently?
Discuss some of the questions below. Use the **present perfect progressive and the present perfect** to talk about them.

EXAMPLE: A: Recently, I've gotten more interested in the environment. I've been recycling paper and other things. I've also been walking or riding my bike more.
B: I've just started a job, so I've been wearing business clothes instead of jeans.
C: You look good, Ben! For myself, I've been . . .

Have you changed . . . ?

- your opinions about society or the environment
- the way you look or dress
- the people you hang out with
- your hobbies or interests
- your goals
- *Other:* _____

FROM GRAMMAR TO WRITING

A BEFORE YOU WRITE Think about your recent activities—things you have been doing and things you have done lately. Complete the lists.

Unfinished Activities	Finished Activities
_____	_____
_____	_____
_____	_____
_____	_____

B WRITE Use the information from your lists to write an email to a friend or family member about your recent activities. Try to avoid the common mistakes in the chart.

EXAMPLE: Hi everyone,

A new semester has started, and I've been pretty busy lately. I've been working really hard on a science project. We're learning how to check the water quality in the lake. I've gotten more interested in the environment because of this project, so I've been . . .

Common Mistakes in Using the Present Perfect Progressive and Present Perfect

Use the **present perfect progressive** for things that are **unfinished**. Do not use the present perfect.	**I've been reading** Owen's book. I'm almost finished. NOT I've read Owen's book. I'm almost finished.
Use the **present perfect** for things that are **finished**. Do not use the present perfect progressive (except for something that ended in the very recent past and whose results you can still see).	**I've read** Owen's book. It was great. NOT I've been reading Owen's book. It was great.

C CHECK YOUR WORK Read your email. Underline the verbs in the present perfect progressive and circle the verbs in the present perfect. Use the Editing Checklist to check your work.

Editing Checklist

Did you use . . . ?

- ☐ the present perfect progressive for things that are unfinished
- ☐ the present perfect for things that are finished
- ☐ the present perfect progressive to show how long something has been happening
- ☐ the present perfect to show how much, how many, and how many times something has happened
- ☐ the present perfect progressive or the present perfect with verbs of duration

D REVISE YOUR WORK Read your email again. Can you improve your writing? Make changes if necessary.

UNIT 12 REVIEW

Test yourself on the grammar of the unit.

Ⓐ Circle the correct words to complete the sentences.

1. Professor Ortiz has been writing / has written ten articles on global warming.

2. Today, he has been writing / has written since 6:00 a.m.

3. I've been reading / I've read one of his books. I'll give it to you when I'm finished.

4. My sister has been reading / has read it twice already.

5. I wanted to finish it today, but I've been having / I've had a headache all day.

6. I've been taking / I've taken aspirin all day.

Ⓑ Complete the conversations with the present perfect progressive or present perfect form of the verbs in parentheses. Use contractions when possible.

1. **A:** How long _____ you _____ in Dallas?
   a. (live)

   B: I _____ here for more than ten years. What about you?
   b. (be)

   A: I moved here last month. I _____ it a lot.
   c. (enjoy)

2. **A:** _____ you _____ any books by Peter Robb?
   a. (read)

   B: Yes. In fact, I'm reading one now.

   A: Really? How many books _____ he _____?
   b. (write)

3. **A:** Why are your books all over the place? I _____ to clean up!
   a. (try)

   B: I _____ for my exam.
   b. (study)

4. **A:** How long _____ Vilma _____ a student here?
   a. (be)

   B: This is her third semester.

   A: _____ she _____ her major?
   b. (choose)

Ⓒ Find and correct five mistakes.

1. Janet hasn't been writing a word since she sat down at her computer.

2. Since I've known Dan, he's been having five different jobs.

3. I've drunk coffee all morning. I think I've been having at least ten cups!

4. We've been lived here for several years, but we're moving next month.

Now check your answers on page 477.

Modals and Similar Expressions

PART 4

OUTCOMES

- Express ability and possibility in the past, present, and future
- Identify main points in a social sciences text
- Identify important details in a job interview
- Compare and contrast different possibilities for improving language skills
- Discuss an academic topic
- Write a paragraph about past, present, and future abilities

OUTCOMES

- Ask for, give, or deny permission
- Identify main points in a short reading
- Recognize when a speaker gives permission or refuses permission
- Come to a resolution with others by asking for and giving permission to do something
- Write a short note, explaining a situation and asking for permission to do something

OUTCOMES

- Make and respond to requests
- Identify important details related to requests in emails and text messages
- Identify details related to a schedule in a conversation
- Discuss a daily schedule that involves making requests of others
- Write and respond to a request in a text or email message

OUTCOMES

- Give and ask for advice
- Identify main points in a short text about rules and advice
- Recognize statements of advice in a radio show
- Discuss possible solutions to everyday situations, giving reasons and explanations
- Write an email or letter of complaint, giving advice on making improvements

OUTCOMES
• Express ability and possibility in the past, present, and future
• Identify main points in a social sciences text
• Identify important details in a job interview
• Compare and contrast different possibilities for improving language skills
• Discuss an academic topic
• Write a paragraph about past, present, and future abilities

STEP 1   GRAMMAR IN CONTEXT

BEFORE YOU READ

Look at the photo. Discuss the questions.

1. What do you think a *polyglot* is?

2. Do you recognize any of these languages?

3. Which languages can *you* speak?

READ

▶ 13|01   Read this article about multilingualism.

Hello!

Bonjour!

Bom dia!

¡Hola!

Hamjambo!

Multilingualism

Do you speak English? Parlez-vous français? Fala português? ¿Habla Usted español? Unaongea Kiswahili? As a child, retired basketball player, Dikembe Mutombo Mpolondo Mukamba Jean-Jacques Wamutombo (known as Dikembe Mutombo for short), could speak several languages. Growing up in a multilingual home in Zaire (today called the Democratic Republic of the Congo), he learned some languages at home and others at school. Today, he can speak nine: English, French, Portuguese, Spanish, Swahili, and four other African languages. Dikembe Mutombo is just one example of the more than 50% of the world population who can communicate in two or more languages. And as the world "gets smaller," thanks to the Internet, increased travel, and large numbers of people moving to other countries, this number will continue to grow.

Bilingualism describes people who speak two languages; *multilingualism* usually describes the ability to speak more than two languages. Being multilingual, or a polyglot, such as Mutombo, does not always mean that a person is able to communicate like a native speaker in each language. In fact, most foreign language speakers, especially people who learn a language as adults, cannot speak like native speakers. The majority of people, even if they become fluent,[1] are not able to totally

---

1 *fluent:* able to speak or write a language very well

**Polyglot
Dikembe Mutombo**

lose their foreign accents, and they will usually make some mistakes when they use the language. But they will be able to communicate well enough to understand and allow people to understand them.

Multilingualism has many advantages in today's world. Speaking other languages can help you get a job in many fields such as tourism, health services, banking, teaching, and sales. And recent research shows that learning a new language can make you smarter and help slow down the signs of aging. But, most of all, learning and knowing other languages can be fun and exciting. You can use your languages when you travel, and you can learn more about other people and cultures. Dikembe Mutombo loves to travel. In an interview with the magazine *Condé Nast Traveler*, he said, "People think of travel for work or play, but it can also be a lesson that will change your life." However, even if you don't travel, you still can enjoy songs, books, and movies in other languages—without ever leaving home.

AFTER YOU READ

A VOCABULARY **Choose the word or phrase that best completes each sentence.**

1. A **retired** language teacher _____.
   a. teaches many classes   b. used to teach   c. works very hard

2. An **adult** is a person who _____.
   a. is not a child   b. is good at languages   c. speaks well

3. People do **research** when they want to _____ about a subject.
   a. learn new facts   b. forget   c. complain

4. One **advantage** of speaking several languages is _____.
   a. a good dictionary   b. hard work   c. more job opportunities

5. "What **field** are you in?" is a question about your _____.
   a. native language   b. occupation   c. country

6. If the **majority** of people speak more than one language, this means that _____ are multilingual.
   a. less than 50%   b. 50%   c. more than 50%

B COMPREHENSION **Circle the correct information to complete each statement.**

1. As a child, Dikembe Mutombo had the ability to speak two / more than two languages.

2. Today, one of the many languages he speaks is French / Chinese.

3. A multilingual person usually speaks / doesn't speak like a native speaker.

4. Most multilingual people lose / don't lose their foreign accent.

5. Knowing other languages helps you in the field of sports / tourism.

6. Learning another language is often enjoyable / difficult.

C DISCUSSION **Work with a partner. Compare your answers in B. Why did you choose each answer?**

ABILITY AND POSSIBILITY: *CAN* AND *COULD*

Statements

Subject	Can/Could (not)	Base Form of Verb	
I You He She We You They	**can (not)**	**speak** French	now.
	could (not)		last year.

Contractions

cannot or can not	=	**can't**
could not	=	**couldn't**

Yes/No Questions

Can/Could	Subject	Base Form of Verb
Can	I you he she we you they	**speak** French?
Could		

Short Answers

Affirmative				Negative			
Yes,	you I he	**can.**		**No,**	you I he	**can't.**	
	she you we they	**could.**			she you we they	**couldn't.**	

Wh- Questions

Wh- Word	Can/Could	Subject	Base Form of Verb
How well	**can**	she	**speak** French?
	could	you	

ABILITY AND POSSIBILITY: *BE ABLE TO*

Statements

Subject	Be	(Not) Able to	Base Form of Verb
I	am		
You	are		
He She	is	**(not) able to**	**practice.**
We You They	are		

Be	Subject	Able to	Base Form of Verb
Is	she	**able to**	**practice?**
Are	you		

Short Answers

Affirmative			Negative		
Yes,	she	**is.**	**No,**	she	**isn't.**
	I	**am.**		I'm	**not.**

Wh- Questions

Wh- Word	Be	Subject	Able to	Base Form of Verb
When	**is**	she	**able to**	**practice?**
How often	**are**	you		

GRAMMAR NOTES

1 Can, Could, Be able to: Forms

Can and its past form *could* are modals. *Be able to* is an expression similar to a modal. Modals are auxiliaries: we use modals with other verbs.

Like all modals, *can* and *could*:

- are followed by the base form of a verb:
  modal + base form of verb

  Marti **can speak** Arabic.
  Marti **could speak** Arabic when he was a child.

- have only **one form**
  (Do not use -*s* for the third-person singular, and do not add -*s* to the base form of the verb.)

  I **can** speak French, and she **can** speak Arabic.
  NOT She ~~cans~~ speak Arabic.
  NOT She can ~~speaks~~ Arabic.

- form the **negative with *not***
  (Do not use *do*, *does*, or *did*.)

  She **can't** understand me.
  NOT She ~~doesn't can~~ understand me.

- go **before the subject** in **questions**
  (Do not use *do*, *does*, or *did*.)

  Can Antonio speak Italian?
  NOT ~~Does~~ can Antonio speak Italian?

Be able to is similar to a modal, but it has different forms (*am, is, are; was, were; will be*).

Was she **able to speak** French as a child?
Will I **be able to learn** French by next year?

IN WRITING *Can* and *could* are more common in conversation than in writing. *Be able to* is more common in formal writing.

A lot of people **can speak** several languages.
(conversation)
Many people **are able to speak** several languages.
(formal writing)

2 Can, Could, Be able to: Meanings

A modal adds meaning (such as the meaning of ability or possibility) to the verb that follows it. For example, *can*, *could*, or *be able to* shows that somebody has the **ability** and/or the **possibility** to do something.

• **ability** (natural or learned)	She **can speak**, but she **can't hear**. We **could read**, but we **couldn't write**. Soon, you**'ll be able to write** to me in English.
• **possibility**	You **can take** English as a second language this year. I **couldn't take** it last year. My school didn't offer it. You**'ll be able to take** that course next semester.
Can, *could*, and *be able to* often have both meanings of **ability and possibility**. This is especially true when we use them with a human or animal subject.	I **can help** you study for your French test. *(I have the ability and the possibility to help you.)*
We sometimes use *can* with a non-human or non-animal subject, but in this case the meaning is just **possibility**.	Speaking a foreign language **can be** fun. *(It has the possibility of being fun.)*

3 Present Ability or Possibility

Use *can* or *am/is/are able to* for present ability or possibility.

• *can* • *am/is/are able to*	She **can speak** English, but she **can't speak** French. She **is able to speak** English, but she **isn't able to speak** French.
USAGE NOTE *Can* is very common. It is much more common than *be able to* in everyday **conversation** about present ability.	**Can** you **speak** French? *(more common)* **Are** you **able to speak** French? *(less common)*
USAGE NOTE We often use *be able to* when the ability to do something comes after a lot of **hard work**.	French was difficult for me, but now I**'m able to have** a conversation because I spent a year studying in France.

4 Future Ability or Possibility

Use *can* or *will be able to* for future ability or possibility.

• *can*	I hope I **can understand** people when I'm in France next month.
• *will be able to*	I hope I**'ll be able to understand** people when I'm in France next month.
BE CAREFUL! Use *will be able to* (not *can*) for things you **learn**.	When I finish this course, I**'ll be able to** speak French well. NOT When I finish this course, I ~~can~~ speak French well.

Use *could* or *was/were able to* for past ability or possibility.

• *could*	**Could** he **speak** Spanish when he was a child?
• *was/were able to*	**Was** he **able to speak** Spanish when he was a child?

BE CAREFUL! Do not use *could* in affirmative statements for a **single event in the past**. Use *was/were able to*.	After a lot of hard work, they **were able to pass** the French test.
	NOT . . . they ~~could~~ pass the French test.
However, it is possible to use the negative *couldn't* for single past events.	They studied hard, but they **couldn't pass** the test.

REFERENCE NOTES

For *can* and *could* for **permission**, see Unit 14 on page 191; for **requests**, see Unit 15 on page 204.

For *can't* and *could* for **present conclusions**, see Unit 32 on page 440.

For *could* for **future possibility**, see Unit 31 on page 429.

For a list of **modals and their functions**, see Appendix 19 on page 460.

STEP 3   FOCUSED PRACTICE

EXERCISE 1   DISCOVER THE GRAMMAR

Ⓐ GRAMMAR NOTES 1–5   **Read this article about two famous polyglots. Underline all the verbs that express ability or possibility.**

Julio Iglesias

Singing in Another Language

What do Spanish-born Julio Iglesias and Canadian-born Celine Dion have in common? They are both world-famous superstars who <u>can sing</u> in many languages. As a young man, Iglesias played football professionally until a serious car accident changed everything. He couldn't walk for two years, and he wasn't able to play football anymore. But he soon discovered that he could sing. Now more than seventy years old, he can still entertain audiences of all ages. He has recorded songs in fourteen languages including French, Portuguese, German, and Japanese. Did he miss football? Maybe, but he's happy with his career. He realized long ago, he said in a recent interview, "I can sing until the end. I won't be able to play football until the end."

Celine Dion

Celine Dion dreamed at an early age of becoming a professional singer, and by the time she was 14, she was able to turn that dream into reality. She entered many singing competitions and was able to take home prizes including the World Music Award for the best-selling female singer of all time. At first, she only sung in her native French, but she took lessons and soon she was able to sing and record in English. Today, she mostly records in French and English, but, like Julio Iglesias, she can also sing in many languages including Spanish, German, Italian, Japanese and Mandarin Chinese. Because of family health problems, she stopped performing for a while. After taking a break from her career, she resumed her schedule. Her fans hope that she will be able to continue entertaining them for many more years.

B Look at the words you underlined in A. Write three sentences about Julio Iglesias and three sentences about Celine Dion. Write one sentence about the present, one sentence about the past, and one sentence about the future.

Julio Iglesias

present: _He can sing in many languages._

past: _____

future: _____

Celine Dion

present: _____

past: _____

future: _____

EXERCISE 2 STATEMENTS AND QUESTIONS

A GRAMMAR NOTES 2–5 Some language students are talking in the school cafeteria. Circle the correct words to complete their conversations.

Conversation 1

A: I heard your sister wants to take Chinese lessons before her trip. (Could she find) / Is she able to find
1.
a class?

B: Yes. In fact, she started classes last month. She can understand a little now, but even with lessons and a lot of practice, she still can say / can't say very much.
2.

Conversation 2

A: How is Chang doing with his English?

B: Good. He's made a lot of progress. Last semester, he can't order / couldn't order
3.
a meal in a restaurant or talk on the phone. His friends helped him do everything.

Now he can speak / could speak English in a lot of situations. It won't be long before
4.
he was able to get / he'll be able to get a part-time job here.
5.

Conversation 3

A: What about Emma? Was she able to pass / Could she pass her final exam?
6.

B: Yes, but she had trouble with her presentation because she got so nervous. She really

can communicate / can't communicate well in small groups, but she still doesn't feel
7.
comfortable in big ones. She plans to take a course in public speaking.

A: That's good. I'm sure that with her dedication she was able to improve / she'll be able to improve
8.
very quickly.

Conversation 4

A: Can you speak / Could you speak Russian as a child, Alex?
9.

B: Yes. We spoke it at home, so I'm able to speak / I could speak it fluently when I was very young.
10.

A: Do your children speak Russian, too?

B: No. Unfortunately, they don't. We always only spoke French at home, so, sadly, they never

was able to become / were able to become really fluent. But they're going to take Russian
11.
lessons next year, so I hope that someday they can speak / they'll be able to speak and
12.
understand it. Languages are so important!

▶13|02 **B** LISTEN AND CHECK Listen to the conversations and check your answers in A.

EXERCISE 3
CAN AND COULD: AFFIRMATIVE AND NEGATIVE STATEMENTS

GRAMMAR NOTES 1–3 Look at the English Language Ability Checklist. Complete the teacher's comments about Andreas. Use *can, can't, could,* and *couldn't* and the correct verb from the checklist.

English Language Ability Checklist

Student: _Andreas Koblin_

	LAST YEAR	NOW
read a newspaper	☑	☑
read a book	☒	☑
write an essay	☑	☑
write an academic paper	☑	☑
understand a movie	☒	☒
understand the words to songs	☒	☑
understand the news on TV	☒	☑
discuss the news with classmates	☒	☑
give a presentation	☒	☒

1. Last year, Andreas _____*could read*_____ a newspaper in English, but he ___*couldn't understand*___ the news on TV.

2. Now, he _____ the news on TV.

3. Last year, he _____ the news with his classmates, but now he _____ the news with other students.

4. Andreas _____ a book in English now. Last year, he _____ a book in English.

5. Andreas _____ an essay now. And he _____ an academic paper, too.

6. Last year, he _____ a movie in English. He still _____ a movie in English today.

7. Now, he _____ the words to songs in English very well, but last year he _____ them.

8. Andreas has improved a lot, but he still _____ a presentation in English. I am sure he will be able to do this with a little more practice.

EXERCISE 4 CAN, COULD, OR BE ABLE TO

GRAMMAR NOTES 1–5 Complete this FAQ (Frequently Asked Questions) about language learning. Use *can, could,* or *be able to* and the correct form of the verb in parentheses. There is often more than one correct answer.

_____*Can*_____ everyone _____*become*_____ multilingual?
                                        1. (become)

Yes. Almost everyone has the ability to learn more than one language, but some people

_____ languages more easily than others.
   2. (learn)

What are some characteristics of good language learners?

Good learners _____ mistakes. This means they accept mistakes as a
        3. (tolerate)

natural part of the language-learning process. They don't feel frustrated or get embarrassed.

They understand that people learn through mistakes. Good learners also enjoy learning

languages. They know that it is hard work, but they also know that after they learn a new

language, they _____ many advantages.
        4. (enjoy)

What is the best way to learn a language?

There is no one "best way." Polyglot, author, language teacher, and world traveler Susanna

Zaraysky says that people _____ any language anywhere. As an example,
        5. (learn)

she describes how people in post-war Bosnia _____ their English by
        6. (practice)

listening to weak radio or TV signals. She also strongly believes that listening to music

_____ with the learning process. In fact, research shows that singing in a
    7. (help)

foreign language _____ people in their fluency and pronunciation.
        8. (assist)

Does knowing one foreign language help you learn another?

Definitely. People who speak a second language _____ a third or fourth
        9. (pick up)

language more easily.

I'm studying French this semester. _____ I _____ Italian
                                        10. (learn)

more easily next semester?

Yes. Especially because French and Italian have a lot in common—similar vocabulary for

example. But even if the third language is unrelated to the second, as with Spanish and

Chinese, it helps to have the experience of "learning to learn" another language.

What about age? Can people learn at any age?

Yes, again. Most people find it much easier to learn when they are younger, but people

_____ a new language at any age. I had a student who, after a lot of hard
    11. (acquire)

work, _____ Portuguese when she was 82. She _____
        12. (learn)   **13.** (not lose)

her accent, but today she _____ with Portuguese language speakers when
        14. (communicate)

she travels.

EXERCISE 5 EDITING

GRAMMAR NOTES 1–5 **Read these postings from an online language-learning message board. There are ten mistakes in the use of** *can*, *could*, **and** *be able to*. **The first mistake is already corrected. Find and correct nine more.**

I just read an article about polyglot Dikembe Mutombo. It's an amazing story. When he first went to the

United States, he was able to speak French and several other languages, but he couldn't ~~spoke~~ *speak* a word of

English. He studied six hours a day and soon he is able to join in discussions in his classes at Georgetown

University. He was also able become a professional basketball player—something he never really planned to

do. Today, he can speak nine languages, and he is able to help a lot of people with the money he made as a

star basketball player!   —Martha O'Neill, Canada

I grew up in Finland, where children learn at least two foreign languages. By the time I was 18, I was able

speaking Finnish, Swedish, English, and German. I'm studying Russian now. Last week, I could get an A on my

final exam. And in a few years, I can speak my fourth foreign language. I think everyone should learn foreign

languages!   —Matias Laine, Finland

In India, we grow up speaking many languages. I was born in Bangalore. As a child, I spoke Gujarati at home

with my parents. In school, I also learned Kannada (the state language) and India's two official languages

(Hindi and English). As a result, today I able to communicate in four languages.   —Tanvi Patel, India

My mother could understands both English and Spanish, but she only spoke Spanish with me. I never really

knew if she couldn't speak English or if she just didn't want to. It had an advantage for me, though. I learned

English at school at an early age, but I was also able to keep my family's native language. Now, I'm fluent in

both languages.   —Lia Gomez, USA

Here in Europe, we generally learn more than one language because there are so many different countries

close together. As a result, we can often communicate with other Europeans when we travel. When I went

to Germany last year, I were able to speak to the people there and I learned a lot about their country. That

wasn't true on my trip to Hungary, though. Hungarian is very different from French. I can't understand a

word when I was there!   —Philippe Michaud, France

EXERCISE 6 LISTENING

▶13|03 **A** Karl is interviewing for the job of office assistant at Lang's Language Lab, a school that teaches foreign languages. Look at the list of job skills and other job requirements. Then listen to the interview. Listen again and check (✓) all the things Karl says he can do now.

Lang's Language Lab

FULL-TIME OFFICE ASSISTANT wanted for busy language school. Must be friendly and speak fluent English. Other languages a definite plus! Computer skills important. Contact us at 555-TALK.

- [✓] **1.** answer the phones
- [ ] **2.** greet visitors to the school
- [ ] **3.** speak fluent English
- [ ] **4.** speak other languages
- [ ] **5.** do word processing
- [ ] **6.** do Excel spreadsheets
- [ ] **7.** type 50 words per minute
- [ ] **8.** design a monthly newsletter
- [ ] **9.** order office supplies
- [ ] **10.** work weekends

▶13|03 **B** Work with a partner. Listen to the interview again. Do you think Karl is a good person for this job? Why or why not? Discuss your answers.

EXAMPLE: A: Well, he seems pretty friendly. That's important for the job.
B: I agree. I think he'll be able to get along well with the students. But will he be able to . . . ?

EXERCISE 7 WHAT ABOUT YOU?

A CONVERSATION Before you talk about your abilities in English, complete the English Language Ability Checklist. Use your own information. Check (✓) things you *could do last year* and/or *can do now*. Put an X next to things you *couldn't do last year* and/or *can't do now.*

English Language Ability Checklist

Student: _____

	LAST YEAR	NOW
read a newspaper	[ ]	[ ]
read a book	[ ]	[ ]
write an essay	[ ]	[ ]
write an academic paper	[ ]	[ ]
understand a movie	[ ]	[ ]
understand the words to songs	[ ]	[ ]
understand the news on TV	[ ]	[ ]
discuss the news with classmates	[ ]	[ ]
give a presentation	[ ]	[ ]

B Work with a partner. Ask and answer questions about your abilities in English. Give examples. Use *can*, *can't*, *could*, *couldn't* or the correct form of *be able to*.

EXAMPLE: A: Can you read a newspaper in English?
B: Sometimes. It all depends on the topic. Sometimes I can understand it, but sometimes I can't. For example, I can understand articles about soccer because I know the vocabulary, but I'm not really able to understand scientific articles very well. What about you?
A: It's the same with me. What about movies? Can you . . . ?

EXERCISE 8 LANGUAGE LEARNING TIPS

PROBLEM SOLVING Work in a group. Look at the list of language learning skills in the box. What can you do to improve your skills? Think of as many suggestions as possible. Make a list of tips. Compare your list of tips with another group's.

SKILLS
- listening comprehension
- grammar
- pronunciation
- reading
- vocabulary
- writing

EXAMPLE: A: For listening comprehension, you can listen to a lot of TV.
B: You can also listen to songs. The more you listen, the more you'll be able to understand!
C: You can also . . .

EXERCISE 9 A WORLD OF ADVANTAGES

A BRAINSTORMING Work in a group. Brainstorm advantages of being multilingual. Think about the topics in the list below.

EXAMPLE: A: You can get a better job.
B: You can talk to customers in their own language.
C: You can . . .

TOPICS
- employment
- travel
- social life
- free-time activities
- politics
- health
- *Other:* _____

B Compare your answers with those of the rest of the class.

EXAMPLE: A: We said languages can help you get a better job.
B: We said that, too. If you're multilingual, you can get specific types of jobs, too.
C: Right. You can become a translator, for example.

A BEFORE YOU WRITE Think about your English. How has it changed? How hasn't it changed? What are your hopes for the future? Complete the outline about your English language abilities.

Past Abilities	Present Abilities	Future Abilities
_____	_____	_____
_____	_____	_____
_____	_____	_____

B WRITE Use your outline to write a paragraph about your English abilities. Compare your language ability now to your abilities at some time in the past. What do you think you'll be able to do in the future that you can't do now? Include examples. Try to avoid the common mistakes in the chart.

EXAMPLE: When I first came to this country five years ago, I couldn't speak a word of English. I wasn't able to . . . and I couldn't . . . Now, I can do many things that I couldn't do then. For example, I can . . . I hope in the future, I will be able to . . .

Common Mistakes in Using *Can, Could,* and *Be able to* for Ability or Possibility

Use the **base form** of the verb after *can* or *could*. Do not add *-s* to the base form after *he, she,* or *it*.	She **can speak** Arabic. NOT She can ~~speaks~~ Arabic.
Use *will be able to* for things you **learn**. Do not use *can*.	Next year, I'**ll be able to speak** Russian. NOT Next year, I ~~can speak~~ Russian.
Use *was/were able to* for a **single event in the past**. Do not use *could*.	Last year, I **was able to get** an A in Spanish. NOT Last year, I ~~could get~~ an A in Spanish.

C CHECK YOUR WORK Read your paragraph. Circle all the verbs with *can* or *could*. Underline all the verbs that use a form of *be able to*. Use the Editing Checklist to check your work.

Editing Checklist

Did you use . . . ?

- ☐ the base form of the verb after *can* or *could*
- ☐ *can, can't,* or *am able to* for present ability
- ☐ *can* or *will be able to* for future ability
- ☐ *could* or *was able to* for past ability
- ☐ *was able to* for a single past event

D REVISE YOUR WORK Read your paragraph again. Can you improve your writing? Make changes if necessary. Give your paragraph a title.

UNIT 13 REVIEW

Test yourself on the grammar of the unit.

Ⓐ Circle the correct words to complete the sentences.

1. How many languages can she <u>speak / speaks</u>?

2. After a lot of studying, Stefan <u>could / was able to</u> get an A on his Russian test.

3. Keep practicing and soon you <u>can / will be able to</u> understand the TV news.

4. Sorry, but I <u>can't / couldn't</u> help you with your Spanish homework right now.

5. I <u>can't / couldn't</u> understand the movie. They spoke too fast.

Ⓑ Complete the paragraph with *can*, *could*, or *be able to* and the verbs in parentheses. Choose between affirmative and negative. There is often more than one correct answer.

As a child, Lia Romano _____ two languages fluently—English and Italian.
            1. (speak)

Then, in high school, she studied French, and after a few years, she _____ an
                                                                      2. (win)

award for "Best Foreign Language Learner." Last year, she took Chinese classes, and now she

_____ a little. But she _____. It's still too difficult for her.
     3. (speak)   **4.** (write)

She's really working very hard, though, and she believes that with some more practice, she

_____ soon. Lia hopes she _____ to China some day, but
     5. (improve)   **6.** (travel)

right now she _____ the air fare. She just got a part-time job, so she hopes that
                  7. (afford)

after she saves some money, she _____ the trip. Last summer, she went to Cuba.
                                   8. (make)

Because she speaks Italian, she _____ well enough to get along. It was a great
                                  9. (communicate)

experience, and Lia hopes she _____ other countries soon.
                                10. (visit)

Ⓒ Find and correct five mistakes.

A: I can't to see the board. The guy in front of me is very tall.

B: Let's change seats. You be able to see from this seat.

A: Thanks. I don't want to miss anything. I no can believe what a great teacher Ms. Acosta is.

B: I know. My sister had her last semester. She could get an A on her final exam!

A: Were your sister able to speak any Spanish before taking that class?

B: No. She couldn't speak a word!

A: That's amazing!

Now check your answers on page 478.

Permission: *Can, Could, May, Do you mind if*
ROOMMATES

OUTCOMES
- Ask for, give, or deny permission
- Identify main points in a short reading
- Recognize when a speaker gives permission or refuses permission
- Come to a resolution with others by asking for and giving permission to do something
- Write a short note, explaining a situation and asking for permission to do something

STEP 1	GRAMMAR IN CONTEXT

BEFORE YOU READ

Look at the cartoon and at the title of the article. Discuss the questions.

1. Where are these people?
2. What is their relationship?
3. How are they getting along? Why?

READ

▶14|01 Read this article about getting along with a roommate.

Always Ask First

Heather immediately liked Tara, her neat, non-smoking college roommate. Their first week together was great. But the second week, the cookies from Heather's mother disappeared. Tara didn't ask Heather, "Could I have one?" She just assumed it was all right. Tara's friends always helped themselves to[1] food without asking for permission. The third week, Heather was halfway out the door when she asked Tara, "Can I wear your new jacket today?" She was already wearing it. Tara was angry, but she stayed calm and answered, "Sorry, but I was planning on wearing it today." The fourth week, Tara looked annoyed whenever Heather's friends stopped by to visit. Heather never asked Tara, "Hey, do you mind if they hang out here for a while?" At

Can I wear your new jacket today?

---
1 *helped themselves to:* took without asking for permission

home, Heather's friends were always welcome. By October, Heather and Tara weren't talking. Luckily, their dorm counselor was able to help them fix their relationship with three simple rules.

1. Always ask for permission before you touch your roommate's stuff. Say: "My computer isn't working. Could I use yours for a few hours?"

2. Establish times when it's OK to have visitors. If it's not "visiting hours," ask for your roommate's permission: "Can Luis and Ming-Hwa work here tonight? We're doing a presentation in class tomorrow."

3. Try to solve problems. Say: "Your music is too loud for me, but you can borrow my headphones."

Follow these guidelines, and who knows? You may gain a happier roommate *and* a good friend.

AFTER YOU READ

A VOCABULARY **Complete the sentences with the words from the box.**

annoyed	assumed	established	gained	guidelines	presentation

1. Ahmed is _____ at his roommate for using his computer without asking first.

2. We didn't get any _____ for our science report. Could you please give us some instructions?

3. I just _____ it was OK to eat the cookies because you left them on the table.

4. We _____ those rules when we became roommates. That means we both agreed to follow them.

5. For his class _____, Raoul showed a video about getting along with roommates.

6. I _____ a better understanding of relationships from my roommate.

B COMPREHENSION **Read the statements. Check (✓) *True* or *False*.**

	True	False
1. Tara didn't ask for permission before taking Heather's cookies.	☐	☐
2. Tara's friends never asked for permission before taking food.	☐	☐
3. Heather asked for permission to wear Tara's jacket.	☐	☐
4. Tara gave Heather permission to wear her jacket.	☐	☐
5. Heather asked for permission before her friends visited.	☐	☐

C DISCUSSION **Work with a partner. Compare your answers in B. Why did you check *True* or *False*?**

PERMISSION: *CAN, COULD, MAY, DO YOU MIND IF*

Yes/No Questions: *Can/Could/May*

Can/Could/May*	Subject	Base Form of Verb	
Can **Could** **May**	I he she we they	**stay**	here?

Short Answers

Affirmative	Negative
Certainly. Of course. Sure. No problem.	Sorry, but . . .

* Can, could, and *may* are modals. Modals have only one form. They do not have *-s* in the third-person singular.

Wh- Questions: *Can/Could/May*

Wh- Word	Can/Could/May	Subject	Base Form of Verb
When	**can** **could** **may**	I he she we they	**call**?

Statements: *Can/May*

Subject	Can/May (not)	Base Form of Verb	
You He She	**can (not)** **may (not)**	**stay**	here.

Contractions*

cannot or can not	=	**can't**

** There is no contraction for **may not**.*

Questions: *Do you mind if*

Do you mind if	Subject	Verb	
Do you mind if	I we they	**stay**	here?
	he she it	**stays**	

Short Answers

Affirmative	Negative
Not at all. **No**, I **don't**. Go right ahead.	Sorry, but . . .

GRAMMAR NOTES

1 Can, Could, May

Use the modals *can*, *could*, and *may* to ask for **permission**.

- *can*
- *could*
- *may*

Can I **borrow** your book?	LESS FORMAL
Could he **come** tomorrow?	↕
May we **leave**, Professor Lee?	MORE FORMAL
(student speaking to teacher)	

USAGE NOTE   *May* is not very common. It is much **more formal** and polite than *can* and *could*. We sometimes use it when we are speaking to a person in authority (for example, a teacher, police officer, doctor, librarian, counselor, etc.).

USAGE NOTE   We often use *please* when we ask for permission. Notice the word order.

Could I **ask** a question, *please*?
or
Could I *please* **ask** a question?

Could refers to the **present** or the **future**. It does not refer to the past (even though *could* is the past form of *can*).

Could I **call** you *tomorrow*?

IN WRITING   **Asking for permission** is much more common in **conversation** than in writing, but you can ask for permission in **informal notes**, **emails**, and **text messages**.

Can I **make** an appointment to discuss my presentation with you? *(conversation)*
Hi Professor Chin. **Could** I **make** an appointment to discuss my presentation with you? *(note / email)*

2 Answers

There are **several ways to answer** when someone asks for permission.

When we **give permission**, we usually use **informal expressions** instead of modals in answers.

A: **Could** I close the window?
B: *Sure.* or *Of course.* or *Go ahead.*

When we use a **modal** in an **affirmative answer**, we almost always use *can*. We do not use *could*, and we rarely use *may* in short answers.

A: **Could** I borrow this pencil?
B: *Yes*, of course you **can**.
   NOT Yes, of course you ~~could~~.

A: **May** I please see your notes?
B: *Sure* you **can**. or *Yes*, you **may**. *(rare)*

USAGE NOTE   When we **refuse permission**, we usually **apologize** and give an **explanation**.

A: **Can** I please use your computer?
B: *I'm sorry*, *but* I need it today.

USAGE NOTE   *No, you can't* and *No, you may not* are **not common** answers, and they don't sound polite. People sometimes use these short negative answers when they are angry. And adults sometimes use them when talking to children.

A: **Can** I wear your new sweater?
B: *No, you can't!* I haven't even worn it yet!

A: Mommy, **can** I have ice cream for breakfast?
B: *No, you can't.*

Use the expression *do you mind if* to ask for permission when an **action may annoy** or inconvenience someone.

Use the **simple present** of the verb after *do you mind if*.	A: **Do you mind if** he *cleans up* later? B: No, I don't. He can do it tomorrow.
BE CAREFUL! Do not use *please* with *do you mind if*.	**Do you mind if** I **ask** a question? **NOT** Do you mind if I ask a question ~~please~~?

BE CAREFUL! When we **give permission**, we use *Not at all* or *No, I don't*, but we're really saying: *It's OK*.
 	
When we **refuse permission**, we can use *Yes, I do*, but we're really saying: *It's not OK*.
	A: **Do you mind if** Ian comes over tonight?
	B: **Not at all.** or **No, I don't.**
	      (It's OK for Ian to come over tonight.)
	
	B: **Yes, I do.**
	      (It's not OK for Ian to come over tonight.)

USAGE NOTE It's **not common** to refuse permission with *Yes, I do*. As with questions with *can*, *could*, and *may*, when we refuse permission to a question with *do you mind if*, we usually **apologize** and give an **explanation**.	A: **Do you mind if** Ian comes over tonight? B: **Sorry, but** I have to study tonight.
IN WRITING As with *can*, *could*, and *may*, *do you mind if* is much more common in **conversation** than in writing, but you can use it in **informal notes**, **emails**, and **text messages**.	Hi. **Do you mind if** I **invite** Paulo to have dinner with us tomorrow night? *(email)*

REFERENCE NOTES

For general information on **modals**, see Unit 13, Grammar Notes 1–2, on page 177.

For *can* and *could* for **ability and possibility**, see Unit 13 on page 176; for **requests**, see Unit 15 on page 204.

For *could* and *may* for **future possibility**, see Unit 31 on page 429; for **present conclusions**, see Unit 32 on page 440.

For a list of **modals and their functions**, see Appendix 19 on page 460.

EXERCISE 1 DISCOVER THE GRAMMAR

GRAMMAR NOTES 1–3 Read the quiz. Underline all the modals and expressions for permission. Then if you'd like to, you can take the quiz. The answers are below.

Are You a Good Roommate?

Take this short quiz and find out.

1. **You want to use your roommate's computer.**
   You say:
   ○ **a.** I may use your computer tonight.
   ○ **b.** Can I use your computer tonight?
   ○ **c.** I'm using your computer tonight.

2. **You don't have any food in the house.**
   You say:
   ○ **a.** Can you make dinner for me?
   ○ **b.** I don't mind eating some of your food.
   ○ **c.** Do you mind if I have some of your food?

3. **You may not have time to wash the dishes tonight.**
   You say:
   ○ **a.** Could you wash the dishes?
   ○ **b.** I can't wash the dishes.
   ○ **c.** Can I wash the dishes tomorrow?

4. **Your roommate asks you: "Could my best friend stay overnight?"**
   You answer:
   ○ **a.** Can she stay in a hotel instead?
   ○ **b.** Sure she can!
   ○ **c.** I'm sure she could, but I don't want her to!

5. **You can find nothing to wear to the party next Friday.**
   You say:
   ○ **a.** Could I borrow your new sweater?
   ○ **b.** I may borrow your new sweater.
   ○ **c.** You could lend me your new sweater.

6. **You want to hang your favorite poster in your dorm room.**
   You say:
   ○ **a.** Could I hang my poster here?
   ○ **b.** Maybe you could hang my poster here.
   ○ **c.** I assume I can hang my poster here.

ANSWERS: 1. b, 2. c, 3. c, 4. b, 5. a, 6. a

EXERCISE 2 QUESTIONS AND ANSWERS

GRAMMAR NOTES 1–3 Look at the signs. Complete each question and answer. Use the words in parentheses and the correct pronouns. Write appropriate short answers. There can be more than one correct short answer.

1. PIERRE: _____Do you mind if_____ I _____eat_____ my lunch here
a. (do you mind if / eat)
while I get on the Internet? I'll be neat.

ASSISTANT: _____Sorry_____. Please look at the sign.
b.

Computer Lab

2. SÉBASTIEN: Those guys next door are making a lot of noise!

_____ they _____ that?
a. (can / do)

NATHANIEL: _____. They aren't going to gain any friends
b.
that way, but according to the guidelines, it's OK to play

music now. It's 8:00 a.m.

SÉBASTIEN: Well, _____ I _____ your
c. (can / borrow)
earplugs? I have to prepare for my English presentation.

Quiet Hours
11:00 p.m. - 7:00 a.m.
Sunday - Saturday

3. CARMEN: _____ we _____ our bikes on
a. (may / ride)
this path?

GUARD: _____.
b.

4. DONOVAN: _____ I _____ my dog next
a. (could / bring)
semester? My roommate doesn't mind.

COUNSELOR: _____. But some of the other dorms
b.
allow pets.

Kent Hall

5. GABRIELLE: _____ I _____ my cell phone
a. (may / use)
in here?

LIBRARIAN: _____. People get really annoyed by cell
b.
phone conversations.

EXERCISE 3 QUESTIONS AND ANSWERS

GRAMMAR NOTES 1–3 Heather and her roommate Tara are planning a party in Kent Hall. Use the words in parentheses to ask for permission. Answer the questions.

1. Tara's friend Troy is in town. She wants him to come to the party.

   TARA: *Do you mind if Troy comes to the party?*
   _____
                                   (do you mind if)
   HEATHER: *Not at all.* _____ I'd love to meet him.

2. Heather wants to borrow her roommate's black sweater.

   HEATHER: I have nothing to wear. _____
                                              (can)
   TARA: _____ I'm planning to wear it myself!

3. Tara's sister is coming from out of town. Tara wants her to stay in their room.

   TARA: _____
                              (do you mind if)
   HEATHER: _____ She can sleep on the couch.

4. Heather and Tara would like to have the party in the dormitory lounge. Heather asks her dormitory counselor for permission.

   HEATHER: _____
                                  (may)
   COUNSELOR: _____ It's available next Friday. We just have to

   establish some guidelines.

5. Heather and Tara would like to hang decorations from the ceiling of the lounge.

   HEATHER: _____
                                  (could)
   COUNSELOR: _____ Fire regulations won't allow it.

6. Heather and Tara want the party to go until midnight.

   HEATHER: _____
                                  (could)
   COUNSELOR: _____ Quiet hours start at 11:00 on Friday.

7. Tara wants to play some of her friend Erica's CDs at the party.

   TARA: _____
                               (could)
   ERICA: _____ Which ones should I bring?

8. It's Friday night. A student wants to study in the lounge.

   STUDENT: _____
                               (can)
   HEATHER: _____ We're having a party. Want to join us?

EXERCISE 4 EDITING

GRAMMAR NOTES 1–3 Read Sharif's English test. There are seven mistakes in the use of *can*, *could*, *may*, and *do you mind if*. The first mistake is already corrected. Find and correct six more.

Class: English 102

Name: Sharif Halabi

Directions: These conversations take place on a train. Find and correct the mistakes.

1. A: May we board the train now?

   B: Sorry, you ~~couldn't~~ *can't* board until 12:30.

2. A: Can he comes on the train with me?

   B: Sorry. Only passengers can board.

3. A: Do you mind if I'm sitting here?

   B: No, I don't. My friend is sitting here.

4. A: Could I looked at your newspaper?

   B: Yes, of course you could.

5. A: Do you mind if my son play his computer game?

   B: No, not at all. It won't disturb me.

   A: Thanks.

   B: No problem.

EXERCISE 5   LISTENING

▶14|02   Ⓐ Listen to seven short conversations. For each one, check (✓) *Permission Given* or *Permission Refused*.

	Permission Given	Permission Refused
Conversation 1	✓	☐
Conversation 2	☐	☐
Conversation 3	☐	☐
Conversation 4	☐	☐
Conversation 5	☐	☐
Conversation 6	☐	☐
Conversation 7	☐	☐

▶14|02   Ⓑ Work with a partner. Read the list of people. Listen again to the conversations. Decide who is speaking. What do you think their relationship is? Match each conversation with the correct people.

EXAMPLE: A: So, Conversation 1 is between a driver and a police officer.
   B: Yes. The driver is very polite. She uses "may." It's clear she's speaking to an authority figure like a police officer. So what about Conversation 2?

Conversation	People
_d_ **1.**	**a.** roommate and roommate
____ **2.**	**b.** child and parent
____ **3.**	**c.** travel agent and customer
____ **4.**	~~**d.**~~ driver and police officer
____ **5.**	**e.** boyfriend and girlfriend's mother
____ **6.**	**f.** employee and employer
____ **7.**	**g.** student and teacher

EXERCISE 6   DO YOU MIND IF . . . ?

BRAINSTORMING   Work in a group. Read each situation and decide what to say. Think of as many things to say as possible.

1. You have a small apartment. Two of your friends are coming to visit your town for a week, and they want to stay with you. What can you say to your roommate?

   EXAMPLE: A: Do you mind if Anton and Eva stay here for a week?
      B: Could Anton practice his guitar in the evening?
      C: Can Eva keep her bike in the hall?

2. You're visiting some good friends. The weather is very cold, but they don't seem to mind. Their windows are open and the heat is off. You're freezing.

3. You're at a concert with some friends. You like the performer very much. You have your smartphone with you and you'd like to take some photos or maybe a short video. Sometimes this performer talks to fans and signs programs after the concert.

4. You have formed a study group with some classmates. You want to use a classroom on Thursday evenings to study. Some of your classmates come directly from work. They would like to eat their dinner in the classroom. What can you say to your teacher?

EXERCISE 7 COULD I . . . ?

ROLE PLAY Work with a partner. Read the situations. Take turns being Student A and Student B.

Student A	Student B
1. You were absent from class yesterday. Student B, your classmate, always takes good notes.	Student A is in your class. You're always willing to help your classmates.

> EXAMPLE: A: Can I copy your notes from class yesterday?
> B: Sure. Here they are.
> A: Could I call you tonight if I have questions?
> B: Of course. I'll give you my number.

Student A	Student B
2. You're at work. You have a terrible headache. Student B is your boss.	Student A is your employee. You have a lot of work for Student A to do today.
3. You're a teenager. You and your friend want to travel to another city to see a concert. Student B is your father/mother. You want to borrow his or her car. Your friend has a license and wants to drive.	Student A is your son/daughter. You like this friend, and you have no objection to lending him or her the car. However, you want the friend to be careful.
4. Student B has invited you to a small party. At the last minute, your two cousins show up. They have nothing to do the night of the party.	Your party is a small party for a few of your close friends. It's also at a restaurant, and you have already arranged for a certain number of people to attend.

FROM GRAMMAR TO WRITING

A BEFORE YOU WRITE Think of two situations for which you need to write a short note asking for permission. Complete the outline.

EXAMPLE: My computer isn't working. I want to borrow my roommate's laptop.

Situation	Reason you will ask for permission
1. _____	_____
2. _____	_____

B WRITE Use the information from your outline to write two notes asking for permission. Then exchange notes with two classmates. Write answers to your classmates' notes. Try to avoid the common mistakes in the chart.

EXAMPLE:

> Ana, my computer isn't working. I have to write a report for my class tomorrow. Could I please borrow your laptop? —Melissa

> Sorry, Melissa. I can't lend you my laptop. I'm going home for the weekend, and I'm taking my laptop with me. —Ana

Common Mistakes in Using *Can, Could, May,* and *Do you mind if* for Permission

Use the **base form** of the verb after *can, could,* or *may*. Do not add *-s* to the base form after *he, she,* or *it*.	**Can** my roommate **come** with us? NOT Can my roommate ~~comes~~ with us?
To be **more polite**, use *please* with *can, could,* or *may*. Do not use *please* with *do you mind if*.	**Could** I *please* borrow your notes? NOT Do you mind if I borrow your notes~~, please~~?
Use **informal expressions** in **answers**. Do not use *can, could,* or *may*.	A: **Can** my roommate come with us? B: *Of course.* NOT ~~Yes, he can.~~

C CHECK YOUR WORK Read your four notes. Circle all the modals or expressions that ask for permission. Underline all the informal expressions in your answers. Use the Editing Checklist to check your work.

Editing Checklist

Did you use...?

☐ the base form of the verb after *can, could,* or *may*

☐ *do you mind if* when an action may annoy or inconvenience someone

☐ *please* with *can, could,* or *may* (but not with *do you mind if*) to be more polite

☐ informal expressions in your answers

☐ an apology and an explanation if you refused permission

D REVISE YOUR WORK Read your notes again. Can you improve your writing? Make changes if necessary.

UNIT 14 **REVIEW**

Test yourself on the grammar of the unit.

A Circle the correct words to complete the questions.

1. Can my roommate come / comes to class with me?

2. Could / Do you mind if I call you at home?

3. Could I borrow / borrowed a pen?

4. Do you mind if / when I ask a question?

5. May I shut please / please shut the door?

B Read the situations in parentheses. Complete the questions to ask for permission.

1. Could _____?
   (You want to borrow a pen.)

2. Can _____?
   (Your sister wants to leave.)

3. Do you mind if _____?
   (You want to open a window.)

4. Could _____?
   (You and a friend want to come early.)

5. May _____?
   (You want to ask a question.)

C Find and correct ten mistakes.

1. A: Do you mind if I changed the date of our next meeting?

   B: Yes, I do. When would you like to meet?

2. A: Could I calling you tonight?

   B: Sorry, but you couldn't. I won't be home.

3. A: Mom, I may have some more ice cream?

   B: No, you mayn't. You've already had a lot. You'll get sick.

4. A: Do you mind if my son turn on the TV?

   B: Not at all. I can't study with the TV on.

5. A: Can my sister borrows your bike?

   B: Could I letting you know tomorrow?

   A: Sure. No problem.

Now check your answers on page 478.

Requests: *Can, Could, Will, Would, Would you mind*
MESSAGES

OUTCOMES
- Make and respond to requests
- Identify important details related to requests in emails and text messages
- Identify details related to a schedule in a conversation
- Discuss a daily schedule that involves making requests of others
- Write and respond to a request in a text or email message

STEP 1   GRAMMAR IN CONTEXT

BEFORE YOU READ

Look at the title of the text messages and the emails. Discuss the questions.

1. What do you think the title means?

2. Why do people use abbreviations in text messages?

3. Do you prefer text messages or emails? Why?

READ

▶15|01   Read these text messages between Marta and her mother. Then read the emails to Marta from her boss and from Marta to her assistant.

Messages 4 u!

Tuesday 9:14 a.m.

Can u drive me to the Rubios' after work today, Marta? They've invited me for dinner. Oh, and will you pick up something special at the bakery before u come? I promised to bring dessert.

Tuesday 10:20 a.m.

I'm sorry, Mom. I can't tonight. I'm working late. Do u want me to ask your favorite son-in-law if he can drive u?

From: JohnSanchez@dataline.com
To: MartaCampos@dataline.com
Subject: Re: Sales Report

Hi, Marta,

I'll be out of town until Thursday. Would you please copy and distribute the monthly sales report? Thank you. I really appreciate your help!

John

AFTER YOU READ

A VOCABULARY Choose the word or phrase that best completes each sentence.

1. A **request** is a polite way of _____ something.
   a. asking for
   b. doing
   c. answering

2. When you **deliver** a report, you _____ it to someone.
   a. promise
   b. describe
   c. bring

3. When you **respond** to a message you give a(n) _____.
   a. answer
   b. report
   c. opinion

4. When a question is **urgent**, you need to react to it _____.
   a. carefully
   b. immediately
   c. slowly

5. When you **distribute** reports, you _____ one to each person in a group.
   a. give
   b. read
   c. talk about

6. When you **appreciate** what someone does for you, you feel _____.
   a. worried
   b. sorry
   c. thankful

B COMPREHENSION Read the statements. Check (✓) *True* or *False*.

	True	False
1. Marta's mother made three requests to her daughter.	☐	☐
2. Marta's mother needs a ride.	☐	☐
3. Marta is going to drive her.	☐	☐
4. John is going to copy and distribute the sales report.	☐	☐
5. Marta wants Ann to give her the copies of the sales report.	☐	☐
6. Marta wants to know how her boss responds to a request.	☐	☐

C DISCUSSION Work with a partner. Compare your answers in B. Why did you check *True* or *False*?

FROM: MartaCampos@dataline.com
TO: AnnChen@dataline.com
SUBJECT: Re: Sales Report

Hi, Ann,

I'm sending you a copy of our sales report. Could you please make 25 copies? And would you mind delivering them to me as soon as you're finished? It's urgent.

One more thing—Will you tell me how the boss responds to our request for another office assistant?

Thanks.

Marta

REQUESTS: *CAN, COULD, WILL, WOULD, WOULD YOU MIND*

Questions: *Can/Could/Will/Would*

Can/Could/ Will/Would*	You	Base Form of Verb	
Can Could Will Would	you	**distribute**	this report for me?
		drive	me to the doctor?
		pick up	some groceries?

Short Answers

Affirmative	Negative	
Sure. Certainly. No problem. Of course. I'd be glad to.	I'm sorry, (but)	**I can't.**
	I'm afraid	

* *Can, could, will,* and *would* are modals. Modals do not have *-s* in the third-person singular.

Questions: *Would you mind*

Would you mind	Gerund	
Would you mind	**distributing**	this report for me?
	driving	me to the doctor?
	picking up	some groceries?

Short Answers

Affirmative	Negative	
Not at all. I'd be glad to. No problem. Of course not.	I'm sorry, (but)	**I can't.**
	I'm afraid	

GRAMMAR NOTES

1 *Can, Could, Will, Would*

Use the modals *can*, *could*, *will*, and *would* to make a **request**.

• *can* • *could* • *will* • *would*	**Can** you **email** me? **Could** you **copy** Danica? **Will** you **call** me tomorrow? **Would** you **remind** me to call Mason?

USAGE NOTE *Could* and *would* are more polite than *can* and *will*. We use *could* and *would* to soften requests.	John, **can** you mail this for me? Ms. Lee, **could** you mail this for me? *(more polite)*

USAGE NOTE You can also use *please* to make the request even more polite. Notice the word order.	**Would** you **close** the door, ***please***? or **Would** you ***please* close** the door?

IN WRITING **Requests** are much more common in **conversation** than in writing, but you can use requests in **informal notes**, **emails**, and **text messages**.	**Can** you **get** two oranges? *(conversation)* Laura, **could** you **pick up** some bread on the way home? *(text message)*

There are **several ways to respond** to requests.

In **affirmative answers** to requests, we usually use expressions such as *sure, of course, certainly, I'd be glad to,* and *no problem*.	A: **Would** you **shut** the window, please? B: *Sure.* or *Of course.* or *Certainly.*
USAGE NOTE *Certainly* and *I'd be glad to* are more formal than other answers. *No problem* is the least formal.	A: Dan, **could** you **help** me carry these books? B: *I'd be glad to,* Professor Chin. *(more formal)* A: **Can** you **lend** me your pen? B: **No problem.** *(least formal)*
USAGE NOTE In **negative answers**, we usually **apologize** and give an **explanation**.	A: **Could** you **deliver** this to Ron, please? B: *I'm sorry, but* I **can't**. I'm expecting a client.
BE CAREFUL! Do not use *would* or *could* in response to polite requests.	NOT Sure I ~~would~~. NOT I'm sorry, but I ~~couldn't~~.

We also use the expression *would you mind* to make **polite requests**.

Use a **gerund** (verb + *-ing*) after *would you mind*.	Would you mind *making* a copy of the report?
Would you mind is even more polite than *could* or *would*.	A: **Would you mind waiting**? Mr. Caras is in a meeting.
BE CAREFUL! When we answer this type of request with *Not at all* or *Of course not*, it means that we will do what the person requests.	B: *Not at all.* or *Of course not.* (OK. I'll do it.)
USAGE NOTE In **negative answers**, we usually **apologize** and give an **explanation**.	C: *I'm sorry,* I **can't**. I have another appointment in a half an hour.

PRONUNCIATION NOTE

▶ 15|02

In **informal conversation**, we often pronounce *could you, would you, will you,* and *can you* as "couldja," "wouldja," "willya," and "canya."	A: **Could you** mail this for me? (couldja) B: Sure. **Would you** remind me later? (wouldja) A: **Will you** type this for me? (willya) B: No problem. **Can you** leave it on my desk? (canya)

REFERENCE NOTES

For general information on **modals**, see Unit 13, Grammar Notes 1–2, on page 177.

For *can* and *could* for **ability and possibility**, see Unit 13 on page 176; for **permission**, see Unit 14 on page 191.

For *can't* and *could* for **present conclusions**, see Unit 32 on page 440.

For *could* for **future possibility**, see Unit 31 on page 429.

For *will* for the **future**, see Unit 6 on page 76 and Unit 7 on page 93.

For a list of **modals and their functions**, see Appendix 19 on page 460.

STEP 3   FOCUSED PRACTICE

EXERCISE 1   DISCOVER THE GRAMMAR

GRAMMAR NOTES 1–3   Raul's roommate, Emil, is having problems today. Underline Emil's requests. Then choose the appropriate response to each request.

1. Raul, <u>would you please drive me to Cal's Computer Shop?</u> I have to bring my computer in.

    a. Yes, I would.   **(b.)** I'd be glad to.

2. Would you mind lending me five dollars? I'm getting paid tomorrow.

    a. Not at all.   **b.** Yes.

3. Raul, can you lend me your laptop for a minute? I have to email my teacher.

    a. Sorry, but I can't.   **b.** No, I can't.

4. Will you pick up some milk on the way home this afternoon?

    a. No, I won't.   **b.** I'm sorry, I can't. I'll be at work until 8:00.

5. Would you explain this text message from Kora? She uses weird abbreviations.

    a. I'd be glad to.   **b.** No, I wouldn't.

6. Could you text me Jana's address? I lost it.

    a. No, I couldn't.   **b.** Sorry, but I don't have it.

7. I'm in a real hurry. Will you help me do the dishes?

    a. Certainly.   **b.** Of course not.

8. Could you lock the door on your way out? My hands are full.

    a. Yes, I could.   **b.** Sure.

9. Kora, can you tell Ethan to come to the phone? It's important.

    a. No problem.   **b.** Not at all.

EXERCISE 2 REQUESTS

Ⓐ GRAMMAR NOTES 1, 3 Look at the pictures. What is each person thinking? Write the letter of the correct thought from the box.

a. Repair the copier.	d. File these reports.	g. Buy some cereal.
b. Call back later.	e. Shut the door.	h. Wait for a few minutes.
c. Get that book.	f. Close the window.	i. Wash your cups and dishes.

1. _d_

2. ____

3. ____

4. ____

5. ____

6. ____

7. ____

8. ____

9. ____

B What are the people in the pictures in A going to say? Complete their requests. Use the words in parentheses and the information from the pictures.

1. _____*Could you file these reports, please?*_____ I've finished reading them.
   (could)

2. _____ I can't think with all that noise in the hall.
   (would)

3. _____ on the way home? We don't have any left.
   (will)

4. _____ It's freezing in here.
   (can)

5. _____ Mr. Rivera is still in a meeting.
   (would you mind)

6. _____ It's getting messy in here.
   (would you mind)

7. _____ I have to leave for a meeting now.
   (could)

8. _____ I can't reach it.
   (can)

9. _____ I need to make copies right away.
   (could)

EXERCISE 3 REQUESTS AND ANSWERS

GRAMMAR NOTES 1–3   Write polite requests. Use *can, could, will, would,* or *would you mind* and the correct form of the words in parentheses. Write appropriate answers. There can be more than one correct answer.

1. MAN: _____*Would you mind lending me your phone*_____? The battery in mine is dead.
   a. (lend me your phone)

   WOMAN: _____*No problem*_____. But I'm in a hurry.
   b.

   _____?
   c. (please / keep your conversation short)

   MAN: _____. I just need to text my friend.
   d.

2. STUDENT: Excuse me, Professor Ruiz. _____?
   a. (explain reflexive pronouns)

   I don't understand them.

   PROFESSOR: _____ right now. I'm expecting a call.
   b.

   _____?
   c. (come back in 20 minutes)

3. WOMAN: _____? It's blocking my driveway.
   a. (move your car)

   MAN: _____. I'll do it right away. I'm really
   b.

   sorry. I didn't notice.

4. MANAGER: _____? Our sales people need it for their
   a. (please / distribute this report)

   meeting this afternoon.

   ASSISTANT: _____. I can't leave my desk right now.
   b.

   But I can ask Tania to do it.

EXERCISE 4 COULD YOU, WOULD YOU (MIND), WILL YOU, CAN YOU

 PRONUNCIATION NOTE Listen to the short informal conversations. What do you hear? Complete the requests with *could you*, *would you (mind)*, *will you*, and *can you*.

1. _____Could you_____ lend me some money?

2. _____ call me when you get home?

3. _____ turning the TV down?

4. _____ explain the meaning of this word to me?

5. _____ give me a ride home?

6. _____ help me carry these books?

EXERCISE 5 EDITING

GRAMMAR NOTES 1–3 Read Marta's response to an email from her boss. (Her answers are in red.) There are eight mistakes in making and responding to requests. The first mistake is already corrected. Find and correct seven more.

Date: 04-11-16 12:14:39 EST
From: MartaCampos@dataline.com
To: JohnSanchez@dataline.com
CC: AnnChen@dataline.com
Subject: sales meeting—Reply

>>><JohnSanchez@dataline.com>   04/11/16 10:37 am>>>

The meetings are going well, but they are going to go on an extra day. Could you
                            please call
~~call please~~ Doug Rogers to try to reschedule our sales meeting?

Not at all. I'll do it right away.

We'll need three extra copies of the monthly sales report. Would you ask Ann to take

care of that?

Yes, I would. (Ann—could you do this?)

I won't have time to return Emma Lopes's call this week. Would you mind to call her and

telling her I'll call her back next week?

No problem. Could you email me her phone number?

I hate to ask, but will you mind working on Saturday? We'll need the extra time to go

over the new information I've gotten.

Sorry, but I couldn't. My in-laws are coming for a visit. But Rob Lin says he can come into the office to help out.

One last thing. I was going to pick up those new business cards, but I won't be back in time. Would you mind asking the printer to deliver them to the office? I'd really appreciate that.

Yes, I would. I'll call and ask him to do it right away.

And this will cheer you up—it looks like our office will receive the award for Communication Excellence this year.

Great! Can I told everyone, or is it a secret?

STEP 4 COMMUNICATION PRACTICE

EXERCISE 6 LISTENING

▶15|04 **A** Marta Campos has planned a busy weekend. Read the list. Then listen to the conversations. Listen again and check (✓) the things that belong on her schedule.

- ☐ **1.** drive Kevin to the library Saturday morning
- ☑ **2.** take Diana to the dentist
- ☐ **3.** take the kids to the library in the afternoon
- ☐ **4.** babysit for Amanda's daughter
- ☐ **5.** go to Amanda's party
- ☐ **6.** go to the movies
- ☐ **7.** walk Mom's dog
- ☐ **8.** pick up the car at the garage
- ☐ **9.** go to the gym with John

▶15|04 **B** Work with a partner. Listen again to the conversations. Discuss your answers in A. Why did or why didn't you check each item?

EXAMPLE: A: I didn't check item 1.
B: Right. Kevin asked his mother to drive him, but she answered, "Sorry, I can't."
A: She's taking Diana to the dentist.

EXERCISE 7 WHAT ABOUT YOU?

A CONVERSATION Before you talk about your plans for the weekend, fill out your schedule.

YOUR DAILY PLANNER
SATURDAY

Morning _____

_____

_____

Afternoon _____

_____

_____

Evening _____

_____

_____

YOUR DAILY PLANNER
SUNDAY

Morning _____

_____

_____

Afternoon _____

_____

_____

Evening _____

_____

_____

B Work in a group. Talk about your weekend plans. Ask group members to help you with some of the things on your schedule.

EXAMPLE: A: Ali, what are you doing Saturday afternoon?

B: I want to go to the mall, but my car broke down. Could you give me a ride?

C: Sure, I'd be glad to . . .

EXERCISE 8 COULD YOU . . . ?

ROLE PLAY Work with a partner. Look at the pictures in Exercise 2. Role-play each situation. Take turns making and responding to requests. Use your imagination.

EXAMPLE: A: Could you please file these reports for me?

B: Sure. I'll be glad to in just a minute. I need to file this one first before I lose it.

A: OK. Thanks.

FROM GRAMMAR TO WRITING

A BEFORE YOU WRITE Read the three situations below. Work with a partner. Brainstorm several requests for each situation.

1. Your roommate is going away for the weekend. Your sister from out of town will be visiting you. What can you ask your roommate?

2. You work at a restaurant on Mondays, Wednesdays, and Fridays. You have to go to the dentist, but the dentist can only see you on Wednesday. What can you ask a coworker?

3. You're in school. You have to leave class early in order to help your parents. What can you ask a classmate?

B WRITE For each situation, write a text or email message making one or more requests. Use ideas from your brainstorming sessions. Then exchange messages with a partner. Write responses to your partner's requests. Try to avoid the common mistakes in the chart.

EXAMPLE:

Hi Viktor. My sister is visiting tomorrow. Could you please lend her your bike for a ride in the park? Thanks. —Kunio	Hi Kunio. I'm really sorry, but I can't. My bike broke down this week. You can rent a bike in the park, though. —Viktor

Common Mistakes Using *Can, Could, Will, Would,* and *Would you mind* for Requests

Use the **base form** of the verb after *can, could, will,* or *would*. Do not use the gerund.	**Will** you **make** copies for me? **NOT** Will you ~~making~~ copies for me?
Put *please* **before the base form** of the verb or at the **end of the sentence**. Do not put *please* after the base form.	Could you ***please* send** me an email? Could you **send** me an email ***please***? **NOT** Could you ~~send please~~ me an email?
Use the **gerund** (verb + *-ing*) after *would you mind*. Do not use the base form of the verb.	Would you mind **texting** me? **NOT** Would you mind ~~text~~ me?

C CHECK YOUR WORK Read your six messages. Underline all the modals and expressions for requests. Circle *please*. Use the Editing Checklist to check your work.

Editing Checklist

Did you use...?

☐ the base form of the verb after *can, could, will,* or *would*

☐ the gerund after *would you mind...*

☐ *please* correctly

☐ an apology and explanation in a negative answer to a request

D REVISE YOUR WORK Read your messages again. Can you improve your writing? Make changes if necessary.

UNIT 15 REVIEW

Test yourself on the grammar of the unit.

Ⓐ Circle the correct words to complete the conversations.

1. A: Would you mind <u>to turn / turning</u> off the TV? I'm trying to read.
                                   _{a.}

    B: <u>Yes, I would. / I'm sorry, I can't.</u> I need to watch the news for a homework assignment.
                               _{b.}

2. A: Will you <u>please text / text please</u> me when you get home?
                          _{a.}

    B: <u>Not at all. / No problem.</u> I'll probably be home by nine.
                       _{b.}

3. A: Could you <u>picked / pick</u> up some dessert on the way home?
                          _{a.}

    B: <u>I'd be glad to. / Yes, I could.</u> How about ice cream?
                     _{b.}

Ⓑ Read the statements in parentheses. Then complete the questions to make requests.

1. Would you mind _____?
                           (Please lend me five dollars.)

2. Could _____?
                   (I'd like you to drive me to school.)

3. Will _____?
                   (Please explain this sentence to me.)

4. Can _____?
                 (I'd like you to carry this suitcase for me.)

5. Would _____?
                   (Please distribute the report.)

6. Would you mind _____?
                   (I'd like you to walk the dog tonight.)

Ⓒ Find and correct eight mistakes.

1. JASON: Hi, Tessa. It's Jason. Could you taking some photos of the game today?

    TESSA: Sorry, Jason, but I couldn't. My camera is broken. Maybe Jeri can help.

2. JASON: Hi, Jeri. Would you came to the game today? I need someone to take photos.

    JERI: Jason, can you mind calling me back in a few minutes? I'm busy right now.

    JASON: Sorry, Jeri, I can't, but I'll email you. Would you give me please your email address?

    JERI: Not at all. It's Rainbows@local.net.

3. JERI: Hi, Jason, it's Jeri. I'm sending you those photos. You could call me when you get them?

    JASON: Thanks, Jeri. The photos are great. Now, will teach me how to put them on Facebook?

Now check your answers on page 478.

Advice: *Should, Ought to, Had better*
INTERNET RULES

OUTCOMES
- Give and ask for advice
- Identify main points in a short text about rules and advice
- Recognize statements of advice in a radio show
- Discuss possible solutions to everyday situations, giving reasons and explanations
- Write an email or letter of complaint, giving advice on making improvements

STEP 1   GRAMMAR IN CONTEXT

BEFORE YOU READ

How do you communicate with people on the Internet? Discuss the questions.

1. Is it important to be polite on the Internet? Why or why not?

2. Do you behave differently online than face-to-face with people?

3. What are some rules you follow?

READ

16|01   Read this article about being polite on the Internet. If you don't understand a cyber[1] word, look up its meaning on the next page.

Netiquette 101

Email, bulletin boards, and chat rooms open up a new world of communication—and sometimes misunderstanding. To avoid problems, you should know these simple rules of netiquette:

- When should you post to a bulletin board or chat room? Newbies shouldn't jump in right away—they really ought to lurk a little first. Look through old messages for answers to common questions. Many websites also have FAQs for basic information. After that, post when you have something new to say. You should keep your post short and simple.

- Should you use capital letters to make a strong statement? NO! A MESSAGE ALL IN CAPITAL LETTERS SEEMS LIKE SHOUTING. You should follow the normal rules for capital (big) and lowercase (small) letters.

- Did someone make you angry? Wait a minute! You'd better not reply right away. Count to 10 first. Don't flame another board or chat room member. You should never forget that people on the Internet are real people with real feelings.

- Emoticons can help avoid misunderstandings. You should learn how to use them to show your feelings.

- Internet safety is part of netiquette. When you post to a bulletin board or a chat room, you should always protect your identity by using a screen name. Never give your real name or other personal information.

Practice these five rules of netiquette, and most of your emoticons will be smileys!

---

1 *cyber:* about computers or the Internet

Cyber Words

bulletin board an Internet site where members can post ideas about a special interest

chat room a site for online conversations in "real" time

emoticon a picture of a feeling, for example: 😟 😠 😁 😟 😴

FAQs Frequently Asked Questions

flame to send insulting messages to someone

lurk to read messages on a bulletin board but not post any messages

netiquette Internet etiquette (rules for polite behavior)

newbie (or newb) someone new to an Internet site

post to send messages to a bulletin board or chat room

AFTER YOU READ

Ⓐ VOCABULARY Complete the sentences with the words from the box.

avoid	behavior	communication	identity	normal	protect

1. Never give your real _____ in a chat room. Always use a screen name.

2. It's _____ for newbies to lurk on a site before they post. Many people do that.

3. _____ websites where members flame other members.

4. Emoticons improve your online _____. They show your feelings.

5. People's _____ in chat rooms is often different from how they act in real life.

6. _____ yourself on the Internet. Never tell anyone your passwords.

Ⓑ COMPREHENSION Read the statements. Check (✓) *OK* or *Not OK*.

	OK	Not OK
1. Read some messages before you post.	☐	☐
2. Reply immediately when you're angry.	☐	☐
3. Use all capital letters in your posts.	☐	☐
4. Use emoticons to show feelings.	☐	☐
5. Use your real name in chat rooms.	☐	☐
6. Write long, complicated messages.	☐	☐
7. Think about people's feelings when you post a message.	☐	☐

Ⓒ DISCUSSION Work with a partner. Compare your answers in B. Why did you check *OK* or *Not OK*?

ADVICE: *SHOULD, OUGHT TO, HAD BETTER*

Statements

Subject	Should/Ought to/ Had better*	Base Form of Verb
I You He She We You They	**should** (not) **ought to** **had better** (not)	**reply**.

Contractions

should not	=	**shouldn't**
had better	=	**'d better**

* *Should* and *ought to* are modals. *Had better* is similar to a modal.
   These forms do not have *-s* in the third-person singular.

Yes/No Questions

Should	Subject	Base Form of Verb
Should	I he she we they	**reply**?

Short Answers

Affirmative			Negative		
Yes,	you he she you they	**should.**	**No,**	you he she you they	**shouldn't**.

Wh- Questions

Wh- Word	Should	Subject	Base Form of Verb	
How When Where	**should**	I he she we they	**send**	it?

GRAMMAR NOTES

1 Should and Ought to

Use the modals *should* and *ought to* to say that something is **advisable** (a good idea).

• *should*	Derek **should answer** that email.
• *ought to*	You **ought to send** Mia a copy, too.

USAGE NOTE *Should* is much more **common** than *ought to* in conversation.	You **should check out** this website!
IN WRITING *Should* is common in both informal and formal writing.	You **should post** some of your vacation photos. *(email)* Internet users **should be** aware of proper Internet etiquette. *(newspaper)*
USAGE NOTE We often soften advice with *maybe*, *perhaps*, or *I think*.	Ryan, **maybe** you **should spend** less time on the Internet.

2 Had better

Use the expression *had better* for **strong advice**—when you believe that something bad will happen if the person does not follow the advice.

• *had better*	Kids, you**'d better get** offline now or you won't have time for your homework.

USAGE NOTE We mostly use the expression *had better* in **conversation**, and we usually use the contraction *'d better*. The full form *had better* is very formal.	You**'d better** choose a screen name. *(common)* You **had better** choose a screen name. *(rare)*
Had better always refers to the **present** or the **future**. It never refers to the past (even though it uses the word *had*).	You**'d better call** them *now*. They're waiting. You**'d better post** that *tomorrow* or it'll be late.

3 Negative Statements

Use *should not* and *had better not* in negative statements.

The negative of *should* is *should not* or *shouldn't*.	You **shouldn't post** right away.
The negative of *had better* is *had better not* or *'d better not*. Notice the word order.	You**'d better not use** your real name. NOT You'd not better use your real name.
USAGE NOTE We do not usually use the negative of *ought to* in American English. We use *shouldn't* instead.	We **shouldn't** post long messages. We **ought not to** post long messages. *(rare)*

Use *should* for questions. We do not usually use *ought to* or *had better* for questions.	
• *should*	When **should** I **sign on**?
Use *should* to ask for advice.	A: **Should** I **join** this chat room?
USAGE NOTE You can use *should* in **short answers**, but we often use other **expressions**.	B: Yes, you **should**. It's fun. C: *Sure. Why not?* D: *Not really.* It's a waste of time.

PRONUNCIATION NOTE

▶16|02 **Pronunciation of *Ought to* and *Had better***

In **informal conversation**, we often pronounce *ought to* "oughta." Notice that the "t" in "oughta" sounds like a quick "d."	A: I **ought to get** a new computer. *(I oughta get)*
For *had better*, we usually pronounce *had* as the contraction *'d*, and sometimes we leave out *had* and just say "better."	B: You **had better get** a flash drive, too. *(You'd better get* or *You better get)*

REFERENCE NOTES

For general information on **modals**, see Unit 13, Grammar Notes 1–2, on page 177.
For a list of **modals and their functions**, see Appendix 19 on page 460.

∨

EXERCISE 1 DISCOVER THE GRAMMAR

A GRAMMAR NOTES 1–4 Read these posts to an online bulletin board for high school students. Underline the words that give or ask for advice.

Subject: HELP!

From: Hothead

MY BRAIN IS EXPLODING!!! SAVE ME!! <u>What should I do?</u> I'm taking all honors courses this year, and I'm on the debate team, in the school congress, and on the soccer team. OH! And, I'd better not forget piano lessons! I'm so busy I shouldn't even be online now. 😞

From: Tweety

First of all, you should stop shouting. You'll feel better. Then you really ought to ask yourself, "Why am I doing all this?" Is it for you, or are you trying to please somebody else?

From: Loki

Tweety's right, Hothead. Do you really want to do all that stuff? No? You'd better not do it then. You'll burn out before you graduate. 🙂

From: gud4me

You're such a loser. You should get a life. I mean a NORMAL life. Do you have any friends? Do you ever just sit around and do nothing?

From: Tweety

Hey, gud4me, no flaming allowed! That's bad cyber behavior. We really shouldn't fight—it never helps communication. 😊

B Check all the advice from the posts in A.

☐ **1.** Take all honors courses.

☑ **2.** Stop shouting.

☐ **3.** Feel better.

☐ **4.** Don't do things you don't want to do.

☐ **5.** Get a life.

☐ **6.** Don't fight.

EXERCISE 2 STATEMENTS WITH *SHOULD*, *OUGHT TO*, AND *HAD BETTER*

GRAMMAR NOTES 1–3 Read these posts to a chat room about learning English. Complete the posts. Use the correct form (affirmative or negative) of the words in parentheses. Use contractions when possible.

CURLY: I think I _____*should watch*_____ more movies to improve my English. Any ideas?
1. (should / watch)

USEDIT: I loved *The Uninvited*. But you _____ it if you don't like scary films.
2. (had better / rent)

AGURL: That's right. And you _____ the remote in your hand. That way you
3. (had better / keep)

can fast-forward through the scary parts.

592XY: I think you _____ *Groundhog Day*. The same thing happens again and
4. (ought to / see)

again. It's an old movie, but it's great listening practice—and it's funny!

PATI: You _____ the English subtitles. They really help.
5. (should / turn on)

USEDIT: But you _____ the subtitles right away. At first, you really
6. (should / use)

_____ a few times. That's what rewind buttons are for!
7. (should / listen)

592XY: Good advice. And you really _____ a plot summary before you
8. (ought to / read)

watch. You can find one online. It's so much easier when you know the story.

AGURL: Curly, you're a math major, right? Then you really _____ my favorite
9. (ought to / watch)

movie, *The Da Vinci Code*. It's about solving a mystery with math clues.

CURLY: Thanks, guys. Those are great ideas. But you _____ me any more
10. (had better / give)

advice, or I'll never work on my other courses!

EXERCISE 3 STATEMENTS WITH *SHOULD*, *OUGHT TO*, AND *HAD BETTER*

GRAMMAR NOTES 1–3 Rewrite the Internet safety tips in parentheses. Use *should*, *ought to*, or *had better*. Choose between affirmative and negative.

> The Internet is a wonderful place to visit and hang out.
> Here are some tips to make your trip there a safe one!

1. **I often use my real name online. Is that a problem?**

   Yes! *You should always use a screen name.*
   (Always use a screen name.)

   Protect your identity!

2. **Someone in my chat group just asked for my address.**

   _____
   (Don't give out any personal information.)

   People can use it to steal your identity and your money.

3. **My brother wants my password to check out a group before joining.**

_____
(Don't give it to anyone.)

Not even your brother! He might share it, and then people can steal your information.

4. **I sent a file to someone, and she told me it had a virus.**

_____
(Get virus protection and use it.)

A virus can hurt your computer and destroy important files (and other people's too).

5. **I update my virus protection every month. Is that really necessary?**

Yes! _____
(Always keep your virus protection up-to-date.)

Program it to update automatically. Remember: *Old* virus protection is *no* virus protection!

6. **I got an email about a home-based business. I could make $15,000 a month.**

_____
(Don't believe any "get rich quick" offers.)

They sound good, but people almost always lose money.

7. **I got an interesting email. I don't know who sent it, but it's got a file attached.**

_____
(Don't open any email attachments from strangers.)

They could contain dangerous viruses.

8. **The Internet sounds too dangerous for me!**

Not really. _____ ,
(Be careful!)

but enjoy yourself—it's an exciting world out there!

EXERCISE 4 QUESTIONS AND SHORT ANSWERS WITH *SHOULD*

GRAMMAR NOTE 4 **Complete these posts to an online bulletin board. Use the words from the box to complete the questions. Give short answers.**

buy one online	forward the email	~~try to repair it~~
check the spelling	say to make them stop	use emoticons
flame him	start posting	use my birthday

1. Q: My computer is seven years old and has problems. _____*Should I try to repair it*_____?

   A: _____*No, you shouldn't*_____. That's very old for a computer! Buy a new one!

2. Q: I just joined an online discussion group. When _____? Right away?

   A: You should really just read for a while. It's always a good idea to "lurk" before you post.

3. Q: I just received a warning about a computer virus. The email says to tell everyone I know

   about it. _____?

   A: _____. These warnings are almost always false.

4. Q: I hate to go shopping, but I really need a jacket. _____?

   A: _____. It's safe. Just buy from a company you know.

5. Q: I type fast and make spelling mistakes. Is that bad? _____?

A: _____. Use a spell checker! Mistakes are bad netiquette!

6. Q: My friends email me a lot of jokes. I don't want to hurt their feelings, but I *really* don't want to keep getting these jokes. What _____?

A: You should be honest and say you are too busy to read them. These jokes can waste an awful lot of time!

7. Q: I always forget my password. _____ so I don't forget?

A: _____. It's too easy to guess. Protect your identity.

8. Q: A newb on our board is asking dumb questions. _____?

A: _____! Your behavior should be as polite online as offline.

9. Q: _____ in emails? Those smileys are awfully cute.

A: Sure, go ahead. They're fun. But don't use them in business emails.

EXERCISE 5 *OUGHT TO* OR *OUGHTA*; *HAD BETTER* OR *BETTER*

▶16|03 PRONUNCIATION NOTE Listen to the sentences. Check (✓) *More Formal* if you hear *ought to* or *had better*. Check (✓) *Less Formal* if you hear "oughta" or "better."

	More Formal	Less Formal
1. Do you think I ought to buy a new computer?	☐	☑
2. I think you had better get good virus protection.	☐	☐
3. Maybe you ought to get a tablet.	☐	☐
4. You had better read some reviews.	☐	☐
5. Do you think I ought to wait until next month?	☐	☐
6. I really think you had better get one now.	☐	☐

EXERCISE 6 EDITING

GRAMMAR NOTES 1–4 Read these posts to a bulletin board for international students in the United States. There are twelve mistakes in the use of *should*, *ought to*, and *had better*. The first mistake is already corrected. Find and correct eleven more.

Justme | My friend asked me to dinner, and she told me I should ~~to bring~~ *bring* some food! What kind of an invitation is that? What I should bring to this strange dinner party?

Sasha | LOL![1] The invitation is totally normal. Your friend is having a potluck—a dinner party where everybody brings something. It's really a lot of fun. You know, you really ought bring a dish from your country. People will enjoy that.

Toby | HELP! My first day of class, and I lost my wallet! What ought I do first? My student ID, credit card, and cash are all gone.

R2D2 | First of all, you'd not better panic because you need to be calm so you can speak clearly. You should to call your credit card company right away. Did you lose your wallet at school? Then you ought to going to the Lost and Found Department at your school.

Smiley | What should an international student does to make friends? At my college, people always smile and say, "Hi, how are you?" but they don't wait for an answer!

4gud | New students should joining some clubs and international student organizations. They also ought to find a student in each class to study with and ask about homework assignments.

Newguy | Hi. I'm new to this board. I'm from Vietnam, and I'm going to school in Canada next year. How should I will get ready?

Smiley | Welcome Newguy! I'm at school in Montreal, and you won't believe how cold it gets here. You're better bring a lot of warm clothes!

Sasha | You ought check the school's website. They might have a Vietnam Students Association. If they do, you should email the association with your questions. Good luck!

---

1 *LOL:* abbreviation for *Laughing out Loud*

EXERCISE 7 LISTENING

16|04 **A** A radio show host, Tim Tommando, is giving advice to callers about buying a new computer. Listen to the show. Then read the advice in the list. Listen again and check (✓) the statements that agree with the host's advice.

- ☐ **1.** Repair a seven-year-old computer.
- ☑ **2.** Read online computer reviews.
- ☐ **3.** Throw away your old computer.
- ☐ **4.** Always buy the cheapest computer.
- ☐ **5.** Order a computer from a big online company.
- ☐ **6.** Shop at a local computer store.
- ☐ **7.** Consider a service contract.
- ☐ **8.** Get the most memory you can afford.

16|04 **B** Listen to the show again. Work with a partner. First, compare your answers in A. Then, discuss Tim's advice. Do you agree with the advice?

EXAMPLE: A: Tim says you shouldn't repair a seven-year-old computer.

B: I agree. You shouldn't repair an old computer. You should buy a new one even if your old one is still working. You should always have the newest technology.

A: I don't agree. I think you should keep using your computer as long as it lasts.

EXERCISE 8 WHAT SHOULD I DO?

PROBLEM SOLVING Work in a group. Each group member chooses a problem to ask the group about. Group members discuss the problem and give advice.

1. I was studying for exams, and I forgot my girlfriend's birthday. She's really angry at me. What should I do?

EXAMPLE: A: You'd better send flowers and take her to a nice restaurant.

B: I think you should apologize and tell her you were really busy.

C: Yes, but you'd better not just send her an email or text. Call her!

D: And in the future, you really should use one of those online apps that remind you about important events. You'll never forget again.

PART 5

OUTCOMES

- Use proper, common, count, and non-count nouns
- Describe quantities and use quantifiers with nouns
- Identify the main points in a text on a scientific topic
- Identify details in a conversation about a day-to-day topic
- Discuss quotes and proverbs
- Write a note or letter that lists and describes quantities of items

OUTCOMES

- Use indefinite and definite articles to describe nouns
- Identify main ideas in a story
- Identify important details in a conversation
- Summarize and give opinions on the moral of a fable
- Write a paragraph about a personal experience that illustrates the meaning of a moral

Nouns and Quantifiers

TIME CAPSULES

OUTCOMES
• Use proper, common, count, and non-count nouns
• Describe quantities and use quantifiers with nouns
• Identify the main points in a text on a scientific topic
• Identify details in a conversation about a day-to-day topic
• Discuss quotes and proverbs
• Write a note or letter that lists and describes quantities of items

---

STEP 1   GRAMMAR IN CONTEXT

BEFORE YOU READ

Look at the photos and at the title of the article. Discuss the questions.

1. What items are in the time capsule?
2. Why is the article called "Time in a Bottle"?

READ

 Read this article about time capsules.

The Westinghouse Time Capsule at the 1939 New York World's Fair

Time in a Bottle

A baseball, a light bulb, a child's doll, a camera, and an electric shaver. Some money (a dollar bill and a few coins). Seeds (such as rice and corn). The Bible, a written message from Albert Einstein, and hundreds of books and newspapers on microfilm.[1]

What do these items have in common? They all went into a capsule 50 feet (15 meters) underground in Flushing Meadows Park, in New York City. The year was 1939; the occasion was the New York World's Fair; and the instructions were not to open the capsule for 5,000 years!

The Westinghouse Time Capsule is just one of many capsules all over the world. They hold hundreds of everyday objects, but they have just one purpose: to tell people of the future about life in the past. To help make this happen, Westinghouse published a book, printed on special paper with ink that will not fade[2] over time. The book tells how to find and open the capsule. It even explains how to interpret the capsule's English, which will be very different from languages 5,000 years from now!

The Westinghouse Time Capsule is an example of an intentional time capsule, but history has given us unintentional time capsules, too. The most famous is the ancient Roman city of Pompeii, in Italy. In the year 79, Vesuvius, a nearby volcano,

---

1 *microfilm:* a special type of film used for making very small photos of important papers
2 *fade:* lose color

erupted.[3] It buried the city under 60 feet (18 meters) of ash and created an instant time capsule. Archaeologists[4] are still studying it today.

Intentional or unintentional, time capsules give us the chance to "communicate" with people from other times. What will people think of us when they open the Westinghouse Time Capsule in 5,000 years? Will they be as impressed with our civilization as we are with ancient Pompeii? Only time will tell—although we certainly won't be there to find out!

---

3 *erupted:* exploded and sent out smoke, fire, and rocks into the sky
4 *archaeologists:* people who study ancient cultures by examining their buildings and objects

Replica of the Westinghouse Time Capsule

AFTER YOU READ

A VOCABULARY Choose the word or phrase that best completes each sentence.

1. A _____ is an example of an **occasion**.
   a. time capsule   **b.** location   **c.** party

2. The **purpose** of the party was a _____ .
   a. cake   **b.** present   **c.** birthday celebration

3. Emily was **impressed**. She thought the time capsule was _____ .
   a. depressing   **b.** great   **c.** terrible

4. If an action was **intentional**, you _____ to do it.
   a. planned   **b.** forgot   **c.** didn't want

5. I really couldn't **interpret** Einstein's message. What was the _____ ?
   a. reason   **b.** language   **c.** meaning

6. _____ is an example of an ancient **civilization**.
   a. Flushing Meadows Park   **b.** Pompeii   **c.** Westinghouse

B COMPREHENSION Read the statements. Check (✓) *True* or *False*.

	True	False
1. Time capsules contain unusual items.	☐	☐
2. There are time capsules all over the world.	☐	☐
3. The Westinghouse Time Capsule is in Italy.	☐	☐
4. The ancient city of Pompeii is an unintentional time capsule.	☐	☐
5. Time capsules teach us about different civilizations.	☐	☐
6. People will soon be able to see the contents of the Westinghouse Time Capsule.	☐	☐

C DISCUSSION Work with a partner. Compare your answers in B. Why did you check *True* or *False*?

NOUNS AND QUANTIFIERS

Count Nouns			
	Noun	Verb	
One	**capsule**	is	in New York.
Two	**capsules**	are	

Non-Count Nouns		
Noun	Verb	
Money	is	inside.

Quantifiers and Count Nouns		
	Quantifier	Noun
It holds	some enough a lot of a few several (a great) many	coins.
It doesn't hold	any enough	coins.
Does it hold	a lot of many	coins?

Quantifiers and Non-Count Nouns		
	Quantifier	Noun
It holds	some enough a lot of a little a great deal of	money.
It doesn't hold	any enough	money.
Does it hold	a lot of much	money?

GRAMMAR NOTES

1 Proper Nouns and Common Nouns

Proper nouns are the **names** of particular people, places, or things.	
• **people:** *Albert Einstein, Columbus, Emily*	**Albert Einstein** was a famous scientist.
• **places:** *New York, Germany, Europe, Vesuvius*	He was born in **Germany**.
• **things:** *Coca Cola, the Statue of Liberty*	We visited **the Statue of Liberty**.
Proper nouns are usually **singular**.	**Pompeii** *is* an amazing place.
IN WRITING **Capitalize** the **first letter** of each word in a proper noun.	**Westinghouse** built a time capsule. It's in **New York City**.
Common nouns refer to people, places, and things, but not by their names.	
• **people:** *scientist, teacher, explorer*	Albert Einstein was a famous **scientist**.
• **places:** *city, country, continent, volcano*	He left his **country** in 1933.
• **things:** *soda, monument, magazine, wool*	The Statue of Liberty is a popular **monument**.
Common nouns can be **singular or plural**.	The time **capsule** *is* in New York. How many time **capsules** *are* there?
IN WRITING Do **not capitalize** the **first letter** of a common noun.	Einstein was a **scientist**. NOT Einstein was a ~~Scientist~~.

2 Count Nouns and Non-Count Nouns

Common nouns can be **count nouns** or **non-count nouns**.

Count nouns refer to people, places, or things that you **can count separately**: *one book, two books, three books . . .* • **people:** *one teacher, twenty students* • **places:** *one country, five cities* • **things:** *one bookcase, a hundred books*	Mr. Lee is my favorite **teacher**. He's lived in three different **countries**. He reads more than fifty **books** a year.
Count nouns can be **singular** or **plural**. They take **singular** or **plural verbs**. You can use *a*, *an*, or *the* before singular count nouns. You can use *the* before both singular and plural nouns.	He read one **book**. She read two **books**. The **book** *is* new, but the **newspapers** *are* old. There's *a* **doll** and *an* **electric shaver** in *the* **box**. *The* **box** contains *the* **objects** I described.
Non-count nouns refer to things that you **cannot count separately**. For example, you can say *rice*, but you cannot say ~~one rice~~ or ~~two rices~~. Here are some categories of non-count nouns: • **abstract words:** *education, love, time* • **activities:** *exploring, farming, sailing* • **courses of study:** *art, history, math* • **foods:** *corn, milk, rice* • **fabrics:** *cotton, silk, wool*	**Education** is very important. **Farming** is a difficult occupation. **Math** was my favorite subject in school. They grow **rice**, but they don't grow **corn**. That sweater is made of **cotton**.
Some **common non-count nouns** do not fit into categories: *equipment, furniture, homework, information, news, work*.	Today's **homework** was very easy. The **information** in this article is interesting. The **news** is on TV now. Let's watch it.
Most non-count nouns have **no plural forms**. They take **singular verbs** and **pronouns**.	She bought a lot of **rice**. NOT She bought a lot of ~~rices~~. **Archaeology** *is* an interesting subject. *It was* his favorite subject.

3 Quantifiers

Quantifiers are **words** or **phrases** such as *some* or *a few* that **show quantity**. Use quantifiers with nouns to express *how many* or *how much*.

Some quantifiers go only with **count nouns**.	*Many* **people** worked on the capsule. *(count)*
Other quantifiers go only with **non-count nouns**.	They did *a great deal of* **work**. *(non-count)*
A few quantifiers can go with both **count** and **non-count nouns**.	It took *a lot of* **people** to finish. *(count)* It took *a lot of* **time**. *(non-count)*

4 Quantifiers in Affirmative Statements

In **affirmative statements**, use these quantifiers:

- *many*, *a lot of*, *a great many*, and *a great deal of* for a large quantity

- *some* and *several* for a moderate quantity (not very large, not very small)

- *enough* for a necessary quantity

- *a few/few* and *a little/little* for a small quantity

PLURAL COUNT NOUNS	NON-COUNT NOUNS
many/a lot of coins	*a lot of* money
a great many jobs	*a great deal of* work
some socks	*some* wool
several books	*some* paper
enough apples	*enough* rice
a few years	*a little* time

BE CAREFUL! The meaning of *a few* and *a little* is different from *few* and *little*. *A few* and *a little* mean *some*.

Few means *not many*. *Little* means *not much*. *Few* and *little* often mean *not enough* or *less than expected*.

We had ***a little* time** to complete the project.
(We had some time, but not a lot.)

We had ***little* time** to complete the project.
(We almost didn't have enough time.)

USAGE NOTE Sometimes people use *much* instead of *a lot of* in affirmative sentences. This is very formal and not common.

They spent ***a lot of* money**. *(very common)*
They spent ***much* money**. *(not common)*

USAGE NOTE In **informal conversation**, we sometimes use *lots of* instead of *a lot of* with both **plural count nouns** and **non-count nouns**.

We have ***lots of* coins**.
We have ***lots of* time**.

IN WRITING You can use *a lot of* and *lots of* in **informal writing**.

However, people **do not use** these quantifiers in very **formal writing**.

The Westinghouse time capsule contains ***a lot of*** everyday objects. *(less formal)*

The Westinghouse time capsule contains ***many*** everyday objects. *(more formal)*

5 Quantifiers in Negative Statements and Questions

In **negative statements** and **questions**, use:

- *many*, *a lot of*, *any*, and *enough* with **count nouns**

There weren't ***many* students** in class.
Did you put ***any* seeds** in the capsule?
There weren't ***enough* books**.

- *much*, *a lot of*, *any*, and *enough* with **non-count nouns**

We didn't have ***much* time** to study.
Did you put ***any* rice** in the capsule?
There wasn't ***enough* paper**.

REFERENCE NOTES

For a list of **irregular plural nouns**, see Appendix 6 on page 456.

For a list of **non-count nouns**, see Appendix 7 on page 456.

For **categories of proper nouns**, see Appendix 8 on page 457.

For **spelling rules** for **regular plural nouns**, see Appendix 25 on page 463.

For **capitalization rules**, see Appendix 27 on page 465.

EXERCISE 1 DISCOVER THE GRAMMAR

Ⓐ GRAMMAR NOTES 1–5 Read this article about Pompeii. Underline the nouns. Circle the quantifiers.

Pompeii: A Window to Ancient History

Pompeii was a rich and lively city on the bay of Naples, south of Rome. Wealthy Romans came to spend the summer there in large and beautiful villas.[1] Then on August 24 in the year 79, Vesuvius erupted. The volcano buried the city under 60 feet (18 meters) of ash and killed thousands of people. It also destroyed (a great many) buildings. But not all of them. The ash preserved many houses, streets, theaters, statues, and a lot of beautiful art.

Pompeii's ruins stayed buried for almost 2,000 years. Then one day in 1748, a Spanish engineer discovered them. Since that time, archaeologists have dug up many everyday objects from this ancient civilization. Furniture, jewelry, money, and even a little food remain from that terrible day. Today, we can "see" the daily lives of people in the first century in a couch made of wood, beautiful bracelets and rings, and bowls and cups made of glass. Preserved fruit, vegetables, bread, eggs, and olives tell us meals then were not so different from meals now!

Today, Pompeii is "alive" again. Millions of tourists walk its streets each year. This amazing unintentional time capsule shows them what everyday life in ancient Rome was like. It is their window to ancient history.

1 *villas*: ancient Roman houses or farms with land surrounding them

Ⓑ Put nouns from the article into the correct columns. Choose only sixteen count nouns.

Proper Nouns	Common Nouns			
	Count Nouns		Non-Count Nouns	
1. _Pompeii_	1. _window_	9. _____	1. _history_	8. _____
2. _____	2. _____	10. _____	2. _____	9. _____
3. _____	3. _____	11. _____	3. _____	10. _____
4. _____	4. _____	12. _____	4. _____	11. _____
5. _____	5. _____	13. _____	5. _____	12. _____
6. _____	6. _____	14. _____	6. _____	13. _____
	7. _____	15. _____	7. _____	
	8. _____	16. _____		

EXERCISE 2 NOUN AND VERB AGREEMENT

GRAMMAR NOTE 2 Emily and James are planning a trip to Pompeii. They are checking a travel website for some tips on packing. Complete these tips. Use the correct form of the words in parentheses. See Appendix 7 on page 456 for help with non-count nouns.

Pompeii Packing Posts

On the road

Your _____*feet need*_____ your help! Good _____ a must! Remember your
1. (foot / need)   2. (shoe / be)

purpose here—you'll be walking for _____ to see the _____
3. (hour)   4. (ruin)

of this ancient civilization. And those _____ very, very old—almost 2,000
5. (street / be)

_____ old!
6. (year)

Hey, it's hot out there!

_____ essential. You can't buy it once you're inside, so don't forget to take
7. (water / be)

several _____ with you. The _____ very, very hot, so
8. (bottle)   9. (sun / be)

_____ very important, too. And don't forget your _____! Both
10. (sunblock / be)   11. (hat)

of these _____ protect you from the sun.
12. (thing / help)

Pompeii—it's picture perfect!

Pompeii is amazing, and you'll want to take lots of _____. So bring a
13. (picture)

camera and an extra memory card. Extra _____ important, too!
14. (battery / be)

What to wear

The right _____ a big difference. Pompeii often _____ cool at
15. (clothing / make)   16. (get)

night, so bring a sweater.

Tempus fugit

That's Latin for _____. Most _____ a whole day at Pompeii.
17. (time / fly)   18. (people / spend)

The _____ huge. Take a map, and take your time!
19. (ruin / be)

EXERCISE 3 QUANTIFIERS

Ⓐ GRAMMAR NOTES 3–5 Emily and James are now in Pompeii. Circle the correct words to complete their conversations.

1. EMILY: There were so (many) / much people at the ruins today. Was it some kind of special
   a.
   occasion or something?

   JAMES: I don't think so. I heard the guide say it's the most popular tourist attraction in Italy.

   EMILY: And I can understand why. I've never seen so much / many fascinating things.
   b.

2. EMILY: My feet hurt! We did a lot of / much walking today!
   a.

   JAMES: Tell me about it! But it sure was amazing.

   EMILY: How many / much pictures did you take?
   b.

   JAMES: I took a few / lots of pictures—over 200!
   c.

3. JAMES: It sure was hot. I'm glad we took some / any water with us. I really drank
   a.

   a lot / much.
   b.

   EMILY: Me too. And I used several / a great deal of sunblock. The sun was *really* strong.
   c.

   JAMES: Do we have some / any water left? I'm still thirsty.
   d.

4. EMILY: Are you hungry? I saw a little / a few nice-looking restaurants nearby.
   a.

   JAMES: OK. But we need to stop at an ATM first. We only have a little / a few money left.
   b.

   EMILY: That's not a problem. Very little / few restaurants don't accept credit cards these days.
   c.

5. JAMES: You know, we should spend some / any time in Naples. Our guidebook says they
   a.

   have a lot of / much art from Pompeii at the Archaeological Museum.
   b.

   EMILY: Do we have little / enough time to do that? Tomorrow is our last day.
   c.

   JAMES: True. But I think we can spend few / a few hours there. We don't need
   d.

   enough / much time to pack, do we?
   e.

   EMILY: No, but I haven't bought some / any souvenirs yet, and I feel like we're running out
   f.

   of time.

   JAMES: Don't worry. We can do some / a few shopping before dinner. How much / many
   g.   h.

   gifts do you need to buy?

   EMILY: Not much / many, I guess. Just some / any things for the family.
   i.   j.

6. EMILY: I'm impressed with our guidebook. It does a great job of interpreting the art.

JAMES: Yes. It has <u>a lot of / many</u> useful information. Maybe it can recommend a restaurant.

　　　　　　　　a.

EMILY: What do you feel like eating?

JAMES: I'd love <u>some / any</u> pasta. What about you?

　　　　　　　b.

EMILY: Sounds good. And <u>a little / a few</u> dessert would be nice, too. Maybe they have that

　　　　　　　　　　　c.

Roman apple cake.

17|02　**B** LISTEN AND CHECK　**Listen to the conversations and check your answers in A.**

EXERCISE 4　EDITING

GRAMMAR NOTES 1–5　**Read Emily's email to her family. There are fifteen mistakes in the use of nouns and quantifiers and in the use of verb and pronoun agreement. The first mistake is already corrected. Find and correct fourteen more.**

● ● ●

Hi Everyone!

　　　　　　　　　　　　　　　　　　a few
James and I got back from Pompeii ~~few~~ days ago. We bought a little souvenirs, which I'll mail to

you all very soon. We're still unpacking and looking over the many, many photograph (hundreds!)

we took of this amazing place. Our Guidebook calls pompeii a "time capsule," and I truly felt that

we were somehow communicating with this rich and vibrant cultures. There are never enough

times for everything on vacation, but that's especially true of Pompeii. Really, there are few places

in the world this amazing. You should all try to go. I was so impressed!

I plan to do a several blog posts and put up a lot photos to show you what I mean. Speaking of

time capsules, I was just in the attic putting away any suitcases, and I discovered a trunk with

much old stuff. The old clothing were still in great shape—I might wear some of the skirts and

blouses. Oh, and I found a great deal of letters that Grandpa wrote to grandma when he was

working in Italy on an archaeological dig. A few of them made me cry, and one of them had a

recipe for Roman apple cake! I think we'll try to make it, and we'll let you know how it turns out.

Love,
Emily

EXERCISE 5 LISTENING

▶17|03 **Ⓐ** Emily and James are discussing a recipe for Roman apple cake. Look at the list of ingredients. Then listen to the first part of their conversation. Listen again and complete the list of ingredients.

Roman Apple Cake
Ingredients

1 ½ cups _sugar_____

½ cup vegetable _____

2 _____

2 _____ flour

1 teaspoon baking powder

1 _____ baking soda

¼ teaspoon _____

½ teaspoon cinnamon

1 cup _____

½ cup _____

½ cup _____

3 _____

Shopping List

eggs

▶17|04 **Ⓑ** Work with a partner. Listen to the rest of the conversation between Emily and James. Listen again and discuss what they have enough of and what they need to buy. Together, complete the shopping list above.

EXAMPLE: A: OK. The first ingredient is sugar. Do they have enough sugar?
   B: Yes. They have a lot of sugar. We don't need to put it on the shopping list.
   A: Good. What about vegetable oil?
   B: They don't have much. But they have enough.
   A: But they need eggs. They don't have any eggs.
   B: It's already on the list. What else?

EXERCISE 6 QUOTABLE QUOTES

DISCUSSION Work with a partner. Read the quotes about time. Choose three quotes and discuss them. What do they mean? Do you agree with them? Why or why not?

1. It takes time to build castles. Rome wasn't built in a day.
   —*Irish proverb*

   EXAMPLE: A: I think this means that you can't do something important quickly.
   B: I agree. Success isn't instant. It takes a lot of time.

2. Time gives good advice.
   —*Maltese proverb*

3. There's no time like the present.
   —*English proverb*

4. Time is money.
   —*Benjamin Franklin (1706–1790, U.S. statesman, scientist, writer)*

5. Time you enjoyed wasting is not wasted time.
   —*T.S. Eliot (1888–1965, U.S.-British poet)*

6. When you sit with a nice girl for two hours, you think it's only a minute. But when you sit on a hot stove for a minute, you think it's two hours. That's relativity.
   —*Albert Einstein (1879–1955, German-U.S. physicist)*

EXERCISE 7 YOUR TIME CAPSULE

Ⓐ PROBLEM SOLVING Work in a group. Imagine that you are going to create a time capsule to tell people in the future about your present life. You have room in your capsule for only eight things. Choose things from the categories in the box. Answer the questions below.

• books	• food	• money	• technology
• clothing	• games	• music	• tools

1. Which eight items will you put in your time capsule? (Give the reasons for your choices.)

   EXAMPLE: A: Let's put in some fast food.
   B: A hamburger will go bad in less than a day!
   C: Well, we could put in *pictures* of popular kinds of fast food.

2. When do you want people to open it?

3. Where will you put your time capsule?

4. What will you call your time capsule? Give it a name.

Ⓑ Compare your choices with the choices of other groups. Have other groups made any of the same choices as your group?

FROM GRAMMAR TO WRITING

A BEFORE YOU WRITE You are going to write a note to put inside a time capsule along with six items. Answer these questions. Use your imagination!

1. Who created this time capsule with you and when? _____

2. What is inside it? How much or how many did you include? (Complete the lists below.)

Item	Quantity	Item	Quantity
_____	_____	_____	_____
_____	_____	_____	_____
_____	_____	_____	_____

4. Why did you choose these items? _____

B WRITE Use your answers to write the note to put inside your time capsule. Your note is to the people who will open the capsule. Try to avoid the common mistakes in the chart.

EXAMPLE: On October 4, 2017, my classmates (Enrique Torres, Tanya Antonov, Ilgin Sadlik) and I (Min Yoon) created this time capsule. It contains six items. Each item tells something about the lives we live today. For example, we put . . . inside to show . . .

Commons Mistakes in Using Nouns and Quantifiers

Use **singular verbs** and **pronouns** with common **non-count nouns**. Do not use plural verbs and pronouns.	We put **money** in the capsule. ***It was*** worth $100. NOT We put money in the capsule. ~~They were~~ worth $100.
Use *many*, *several*, and *a few* with **count nouns**. Do not use *much* and *a little* with count nouns.	The capsule contains *many* everyday **items**. NOT The capsule contains ~~much~~ everyday items.
Use *much* (in questions and negative statements) and *a little* with **non-count nouns**. Do not use *many*, *several*, and *a few* with non-count nouns.	We didn't have ***much* time** to create the capsule. NOT We didn't have ~~many~~ time to create the capsule.

C CHECK YOUR WORK Read your note. Underline the nouns (once for count nouns, twice for non-count nouns, and three times for proper nouns). Circle the quantifiers. Use the Editing Checklist to check your work.

Editing Checklist

Did you use . . . ?

☐ non-count nouns with singular verbs and pronouns

☐ the correct verb (singular or plural) after count nouns

☐ the correct quantifiers

D REVISE YOUR WORK Read your note again. Can you improve your writing? Make changes if necessary. Give your note a title.

UNIT 17 REVIEW

Test yourself on the grammar of the unit.

A Choose the correct answer to complete each sentence.

1. Where would you like to go today? We only have a _____ time.
   a. little   **b.** few   **c.** great deal of

2. Do we have _____ time for the photography museum?
   a. several   **b.** enough   **c.** few

3. Sure! They have _____ old photographs of the city, and I'd love to see them.
   a. any   **b.** much   **c.** a lot of

4. The museum is _____ miles from here. Let's take our bikes.
   a. few   **b.** a great deal of   **c.** several

5. OK. And we should remember to bring _____ water. It's hot today.
   a. some   **b.** a few   **c.** little

B Complete the suggestions for items to put in a time capsule. Use the correct form of the words in parentheses.

1. _____ essential. Include different kinds.
   (music / be)

2. Family _____ relationships, personalities, and a lot more.
   (photo / show)

3. _____ a great item. Include bills and coins.
   (money / make)

4. _____ the popular styles and the fabrics of the time.
   (clothing / show)

5. _____ bad fast, so put in pictures of food instead.
   (food / go)

C Find and correct ten mistakes.

One night in june, 1,400 Years ago, a volcano erupted in today's El Salvador and buried a village of the great Mayan civilization. Archaeologists have already found many large building from this time, but only a little homes of farmers and workers. The village of El Ceren contains perfect examples of a great deal of everyday objects. The archaeologists have found some knives (with foods still on them), much pots, a lot garden tools, some fabrics, and a book. On the wall of one room, they found a few word in an unknown language. There is still a lot to learn from this time capsule, called "the pompeii of Latin America."

Now check your answers on page 479.

Articles: Indefinite and Definite

STORIES

OUTCOMES
- Use indefinite and definite articles to describe nouns
- Identify main ideas in a story
- Identify important details in a conversation
- Summarize and give opinions on the moral of a fable
- Write a paragraph about a personal experience that illustrates the meaning of a moral

---

STEP 1   GRAMMAR IN CONTEXT

BEFORE YOU READ

Look at the picture and at the title of the story. Discuss the questions.

1. What kind of a story is a fable?
2. Which mouse is the town mouse? Which is the country mouse? Give reasons for your answers.

READ

▶ 18|01   Read this fable.

A Fable by Aesop

Aesop was a famous storyteller in Greece more than 2,000 years ago. The fables he told are still famous all over the world.

The Town Mouse and the Country Mouse

A town mouse went to visit his cousin in the country. The country cousin was poor, but he gladly served his town cousin the only food he had—some beans and some bread. The town mouse ate the bread and laughed. He said, "What simple food you country mice eat! Come home with me. I'll show you how to live." The moon was shining brightly that night, so the mice left immediately.

As soon as they arrived at the town mouse's house, they went into the dining room. There they found the leftovers of a wonderful dinner. The mice were soon eating jelly and cake and many nice things. Suddenly, the door flew open, and an enormous dog ran in. The mice ran away quickly. "Good-bye, Cousin," said the country mouse. "Are you leaving so soon?" asked the town mouse. "Yes," his honest cousin replied. "This has been a great adventure, but it's been a little too dangerous for me."

Moral:[1] It's better to eat bread in peace than cake in fear.

---

[1] *moral:* a practical lesson that you learn from a story or from something that happens to you

AFTER YOU READ

A VOCABULARY **Complete the sentences with the words from the box.**

enormous	famous	honest	immediately	wonderful

1. Aesop's fables are _____ all over the world. Millions of people have read them.

2. I think *The Town Mouse and the Country Mouse* is a(n) _____ fable. I really enjoyed it.

3. To be _____, I didn't really understand the moral of the fable.

4. After I read the fable, I _____ went online to search for other ones. I couldn't wait to read more!

5. I ordered a book of Aesop's fables. It's _____—almost 400 pages!

B COMPREHENSION **Read the statements. Check (✓)** *True* **or** *False.*

	True	False
1. The country mouse made a wonderful meal for his cousin.	☐	☐
2. The town mouse was happy with the meal.	☐	☐
3. It was a beautiful, bright night.	☐	☐
4. The mice left the country and went to the town mouse's house.	☐	☐
5. They ate in the town mouse's kitchen.	☐	☐
6. A dog came in and frightened the mice away.	☐	☐

C DISCUSSION **Work with a partner. Compare your answers in B. Why did you check** *True* **or** *False?*

ARTICLES: INDEFINITE AND DEFINITE

Indefinite

Singular Count Nouns

	A/An	(Adjective) Noun
Let's read	a	story.
This is	an	old story.

Plural Count Nouns / Non-Count Nouns

	(Some)	(Adjective) Noun
Let's listen to	(some)	stories on this CD.
This CD has		nice music, too.

Definite

Singular Count Nouns

	The	(Adjective) Noun
Let's read	the	story by Aesop.
It's		oldest story.

Plural Count Nouns / Non-Count Nouns

	The	(Adjective) Noun
Let's listen to	the	stories by Aesop.
I like		old music on this CD.

GRAMMAR NOTES

1 Indefinite and Definite Nouns

Nouns can be **definite** or **indefinite**.

A noun is **indefinite** when you and your listener do not have a specific person, place, or thing you are thinking about.	A: Let's buy **a book**. B: Good idea. Which one should we buy? _(A and B are not thinking about a specific book.)_
A noun is **definite** when you and your listener both know which person, place, or thing you are talking about.	A: I bought **the book** yesterday. B: Good. You've wanted it for a while. _(A and B are talking about a specific book.)_

2 Indefinite Article A/An, No Article, and Some

To show that a noun is **indefinite**, use the indefinite article **a/an**, **no article**, or _some_.

Use the **indefinite article** _a/an_ with **singular count nouns** that are indefinite.	A: I'm reading **a fable**. B: Oh really? Which one?
• _a_ before **consonant** sounds • _an_ before **vowel** sounds	**a** mouse, **a s**imple meal **an a**dventure, **an e**normous dog
BE CAREFUL! It is the **sound**, not the letter, that determines if you use _a_ or _an_.	**a E**uropean writer (a "Yuropean") NOT ~~an~~ European writer **an h**onest man (an "ahnest") NOT ~~a~~ honest man
Use **no article** or _some_ with **plural count nouns** and with **non-count nouns** that are indefinite. _Some_ means an indefinite number or amount.	PLURAL COUNT NON-COUNT A: We could have **beans** and maybe **salad** for dinner. B: All we have are **some peas** and **some spinach**.

3 Indefinite Article or No Article for Identification and General Statements

Use *a/an* or **no article** to identify people or things and to make general statements.

To **identify people or things** (say what someone or something is), use:

- *a/an* with **singular count nouns**

A: What do you do?
SINGULAR COUNT
B: I'm **a cook**.

- **no article** with **plural count nouns** and **non-count nouns**

A: What are you doing?
PLURAL COUNT   NON-COUNT
B: I'm baking **cookies** and making **tea**.

BE CAREFUL! A singular count noun always needs an article (*a*, *an*, or *the*) before it.

I'm **a cook**.   NOT   I'm ~~cook~~.

Do not use *a* or *an* before non-count nouns.

I'm making **tea**.   NOT   I'm making ~~a tea~~.

To **make general statements**, use:

- *a/an* with **singular count nouns**

SINGULAR COUNT
A cook has a difficult job.

- **no article** with **plural count nouns** and **non-count nouns**

PLURAL COUNT   NON-COUNT
Ava loves **stories** and **music**.
(stories and music in general)

4 Definite Article *The*

To show that a noun is **definite**, use the definite article *the*.

Use the **definite article** *the* with most **common nouns** (count and non-count, singular and plural) when:

- a person, place, or thing is **unique**—there is only one

The author of this fable is very famous.
The moon was shining brightly.

- the **context** or situation makes it clear which person, place, or thing you mean

A: Who is she?
B: She's *the* teacher.
(A and B are in class. A is a new student.)

- you mention the noun for the **second time** (it is often indefinite the first time you mention it)

A mouse lived in the town. One day, *the* mouse went to the country to visit his cousin.

- a phrase or adjective such as *first*, *best*, *right*, *wrong*, or *only* identifies the noun

It was *the first* time he visited his cousin.
He served *the only* food he had.

Use the **definite article** *the* with some **proper nouns**, for example, the names of:

- certain books and documents
- countries and geographical features

the *Encyclopedia Britannica*, **the** U.S. Constitution
the United Arab Emirates, **the** Alps

REFERENCE NOTES

For a list of **non-count nouns**, see Appendix 7 on page 456.
For more information on *the* with **proper nouns**, see Appendix 8 on page 457.

EXERCISE 1 DISCOVER THE GRAMMAR

GRAMMAR NOTES 1–4 **Read the conversations. Choose the statement that best describes each conversation.**

1. CORA: Dad, could you read me a story?
   DAD: Sure, I'd love to.

   a. Dad knows which story Cora wants him to read.

   (b.) Cora isn't talking about a particular story.

2. IGOR: Mom, where's the new book?
   MOM: Sorry, I haven't seen it.

   a. Mom knows that Igor bought a new book.

   b. Mom doesn't know that Igor bought a new book.

3. DAD: I'll bet it's in the hall. You always drop your things there.
   IGOR: I'll go look.

   a. There are several halls in the house.

   b. There is only one hall in the house.

4. DAD: Was I right?
   IGOR: You weren't even close. It was on a chair in the kitchen.

   a. There is only one chair in the kitchen.

   b. There are several chairs in the kitchen.

5. DAD: Wow! Look at that! The pictures are great.
   IGOR: So are the stories.

   a. All books have great pictures and stories.

   b. The book Igor bought has great pictures and stories.

6. IGOR: Oh, I forgot . . . I also got a video game. Do you want to play?
   DAD: You know I love video games. But, to be honest, I'm too tired right now.

   a. Dad is talking about video games in general.

   b. Dad is talking about a particular video game.

EXERCISE 2 DEFINITE ARTICLE OR NO ARTICLE

Ⓐ GRAMMAR NOTES 1–4 Pilar is in a bookstore to buy books for her young niece. An assistant, Jason, is trying to help her. Complete their conversation. Use *the* where necessary. Leave a blank if you don't need an article.

PILAR: I'm looking for _____ books for my
1.
14-year-old niece. Do you have

any recommendations?

JASON: Let's go to __*the*__ young adult
2.
section. Does she like _____
3.
mysteries? Doris Duncan wrote some

good ones for teenagers.

PILAR: She's read all _____ mysteries by
4.
Duncan. She's _____ fastest reader
5.
in our family!

JASON: It's hard to keep up with _____ fast
6.
readers. Here's a good one by Gillian

Cross—*Born of* _____ *Sun*. It's about finding a lost Inca city.
7.

PILAR: She'll like that one. She loves _____ books about _____ history—and
8.   9.
science, too.

JASON: Then how about *A Short History of* _____ *Universe*? It's in _____
10.   11.
science section.

PILAR: This is great! She likes _____ books with beautiful pictures.
12.

JASON: Well, _____ pictures in this one are wonderful. *Nature Magazine* called this book
13.
_____ best introduction to this subject.
14.

PILAR: OK, I'll take _____ mystery by Cross and _____ science book. Anything else?
15.   16.

JASON: Well, _____ kids have fun with _____ trivia games. Here's a good one.
17.   18.

PILAR: Great. I'll get _____ trivia game, too. Thanks. You've been very helpful.
19.

▶ 18|02 **Ⓑ LISTEN AND CHECK** Listen to the conversation and check your answers in A.

EXERCISE 3 INDEFINITE OR DEFINITE ARTICLE

(A) **GRAMMAR NOTES 1–4** Read this story about a famous character in Turkish literature, Nasreddin. Complete the text with *a*, *an*, or *the*.

Nasreddin lived ___*a*___ long time ago in Turkey. He is one of _____ most famous
            1.   2.

characters in literature. People often thought he was _____ fool, but he was _____
                                                                      3.   4.

very wise man. Here is _____ funny story about him:
                                 5.

Nasreddin Solves _____ Difficult Problem
                          6.

Nasreddin had _____ little donkey. There was _____ market
                       7.   8.

in _____ only nearby town, and Nasreddin and his grandson often
        9.

went there with _____ donkey. One day, they were traveling to
                        10.

_____ market when _____ group of people passed by. Someone
   11.   12.

shouted, "Look! _____ old man is walking while _____ boy
                         13.   14.

rides!" So _____ boy got down, and Nasreddin rode. Then they
                15.

passed _____ storyteller sitting under _____ tree. _____
              16.   17.   18.

storyteller called out, "Why is that poor child walking in _____
                                                                          19.

hot sun?" So they both rode. Next, they met _____ old woman.
                                                        20.

"_____ little donkey is tired!" she shouted. So Nasreddin said,
    21.

"_____ best thing is for both of us to walk." Soon they met
    22.

_____ merchant. _____ merchant's donkey was carrying
   23.   24.

_____ enormous bag. _____ merchant laughed and said,
   25.   26.

"Why are you two walking? That's _____ strong little
                                            27.

donkey!" Nasreddin immediately picked up _____
                                                        28.

donkey and carried it on his shoulders. "These people

will never leave us alone," he told his grandson. "So

this is _____ only way to solve _____ problem."
            29.   30.

▶18|03 (B) LISTEN AND CHECK Listen to the story
about Nasreddin. Check your answers in A.

EXERCISE 4 INDEFINITE, DEFINITE, NO ARTICLE, OR *SOME*

GRAMMAR NOTES 1–4 Read this short biography of Aesop, the famous Greek storyteller.
Circle the correct article or *some* to complete the text. Circle Ø if you don't need an article.

People all over (the)/ Ø world know a / the fables of Aesop, but
          1.   **2.**

there is very little information about the / Ø life of this famous Greek
                                3.

storyteller. Scholars agree that Aesop was born around 620 B.C.E.[1] In

his early years, he was a / the slave, and he lived on Samos, an / a island
                     4.   **5.**

in an / the Aegean Sea. Even as a / the slave, Aesop had the / Ø wisdom
  6.   **7.**   **8.**

and knowledge. His master respected him so much that he freed him.

When Aesop became a / Ø free man, he traveled to many countries in
                        9.

order to learn and to teach. In Lydia, the / Ø king invited him to stay in
                               10.

that country and gave Aesop some / a difficult jobs in a / the government.
                           11.   **12.**

In his work, Aesop often struggled to convince people of

his ideas. Sometimes he used a / Ø fables to help people
                      13.

understand what he meant. One time, a / the king sent
                           14.

Aesop to Delphi with a / some gold for a / the people of
                     15.   **16.**

that city. Aesop became disgusted with the / Ø people's
                                17.

greed, so he sent the / Ø gold back to a / the king.
          18.   **19.**

A / The people of Delphi were very angry at
 20.

Aesop for this, and they killed him. After his

death, a / the famous sculptor made a / the
      21.   **22.**

statue of Aesop you see in a / the photo.
                     23.

---

1 *B.C.E.:* the abbreviation for *Before Common Era*, a year-numbering
system used in many parts of the world

EXERCISE 5 INDEFINITE, DEFINITE, OR NO ARTICLE

GRAMMAR NOTES 1–4 This is a trivia game. Complete the clues for each item. Then, using the clues and the appropriate picture, write the answer. Use *a*, *an*, or *the* where necessary. Leave a blank if you don't need an article. The answers to this trivia game are on page 254.

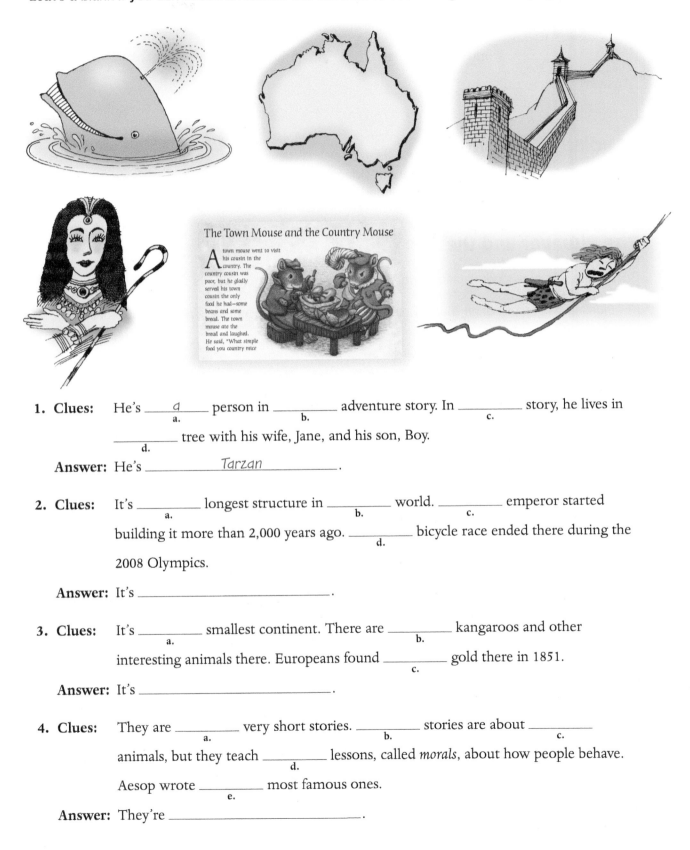

1. **Clues:** He's _____ person in _____ adventure story. In _____ story, he lives in

  a. b. c.
   _____ tree with his wife, Jane, and his son, Boy.

  d.

   Answer: He's _____ *Tarzan* _____.

2. **Clues:** It's _____ longest structure in _____ world. _____ emperor started

  a. b. c.
   building it more than 2,000 years ago. _____ bicycle race ended there during the

  d.
   2008 Olympics.

   Answer: It's _____.

3. **Clues:** It's _____ smallest continent. There are _____ kangaroos and other

  a. b.
   interesting animals there. Europeans found _____ gold there in 1851.

  c.

   Answer: It's _____.

4. **Clues:** They are _____ very short stories. _____ stories are about _____

  a. b. c.
   animals, but they teach _____ lessons, called *morals*, about how people behave.

  d.
   Aesop wrote _____ most famous ones.

  e.

   Answer: They're _____.

5. Clues: She was _____ intelligent and beautiful woman. She was _____ most famous
a.   b.

queen of Egypt. She ruled _____ country with her brother.
c.

Answer: She was _____.

6. Clues: They are _____ biggest living animals on Earth. They live in all the oceans of
a.

_____ world, but they aren't _____ fish.
b.   c.

Answer: They're _____.

EXERCISE 6 EDITING

GRAMMAR NOTES 1–4 Read this article about video games. There are twelve mistakes in the
use of *a*, *an*, and *the*. The first mistake is already corrected. Find and correct eleven more.

The Plumber and the Ape

Once there was a plumber named Mario.

~~Plumber~~ *The plumber* had beautiful girlfriend. One day, a ape fell in love with the girlfriend and kidnapped

her. The plumber chased ape to rescue his girlfriend. This simple tale became *Donkey Kong*, a

first video game with a story. It was invented by Shigeru Miyamoto, an artist with Nintendo, Inc.

Miyamoto loved the video games, but he wanted to make them more interesting.

He liked fairy tales, so he invented story similar to a famous fairy tale. Some

story was an immediate success, and Nintendo followed it with *The*

Mario Brothers and then with *Super Mario*. The third game became

popular all over a world, and it is still one of the most famous games

in video history. Nintendo has continued to add

the new adventures and new ways to play game.

Now players can follow Mario to outer space and

play the game on their Wii.[1] But success and

space travel do not change Mario. He is

still brave little plumber in a red hat.

---

1 *Wii (pronounced "we")*: a game system in which
players hold a wireless controller and control the
game by their movements and by pressing buttons

**Mario and his creator,
Shigeru Miyamoto**

EXERCISE 7 LISTENING

▶18|04 **A** **Read the sentences. Then listen to the short conversations. Listen again and circle the words that you hear.**

1. I just finished a / (the) story about Nasreddin.

2. It's a / the new video game. Do you want to try it?

3. To be honest, I don't really like the video games / video games.

4. She's a / the princess with magic powers.

5. What about Aesop? Have you read a / the fable?

6. You know, I'd like to buy a / the book of fables for Ava.

7. Let's go to a / the bookstore this weekend.

8. Why don't you have a / the sandwich?

9. I think I put it on a / the shelf above the sink.

▶18|04 **B** **Work with a partner. Read the statements about the conversations. Then listen again to each conversation. Together, decide which answer is correct and give your reasons.**

1. (a.) Narno already knows about the story.
   b. Narno and Pilar haven't spoken about the story before.

   EXAMPLE: A: The answer to number 1 is *a*. Narno already knows about the story.
   B: Right. Narno says he just finished *the* story. That means he thinks Pilar knows which story he's talking about.

2. a. Narno and Pilar have already spoken about this video game.
   b. Narno has never mentioned this video game before.

3. a. Pilar doesn't like video games in general.
   b. Pilar doesn't like some specific video games.

4. a. The story has several princesses. One of them has magic powers.
   b. The story has just one princess.

5. a. Narno and Pilar have already spoken about this fable.
   b. Pilar has never mentioned this fable before.

6. a. Pilar has a specific book of fables in mind.
   b. Pilar isn't thinking of a particular book of fables.

7. a. Pilar has a specific bookstore in mind.
   b. Pilar isn't thinking of a particular bookstore.

8. a. There is only one sandwich.
   b. There are several sandwiches.

9. a. There is only one shelf above the sink.
   b. There is more than one shelf above the sink.

EXERCISE 8 QUIZ SHOW

GAME Work in a group. Choose five interesting or famous things. Write three clues for each thing. Then join another group. Give your clues and ask the other group to guess what each thing is. Look at Exercise 5 on page 251 for ideas. You can use the Internet or a library to find information.

EXAMPLE: A: It's a planet. It's the closest one to the sun. There might be water there.
B: Does it have rings?
C: No, it doesn't.

EXERCISE 9 THE MORAL OF THE STORY

DISCUSSION Fables often have a moral—a sentence at the end that explains the lesson of the story. Work in a group. Read this list of morals. Discuss their meanings. Do you agree with them?

1. It's better to eat bread in peace than cake in fear.

   EXAMPLE: A: "It's better to eat bread in peace than cake in fear." That's the moral of *The Town Mouse and the Country Mouse*.
   B: I think this means it's better to have simple things and a peaceful life than to have nicer things but a dangerous life.
   C: I agree. You can't enjoy the better things in life if you're always living in fear.

2. Look before you leap.

3. Self-help is the best help.

4. You can't please everyone.

5. Sometimes a little friend is a great friend.

6. Slow and steady wins the race.

7. Necessity is the mother of invention.

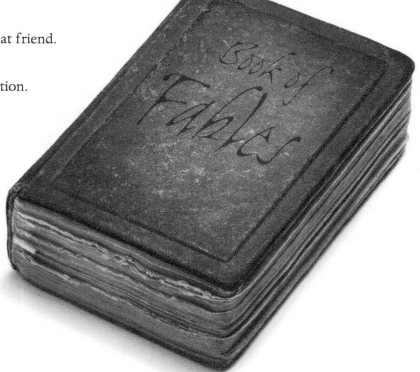

Answers to Exercise 5, pages 251–252:
2. the Great Wall of China
3. Australia   4. fables
5. Cleopatra   6. whales

EXERCISE 10 STORY TIME

A INFORMATION GAP Work with a partner. Student A will follow the instructions below. Student B will follow the instructions on page 487.

STUDENT A

- Look at the picture. Ask your partner for the information you need to finish labeling the picture.

  EXAMPLE: A: Who's the man in the black cape?
  B: He's the magician.

- Answer your partner's questions.

  EXAMPLE: B: What's the magician holding?
  A: A magic wand.

- If you don't know how to spell something, ask your partner.

  EXAMPLE: A: How do you spell "magician"?
  B: m, a, g, i, c, i, a, n

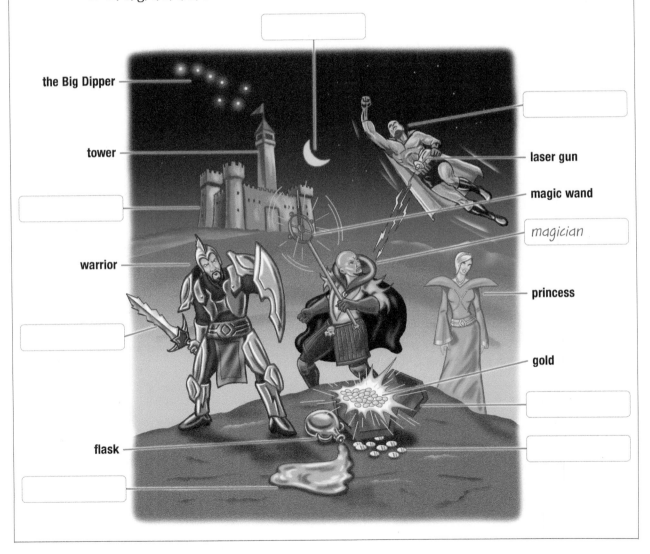

the Big Dipper

tower

warrior

flask

laser gun

magic wand

magician

princess

gold

B When you are finished, compare pictures. Are the labels the same?

FROM GRAMMAR TO WRITING

Ⓐ BEFORE YOU WRITE Choose a moral to write about. You can use one of the morals in Exercise 9 or you can look up other morals online. Think about an experience that illustrates the meaning of the moral. Answer the questions below.

_____
(the moral)

1. When did the experience happen? _____

2. What happened? _____

3. What was the result? _____

4. What did you learn from the experience? _____

_____

Ⓑ WRITE Use your answers to write a paragraph about an experience that illustrates the meaning of the moral you chose. Try to avoid the common mistakes in the chart.

EXAMPLE: "Slow and steady wins the race."

> When I was in high school, I was a good student, but I always waited until the night before a test to study. I learned very fast, so I never had trouble. Then I took a science class from Mr. Fox, the toughest teacher in the school . . .

Common Mistakes in Using Articles

Use an **article** before all **singular count nouns**. Do not forget the article.	I was **a good student**. NOT I was ~~good student~~. I was **the best student** in my class. NOT I was ~~best student~~ in my class.
Use **the** or **no article** before **non-count nouns**. Do not use *a* or *an* before non-count nouns.	**The soup** in the school cafeteria is good today. NOT ~~A soup~~ in the school cafeteria is good today. I love **soup**. NOT I love ~~a~~ soup.

Ⓒ CHECK YOUR WORK Read your paragraph. Underline all the indefinite nouns and circle the definite nouns. Use the Editing Checklist to check your work.

Editing Checklist

Did you use . . . ?

☐ *a, an, some,* or no article with indefinite nouns

☐ *the* with definite nouns

☐ *a, an, some,* or no article to identify and make general statements

☐ *the* when a noun is unique, or it is clear which person, place, or thing it is

Ⓓ REVISE YOUR WORK Read your paragraph again. Can you improve your writing? Make changes if necessary.

UNIT 18 REVIEW

Test yourself on the grammar of the unit.

A Circle the correct articles to complete the sentences. Circle Ø if you don't need an article.

1. Is there a / the good bookstore around here?
2. I want to buy a / the book for my niece.
3. She really enjoys the / Ø fables.
4. I just read a / an excellent collection of fables.
5. Some / A fables have mice in them.
6. My niece is afraid of Ø / the mice.
7. This is a / the best story I've ever read.
8. It's famous all over a / the world.

B Complete the conversations with *a*, *an*, or *the*.

1. A: Did anyone feed _____ cat today?
   a.

   B: I did. Why?

   A: He's still hungry.

   B: Well, there's more food in _____ kitchen.
   b.

2. A: Look at this picture of Boots.

   B: It's really cute. What kind of cat is it?

   A: It's not _____ cat. It's _____ dog.
   a.   b.

   B: You're kidding! What _____ unusual animal!
   c.

C Find and correct seven mistakes.

Yesterday, I downloaded two movies. One was comedy, the other was a Argentinian thriller. We watched a comedy first. It was really funny. A thriller wasn't that good. There wasn't enough action in it. Tonight, I think I'd rather read the book than watch a movie. I recently bought the book of fables and a mystery. I think I'll read a mystery before I go to sleep.

Now check your answers on page 479.

Adjectives and Adverbs

PART 6

OUTCOMES

- Describe people, objects, and places, using adjectives and adverbs
- Form and use basic adverbs and participial adjectives
- Recognize important points in an advertisement
- Identify speakers' opinions in a conversation
- Discuss places to live, comparing and contrasting different options
- Write a description of one's ideal home

OUTCOMES

- Form and use comparative adjectives
- Express how two people, places, or things are similar or different
- Identify main ideas in a short newspaper article
- Recognize speakers' preferences in a conversation
- Discuss different food options
- Write a paragraph that compares and contrasts foods from different cities or countries

OUTCOMES

- Form and use superlative adjectives
- Compare one person, place, or thing to others in a group
- Identify key details in an article about a city
- Identify places and locations by their descriptions in a conversation
- Describe and express opinions about places
- Write a description of one's hometown or city

OUTCOMES

- Form and use comparative and superlative adverbs
- Express how two actions are similar or different
- Identify main ideas in an opinion article and in a debate
- Discuss issues in a debate, supporting opinions
- Describe and compare people's abilities
- Write arguments for and against a statement

Adjectives and Adverbs

HOME

OUTCOMES
- Describe people, objects, and places, using adjectives and adverbs
- Form and use basic adverbs and participial adjectives
- Recognize important points in an advertisement
- Identify speakers' opinions in a conversation
- Discuss places to live, comparing and contrasting different options
- Write a description of one's ideal home

STEP 1   GRAMMAR IN CONTEXT

BEFORE YOU READ

Look at the photo of a house. Discuss the questions.

1. Is this a good place to live? Why or why not?
2. What is important when looking for a home?

READ

▶19|01   Read this ad for two apartments in a private house.

Wakefield House

Are you looking for a nice neighborhood with safe, quiet streets? Do you love the big sunny rooms and high ceilings in interesting old buildings—but want modern appliances[1] and high-speed Internet, too? Apartments in Wakefield House offer that and more. Here's your place to relax completely after a long hard day at school or work. We are located in a peaceful residential area near famous Lake Forest Park. And it's so convenient! An easy drive or bus ride takes you downtown and to the university. Exciting nightlife, shopping, and museums are only minutes away.

---

1 *appliances:* pieces of equipment, such as washing machines or stoves, that people use in their homes

It sounds very expensive, right? But it's not! A comfortable one-bedroom apartment is surprisingly affordable. We have two beautifully furnished apartments available right now. But don't wait! Our apartments rent very quickly.

Call 555-1234 now for an appointment.

Here's what some of our satisfied tenants[2] are saying about life at Wakefield House:

"The neighborhood is like a small village with really friendly people and beautiful, charming[3] houses."

—Maggie Chang

"This place is absolutely perfect. I can easily get everywhere on my bike. It's my ideal home away from home. It's awesome."

—Luis Rivera

"Weekends here are so peaceful—no annoying traffic noise. I love sitting on the front porch and reading a good book."

—Alice Thompson

---

2 *tenants:* people who live in a house, apartment, or room and pay rent to the owner
3 *charming:* very nice or attractive

AFTER YOU READ

Ⓐ VOCABULARY Choose the word or phrase closest in meaning to the word in **bold**.

1. We found the **ideal** house today.
   a. perfect
   b. expensive
   c. nearby

2. The bus to town is very **convenient**.
   a. safe
   b. easy to use
   c. comfortable

3. The house is **located in** a residential area.
   a. close to
   b. far from
   c. part of

4. It's on a **peaceful** street.
   a. dangerous
   b. quiet
   c. crowded

5. We were very **satisfied** with the neighborhood.
   a. happy
   b. unhappy
   c. relaxed

6. It's **absolutely** perfect for us.
   a. almost
   b. completely
   c. very

COMPREHENSION Read the statements. Check (✓) *True* or *False*.

	True	False
1. Wakefield House is in a dangerous neighborhood.	☐	☐
2. It's in an exciting area of the city.	☐	☐
3. The apartments are not dark.	☐	☐
4. You'll be surprised that the rent is so low.	☐	☐
5. It's difficult to get to the university.	☐	☐
6. One tenant likes to spend weekends at home.	☐	☐

C DISCUSSION Work with a partner. Compare your answers in B. Why did you check *True* or *False*?

STEP 2 GRAMMAR PRESENTATION

ADJECTIVES AND ADVERBS

Adjectives	Adverbs of Manner	Adverbs of Degree
They are **quiet** tenants.	They talk **quietly**.	They're **very** quiet. They talk **very** quietly.
The house is **nice**.	They decorated it **nicely**.	It's **so** nice. They decorated it **so** nicely.
It looks **good**.	She described it **well**.	This looks **really** good. She described it **really** well.
It's a **fast** elevator.	It moves **fast**.	It's **awfully** fast! It moves **awfully** fast!

Participial Adjectives

-ing Adjective	*-ed* Adjective
The apartment is **interesting**.	One couple is **interested** in the apartment.
It's an **interesting** one-bedroom apartment.	The **interested** couple called again.
My neighbor is **annoying**.	I'm **annoyed** by his loud music.
He's an **annoying** neighbor.	Another **annoyed** tenant complained.

Word Order: Adjectives before Nouns

	Opinion	Size	Age	Shape	Color	Origin	Material	Purpose	Noun (as Adj.)	NOUN
a	**peaceful**	**little**						**residential**		area
some	**interesting**		**young**							tenants
your				**round**	**blue**	**Chinese**				vase
the		**large**	**old**				**wooden**		**kitchen**	table

GRAMMAR NOTES

1 Adjectives and Adverbs

Adjectives and adverbs **describe** or give information about **other words**.

Use **adjectives** to describe **nouns** (people, places, or things).	ADJECTIVE NOUN NOUN ADJECTIVE They are **safe** streets. or The **streets** are **safe**. *(Safe gives you information about the streets.)*
Use **adverbs** to describe: • verbs • adjectives • other adverbs	VERB ADVERB The manager **talks** *quietly*. ADVERB ADJECTIVE He's *extremely* **quiet**. ADVERB ADVERB He works *very* **quietly**.
BE CAREFUL! Use an adjective after a **non-action verb** such as *be, look, seem, appear, smell,* or *taste.* Do not use an adverb.	VERB ADJECTIVE This house **looks** *beautiful*. NOT The house looks ~~beautifully~~.

2 Adverbs of Manner

Adverbs of manner **describe** or give information about **action verbs**.

Adverbs of manner often **answer the question "How?"**	A: How did they decorate the apartment? ACTION VERB ADVERB B: They **decorated** it *beautifully*.
Form most adverbs of manner by **adding** *-ly* to the adjective.	ADJECTIVE ADVERB I need a **quick** decision. Please decide *quickly*.
Some adverbs of manner also have a **form without** *-ly*. The form is the **same as the adjective**.	ADVERB WITH *-LY* ADVERB WITHOUT *-LY* slowly or slow quickly or quick loudly or loud clearly or clear
USAGE NOTE The adverb form **without** *-ly* is **less formal**.	Don't speak so **loudly**. *(more formal)* Don't speak so **loud**. *(less formal)*
BE CAREFUL! Some **adjectives** also end in *-ly*, for example, *friendly, lonely, lovely,* and *silly*.	ADJECTIVE It's a **lovely** apartment.
Some common adverbs of manner are **not formed by adding** *-ly* to adjectives: The adverb form of *good* is *well*.	ADJECTIVE He's a **good** building manager. ADVERB He manages the building **well**.
Early, **fast**, **hard**, *late,* and *wrong* have the **same** adjective and adverb forms.	ADJECTIVE ADVERB She is a **hard** worker. She works **hard**.
BE CAREFUL! *Hardly* is not the adverb form of *hard*. *Hardly* means "almost not." *Lately* is not the adverb form of *late*. *Lately* means "recently."	There's **hardly** enough room for a bed. *(There's almost not enough room for a bed.)* We haven't seen any nice houses **lately**. *(We haven't seen any nice houses recently.)*

3 Adverbs of Degree

Adverbs of degree make adjectives, other adverbs, and verbs **stronger** or **weaker**.

100%	*absolutely, completely, totally*
	awfully, terribly, too
	really, so, very, extremely
	pretty, quite, fairly
0%	*not at all*

ADVERB   VERB
A: I *absolutely* love it here.

ADVERB   ADVERB
B: You can get to work *awfully* easily.

ADVERB   ADJECTIVE
A: We are *pretty* lucky to live here.

ADVERB   ADJECTIVE
B: And it's *not at all* expensive!

USAGE NOTE *Awfully* and *terribly* can describe something good or bad.

The apartment was *awfully* nice.
The landlord was *awfully* rude.

USAGE NOTE In informal conversation, we often use *real* instead of *really* before an adjective.

The house is in a *real* good neighborhood.
(The house is in a really good neighborhood.)

Not at all means "totally not."

I did*n't* like the apartment *at all*.
(I totally didn't like it.)

Notice the word order for *not at all*.
- **after a verb** or verb + object
- **after or before an adjective** or another adverb

They did*n't* decorate (the place) *at all*.

It was*n't* nice *at all*. or It was*n't* *at all* nice.

BE CAREFUL! Not all adverbs of degree can go with verbs. Do not use *extremely, very, pretty, awfully, terribly, fairly,* or *too* before a verb.

I *absolutely* love it.
NOT I ~~extremely~~ love it.
I *totally* agree with you.
NOT I ~~terribly~~ agree with you.

---

4 Participial Adjectives

Participial adjectives are adjectives that **end with** *-ing* or *-ed*.

Participial adjectives **come from verbs**.

VERB
This neighborhood **amazes** me.
ADJECTIVE   ADJECTIVE
It's an **amazing** neighborhood. I'm **amazed**.

Use participial adjectives to **describe feelings**:
- the **-ing** form shows that someone or something **causes** a feeling

The house is **disappointing**.
(The house causes a feeling of disappointment.)

- the **-ed** form shows that someone **has** a feeling

I'm **disappointed**.
(I have a feeling of disappointment.)

---

5 Word Order with One Adjective

An **adjective** usually goes right **before the noun** it describes.

ADJECTIVE   NOUN
This is a *beautiful* house.

It can also go **after a non-action verb** such as *be, look, seem, appear, smell,* or *taste*.

VERB   ADJECTIVE
This house **looks** *beautiful*.

6 Word Order with Several Adjectives

Sometimes we use **two or three adjectives before a noun**.

If adjectives belong to **different categories**, we usually **follow this order**: **opinion + size + age + shape + color + origin + material + purpose + noun (used as adjective) + NOUN**	(OPINION) (AGE) (PURPOSE) It's in a **beautiful old residential** neighborhood. (OPINION) (COLOR) (MATERIAL) I bought a **nice black leather** couch.
Size adjectives (such as *big* and *small*) are an exception. They often go first in a series of adjectives.	(SIZE) (OPINION) (NOUN AS ADJ.) It's a **small affordable one-room** apartment. or (OPINION) (SIZE) (NOUN AS ADJ.) It's an **affordable small one-room** apartment.
IN WRITING **Do not use commas** between adjectives that belong to different categories.	(SIZE) (SHAPE) (ORIGIN) I got a **large round Mexican** mirror. NOT I got a large‚ₓ round‚ₓ Mexican mirror.
For adjectives that belong to the **same category**, the **order is not important**. IN WRITING **Use commas** between adjectives that belong to the same category.	She's a **friendly, helpful, nice** woman. or She's a **helpful, friendly, nice** woman. or She's a **nice, helpful, friendly** woman. *(All the adjectives are opinion adjectives, so the order can change.)*

7 Word Order with Adverbs of Manner or Degree

An **adverb of manner** usually goes **after the verb** it describes.	VERB ADVERB The apartment **rented** *quickly*.
When the verb has an object, the adverb goes **after the object**. BE CAREFUL! Do not put an adverb between the verb and the object.	VERB OBJECT ADVERB She **decorated** the house *nicely*. NOT She decorated ~~nicely the house~~.
An **adverb of degree** usually goes right **before the adjective, adverb, or verb** it describes.	ADVERB ADJECTIVE It's an *extremely* nice house. ADVERB ADVERB They found it *very* quickly. ADVERB VERB They *really* liked it.

REFERENCE NOTES

For a list of **non-action verbs**, see Appendix 2 on page 454.

For **adverbs of frequency**, see Unit 1, Grammar Note 3, on page 7.

For a list of **participial adjectives**, see Appendix 11 on page 458.

For the **order of adjectives before a noun**, see Appendix 12 on page 458.

For **spelling rules** for **adverbs ending in -*ly***, see Appendix 24 on page 463.

EXERCISE 1 DISCOVER THE GRAMMAR

GRAMMAR NOTES 1–7 Read this notice from a university bulletin board. Underline the adjectives and circle the adverbs. Then draw an arrow from the adjective or adverb to the word it is describing.

APARTMENT FOR RENT
140 Grant Street, Apt. 4B

Are you looking for a place to live? This amazing apartment is in a new

building and has two large comfortable bedrooms and a small sunny

kitchen. The building is very quiet—absolutely perfect for two serious

students. It's near the campus on a peaceful street. There's convenient

transportation. The bus stop is an easy, pleasant walk, and the express bus

goes directly into town. You can run or ride your bike safely in nearby

parks. The rent is very affordable. Small pets are welcome. The apartment

is available on June 1. Interested students should call Megan at 555-5050.

We're sure you'll be satisfied. Don't wait! This beautiful new apartment

will rent fast. Nonsmokers, please.

EXERCISE 2 ADJECTIVE OR ADVERB

GRAMMAR NOTES 1–4 Circle the correct words to complete Maggie's email to her brother.

Hi Roger!

I wasn't sure I'd like living in a large / largely city, but I real / really love it! Maybe that's
          1.   **2.**

because my new / newly neighborhood is located in such a beautiful / beautifully residential
          3.   **4.**

area with lots of nice old trees.

Last Saturday, I worked hard / hardly and unpacked all my stuff. Then I spent Sunday
                       5.

happy / happily exploring my new neighborhood. I couldn't believe the gorgeous / gorgeously
6.   **7.**

houses on these streets. I feel very lucky / luckily to live in one of them.
                                    8.

Here's a photo of "my" house. What do you think?

My apartment is on the second floor. It's really great / greatly. I'm total / totally satisfied
                                                        9.   **10.**
with it. The other tenants are very nice / nicely. My next-door neighbor, Alice, seemed pretty
                                              11.
shy / shyly at first, but I think we're going to become good / well friends very quick / quickly.
12.   **13.**   **14.**
She's an art student, and she likes to visit museums. We're going to the Modern Art Museum

together next Saturday. Life in the city is exciting / excitingly, but I get terrible / terribly
                                              15.   **16.**
homesick. So I real / really hope you visit me soon!
          17.

Love,
Maggie

EXERCISE 3 ADVERBS BEFORE ADJECTIVES AND OTHER ADVERBS

GRAMMAR NOTES 2–3 Many different people went to see the apartment described in
Exercise 1. Complete their comments about the apartment. Use the correct form of
the words in parentheses. See Appendix 24 on page 463 for help with spelling adverbs
ending in *-ly*.

1. I am very interested. I think the apartment is _____ *extremely nice* _____ .
                                                        (extreme / nice)

2. I was expecting much bigger rooms. I was _____ .
                                                        (terrible / disappointed)

3. I thought it would be hard to get to, but the bus was _____ .
                                                        (surprising / convenient)

4. I think it's a great place. I'm sure it will rent _____ .
                                                        (incredible / fast)

5. The ad said it was quiet, but I heard the neighbors _____ .
                                                        (very / clear)

6. I heard them, too. I thought their voices were _____ .
                                                        (awful / loud)

7. The ad described the apartment _____ .
                                                        (pretty / accurate)

8. To be honest, this place is _____ for me!
                                                        (absolute / perfect)

9. I'm going to feel _____ if I don't get it.
                                                        (real / upset)

EXERCISE 4 PARTICIPIAL ADJECTIVES

A GRAMMAR NOTE 4 Luis is talking to his friend Sylvie. Read their conversation. Complete it with the correct participial adjective form (-ing or -ed) of the verbs in parentheses.

SYLVIE: These apartment ads are really _____*annoying*_____ . Just look at this one.
1. (annoy)

LUIS: Hmmm. It says, "cozy and _____ apartment." Why are you
2. (charm)

_____ at that?
3. (annoy)

SYLVIE: I saw the place—it's *tiny*, not cozy! And I wasn't _____ at all. In fact, I was
4. (charm)

pretty _____ .
5. (disgust)

LUIS: Take it easy. It sounds like you had an _____ day. Let's relax and watch a
6. (exhaust)

movie tonight.

SYLVIE: You're right. I'm completely _____ . I could use a _____
7. (exhaust)   8. (relax)

evening. What do you want to watch?

LUIS: There's a movie called *Lake House*. I hear it's pretty _____ .
9. (interest)

SYLVIE: *Lake House*? Great title! I'm _____ already. What's it about?
10. (interest)

LUIS: Well, the story's a little _____ , but it happens in a beautiful glass house on
11. (confuse)

a peaceful lake.

SYLVIE: Glass? That sounds like an _____ house. I wonder if *they're* looking
12. (amaze)

for tenants.

19|02 **B** LISTEN AND CHECK **Listen to the conversation and check your answers in A.**

EXERCISE 5 WORD ORDER

GRAMMAR NOTES 5, 7 **Put the words in the correct order to complete the entry from Sylvie's journal.**

I'm a _____*fairly cheerful person*_____ most of the time, but I must say that yesterday some
1. (cheerful / person / fairly)

_____ happened. The bus _____ ,
2. (things / upsetting / pretty)   3. (late / arrived / really)

so I missed an _____ at work. However, to my surprise, my boss
4. (important / meeting / awfully)

_____ . She _____ . Later I
5. (well / quite / reacted)   6. (at all / angry / didn't / seem)

looked at a(n) _____ . I thought it was exactly what I wanted, but I
7. (apartment / charming / absolutely)

needed to _____ . When I called early this morning, I found out
8. (it / think about / carefully / very)

that the apartment was already rented! Wow! It _____ ! Next time I
9. (so / happened / quickly)

see a _____ , I won't wait!
10. (place / great / really)

268 Unit 19

EXERCISE 6 WORD ORDER WITH SEVERAL ADJECTIVES

GRAMMAR NOTE 6 Sylvie has found a great place, and she's already moved in. Put the words in the correct order to complete the new entry in her journal. Remember to use commas when necessary.

I found a _____*nice, comfortable apartment*_____ in this _____!
        1. (apartment / nice / comfortable)   **2.** (old / house / charming)

It's in a _____, just a short bus ride into town. And I can see a(n)
        3. (residential / neighborhood / peaceful)

_____ outside my _____.
     4. (tree / enormous / old)   **5.** (bedroom / wide / window)

There's even a very lovely garden with a _____. The apartment is
                6. (stone / bench / Japanese)

nicely furnished, too. The kitchen has a(n) _____. I always do my
              7. (beautiful / table / antique / large)

homework there. And the people here are really great. The manager, Alberto Velazquez, is a

_____. I've already met most of my neighbors. Across the hall
     8. (man / friendly / helpful)

from me is a _____. My first night here, she took me to a(n)
        9. (Polish / young / woman)

_____ for dinner. I know I'll be happy in this apartment.
   10. (nice / neighborhood / restaurant / Italian)

EXERCISE 7 EDITING

GRAMMAR NOTES 1–7 Read reviews of school dormitories. There are fifteen mistakes in the use of adjectives and adverbs. The first mistake is already corrected. Find and correct fourteen more.

RATE YOUR DORM

★★★★★ **Jeff W.** The Northwood dorms are pretty ~~awesomely~~ *awesome*. They're clean and modern, and they're a convenient walk to class and the dining hall. The halls get noisy terribly sometimes, though. When I'm studying hardly for exams, I have to go to the library.

★★★★★ **Sheryl** Miller Hall is the ideal dorm for freshmen. It's quite small, so I was able to make friends fastly there. Also, the floor counselors are great. Ours explained clearly the rules. She was a young French nice woman, and she was always available when you needed to talk. I was extreme satisfied. I recommend absolutely this dorm amazing to anyone.

★★★★★ **Tania** Warning! Keep away! Wyeth Hall is totally disgusted. The lounges are incredible dirty. The toilets don't work good, and the halls smell badly. I had a small brown depressing room on the ground floor. My parents were shocking when they saw the place.

EXERCISE 8 LISTENING

A A couple is discussing online apartment ads. Read the ads and guess the missing adjectives and adverbs.

Janslist > bay area > housing > apts/housing for rent

$700 a month _____*small*_____ **, charming 2 bedroom in Smithfield.**
1.

This is an _____ building very _____ all public transportation. Keep
2.   3.

your car in the garage and relax on the train!

Date: 12-10-2017 posted 10:00 PM PST
Call 555-3296 for an appointment today

FOSTER $750 Light and bright 2 BR on beautiful tree-lined street

This lovely apartment has been newly painted and is in _____ condition.
4.

_____ near stores and schools.
5.

Date: 12-09-2017 posted 1:00 PM PST
Apply Online   Email for Appointment   See Photos

$650 Cute and Cozy 2 BR in Cumberland!

Our last 2-bedroom apartment has all _____ appliances. Enjoy the
6.

_____ residential area of Cumberland. No pets, please!
7.

Date: 12-14-2017 posted 8:53AM PST
Call 555-2343 ext. 27 OR email blanders@goodproperties.com CLICK for photos.

LINCOLN Beautiful 2 bedroom only $850

Completely renovated building with beautiful

_____ kitchen and bath. All
8.

_____ appliances. Well-behaved
9.

pets welcome. Available _____ .
10.

Date: 12-09-2017 posted 7:00 AM PST
Call 555-4478 email: edgar.hodgins@Lincolntownhouse.com

▶19|03 **B** Listen to the couple's conversation. Did you guess the same adjectives that they used to describe the apartments? If not, write the adjectives you hear in the conversation.

▶19|03 **G** Work with a partner. Read the information in the chart. Then listen again to the conversation and, together, check (✓) the couple's opinion of each apartment. Give your reasons. Then give *your* opinion of the apartment.

EXAMPLE: **A:** What do they think of the first apartment?

B: They think there's not enough information in the ad.

A: Right. It just says it's small and in an old building.

B: But it's near public transportation. That's important if you don't have a car.

A: What about the second apartment?

Opinion	Apt 1	Apt 2	Apt 3	Apt 4
Sunny				
Sounds terrific!				
Not enough information	✓			
Very small				
Can't bring Loki				
Not near stores				

EXERCISE 9 WHAT ABOUT YOU?

CONVERSATION Work with a partner. Talk about the place where you live. Answer the questions.

1. How did you find your place?

EXAMPLE: **A:** How did you find your place, Maria?

B: I was taking a walk one day in a beautiful neighborhood, and I saw a For Rent sign. What about you, Alex? How did you find your place?

A: I was very lucky. I . . .

2. How did you first feel about it (pleased, disappointed, etc.)?

3. What does it look like?

4. How did you decorate it?

5. What is special about your place?

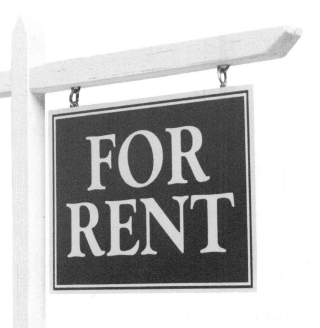

EXERCISE 10 HOME SWEET HOME

COMPARISON Work with a partner. There are many different types of housing. Describe the different types in the list. How are they similar? How are they different? Use your dictionary to help you. Do these types of housing exist in other places you have lived?

EXAMPLE: A: A mobile home is very different from the other homes. It's very convenient. You can move it from place to place.
B: And it's easy to get away from noisy—or nosy[1]—neighbors!

- apartment
- boarding house
- dorm (dormitory)
- mansion
- mobile home
- private home
- rented room in someone's house
- studio apartment

---

1 *nosy:* always trying to find out private information about someone or something

EXERCISE 11 YOUR IDEAL HOME

CONVERSATION What is your ideal home? What does it look like? What kind of roommates, neighbors, and landlord does it have? Work with a partner. Take turns describing this perfect place. Talk about the people and their activities. Use some of the words in the boxes below.

EXAMPLE: A: My ideal home is large and modern. What about you?
B: My ideal home is sunny and cheerful. What kind of neighbors does your ideal home have?
A: My ideal neighbors are considerate and helpful. What about yours?
B: They're very friendly, but they're not at all nosy.

Adjectives

affordable	convenient	honest	messy	peaceful
boring	cozy	interesting	modern	relaxed
cheerful	friendly	large	neat	reliable
considerate	helpful	loud	nosy	sunny

Adverbs of Manner

carefully	honestly	quickly
early	late	politely
easily	loudly	seriously
happily	noisily	well

Adverbs of Degree

awfully	really
not . . . at all	so
pretty	totally
quite	very

EXERCISE 12 A STRANGE STORY

GAME Work in a group. Student A keeps his or her book open. All the other students close their books. Student A asks each member of the group, in turn, for a type of adjective. Student A fills in the blanks with the words the group members give. At the end, Student A will read the story to the group. Expect a very strange story!

EXAMPLE: A: Enrique, I need a size adjective.
B: How about *enormous*?
A: OK. Lee, now I need an opinion adjective...

I was walking down the street one day when I saw a(n) _____*enormous*_____
                                                              1. (size adj)

_____ _____ house. It was _____
2. (opinion adj)   **3.** (color adj)   **4.** (degree adv)

_____. I took out my phone and _____ called my friend.
5. (participial *-ing* adj)   **6.** (*-ly* adv of manner)

He wasn't at home, so I took a picture.

The house was _____ _____. It had three
                    7. (degree adv)   **8.** (opinion adj)

_____ _____ windows and a _____
9. (size adj)   **10.** (shape adj)   **11.** (size adj)

_____ door. There were two _____ _____
12. (material adj)   **13.** (size adj)   **14.** (age adj)

trees and a lot of _____ _____ flowers. Under the tree,
                        15. (opinion adj)   **16.** (color adj)

was a(n) _____ _____ _____ bench. I was
              17. (age adj)   **18.** (material adj)   **19.** (origin adj)

_____. I'd never seen anything like it before!
20. (participial *-ed* adj)

Source: This game is based on the popular game Mad Libs invented in 1953 by Leonard Stern and Roger Price. Mad Libs books are published by Price Stern Sloan, an imprint of Penguin Group.

FROM GRAMMAR TO WRITING

A BEFORE YOU WRITE Complete the lists with adjectives that describe your ideal home, neighborhood, and neighbors.

Home _____ _____ _____ _____ _____

Neighborhood _____ _____ _____ _____ _____

Neighbors _____ _____ _____ _____ _____

B WRITE Use your lists to write a paragraph describing your ideal home, neighborhood, and neighbors. How do you feel living there? Include adverbs of degree and participial adjectives. Try to avoid the common mistakes in the chart.

EXAMPLE: My ideal home is in a beautiful old house. It has large comfortable rooms and a very big stone fireplace. Although the house is old, the kitchen has all new modern appliances. The house is located in a nice safe neighborhood filled with old trees and colorful flowers. My neighbors are very friendly and helpful, and we quickly become good friends. I feel happy and relaxed being there. I imagine living in my ideal home for a very long time.

Common Mistakes in Using Adjectives and Adverbs

Use an **adjective after a non-action verb**. Do not use an adverb.	The house **looks** *beautiful*. NOT The house looks ~~beautifully~~.
Put the **adjective before the noun** it describes. Do not put the adjective directly after the noun.	It's a *large* house. NOT It a ~~house large~~.
Use an **adverb to describe an action verb**. Do not use an adjective.	He **described** the house *perfectly*. NOT He described the house ~~perfect~~.
Put an **adverb after the object**. Do not put it between the verb and the object.	He described **the house** *perfectly*. NOT He described ~~perfectly the house~~.

C CHECK YOUR WORK Read your paragraph. Underline the adjectives and circle the adverbs. Use the Editing Checklist to check your work.

Editing Checklist

Did you use...?

☐ adjectives to describe people, places, and things

☐ participial adjectives to describe feelings

☐ adverbs of manner to describe action verbs

☐ adverbs of degree to describe adjectives and other adverbs

D REVISE YOUR WORK Read your paragraph again. Can you improve your writing? Make changes if necessary. Give your paragraph a title.

UNIT 19 REVIEW

Test yourself on the grammar of the unit.

Ⓐ Circle the correct words to complete the sentences.

1. My neighbor is so annoyed / annoying. He plays loud music all night long.

2. The bus came late / lately, and I missed my class.

3. This apartment seems perfect / perfectly for you. Are you going to take it?

4. Ken worked very hardly / hard on his new apartment. It looks great.

5. My roommate is surprising / surprisingly shy. She doesn't even like to answer the phone.

Ⓑ Unscramble the words to complete the sentences.

1. Today, I looked at a(n) _____.
   (old / house / interesting)

2. I loved the _____.
   (yellow / big / kitchen / cheerful)

3. The house is on a _____.
   (residential / peaceful / street)

4. Two _____ live next door.
   (international / nice / students / young)

5. But the landlord _____.
   (seem / friendly / didn't / at all)

6. There's a _____ on the corner.
   (little / restaurant / charming / Greek)

7. It has a _____ in the back.
   (garden / beautiful / really)

8. We sat at a(n) _____.
   (round / table / wonderful / wooden / old)

9. I think I have to _____ about this house.
   (quickly / pretty / decide)

10. I have a feeling that it's going to _____.
    (fast / awfully / rent)

Ⓒ Find and correct five mistakes.

The conditions in Parker Dorm are pretty shocked. The rooms are terrible small, and the furniture is incredibly ugly. The locks on the doors don't work good, so your stuff is never safely. The dorm counselors are great—they're all really nice, friendly people—but they can't make up for the badly conditions.

Now check your answers on page 479.

Adjectives: Comparisons with *As...as* and *Than*

FOOD

OUTCOMES
- Form and use comparative adjectives
- Express how two people, places, or things are similar or different
- Identify main ideas in a short newspaper article
- Recognize speakers' preferences in a conversation
- Discuss different food options
- Write a paragraph that compares and contrasts foods from different cities or countries

STEP 1   GRAMMAR IN CONTEXT

BEFORE YOU READ

Look at the photo. Discuss the questions.

1. Would you like to order the pizza in the photo? Why or why not?
2. How often do you eat out?
3. What types of restaurant food do you enjoy?

READ

▶20|01   Read this newspaper restaurant review.

A New Place for Pizza

Pizza Place, the chain of popular restaurants, has just opened a new one on Main Street, two blocks from the university. The last time that I ate there, the service was not as good as at the other Pizza Place restaurants in town. The young staff (mostly students) probably needs time to become more professional. It's evident they don't have much experience. But

As fresh as it gets!

the pizza was incredible! It seemed bigger and better than at the other six locations in town. As with all food, the fresher the ingredients,[1] the better the pizza. The ingredients at the new Pizza Place are as fresh as you can get (absolutely no mushrooms from a can here!), and the choices are much more varied than at their other locations. We ordered two different types. The one with mashed potatoes and garlic was a lot more interesting than the traditional pizza with cheese and tomato sauce, but both were delicious.

Each Pizza Place is different. The one on Main Street is a little larger (and louder) than the others. It's also a lot more crowded because students love it. At lunchtime, the lines outside this new eatery are getting longer and longer. Go early for a quieter, more relaxed meal.

---

1 *ingredients:* things that go into a recipe (example: tomatoes, cheese, mushrooms, salt...)

AFTER YOU READ

Ⓐ VOCABULARY Choose the word or phrase that best completes each sentence.

1. **Delicious** food _____.
   a. is healthy
   b. tastes good
   c. costs a lot

2. If something is **evident**, you can easily _____ it.
   a. understand
   b. eat
   c. pay for

3. If a meal is **relaxed**, you don't feel _____.
   a. in a hurry
   b. too full
   c. comfortable

4. A **varied** menu has _____.
   a. pizza and hamburgers
   b. very good food
   c. many different types of food

5. In a **crowded** restaurant, people or things are _____.
   a. close together
   b. not interesting
   c. far apart

Ⓑ COMPREHENSION Check (✓) all the words that describe each item.

1. **the restaurant**	☐ crowded	☐ new	☐ quiet	☐ popular
2. **the staff**	☐ professional	☐ young	☐ relaxed	☐ loud
3. **the food**	☐ delicious	☐ fresh	☐ expensive	☐ good
4. **the choices**	☐ boring	☐ small	☐ varied	☐ interesting

Ⓒ DISCUSSION Work with a partner. Compare your answers to the questions in B. Why did you check these words?

ADJECTIVES: COMPARISONS WITH *AS . . . AS* AND *THAN*

Comparisons with *As . . . as*

	(Not) As	Adjective	As	
The new restaurant is	(not) as	large busy good interesting expensive	as	the other ones.

Comparisons with *Than*

	Comparative Adjective Form	*Than*	
The new restaurant is	larger busier better more interesting less expensive	than	the other ones.

GRAMMAR NOTES

1 Comparisons with *As . . . As*

Use *as* + **adjective** + *as* to show how people, places, or things are **the same or equal**.	The new menu is **as good as** the old. *(The new menu and the old menu are equally good.)*
You can add *just* before the comparison to make it stronger.	The new menu is *just* **as good as** the old. *(The new menu and the old menu are really equally good.)*
Use *not as* + **adjective** + *as* to show how people, places, or things are **not the same or equal**.	The new menu isn't **as varied as** the old. *(The old menu was more varied.)*
USAGE NOTE We often leave out the second part of the comparison when the meaning is clear.	A: I like the old menu. It had more choices. B: Too bad the new one isn't **as varied**. *(It isn't as varied as the old menu.)*

2 Comparisons with *Than*

Use **comparative adjective + *than*** to show how people, places, or things are **different**.	The new room is **bigger than** the old room. The new waiters are **more professional than** the old waiters. The lunch menu is **less expensive than** the dinner menu.
You can add *even* before the comparison to make it stronger. *Even* expresses that something is surprising or unexpected.	The old waiters were very professional, but the new waiters are ***even* more professional than** the old waiters.
USAGE NOTE We usually do not use *less . . . than* with one-syllable adjectives. Instead we use: • *not as . . . as* • another adjective with the opposite meaning	Our server isn't **as fast as** theirs. or Our server is **slower than** theirs. NOT Our server is ~~less fast than~~ theirs.
Remember that it is not necessary to mention the second part of the comparison when the meaning is clear.	The new tables are **smaller**. *(They are smaller than the old tables.)*

3 Forming Comparative Adjectives

There are several ways of forming comparative adjectives.

	ADJECTIVE	COMPARATIVE
For **short adjectives** (one syllable and two syllables ending in *-y*), use **adjective + *-er***.	loud friendly	loud**er** friendl**ier**
IN WRITING There are often **spelling changes** when you add *-er*.	late big early	lat**er** big**ger** earl**ier**
Some short adjectives have **irregular** comparative forms.	good bad far	**better** **worse** **farther**
For **long adjectives** (two or more syllables), use ***more/less* + adjective**.	expensive	**more** expensive **less** expensive
An exception is the short adjective *fun*. It forms the comparative in the same way as a long adjective.	fun	**more** fun NOT ~~funner~~ **less** fun

For **some adjectives**, such as *lively, lovely, friendly,* and *quiet*, you can use *-er* or *more*. The *-er* form is more common.	The Inn is **livelier** than Joe's. *(more common)* The Inn is **more lively** than Joe's. *(less common)*
BE CAREFUL! Do not use *more* or *less* with the comparative form of the adjective.	It's **louder than** Joe's. NOT It's ~~more louder~~. NOT It's ~~less noisier~~.

4 To Show an Increase or Decrease

Repeat the comparative adjective to show an increase or a decrease.

comparative adjective + *and* + comparative adjective	The lines are getting **longer and longer**. *(Their length is increasing.)*

USAGE NOTE This form of comparison is common with the verbs *get*, *grow*, and *become*.

The food quality is getting **worse and worse**. *(The quality is decreasing.)*

BE CAREFUL! With **long adjectives**, repeat only *more* or *less*.

It's becoming **more and more popular**.
NOT It's becoming more ~~popular~~ and more popular.

5 To Show Cause and Effect

Use **two comparative adjectives** to show cause and effect.

the + comparative adjective + *the* + comparative adjective	The **more crowded** the restaurant, **the slower** the service. *(The service is slower because the restaurant is more crowded.)*

USAGE NOTE When both comparative adjectives describe the same person, place, or thing, we often leave out the nouns.

A: The service is really fast here.
B: **The faster, the better.**
(The faster the service, the better the service.)

REFERENCE NOTES

For a list of **adjectives** that use **both forms of the comparative**, see Appendix 9 on page 457.
For a list of **irregular comparative adjectives**, see Appendix 10 on page 458.
For **spelling rules** for the **comparative form of adjectives**, see Appendix 23 on page 463.

EXERCISE 1   DISCOVER THE GRAMMAR

GRAMMAR NOTES 1–3   Read the information about two brands of frozen pizza. Then read each statement. Check (✓) *True* or *False*.

Size	Medium	Medium
Weight	765 grams	680 grams
Price	$6.99	$7.99
Calories*	364	292
Salt content*	731 milligrams	600 milligrams
Fat content*	11 grams	11 grams
Baking time	20 minutes	16 minutes
Taste	★★★☆☆	★★★★☆

*for one slice

	True	False
1. Maria's Pizza is bigger than John's Pizza.	☐	☑
2. John's Pizza is just as big as Maria's Pizza.	☐	☐
3. John's Pizza isn't as heavy as Maria's.	☐	☐
4. Maria's Pizza is just as expensive as John's.	☐	☐
5. John's is more expensive than Maria's.	☐	☐
6. Maria's is higher in calories than John's.	☐	☐
7. Maria's Pizza is saltier than John's.	☐	☐
8. John's Pizza is just as high in fat as Maria's Pizza.	☐	☐
9. The baking time for Maria's isn't as long as the baking time for John's.	☐	☐
10. John's Pizza tastes better than Maria's Pizza.	☐	☐

EXERCISE 2 COMPARISONS WITH *AS . . . AS*

GRAMMAR NOTE 1 Look at the consumer magazine chart comparing three brands of pizza cheese. Complete the sentences. Use *(just) as . . . as* or *not as . . . as* and the correct form of the words in parentheses.

PIZZA CHEESE		Better ⟷ Worse	
Brand	**Price** (per serving)	**Taste**	**Smell**
X	45¢	◐	●
Y	30¢	◐	◑
Z	30¢	○	◑

1. Brand Z ___*is as expensive as* **or** *is just as expensive as*___ Brand Y.
   (be / expensive)

2. Brand Y _____ Brand X.
   (be / expensive)

3. Brand X _____ Brand Y.
   (taste / good)

4. Brand Z _____ Brand Y.
   (taste / good)

5. Brand Y _____ Brand X.
   (smell / delicious)

6. Brand Y _____ Brand Z.
   (smell / delicious)

EXERCISE 3 COMPARISONS WITH *THAN*

GRAMMAR NOTES 2–3 Look at the menu on the next page. Then complete these sentences comparing items on the menu. Use the appropriate comparative form of the adjectives in parentheses and *than* where necessary.

1. The sweet-and-sour shrimp is ____*more expensive than*____ the steamed scallops.
   (expensive)

2. The beef with red pepper is _____ the beef with broccoli.
   (hot)

3. The pork with scallions is _____ the sweet-and-sour shrimp.
   (expensive)

4. The chicken with orange sauce is _____ the steamed scallops.
   (spicy)

5. The steamed vegetables are _____ the pork with scallions.
   (salty)

6. The steamed vegetables are _____ the beef with red pepper.
   (healthy)

7. The broccoli with garlic is _____ the chicken with broccoli.
   (cheap)

8. The shrimp dish is _____ the scallop dish.
   (sweet)

9. The restaurant's hours on Sunday are _____ on Saturday.
   (short)

10. The children's menu is _____ the adult's menu.
    (varied)

11. The children's menu is _____, too.
    (expensive)

12. The chicken wings are _____ the macaroni and cheese slices.
    (sweet)

The Golden Palace

TAKE-OUT MENU

2465 Mineral Springs Rd. • Tel: (401) 555-4923

Open 7 days a week

Mon–Thurs: 11 a.m.–10 p.m. • Fri–Sat: 11 a.m.–11 p.m. • Sunday: 12 noon–10 p.m.

Broccoli with Garlic Sauce	$7.25
Beef with Broccoli	$8.75
Beef with Dried Red Pepper	$8.25
Chicken with Broccoli	$8.75
Chicken with Orange Sauce	$8.25
Sweet-and-Sour Shrimp	$9.25
Pork with Scallions	$7.25
Steamed Mixed Vegetables	$6.50
Steamed Scallops with Broccoli	$8.75

Hot and Spicy

No sugar, salt, or oil

Kids Corner

Honey Chicken Wings	$5.75
Pizza-Style Spring Roll	$4.50
Macaroni and Cheese Slices	$4.00

Place your order by phone and it will be ready when you arrive.

EXERCISE 4 INCREASE OR DECREASE; CAUSE AND EFFECT

GRAMMAR NOTES 4–5 Complete the conversations. Use the comparative form of the adjectives in parentheses to show an increase or decrease or a cause and effect.

1. A: Wow! The lines here are growing

   _____*longer and longer*_____ .
                  (long)

   B: Tell me about it. And, unfortunately,

   _____*the longer*_____ the wait,
           (long)

   _____*the hungrier*_____ I get.
         (hungry)

2. A: It's worth the wait. The food here is getting

   _____ .
              (good)

   B: But _____ the food,
            (good)

   _____ the bill!
       (high)

3. A: Some of the servers look like they're not a day older

   than fifteen. They seem to be getting

   _____ .
            (young)

   B: I know. And each time I come here, I feel _____ !
                  (old)

4. A: It's now evident that the cook is really very creative. The menu is definitely becoming

   _____ .
         (interesting)

   B: I know, but that means it's also _____ to choose something.
           (difficult)

5. A: There's Professor Lee. You know, his course is getting _____ .
            (popular)

   B: It's absolutely amazing. _____ his classes are,
           (hard)

   _____ the course gets. He's an incredible teacher.
       (popular)

6. A: Is it the hot sauce, or has your cough been getting _____ .
            (bad)

   B: It's the hot sauce, but I love it. For my taste, _____ ,
           (spicy)

   _____ .
       (good)

7. A: The service used to be slow here, but it's getting _____ .
           (fast)

   B: And that's good news. _____ the service,
           (fast)

   _____ the lines!
       (short)

EXERCISE 5 EDITING

GRAMMAR NOTES 1–5 Read the student's essay. There are ten mistakes in the use of *as...as* and comparatives with *than*. The first mistake is already corrected. Find and correct nine more.

Changing Tastes

When I was a teenager in the Philippines, I was an expert on snacks

and fast foods. I was growing fast, so the more I ate, the ~~hungry~~ *hungrier*

I felt. The street vendors in our town had the better snacks than

anyone else. In the morning, I used to buy rice muffins on the way

to school. They are even more sweeter that American muffins.

After school, I ate fish balls on a stick or *adidas* (chicken feet).

Snacks on a stick are small than traditional American hot dogs and

burgers, but they are much varied, and the food is much fresher. My

friend thought *banana-cue* (banana on a stick) was really incredible.

However, they weren't as sweet from *kamote-cue* (fried sweet

potatoes and brown sugar), my favorite snack.

When I came to the United States, I didn't like American fast

food at first. To me, it was interesting than my native food and less

tastier, too. Now I'm getting used to it, and in many ways it seems

just as good. In fact, it seems deliciouser and deliciouser.

EXERCISE 6 LISTENING

▶20|02   Ⓐ A couple is discussing two brands of pizza. Listen to their conversation. Read the list. Then listen again and check (✓) the pizza that is better in each category.

	Di Roma's	Angela's			Di Roma's	Angela's
1. cheap	✓	☐	**4.** tasty		☐	☐
2. big	☐	☐	**5.** fresh		☐	☐
3. healthy	☐	☐	**6.** interesting		☐	☐

▶20|02   Ⓑ Listen to the conversation again. Then work with a partner. Which pizza do *you* think is the better choice? Why?

EXAMPLE: A: I think Di Roma's is the better choice. For one thing, it's cheaper. It only costs $4.59. Angela's costs $5.59. It's a dollar more expensive.
B: True. But . . .

EXERCISE 7 PIZZA AROUND THE WORLD

PICTURE COMPARISON   Look at some of these favorite international pizza toppings. Discuss them with a partner. Make comparisons using some of the adjectives from the box.

EXAMPLE: A: The pizza from Hong Kong looks less filling than the one from Mexico.
B: Yes, but it looks just as spicy.

delicious	filling	healthy	interesting	spicy	tasty	traditional	unusual

1. Australia   2. Mexico   3. Hong Kong

4. Greece   5. Poland   6. Indonesia

EXERCISE 8 POPULAR FOODS

CONVERSATION Work in a group. Talk about the popularity of some foods in a country you know. Compare them to pizza.

EXAMPLE: A: Tacos are very popular in the United States, but probably not as popular as pizza.
B: Because of all the different kinds of pizza toppings, the choice of pizza types is more varied than the kinds of tacos.
C: I'm not sure I agree. I think tacos can be just as varied as pizza. There are lots of different taco fillings.

EXERCISE 9
YOUR RESTAURANT

A ROLE PLAY Work in a group. Before you role-play, imagine that you have a small restaurant. Give your restaurant a name and decide what to put on the menu. Discuss dishes and prices for each category. Use comparisons in your discussion.

EXAMPLE: A: We need a soup. How about chicken noodle?
B: Too boring! Gazpacho is more interesting.
C: How about black bean soup? It's a little more unusual.

B With your group, role-play ordering from your menu. One person is the server; the others are customers.

EXAMPLE: A: Is the gazpacho as spicy as the black bean soup?
B: No, the black bean soup is much spicier.
C: Great! I love spicy food. The spicier the better.

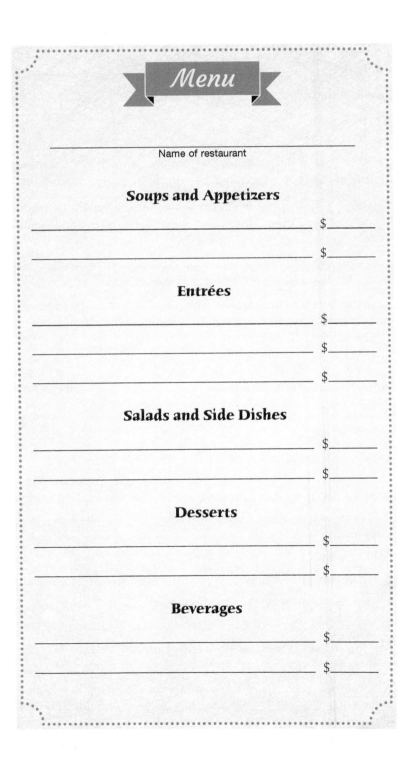

Menu

Name of restaurant

Soups and Appetizers
_____ $_____
_____ $_____

Entrées
_____ $_____
_____ $_____
_____ $_____

Salads and Side Dishes
_____ $_____
_____ $_____

Desserts
_____ $_____
_____ $_____

Beverages
_____ $_____
_____ $_____

FROM GRAMMAR TO WRITING

Ⓐ BEFORE YOU WRITE Think about the food from your city or country. Then think about another city's or country's food. Complete the lists with adjectives that describe the food in both cities or countries.

	(Your City or Country)	(Another City or Country)
Taste:		
Price:		
Variety:		
Popularity:		
Portion Sizes:		
Healthiness:		

Ⓑ WRITE Use the information from your lists to write a paragraph comparing your city's or country's food with the food of another city or country. Try to avoid the common mistakes in the chart.

EXAMPLE: The food in Turkey is fresher than the food in the United States. Turkey is not as big as the United States, but it has many farms and a lot of agriculture. There are many local food markets and . . .

Common Mistakes in Using Comparisons of Adjectives

Use the **correct comparative spelling**. Do not forget that the spelling sometimes changes when you add -er to an adjective.	The food in India is **hotter** than the food in England. NOT The food in India is ~~hoter~~ than the food in England.
Use *not as . . . as* with most **one-syllable adjectives**. Do not use *less than*.	The food in New York is**n't as cheap as** the food in Los Angeles. NOT The food in New York is ~~less cheap than~~ the food in Los Angeles.

Ⓒ CHECK YOUR WORK Read your paragraph. Underline the forms with *(not) as . . . as*. Circle the comparative adjective forms. Use the Editing Checklist to check your work.

Editing Checklist

Did you use . . . ?

☐ comparisons with *as . . . as* to show how food is or is not similar

☐ comparisons with *than* to show how food is different

☐ the correct form of comparative adjectives (long and short)

☐ the correct spelling of the comparative

Ⓓ REVISE YOUR WORK Read your paragraph again. Can you improve your writing? Make changes if necessary. Give your paragraph a title.

UNIT 20 **REVIEW**

Test yourself on the grammar of the unit.

Ⓐ Circle the correct words to complete the sentences.

1. Rosa's spaghetti is just as good as / than Maria's.
2. My mother's tomato sauce is good / better than Rizzo's bottled sauce.
3. These chairs are more / as comfortable than the old ones.
4. I don't like the new menu. It's more / less interesting than the old one.
5. The lines in my supermarket are getting long / longer and longer.
6. The longer the line, the more impatient / more impatient I get.

Ⓑ Complete the sentences with the comparative form of the words in parentheses. Use _than_ where necessary.

1. Tony's pizza is _____ Sal's, so I can't buy it often.
   (expensive)
2. It's also _____, so it's worth the price.
   (big)
3. Tony's restaurant is _____ Sal's. They have more tables.
   (large)
4. But Sal's hours are _____. They're open until midnight.
   (convenient)
5. Tony's is _____ from school. It's ten blocks away.
   (far)

Ⓒ Find and correct nine mistakes.

Last night, I had dinner at the new Pasta Place on the corner of Main Street and Grove. This new Pasta Place is just as good than the others, and it has just as many sauces to choose from. No one makes a more good traditional tomato sauce them. But there are much interestinger choices. Their mushroom cream sauce, for example, is as better as I've ever had. Try the mushroom and tomato sauce for a healthier than meal. It's just as delicious. The new branch is already popular. The later it is, longer the lines. My recommendation: Go early for a more short wait. And go soon. This place will only get more popular and more popular!

Now check your answers on page 479.

UNIT

21

OUTCOMES
- Form and use superlative adjectives
- Compare one person, place, or thing to others in a group
- Identify key details in an article about a city
- Identify places and locations by their descriptions in a conversation
- Describe and express opinions about places
- Write a description of one's hometown or city

Adjectives: Superlatives
CITIES

STEP 1   GRAMMAR IN CONTEXT

BEFORE YOU READ

Look at the photo. Discuss the questions.

1. Do you recognize this city? Where do you think it is?

2. What are some important features for a city to have?

READ

21|01   Read this travel brochure.

The biggest! The best!
The safest! The most exciting!

AFTER YOU READ

A VOCABULARY **Choose the word or phrase that best completes each sentence.**

1. A **financial** center has a lot of _____.
   - **a.** banks
   - **b.** parks
   - **c.** hospitals

2. A **multicultural** city has people from many different _____.
   - **a.** schools
   - **b.** theaters
   - **c.** countries

3. An important **feature** of Toronto is its _____.
   - **a.** city
   - **b.** safety
   - **c.** name

4. The transportation system is **public**. _____ can use it.
   - **a.** Everyone
   - **b.** No one
   - **c.** Only rich people

5. A **dynamic** city is not _____.
   - **a.** interesting
   - **b.** exciting
   - **c.** boring

6. _____ is one of the seven **continents** of the world.
   - **a.** Canada
   - **b.** North America
   - **c.** Toronto

A Superlative[1] City

TORONTO. It's the capital of the province of Ontario. It's also . . .

- the largest city in Canada
- the most important economic and financial center of the country
- one of the most multicultural places on earth[2] (Almost 50% of its population was born outside Canada, and over 100 languages are spoken in the city.)
- one of the easiest places to get around (It has the second largest public transportation system in North America.)
- the city that built the CN Tower, for many years the tallest free-standing structure in the world
- home to the Eaton Centre, a huge shopping mall (With more than fifty-two million visitors a year, it is one of the most popular tourist attractions in the city.)
- the safest city on the continent, and one of the most peaceful of all large, international cities on the planet

All of these features, and many more, make Toronto one of the most dynamic, exciting cities in the world and a major tourist destination.

1 *superlative:* excellent
2 *on earth:* on planet Earth (Earth is one of several planets, such as Mars or Jupiter, moving around the sun.)

B **COMPREHENSION** Read the statements. Check (✓) *True* or *False*.

	True	False
1. Some Canadian cities are larger than Toronto.	☐	☐
2. Some Canadian cities are more important financially than Toronto.	☐	☐
3. Many cities in the world aren't as multicultural as Toronto.	☐	☐
4. It's easy to get around Toronto.	☐	☐
5. Some cities on the North American continent are safer than Toronto.	☐	☐
6. The Eaton Centre attracts the most number of visitors in Toronto.	☐	☐

C **DISCUSSION** Work with a partner. Compare your answers in B. Why did you check *True* or *False*?

STEP 2 — GRAMMAR PRESENTATION

ADJECTIVES: SUPERLATIVES

Superlatives

	Superlative Adjective Form		
This is	the largest the busiest the best	city	*in* the world. *on* earth. *of* all. I've *ever* visited.
	the most interesting the least expensive		

GRAMMAR NOTES

1 Meaning of Superlative Adjectives

Use superlative adjectives to compare one person, place, or thing with other people, places, or things in a group.

• **people**	Canadians are **the friendliest** people I know. *(Canadians are friendlier than all other people I know.)*
• **places**	Toronto is **the largest** city in Canada. *(All other cities in Canada are smaller.)*
• **things**	The CN Tower is **the tallest** building in Canada. *(No other building in Canada is taller.)*

2 Forming Superlative Adjectives

There are several ways of forming superlative adjectives.

	ADJECTIVE	SUPERLATIVE
For **short adjectives** (one syllable and two syllables ending in -y), use *the* + adjective + -*est*.	tall	**the** tall**est**
	easy	**the** eas**iest**

IN WRITING There are often **spelling changes** when you add -*est*.	large	**the** larg**est**
	big	**the** big**gest**
	early	**the** earl**iest**

Some adjectives have **irregular** superlative forms.	good	**the best**
	bad	**the worst**
	far	**the farthest**

For **long adjectives** (two or more syllables), use *the most/the least* + adjective.	expensive	**the most** expensive
		the least expensive
An exception is the short adjective *fun*. It forms the superlative in the same way as a long adjective.	fun	**the most** fun NOT the ~~funnest~~

For **some adjectives**, such as *lively, lovely, friendly*, and *quiet*, you can use *the...-est* or *the most/ the least*. The -*est* form is more common.	Rio is **the liveliest** city on earth. *(more common)*
	Rio is **the most lively** city on earth. *(less common)*

BE CAREFUL! Do not use *most* or *least* with the superlative form of the adjective.	It's **the tallest** building.
	NOT It's the ~~most~~ tallest building.

3 Superlative Adjectives with Other Words and Expressions

We often use superlative adjectives with other words and expressions.

• **phrases with** *in*, *on*, or *of*	It's **the greatest** city *in the world*.
	It's **the safest** place *on earth*.
	This was **the best** day *of our visit*.
• *one of* + **plural count noun**	Toronto is *one of* **the most dynamic** *cities* in the world.
• *some of* + **plural count noun** + **non-count noun**	*Some of* **the best** *cities* have large parks.
	Toronto has *some of* **the best** *food* in Canada.
• *second (third, fourth...)*	It has **the** *second* **largest** transportation system.
• *ever* + **present perfect**	This is **the biggest** building I*'ve ever seen*.

REFERENCE NOTES

For a list of **adjectives** that use **both forms of the superlative**, see Appendix 9 on page 457.
For a list of **irregular superlative adjectives**, see Appendix 10 on page 458.
For **spelling rules** for the **superlative form of adjectives**, see Appendix 23 on page 463.

EXERCISE 1
DISCOVER THE GRAMMAR

A GRAMMAR NOTES 1–3
Read more information about Toronto. Underline all the superlative adjectives.

What to Do and See in Toronto

- **Go to the CN Tower.** It's one of <u>the tallest</u> buildings in the world. From there, you can get the best view of the city and countryside.
- **Drive along Yonge Street.** At 1,200 miles (1,800 km), it's one of the longest streets in the world. For one weekend in July, it's one of the liveliest, too. Come and join one million others for the exciting Yonge Street Festival.
- **Visit PATH,** the world's largest underground shopping complex.
- **Explore the Old Town of York.** It has the most historic buildings in the whole city.
- **Take the Yuk Yuk's Comedy Tour** of the Entertainment District— you'll have a good time on the funniest bus ride in town.
- **Visit the Toronto Zoo.** There's always something new and fascinating going on. Local people call it the best family outing in Toronto.

B Check (✓) all the true statements.

☑ **1.** There are buildings taller than the CN Tower.

☐ **2.** There are better views of the city than the views from the CN Tower.

☐ **3.** There are longer streets than Yonge Street.

☐ **4.** Yonge Street is the liveliest street in the world.

☐ **5.** PATH is larger than all other underground shopping complexes.

☐ **6.** The Old Town of York has more historic buildings than other sections of Toronto.

☐ **7.** There is no funnier bus ride in town than the Yuk Yuk's Comedy Tour.

☐ **8.** There are better family outings than the zoo.

EXERCISE 2 SUPERLATIVE ADJECTIVES

GRAMMAR NOTES 1–2 Look at the chart. Complete the sentences. Use the superlative form of the correct adjectives in parentheses.

CITY STATISTICS[1]

		ISTANBUL	MEXICO CITY	SEOUL	TORONTO
	Population	14,377,019	8,693,387	10,388,055	2,791,140
	Area	2,063 sq mi (5,343 sq km)	573 sq mi (1,485 sq km)	234 sq mi (605 sq km)	243 sq mi (630 sq km)
	Average January Temperature	42°F (5.5°C)	54°F (12.2°C)	27°F (-2.7°C)	23.5°F (-4.7°C)
	Average July Temperature	71°F (21.6°C)	63°F (17.22°C)	76.5°F (24.7°C)	69.5°F (20.83°C)
	Average Rainfall per Year	25.1 in (640 mm)	30 in (762 mm)	49 in (1,242 mm)	35.5 in (852.9 mm)
	Cost of a Cup of Coffee[2] ($US)	$3.92	$3.22	$4.54	$4.08
	Cost of a Bus Ticket ($US)	$1.30	$0.27	$0.86[3]	$2.39

1 based on 2013–2015 statistics
2 based on the cost of Starbuck's "grande latte" (a large cup of strong coffee with steamed milk)
3 based on the cost of the "yellow" city bus

1. Of all four cities, Toronto is _____*the smallest*_____ city in population, but not
   (large / small)
   in area.

2. The _____ city in area is Seoul.
   (big / small)

3. Istanbul has _____ population of all four cities, and it is
   (large / small)
   _____ city in area.
   (big / small)

4. In January, _____ city is Toronto.
   (warm / cold)

5. Seoul has _____ July temperatures.
   (hot / cool)

6. After Seoul, Istanbul has _____ July temperatures.
   (warm / cool)

7. _____ city is Seoul. _____
   (dry / rainy)   (dry / rainy)
   city is Istanbul.

8. You'll find _____ cup of coffee in Mexico City, and you'll find
   (cheap / expensive)
   _____ in Seoul.
   (cheap / expensive)

9. The city with _____ public buses is Mexico City. Toronto has
   (cheap / expensive)
   _____.
   (cheap / expensive)

EXERCISE 3 SUPERLATIVE ADJECTIVES

GRAMMAR NOTES 1–3 **Read about the CN Tower. Complete the information. Use the superlative form of the correct adjective from the box.**

clear	famous	fast	heavy	long	popular	~~tall~~

The CN Tower / *La Tour CN*

1. At 1,815 feet, 5 inches (553.33 m), the CN Tower is one of _____ *the tallest* _____ structures in the world.

2. Everyone recognizes Toronto's CN Tower. It is certainly _____ building in Canada.

3. At 130,000 tons (117,910 metric tonnes), the impressive CN Tower is one of _____ buildings on the planet.

4. With two million visitors every year, the CN Tower is one of _____ tourist attractions in the country.

5. Because of its very high antenna, the tower provides the people of Toronto with some of _____ radio and TV reception in North America.

6. Moving at 15 miles (22 km) per hour, the six elevators are among _____ in the world. The ride to the Look Out Level takes just 58 seconds.

7. If you don't want to take the elevator, you can try the stairs! The CN Tower has _____ metal staircase on earth.

EXERCISE 4 *THE MOST* AND *THE LEAST* + *EVER*

GRAMMAR NOTE 3 **Write superlative sentences about your own experiences. Use the words in parentheses with *the most* or *the least* + *ever* and the present perfect. Write two sentences for each item. See Appendix 1, page 453, for help with the irregular past participles.**

EXAMPLE: Toronto is the most multicultural city I've ever visited.
Meadville is the least multicultural city I've ever visited.

1. (multicultural / city / visit)

_____

_____

2. (comfortable / place / stay)

_____

_____

3. (friendly / people / meet)

_____

_____

4. (expensive / trip / take)

_____

_____

5. (interesting / place / see)

_____

_____

6. (exciting / team / watch)

_____

_____

EXERCISE 5 EDITING

GRAMMAR NOTES 1–3 **Read this email. There are eight mistakes in the use of superlative adjectives. The first mistake is already corrected. Find and correct seven more.**

● ○ ○

Greetings from Toronto—the ~~beautifulest~~ *most beautiful* city I've visited on the North American

continent. Yesterday, we went to the CN Tower—the more recognizable structure in

Canada. From there, you get the best view of the city—the different neighborhoods,

the harbor, the fast traffic. It made my head spin! This is one of most dynamic

places I've ever visited! The restaurant was the most expensivest I've ever seen, so

we just enjoyed the view and then went to Kensington Market to eat. This place has

the baddest crowds, but the cheapest and the goodest food we've had so far. We're

staying in East Toronto. It's not the closer place to downtown, but it has some of

most historic buildings. In fact, our bed-and-breakfast is called 1871 Historic House.

John Lennon slept here!

Love, Marissa

EXERCISE 6 LISTENING

▶21|02 **A** A couple is trying to choose a hotel for their trip to Toronto. Listen to their conversation. Look at the list below. Then listen again and check (✓) the correct hotel for each item.

	Westin Harbour Castle	Hôtel Le Germain	Eaton Chelsea
the best view	✓		
the most convenient			
the least convenient			
the most comfortable			
the most expensive			
the least expensive			
the biggest			
the smallest			

▶21|02 **B** Listen to the conversation again. Then work with a partner. Compare your answers. Give reasons.

EXAMPLE: A: The Westin has the best views.
B: Yes. You can see the lake from a lot of the rooms.
A: And their restaurant has a good view, too.

C Work in a group. Which hotel would *you* like to stay at? Why?

EXAMPLE: A: I'd like to stay at the Hôtel Le Germain.
B: Oh. Why is that?
A: Because it's the smallest of the three. I don't like big hotels. What about you?
B: I'd prefer . . .

EXERCISE 7 WHAT ABOUT YOU?

CONVERSATION Work with a partner. Talk about your answers to Exercise 4 on page 296. Keep the conversation going by asking questions like the ones below.

EXAMPLE: A: What's the most interesting city you've ever visited?
B: Toronto.
A: Why do you say that?
B: People from all over the world live there. It's very multicultural.

- What's the most interesting city you've ever visited?
- Which . . . did you like best?
- Why do you say that?
- Sounds great! What else did you like?
- Who did you meet?
- What was . . . ?

EXERCISE 8 CITIES IN YOUR COUNTRIES

DISCUSSION Work in a group. Discuss cities in your countries. You can use some of the adjectives from the box.

EXAMPLE: A: Madela, what's the most interesting city in your country?
B: I think Buenos Aires is the most interesting city in Argentina. There's so much to do—theater, sports, movies. It's also the most multicultural city in the country. People from all over the world live there. There are some really colorful neighborhoods, like La Boca.
C: It sounds very exciting. What's the most exciting city in your country, Chen?

| beautiful | colorful | exciting | important | modern | old |
| clean | dangerous | friendly | interesting | multicultural | popular |

La Boca neighborhood in Buenos Aires

Ⓐ BEFORE YOU WRITE Complete this list with facts about your hometown or city.

_____
(name of place)

Location _____

Population _____

Famous Places _____

Views _____

Transportation _____

Place(s) to Stay _____

Place(s) to Eat _____

Ⓑ WRITE Use the facts in your list to write a paragraph about your hometown or city. Include superlative adjectives. Try to avoid the common mistakes in the chart.

EXAMPLE: My hometown of Kochel am See is located in southern Germany. With a population of only about 4,000 people, it is one of the smallest towns in the area. It is also one of the most beautiful towns. It doesn't have any really famous places, but it has wonderful views. The nicest view is from . . .

Common Mistakes in Using Superlative Adjectives

Use the **correct superlative spelling**. Do not forget that the spelling sometimes changes when you add **-est** to an adjective.	She lives in the **prettiest** town in Germany. NOT She lives in the ~~prettyest~~ town in Germany.
Use only **one form of the superlative**. Do not use *most* or *least* with the superlative form of the adjective.	Toronto is **the most lively** city in Canada. or Toronto is **the liveliest** city in Canada. NOT Toronto is the ~~most~~ liveliest city in Canada.

Ⓒ CHECK YOUR WORK Read your paragraph. Underline the superlative adjectives. Use the Editing Checklist to check your work.

Editing Checklist

Did you use . . . ?

☐ superlative adjectives

☐ the correct form of superlative adjectives (long and short)

☐ the correct spelling of the superlative

☐ words and expressions such as *in the city, one of, some of,* or *ever*

Ⓓ REVISE YOUR WORK Read your paragraph again. Can you improve your writing? Make changes if necessary. Give your paragraph a title.

UNIT 21 REVIEW

Test yourself on the grammar of the unit.

A Complete each sentence with the superlative form of the correct word from the box.

| cheap | cold | dry | expensive | high | rainy |

1. Yakutsk, Russia, is _____ city in the world. The average January temperature is –37.5°F (–38.6°C).

2. At 16,732 ft (5,100 m), La Rinconada, Peru, is _____ city in the world.

3. Calama, Chile, is one of _____ towns on earth. It gets only .020 in (5 mm) of rain a year.

4. Cherrapunji, India, is one of _____. It gets around 463 in (11,777 mm).

5. Oslo, Norway, is one of _____ cities. A cup of Starbuck's coffee costs $9.83.

6. New Delhi, India, is one of _____. A cup of Starbuck's is $2.80.

B Complete the conversation with the superlative form of the adjectives in parentheses.

A: Welcome back! You just missed _____ week of the year so far. It
1. (bad)
   snowed every day! How was your trip?

B: Orlando was great! The Magic Kingdom is _____ place.
2. (fantastic)

A: It's _____ amusement park. It's also _____.
3. (popular)   **4. (crowded)**

B: True. The long lines were _____ part of the trip.
5. (difficult)

A: What was _____ part?
6. (good)

B: Monsters, Inc. It's not _____ show in the world, but it's quite good.
7. (funny)

C Find and correct seven mistakes.

Small towns aren't most dynamic places to visit, and that's just why we love to vacation on

Tangier Island. This tiny island is probably the less popular vacation spot in the United States.

Almost no one comes here. But it's also one of the most safest places to visit. And you'll find some

of the goodest seafood and the beautiful beaches here. It's one of the easy places to get around

(there are no cars on the island). If you get bored, just hop on the ferry. You're only a few hours

from Washington, D.C., and a few more hours from New York and the excitingest nightlife ever.

Now check your answers on page 480.

Adverbs: *As...as*, Comparatives, Superlatives

SPORTS

OUTCOMES
- Form and use comparative and superlative adverbs
- Express how two actions are similar or different
- Identify main ideas in an opinion article and in a debate
- Discuss issues in a debate, supporting opinions
- Describe and compare people's abilities
- Write arguments for and against a statement

STEP 1   GRAMMAR IN CONTEXT

BEFORE YOU READ

Look at the photo. Discuss the questions.

1. What sport is this?

2. Describe the pitcher (the person holding the ball).

3. Is there anything unusual about the pitcher? If yes, what?

READ

22|01   Read this newspaper opinion piece.

SPORTS

Separation of the Sexes?

Pitcher Eri Yoshida

Can women compete in sports as well as men? Can they run as fast as men or throw a ball as far? Should they be able to compete against men or play with men on the same team? These questions have been the source of debate for ages. And people on both sides of the debate are arguing more passionately[1] than ever.

Many sports require upper-body strength. The average man has more upper-body strength than the average female. But some women can use their strength more efficiently than men. In 1973, in a tennis

---

1 *passionately:* with strong feelings

match called the "Battle of the Sexes," Billie Jean King (female) beat Bobby Riggs (male) in front of 30,000 people. In more recent years, pitcher Eri Yoshida has been playing professionally on all-male baseball teams, and she has won several games.

Physical strength does not tell the whole story. Society does not value female athletes as much as male athletes. As a result, women have not had enough opportunity to play. They do not compete as frequently as men, and when they play, they aren't taken as seriously as men. Professional female athletes have even received insults from their male teammates and from spectators.[2] This attitude is changing, however, especially among younger people. As a result, women will have more opportunities to play. And the more they play, the better they'll be able to compete.

So, should women and men play on separate teams, or should women be allowed to play with men on the same teams? The answer is clear: If an athlete plays well enough to compete in a sport, that person, male or female, should be allowed to. On the other hand, if an athlete plays the best he or she can, but still cannot meet the qualifications[3] of the team, then that person should not be on the team. Sports should be an equal opportunity activity. It's that simple. No ifs, ands, or buts.[4]

---

[2] *spectators:* people who watch sports events

[3] *qualifications:* the skills necessary for a job or position
[4] *no ifs, ands, or buts:* without any questions or doubts

AFTER YOU READ

A VOCABULARY **Complete the sentences with the words from the box.**

competes	debate	insults	requires	source	values

1. Tennis _____ a lot of upper-body strength.

2. The manager _____ her. He thinks she's an important member of the team.

3. The two sides in the TV _____ had very different opinions.

4. My school's baseball team often _____ against the Blues.

5. I think the _____ of the problem is that the team hasn't practiced enough.

6. The crowd shouted _____ at the losing players. It was terrible.

B COMPREHENSION **Read the statements. Check (✓) True or False.**

	True	False
1. People are not interested in the role of women athletes in sports.	☐	☐
2. Some women make more efficient use of their strength than men do.	☐	☐
3. Women need more opportunities to compete.	☐	☐
4. Society takes female athletes seriously.	☐	☐
5. All women should be allowed to compete against men.	☐	☐

C DISCUSSION **Work with a partner. Compare your answers in B. Why did you check** *True* **or** *False***?**

ADVERBS: *AS ... AS*, COMPARATIVES, SUPERLATIVES

As ... as

		As	Adverb	As	
Women	play don't play	as	hard well aggressively consistently	as	men.

Comparatives

		Comparative Adverb Form	*Than*	
Alexis	played	harder better more aggressively less consistently	than	Tyler.

Superlatives

		Superlative Adverb Form	
The star player	played	the hardest the best the most aggressively the least consistently	*of* anyone in the game.

GRAMMAR NOTES

1 Comparisons with *As . . . As*

Use *as* + **adverb** + *as* to show how the actions of two people or things are **the same or equal**.	Gilbert plays **as well as** Miller. *(Gilbert and Miller play equally well.)*
You can add *just* before the comparison to make it stronger.	Gilbert plays **just as well as** Miller. *(Gilbert and Miller really play equally well.)*
Use *not as* + **adverb** + *as* to show how the actions of two people or things are **not the same or equal**.	Gilbert didn't play **as aggressively as** Jones. *(Gilbert and Jones didn't play the same. Jones played more aggressively.)*
Notice that *not* goes before the main verb.	NOT Gilbert played ~~not~~ as aggressively as Jones.
USAGE NOTE We often leave out the second part of the comparison when the meaning is clear.	A: Gilbert hit the ball as well as Miller. B: But she didn't run **as fast**. *(She didn't run as fast as Miller.)*

2 Comparisons with *Than*

Use **comparative adverbs** + *than* to show how the actions of two people or things are **different**.	The Mets played **better than** the Pirates. Clark played **more skillfully than** Brown. He played **less skillfully than** Rogers.
You can add *even* before the comparison to make it stronger. *Even* expresses that something is surprising or unexpected.	The Pirates played aggressively, but the Mets played **even more aggressively than** the Pirates.
USAGE NOTE We usually do not use *less . . . than* with one-syllable adverbs. Instead we use:	NOT Clark runs ~~less fast than~~ Brown.
• *not as . . . as*	Clark doesn't run **as fast as** Brown. or
• another adverb with the opposite meaning	Clark runs **slower than** Brown.
Remember that it is not necessary to mention the second part of the comparison when the meaning is clear.	Brown didn't play as hard as Clark, but she hit the ball **more consistently**. *(. . . more consistently than he hit the ball)*

3 Superlative Adverbs

Use **superlative adverbs** to compare one action with the actions of other people or things in a group.	All the players worked hard, but Robins worked **the hardest**.
We often use a **phrase with** *of* after a superlative adverb.	She scored **the most frequently *of any player*** on the team.
USAGE NOTE We don't use superlative adverbs very often. Instead, we use a comparison with *than* to compare an action with the actions of a group.	Robins worked **the hardest** of anyone on the team. *(less common)* Robins worked **harder than** anyone on the team. *(more common)*

4 Forming Comparative and Superlative Adverbs

There are several ways of forming comparative and superlative adverbs.

	ADVERB	COMPARATIVE	SUPERLATIVE
For most **short adverbs** (one syllable), use **adverb** + -*er* or *the* + **adverb** + -*est*.	fast	fast**er**	**the** fast**est**
	hard	hard**er**	**the** hard**est**
Some short adverbs have **irregular** comparative and superlative forms.	well	**better**	**the best**
	badly	**worse**	**the worst**
	far	**farther**	**the farthest**
	much / a lot	**more**	**the most**
	little	**less**	**the least**
For **long adverbs** (two or more syllables), use *more/less* + **adverb** or *the most/the least* + **adverb**.	skillfully	**more/less** skillfully	**the most/the least** skillfully
Some **adverbs of manner** have two comparative and two superlative forms.	quickly	**more** quickly	**the most** quickly
		quicker	**the quickest**

IN WRITING In formal writing, the forms with *more/less* and *the most/the least* are more common. The -*er*/-*est* forms are more common in spoken English and informal writing.

He got there **more quickly than** the ball. *(newspaper)*
He got there **quicker than** the ball. *(conversation)*

BE CAREFUL! Do not put an **adverb of manner** between the verb and the object.

She *threw the ball* **farther** than Tommy.
NOT She ~~threw farther the ball~~ . . .

5 To Show an Increase or Decrease

Repeat the comparative adverb to show an increase or a decrease.

| comparative adverb + *and* + comparative adverb | Yoshida is playing **better and better**. *(Her performance keeps getting better.)* |

BE CAREFUL! With **long adverbs**, repeat only *more* or *less*.

She's playing **more and more aggressively**.
NOT She's playing more ~~aggressively~~ and more aggressively.

6 To Show Cause and Effect

Use **two comparative adverbs** to show cause and effect.

| *the* + comparative adverb + *the* + comparative adverb | **The harder** she played, **the better** she got. *(When she played harder, she got better.)* |

REFERENCE NOTES

For a list of **irregular comparative and superlative adverbs** see Appendix 10 on page 458.
For more information on **adverbs**, see Unit 19 on page 262.

EXERCISE 1   DISCOVER THE GRAMMAR

 GRAMMAR NOTES 1–6 Read this letter to the editor. Underline all the comparisons with *(not) as* + adverb + *as*, and all the comparative and superlative adverbs forms.

To the Editor:

I read with interest last week's article "Sports: Separation of the Sexes?" The author claims that female athletes can compete <u>as well as</u> males. I cannot disagree more strongly! Women are simply not as powerful as men. That's not an insult. It's a fact. And it's the source of the problem. Even the best female athlete cannot throw a ball as hard or run as fast as the average male athlete. It's true that in some sports that don't require great strength, some women can compete as effectively as men. But those are the exceptions, not the rule. There are many examples of women who play the best of anyone on their team, but still play worse than the average male athlete. Women are trying harder and harder to enter the sports world of men. And the harder they try, the more they will fail. Clearly, women can be great athletes. I just think that they should play with women against other women.

Mary Kennedy, Student
Bryant University, Smithfield, RI

B Which underlined words in the letter to the editor express...

1. equal ability: *as well as* _____

2. unequal ability: _____

3. a comparative: _____

4. a superlative: _____

5. an increase: _____

6. cause and effect: _____

EXERCISE 2 COMPARISONS WITH *AS ... AS*

GRAMMAR NOTE 1   Read this chart comparing three brands of basketball shoes. Complete the sentences. Use *(not) as* + adverb + *as* and the words in parentheses.

Brand	Comfort	Support	Protection	Durability*	Cost
X	●	◗	●	◗	$98
Y	●	○	●	○	$72
Z	○	○	◗	◗	$72

SHOES   BETTER ● ⟷ ◗ ○ WORSE

*how long the product lasts

1. Brand X _____ *fits as comfortably as* _____ Brand Y.
   (fit / comfortable)

2. Brand Z _____ Brand X or Y.
   (fit / comfortable)

3. Brand Y _____ Brand Z.
   (support / the ankles / good)

4. Brands Y and Z _____ Brand X.
   (support / the ankles / good)

5. Brand Z _____ Brand X or Y.
   (protect / the feet / effective)

6. Brand X _____ Brand Y.
   (protect / the feet / effective)

7. Brand X _____ Brand Z.
   (last / long)

8. Brand Y _____ Brand X or Z.
   (last / long)

9. Brands Y and Z _____ Brand X.
   (cost / much)

EXERCISE 3 *AS ... AS*, COMPARATIVE AND SUPERLATIVE ADVERBS

Ⓐ GRAMMAR NOTES 1–6   Complete this conversation between sports commentator Carla Lobo and player Elena Bard. Change the adjectives in parentheses to adverbs. Use them with *as ... as* or with the comparative or superlative forms. Add *the* or *than*, and choose between *more* or *less* where necessary.

LOBO: Why do people still take female basketball players _____ *less seriously than* _____
   1. (serious)

   male players? Do women really play _____ men?
   2. (aggressive)

BARD: Absolutely not! We play just _____. And when we fall, we
   3. (aggressive)

   hit the floor just _____ the guys do.
   4. (hard)

LOBO: You could sure see that in tonight's game. Jackson played _____
   5. (effective)

   of all the players I've seen—male or female. She never let Cash anywhere near the basket.

BARD: Yes. And she performs like that much _____ a lot of men.
              6. (consistent)

Jackson always gets the job done.

LOBO: Some people say women play _____ men.
            7. (cooperative)

BARD: I agree. I think we have better teamwork—we play _____
              8. (good)

on a team. We're also more patient. I've noticed that most women players are able to wait

_____ for a good chance to shoot.
    9. (long)

LOBO: Tickets for women's basketball games cost _____ tickets for
             10. (little)

men's games. Does that bother you?

BARD: Sure. It shows that society doesn't value female athletes as much as they value males. But

_____ women players are able to attract fans,
   11. (fast)

_____ the women's leagues will make money.
   12. (fast)

▶22|02 **B** LISTEN AND CHECK **Listen to the conversation and check your answers in A.**

EXERCISE 4 COMPARATIVE AND SUPERLATIVE ADVERBS

GRAMMAR NOTES 2–4 **Read this chart comparing the performances of four athletes. Then complete the sentences. Use the comparative or superlative adverb form of the words from the box. You will use some words more than once.**

bad	far	fast	good	high	slow

	Broad Jump [distance]	**Pole Vaulting** [height]	**5-mile (8-km) Run** [speed]
Nolan	10.3 ft (3.14 m)	17.3 ft (5.27 m)	26 minutes
Smith	10.1 ft (3.08 m)	17.2 ft (5.24 m)	28 minutes
Costas	11.2 ft (3.42 m)	17.8 ft (5.43 m)	30 minutes
Olsson	11.4 ft (3.48 m)	18.2 ft (5.55 m)	25 minutes

1. Nolan jumped _____*farther than*_____ Smith.

2. Olsson vaulted _____*the highest*_____ of all.

3. Costas ran _____.

4. Smith ran _____ Olsson.

5. Olsson jumped _____.

6. Nolan ran _____ Smith.

7. Olsson vaulted _____ Smith.

8. All in all, Olsson did _____.

9. All in all, Smith did _____.

EXERCISE 5 EDITING

GRAMMAR NOTES 1–6 Read this transcript of a TV sports program. There are eight mistakes in the use of adverbs. The first mistake is already corrected. Find and correct seven more.

CINDY: What a game! Spero, have you ever seen two teams play more aggressively ~~than~~?

SPERO: No, I haven't, Cindy. Folks, we're in Bangkok, Thailand, watching the Australian and French teams battle for the Women's World Basketball Championship. It's halftime, and just listen to that crowd! I think the Australians cheer the most loudest of any fans in the game!

CINDY: Well, the court really belonged to France for the first part of the game, Spero. And without question, Maud Medenou of France was playing the better of all the players on both teams. But the Australian team recovered more quickly than I thought possible. They've scored almost as frequently than the French in the first half. The score is now 30-28, France, and no one can predict a winner at this point.

SPERO: I heard that Elizabeth Cambage, Australia's star player, injured her arm yesterday, but you can't tell from the way she's playing today. So far, she's scored the least of any player on her team. She's playing a great game.

CINDY: And with an injury, too! Spero, I have to say that's pretty amazing. But Medenou isn't that far behind. Did you notice that she's been playing more intensely and more intensely in this tournament? You can see that she really wants the ball, and she's getting it more consistently in every game.

SPERO: You're right, Cindy. And the more hard she plays, the more she scores. The spectators love her. They're cheering more and less enthusiastically.

CINDY: The Australians have really been playing a great defense tonight. They've been blocking Medenou more effectively than any other team this season. But can they stop her?

SPERO: We'll find out soon! The second half is ready to begin. See you again after the game.

Elizabeth Cambage

EXERCISE 6
LISTENING

22|03 **A** Two students are having a debate. The question is: Do you think women should play with men on the same teams? Listen to the debate. Then listen again. Read and circle the words you hear. Listen again and check (✓) the person who made each statement.

Marta   Chin

		Marta	Chin
1.	Women can't hit a ball as ⓕⓐⓡ / fast as men.	☐	☑
2.	They can't run as far / fast as men.	☐	☐
3.	Women don't play as regularly / skillfully as men.	☐	☐
4.	Women are playing more and more aggressively / frequently.	☐	☐
5.	The more fairly / frequently they play, the better they get.	☐	☐
6.	Some women run farther / faster than men.	☐	☐
7.	The fastest woman doesn't run as fast / far as the average man.	☐	☐
8.	Many women can play more skillfully / successfully than men.	☐	☐
9.	Women can shoot the ball as accurately / well as men.	☐	☐
10.	Some women can aim a ball better / more accurately than some men.	☐	☐
11.	They don't play as aggressively / seriously as men.	☐	☐
12.	Many male athletes will be afraid to play as aggressively / passionately against females.	☐	☐

B Work with a partner. Discuss the debate. Which opinions do you agree with? Which do you disagree with? Which of the debaters argued better? Which of the debaters argued more passionately? Did either of the debaters change your opinion?

EXAMPLE: **A:** Chin said that women can't hit the ball as far as men. I think that is generally true. Men usually have more upper-body strength.

B: I think it depends on the man and it depends on the woman. Some women can hit the ball farther than some men.

A: True, but they are the exception. . . .

EXERCISE 7
GOOD, BETTER, BEST!

COMPARISON Work in a group. Name several famous athletes for one sport. Compare their abilities. Use some of the verbs and adverbs in the list below.

EXAMPLE: Usain Bolt is a runner from Jamaica. In 2015, he could run faster than anyone else on earth.

Verbs	Adverbs
catch	carefully
hit	defensively
kick	easily
race	fast
run	hard
play	powerfully
throw	straight
train	successfully

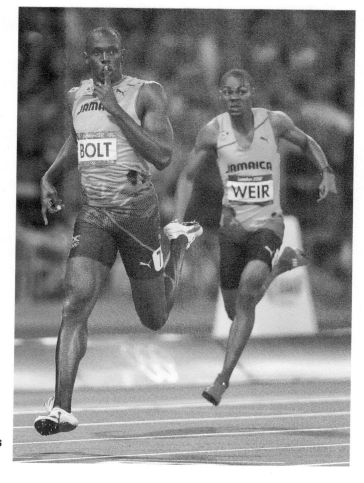

Usain "Lightning" Bolt sets a world record in London.

EXERCISE 8 THE IMPORTANCE OF SPORTS

A QUESTIONNAIRE How important is sports in your life? How well do you balance[1] work (job or school) with your enjoyment of sports? Complete the questionnaire.

1 *balance:* give equal importance to

HOW IMPORTANT IS SPORTS IN YOUR LIFE?

1. How many hours do you play sports a week? _____

2. How many hours do you study a week? _____

3. How many hours do you work a week? _____

4. How often do you attend a sports event? _____

5. How many hours a week do you watch sports on TV? _____

6. When was the last time you watched a sports event? _____

B Work in a group. Compare your answers to the questionnaire with those of your classmates. Then answer the questions below.

EXAMPLE: A: Sharif plays sports the most regularly.
B: Yes. He's on the basketball team and he practices or competes almost every day.
C: Who studies the hardest?

1. Who plays sports the most regularly?
2. Who studies the hardest?
3. Who works the hardest?
4. Who attends sports events the most frequently?
5. Who watches sports on TV the most often?
6. Who watched a sports event the most recently?
7. Who balances work (or school) with their interest in sports the most successfully?

EXERCISE 9 WOMEN AND MEN

DISCUSSION Work in a group. Discuss these questions.

1. Can women compete as well as men? Why or why not?

EXAMPLE: A: I think some women can compete as well as men.
B: I agree. Especially in sports like tennis or skating.
C: I'm not so sure. I think women . . .

2. Should men compete *against* women?

3. Should men and women play on the same teams?

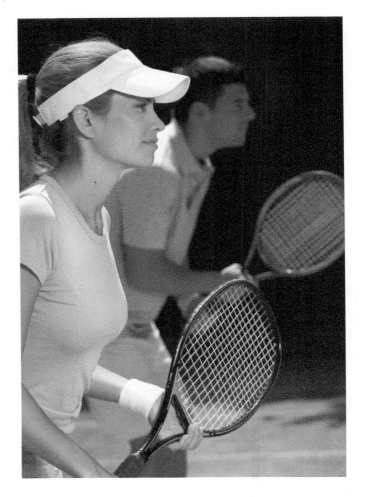

FROM GRAMMAR TO WRITING

A BEFORE YOU WRITE Choose one of the statements below. Complete the outline with arguments *For* and *Against* the statement.

1. Women should play on the same team as men.

2. Women should play against men in one-on-one sports such as tennis.

_____
(write the statement you chose)

Arguments For   **Arguments Against**

_____   _____

_____   _____

B WRITE Use your outline to write a paragraph about the statement you chose. Give reasons for and against the statement. Try to avoid the common mistakes in the chart.

EXAMPLE: People have very strong opinions about male and female athletes. Should women, for example, play on the same baseball team as men? It's true that most women cannot throw the ball as hard as men, and . . . However, women can throw just as accurately as men, and . . .

Common Mistakes in Using *As . . . as*, and Comparative and Superlative Adverbs

Put an **adverb of manner** after the object. Do not put it between the verb and the object.	She ***throws the ball* harder** than him. NOT She ~~throws harder the ball~~ than him.
With **one-syllable adverbs**, use *not as . . . as* or an adverb with the opposite meaning. Do not use *less . . . than*.	She does **not** run **as fast as** Lee She runs **more slowly than** Lee. NOT She runs ~~less fast than~~ Lee.
To show an **increase or decrease** with long adverbs, repeat only *more* or *less*. Do not repeat the adverb.	They are playing **more and more aggressively**. NOT They are playing more ~~aggressively~~ and more aggressively.

C CHECK YOUR WORK Read your paragraph. Underline the comparative adverbs once. Underline the superlative adverbs twice. Circle the form with *as* + adverb + *as*. Use the Editing Checklist to check your work.

Editing Checklist

Did you use . . . ?

☐ *as . . . as* to show how two actions are the same or equal

☐ comparative adverbs with *than* to show how actions are different

☐ superlative adverbs to compare one person's actions to actions of a group

D REVISE YOUR WORK Read your paragraph again. Can you improve your writing? Make changes if necessary. Give your paragraph a title.

UNIT 22 REVIEW

Test yourself on the grammar of the unit.

A Circle the correct words to complete the sentences.

1. Chen plays just as good / well as Sanchez.

2. Maya is a slow runner. She runs / doesn't run as fast as her teammates.

3. Dan always shoots the ball more accurately / the most accurately than Will.

4. Inez plays the most aggressively of / than all the other players.

5. Our team didn't play the worst / as well as I expected. I was disappointed.

6. The faster Tranh runs, the more tired he gets / he gets more tired.

7. We need to practice harder / hardly if we want to win.

8. You're playing well / better and better!

B Complete the sentences with the correct form of the words in parentheses.

1. You play just as _____ as Tomás.
(good)

2. Olga runs _____ than any of her teammates.
(fast)

3. Diego shoots the ball _____ of all the players.
(accurate)

4. He practices _____ of all.
(hard)

5. Their team played _____ of all the teams.
(bad)

C Find and correct seven mistakes.

Last night's game was a very exciting one. The Globes played the best they've played all season. But they still didn't play as good as the Stars. The Stars hit the ball more frequent and ran more fast than the Globes, and their pitcher, Kevin Rodriguez, threw the ball more accurately. Their catcher, Scott Harris, handled better the ball than the Globes' catcher. The Globes are good, but they are less good than the Stars. All in all, the Stars just keep playing good and better. And the better they play, the hardest it is for their fans to get tickets! These games sell out quicker than hotcakes, so go early if you want to get a chance to see the Stars.

Now check your answers on page 480.

Gerunds and Infinitives

PART 7

OUTCOMES

- Use gerunds as the subject or object of a verb
- Recognize main ideas in an article about a habit and trend
- Recognize whether an action is recommended or not recommended in a conversation
- Discuss health and exercise habits
- Discuss one's opinion on a controversial topic
- Write a short opinion essay on a controversial topic

OUTCOMES

- Use verbs that are followed by infinitives
- Identify statistics in a short article
- Evaluate speakers' attitudes in a conversation
- Discuss tendencies and preferences
- Give an opinion in response to a literary quote
- Write a paragraph on a personal topic, using transition words

OUTCOMES

- Express purpose with an infinitive or *in order to*
- Use adjectives/adverbs + infinitives
- Identify important details and opinions in a short text with quotes
- Identify key details in a TV ad
- Discuss the pros and cons of new technologies
- Write a paragraph describing the pros and cons of a smart device

OUTCOMES

- Use verbs that can be followed by gerunds or infinitives
- Use prepositions/phrasal verbs + gerunds
- Identify key points in an article and in an interview
- Discuss solutions to common problems
- Give an opinion in response to a literary quote
- Write several paragraphs about how to achieve one's goals

Gerunds: Subject and Object

HEALTH ISSUES

OUTCOMES
- Use gerunds as the subject or object of a verb
- Recognize main ideas in an article about a habit and trend
- Recognize whether an action is recommended or not recommended in a conversation
- Discuss health and exercise habits
- Discuss one's opinion on a controversial topic
- Write a short opinion essay on a controversial topic

STEP 1 **GRAMMAR IN CONTEXT**

BEFORE YOU READ

Look at the cartoon. Discuss the questions.

1. Why are the people standing on the ledge of the building?

2. How do you think they feel about it?

3. How do *you* feel about it?

READ

▶ 23|01 Read this article about smoking regulations.

No Smoking: Around the World from **A** to **Z**

In the past few decades,[1] life has become more and more difficult for people who enjoy lighting up.[2] At the same time, it has become more comfortable for people who don't smoke. And for those who want to quit smoking, it has become easier as countries around the world introduce laws that limit or ban smoking in public, and sometimes even private spaces. Here are some examples, from **A** to **Z**:

- **AUSTRIA:** In Austria, the law prohibits smoking in many public places, including trains and train stations. It's also banned in offices unless all employees are in favor of permitting it. Large restaurants must provide areas for non-smokers, but smaller ones can choose between permitting smoking or being smoke-free.

- **JAPAN:** Smoking is illegal on the streets in some cities in Japan.

- **MEXICO:** In Mexico, smoking is not permitted at all in restaurants. The government has also banned advertising tobacco products on TV or radio.

- **UAE:** The United Arab Emirates has recently started banning cigarettes in shopping malls and other public places. Selling cigarettes to minors[3] has also become illegal.

- **ZAMBIA:** In Zambia, the law bans smoking in all public places. Not obeying the law can result in fines and even jail time.

---

1 *decades:* ten-year periods
2 *lighting up:* smoking
3 *minors:* people under the age of eighteen

By now, almost everyone agrees that smoking is bad for your health. But, although many people approve of the new laws, not everyone is in favor of prohibiting public smoking. "It's one thing to try to discourage the habit by putting a high tax on cigarettes," says one smoker, "but some of the new laws go too far." Smokers argue that the laws limit personal freedom. They say everyone today knows the dangers of lighting up. So, if someone won't quit smoking and wants to smoke outdoors in a park or on the beach, it is that person's choice. Those smokers are only hurting themselves. There are many things that people do that are not good for them, such as eating junk food[4] and not exercising. But there are no laws that regulate[5] those behaviors.

4 *junk food:* food that is bad for you (usually with a lot of sugar and fat)
5 *regulate:* control (with rules or laws)

AFTER YOU READ

A VOCABULARY **Look at the words in the box. Which words can you use for something that is *OK to Do*? Something that is *Not OK to Do*? Write the words in the appropriate column.**

approve of	ban	illegal	in favor of	permit	prohibit

OK to Do   **Not OK to Do**

_____   _____

_____   _____

_____   _____

B COMPREHENSION **Complete each statement with the name of the correct country.**

1. Smoking outside is illegal in some parts of _____ .

2. In _____ , workers can decide on permitting smoking in the workplace or not.

3. _____ bans smoking in shopping malls.

4. Breaking non-smoking laws is a very serious crime in _____ .

5. In _____ , people can choose between dining in a smoke-free restaurant or in a smaller cigarette-friendly place.

6. You won't see any cigarette ads on TV in _____ .

7. _____ has recently banned selling cigarettes to young people.

C DISCUSSION **Work with a partner. Compare your answers in B. Why did you choose each country?**

GERUNDS: SUBJECT AND OBJECT

Gerund as Subject

Gerund (Subject)	Verb	
Smoking	causes	health problems.
Not smoking	is	healthier.

Gerund as Object

Subject	Verb	Gerund (Object)
You	should quit	**smoking.**
We	suggest	**not smoking.**

Gerund as Object of a Preposition

	Preposition	Gerund	
Are you	**against**	**smoking**	in public?
I plan	**on**	**quitting**	next month.
I'm in favor	**of**	**permitting**	smoking.

GRAMMAR NOTES

1 Forming Gerunds

A gerund is **the base form of the verb** + *-ing*.	**Smoking** is bad for your health. I enjoy **having** a cigarette in the park. She's against **allowing** cigarettes in the office.
IN WRITING There are often spelling changes when you add *-ing*.	**BASE FORM** **GERUND** smoke smok**ing** permit permit**ting** die **dying**
Form the **negative** by placing *not* before the gerund: *not* + *gerund*.	**Not exercising** is bad for you. The doctor suggested **not drinking** coffee. She's happy about **not working** today.
Do not confuse the gerund with the **progressive**. The progressive needs a form of the verb *be*.	GERUND **Drinking** a lot of coffee is unhealthy. PROGRESSIVE He **is drinking** coffee right now.

A gerund is a verb form that you use **like a noun**—as a **subject** or an **object**.

A gerund can be the **subject** of a sentence. It is always singular. Use the third-person-singular form of the verb after gerunds.	**Eating** junk food **makes** me sick. **Advertising** cigarettes on TV **is** illegal.

A gerund can be the **object** of certain verbs. Use a gerund after these verbs:

admit	can't stand	like	recommend	He **can't stand** seeing all the no smoking signs.
advise	consider	limit	resist	Have you **considered** quitting?
allow	deny	mind	risk	Do they **allow** smoking in malls?
appreciate	dislike	miss	start	I **dislike** sitting near smokers in cafés.
avoid	enjoy	permit	stop	She **stopped** smoking last year.
ban	finish	prohibit	suggest	Dr. Ho **suggested** not staying up late.
begin	keep	quit	support	She **kept** trying to quit.

USAGE NOTE We often use *go* + *gerund* to describe activities such as *shopping, dancing, fishing, skiing, swimming,* and *camping.*	Let's **go swimming** in the lake. I **went** shopping for running shoes at the mall.

A gerund can also be the **object of a preposition**.

Use a gerund **after prepositions** such as:

about	at	by	in	to	He spoke to the doctor **about** quitting.
after	before	for	of	with	She's **for** banning tobacco ads.
against	between	from	on	without	I'm **against** smoking in public places.

There are many **expressions with prepositions**. You can use a gerund after expressions with:

• **verb + preposition** *advise against* *believe in* *count on*	I **believe in** taking care of my health.
• **adjective + preposition** *afraid of* *bored with* *excited about*	I'm **excited about** joining the health club.
BE CAREFUL! Use a **gerund**, not the base form of the verb, after expressions with the preposition *to*: *look forward to* *be opposed to* *object to*	I **look forward to** seeing you. NOT I look forward to ~~see~~ you.

REFERENCE NOTES

For **spelling rules for verb + *-ing***, see Appendix 21 on page 462.

For a list of **verbs followed by gerunds**, see Appendix 13 on page 459.

For a list of **adjectives followed by prepositions**, see Appendix 17 on page 459.

For a list of **verbs followed by prepositions**, see Appendix 18 on page 460.

EXERCISE 1 DISCOVER THE GRAMMAR

GRAMMAR NOTES 1–3 Read this online bulletin board about smoking. Underline all the gerunds.

Re: Can't Stand <u>Seeing</u> Those Signs!

Posted by Grofumeur on February 16, 2016 at 15:30:03

I can't stand seeing all the new No Smoking signs. It's getting harder and harder to have a good time. Next thing you know, they'll ban laughing! Eating in a restaurant or having an espresso in a café is just no fun anymore! Junk food is worse than smoking. But I bet the government won't prohibit people from ordering burgers and fries for lunch!

Reply posted by Nuffsed on February 17, 2016 at 12:15:22

Hey, Grofumeur—I'm against smoking in public places. I'm even in favor of banning smoking in apartment buildings. I don't get sick when my boyfriend has a Big Mac, but sitting in a room full of his cigarette smoke makes my hair and clothing stink. I'm really enjoying the new regulations.

Reply posted by Swissfriend on February 17, 2016 at 20:53:11

Hi, Smokers! I am a member of Freunde der Tabak, a Swiss group of smokers and non-smokers. We always suggest practicing courtesy to non-smokers and tolerance of smokers. I enjoy smoking, but I dislike inhaling secondhand smoke. I don't see a problem with people smoking outside, and I'm against banning it.

Reply posted by Cleanaire on February 18, 2016 at 9:53:11

Friend—Have you ever tried to stop smoking? If so, then you know you are addicted to nicotine. The younger you start smoking, the harder it is to quit. I definitely don't approve of advertising cigarettes or selling them to young people. That should be illegal!

EXERCISE 2 AFFIRMATIVE OR NEGATIVE GERUNDS

GRAMMAR NOTES 1–2 **Complete this article with gerunds. Use the verbs from the box. Choose between affirmative and negative.**

drink	eat	exercise	go	increase	join	~~pay~~	smoke	start	stay

_____Not paying_____ attention to their health is a mistake a lot of college students make.
         1.
_____ healthy will help you do well in school and help you enjoy your
         2.
college experience. Here are some tips:

- Smokers have more colds and less energy. Quit _____ now or don't start.
                                                              3.
- _____ regularly reduces stress and brings more oxygen to your brain. If
         4.
  you don't exercise, I suggest _____ every day with a walk or run
                                        5.
  around campus.
- _____ breakfast is a common mistake. It's the most important meal of
         6.
  the day.
- Avoid _____ soda and other sugary beverages. Your body will thank you!
              7.
- Health experts advise _____ the fruits and vegetables in your diet. You
                                8.
  need at least four and a half cups a day, but more is better.
- _____ to the doctor when you're sick is another common mistake. Know
         9.
  where your school Health Service is, and use it when you need it.
- Better yet—consider _____ Healthy Campus—a program for
                             10.
  staying healthy.

EXERCISE 3 GERUND AS OBJECT

GRAMMAR NOTE 2 **Write a summary sentence for each conversation. Use the correct form of the verbs from the box and the gerund form of the verbs in parentheses.**

admit	avoid	deny	enjoy	go	keep	mind	~~stop~~

1. DANTE: Would you like a cigarette?
   MARTA: Oh, no, thanks. Since restaurants have banned cigarettes, I don't smoke anymore.

   Summary: Marta _____*has stopped smoking*_____.
                                        (smoke)

2. BRIAN: Where are the cookies I bought? You ate them, didn't you?
   LYDIA: No, I didn't.

   Summary: Lydia _____ the cookies.
                                  (eat)

3. ANGELA: Do you want to go running with me before work?
   SERGEY: Running? Are you kidding? I hate running!

   Summary: Jan doesn't _____.
                                     (run)

4. CHEN: What are you doing after work?
AN-LING: I'm going to that new swimming pool. Would you like to go with me?

Summary: An-ling is going to _____.
                                          (swim)

5. LARA: You're lazy. You really need to exercise more.
ROMAN: You're right. I *am* lazy.

Summary: Roman _____ lazy.
                          (be)

6. MONICA: Would you like a piece of chocolate cake?
PAULO: No, thanks. I try to stay away from sweets.

Summary: Paulo _____ sweets.
                          (eat)

7. CRAIG: I know exercise is important, but I hate it. What about you?
VILMA: Well, I don't *love* it, but it's OK.

Summary: Vilma doesn't _____.
                                  (exercise)

8. DORA: How's your new exercise program going?
ERIK: Not great. But I won't give up!

Summary: Erik is going to _____.
                                    (try)

EXERCISE 4 GERUND AS OBJECT OF A PREPOSITION

GRAMMAR NOTE 3 Combine the pairs of sentences to make statements about the Healthy Campus Program. Use the prepositions in parentheses plus a gerund.

Bo's Tips for Freshmen

Bo Yang

Many college freshmen develop unhealthy habits. It doesn't have to happen!

If *you're interested in staying healthy* _____,
                      1. You're interested. You want to stay healthy. (in)
join **Healthy Campus**.

Read what members are saying about the program:

Lisa Suarez: _____. I did, and
                  2. You can improve your health. Quit smoking. (by)

   I feel great.

Omar Sisane: _____. It's fun.
                  3. I'm very happy. I'm starting an exercise program (about)

Zhang Feng: _____.
                 4. This program gives you great ideas. Those ideas solve health issues (for)

324 Unit 23

Mee-Yon Go: I *was* a couch potato! _____.

5. Now I'm proud of myself. I swim a mile every day. (for)

Amy Kaplan: The doctors are great. _____.

6. They can help. They listen to your concerns. (by)

Leon Zimmer: _____.

7. I ran my first 10 km race. I didn't stop. (without)

REMEMBER: _____,

8. You should ask a doctor. Then you can start an exercise program. (before)

EXERCISE 5 EDITING

GRAMMAR NOTES 1–3 **Read part of an ex-smoker's journal. There are fifteen mistakes in the use of gerunds. The first mistake is already corrected. Find and correct fourteen more. Remember to check for spelling mistakes.**

DAY 1: I quit ~~to smoke~~ *smoking*! This was the first day of the rest of my life as a non-smoker. Get through the day wasn't too difficult. I quit drinking coffee today, too, and I think that helped. I used to enjoy had a cigarette with a cup of coffee in the morning. But now I'm looking forward to get healthier.

DAY 3: Today was harder. I kept wanting a cigarette. I called Dinah. She told me to take deep breaths and stay busy. That worked. I have to resist eat too much. Gaining 5 pounds aren't a big deal, but I don't want to gain more than that.

DAY 5: I got through the workweek smoke free. My boss definitely approves of the new me. She keeps tells me, "You can do it." I really appreciate to have her support. I miss smokeing, but I DON'T miss to standing outside in the cold just to have a cigarette. I also don't mind don't burning holes in my clothes!

DAY 7: Dinah suggested to go out to dinner, but I can't risk be around smokers. Instead, we went shoping, and I bought a shirt with the money I saved during my first week as a non-smoker. Also, I'm happy about have clothes that smell fresh! Not smoking has advantages.

EXERCISE 6 LISTENING

▶ 23|02 Ⓐ A doctor is giving advice to a patient. Some things are OK for this patient to do, but other things are not OK to do. Read the list. Then listen to the conversation between the doctor and the patient. Listen again and check (✓) *OK to Do* or *Not OK to Do*.

	OK to Do	Not OK to Do
1. smoking	☐	☑
2. drinking a little coffee	☐	☐
3. losing more weight	☐	☐
4. eating more complex carbohydrates	☐	☐
5. running every day	☐	☐
6. riding a bike every day	☐	☐
7. working eight hours a day	☐	☐

Ⓑ Work with a partner. Compare your answers to the questions in A. Why did you check *OK to Do* or *Not OK to Do*?

EXAMPLE: A: Number 1, smoking, is not OK to do. The doctor told the patient to stop smoking.
B: Right. The doctor said smoking causes a lot of health problems.

EXERCISE 7 WHAT ABOUT YOU?

CONVERSATION Work with a partner. Talk about what you do for your own health. Use the ideas below.

EXAMPLE: A: I stopped drinking soda because it has so much sugar.
B: I couldn't quit drinking soda completely, but I limited it to just a can a day.

- I stopped . . .
- I quit . . .
- I avoid . . .
- I keep . . .
- I dislike . . . , but I . . .
- I enjoy . . .
- *Other:* . . .

EXERCISE 8 WHAT DO YOU THINK?

A SURVEY Take a class survey. How many students agree with the statements? How many students disagree? How many don't have an opinion? Take turns asking the questions about each statement in the chart. Write the numbers in the appropriate columns.

EXAMPLE: A: How many students agree that smoking a few cigarettes a day is safe?
B: *(counting)* One, two, three . . .
C: OK. So, ten students agree. How many students disagree that smoking a few cigarettes a day is safe?

	Agree	Disagree	No Opinion or Don't Know
1. Smoking a few cigarettes a day is safe.			
2. Quitting is very difficult.			
3. Increasing the price of cigarettes encourages quitting.			
4. Banning all cigarette ads is a good idea.			
5. TV programs shouldn't allow scenes with smoking.			
6. Raising health insurance rates for smokers is a good idea.			
7. They should allow smoking on the street.			
8. Selling cigarettes to teenagers should be illegal.			
9. Not smoking is the best thing you can do for your health.			

B Work in a group. Discuss the survey results.

EXAMPLE: A: Only three students agree that smoking a few cigarettes a day is safe. Ten students disagree. Three students have no opinion or don't know.
B: It seems that most students think that smoking is bad for people's health.
C: Great! . . . Now how do they feel about quitting smoking?

EXERCISE 9 FOR OR AGAINST?

DISCUSSION Many people agree with laws that prohibit smoking. What is your opinion? Work in a group. Think of arguments for and against allowing smoking in the places listed below.

EXAMPLE: A: I'm in favor of banning smoking in restaurants.
B: I agree. Sitting in a room full of smoke is unhealthy. And it makes your hair and clothing stink.
C: But some restaurants have outdoor seating. I'm not against allowing smoking at tables outside.

- in restaurants
- outside of schools
- at outdoor bus stops
- in parks
- in a car with children under eighteen

- in elevators
- in outdoor sports arenas
- in indoor shopping malls
- in your own home
- at an outdoor café

FROM GRAMMAR TO WRITING

A BEFORE YOU WRITE Smoking is a topic many people disagree about. Choose another topic from the list below to write about. List arguments for or against it.

- allowing dogs in restaurants and stores
- texting while driving
- riding a motorcycle without a helmet
- selling candy and soda in schools

(your topic)	
For	**Against**

B WRITE Use your lists to write two paragraphs. In your first paragraph, give arguments for and against the topic. In the second paragraph, give your own opinion along with your reasons. Remember to use gerunds. Try to avoid the common mistakes in the chart.

EXAMPLE: In the United States, bringing your dog into a restaurant is illegal in most places. Some people don't like dogs. They don't want to eat dinner with one nearby. Other countries are more "dog friendly." In France, for example, many people . . .

Common Mistakes in Using Gerunds

Use the **correct spelling**. Do not forget that the spelling sometimes changes when you add *-ing* to a verb to form a gerund.	I don't like **shopping** in stores that allow dogs. NOT I don't like ~~shoping~~ in stores that allow dogs.
Use a **gerund** after expressions with the **preposition** *to*. Do not use the base form of the verb.	I *look forward to* **relaxing** at a café. NOT I look forward to ~~relax~~ at a café.
Use a **third-person-singular verb** after **gerund + plural noun**. Do not use a plural verb.	**Smoking cigarettes** *is* not allowed in the café. NOT Smoking cigarettes ~~are~~ not allowed . . .

C CHECK YOUR WORK Read your paragraphs. Underline all the gerunds. Circle the prepositions that come before the gerunds. Use the Editing Checklist to check your work.

Editing Checklist

Did you use . . . ?
- [ ] gerunds as subjects
- [ ] gerunds as objects after certain verbs
- [ ] gerunds after prepositions
- [ ] third-person-singular verbs after gerunds

D REVISE YOUR WORK Read your paragraphs again. Can you improve your writing? Make changes if necessary. Give your paragraphs a title.

UNIT 23 REVIEW

Test yourself on the grammar of the unit.

A Complete each sentence with the gerund form of the correct verb from the box. Choose between affirmative and negative.

| eat | feel | improve | join | like | smoke | swim |

1. I admit _____ exercise. I've never enjoyed it.

2. I'm going to quit _____ on my birthday. This is my last pack.

3. You can count on _____ better as soon as you quit. You'll sleep better, too.

4. Are you interested in _____ a gym?

5. Rafe goes _____ almost every day.

6. Sally doesn't mind _____ sweets anymore. She doesn't miss them.

7. I'd like some ideas for _____ my health. I catch too many colds.

B Complete the sentences with the correct form of the words in parentheses.

1. _____ good for your health.
   (laugh / be)

2. My doctor _____ funny movies.
   (suggest / watch)

3. _____ jokes _____ your blood pressure.
   (tell)   (help)

4. One expert _____ too much coffee.
   (advise against / drink)

5. We _____ long walks.
   (enjoy / take)

6. What do you _____ in restaurants?
   (think about / smoke)

C Find and correct seven mistakes.

1. You look great. Buying these bikes were a good idea.

2. I know. I'm happy about lose weight, too. Didn't exercising was a bad idea.

3. It always is. Hey, I'm thinking of rent a movie. What do you suggest to see?

4. I've been looking forward to see *Grown Ups*. Have you seen it yet?

5. Not yet. Do you recommend it? You're so good at choose movies.

Now check your answers on page 480.

Infinitives After Certain Verbs

HAPPINESS

OUTCOMES
• Use verbs that are followed by infinitives
• Identify statistics in a short article
• Evaluate speakers' attitudes in a conversation
• Discuss tendencies and preferences
• Give an opinion in response to a literary quote
• Write a paragraph on a personal topic, using transition words

STEP 1 GRAMMAR IN CONTEXT

BEFORE YOU READ

Look at the photo. Discuss the questions.

1. What is the relationship of these people?

2. Do you think they are happy? Why?

3. What makes *you* feel happy?

READ

▶ 24|01 Read this magazine article about happiness.

Can People Learn to Be Happy?

WE ALL KNOW people who have problems in life, but who still seem to be happy most of the time. On the other hand, there are people who appear to have it all—money, health, good friends, and family, but still seem unhappy. What makes one person happy and another unhappy? According to psychologist[1] Martin Seligman, 50 percent of happiness is genetic—you are born with a certain disposition.[2] This means that you are "programmed" from birth to feel a certain way. Another 10 percent of happiness is situational—if bad things happen, people tend to feel bad; if good things happen, they feel good, at least for a while. Interestingly, research shows that after some time, people seem

---

1 *psychologist:* a person whose job it is to study the mind and how it works
2 *disposition:* the way a person usually feels or acts

Sources of Happiness

- 10% situational
- 50% genetic
- 40% under our control

to return to their pre-set genetic levels of happiness. But perhaps the most significant finding is that 40 percent of our feelings is under our control—we can choose to react to life's situations one way or another.

If 40 percent of happiness is under our control, what can we do to feel happier? Studies show that happy people tend to do the following:

- interact with friends and people they like
- stay healthy
- focus on goals
- participate in enjoyable activities
- do meaningful work
- show compassion[3] to themselves and others

Most people want to be happy. Life is not always easy, however, and it is appropriate to feel sad in reaction to a life-changing event such as illness, death, or other losses. We can, however, try to feel better even when we have problems. And it's good to know that although genetics play a large role in how we feel, there is still a lot we can do to increase our chances at happiness.

---

3 *compassion:* a strong feeling of sympathy for someone who feels bad or has problems

AFTER YOU READ

A VOCABULARY Match the underlined words with the words in **bold**.

_____ **1.** You'll feel better if you talk and work with other people.

_____ **2.** Don't keep your attention on your problems.

_____ **3.** Sometimes it is a normal reaction to feel sad.

_____ **4.** Good friends and family usually make people feel better.

_____ **5.** The research on happiness is important.

_____ **6.** People who do more enjoyable activities are happier.

a. focus

b. tend to

c. significant

d. appropriate

e. participate in

f. interact

B COMPREHENSION Read the statements. Check (✓) *True* or *False*.

	True	False
1. People who have money and health are always happy.	☐	☐
2. People always feel bad in reaction to bad events.	☐	☐
3. Participating in enjoyable activities usually increases happiness.	☐	☐
4. People's attitudes can affect their happiness.	☐	☐
5. Feeling good is one of life's goals.	☐	☐
6. People can't change the way they feel.	☐	☐

C DISCUSSION Work with a partner. Compare your answers in B. Why did you check *True* or *False*?

INFINITIVES AFTER CERTAIN VERBS

Statements

Subject	Verb	(Object)	Infinitive	
I	**decided**		**(not) to stay**	home.
You	**advised**	John	**(not) to change**	jobs.
He	**wanted**	(her)	**(not) to be**	happy.

GRAMMAR NOTES

1 Forming Infinitives

An infinitive is *to* + **the base form of the verb**.	She decided **to join** a health club.
Form the **negative** by placing *not* before the infinitive: *not to* + **base form**.	She decided **not to join** the math club.

2 Verb + Infinitive

An infinitive can directly **follow certain verbs**.

agree	*fail*	*manage*	*seem*
attempt	*forget*	*offer*	*tend*
begin	*hope*	*plan*	*try*
can't wait	*learn*	*refuse*	*volunteer*
choose	*like*	*remember*	*wait*
decide	*love*	*rush*	*want*

VERB + INFINITIVE
They **seemed to enjoy** it.
He **tends to be** happy.
She **tried not to arrive** late.
I **can't wait to see** you.
We **like to go** to the movies.
Did they **decide to take** a dance class?

BE CAREFUL! When there is **more than one infinitive** in a clause, **do not repeat** *to*.

He **wants to move** and **get** a job.
NOT He wants to move and ~~to~~ get a job.

3 Verb + Object + Infinitive

Some verbs need an **object (noun or pronoun)** before the infinitive.

advise	*encourage*	*permit*	*tell*
allow	*force*	*persuade*	*urge*
convince	*invite*	*remind*	*warn*

VERB + OBJECT + INFINITIVE
I **advised Jason to take** the train to the party.
Ana **persuaded me to try** the desert.
She **convinced me to take** another piece of cake.

The **object** can be a noun or a pronoun.

- **noun**

VERB + NOUN + INFINITIVE
We **invited Marta to have** dinner with us.

- **pronoun**

VERB + PRONOUN + INFINITIVE
We **invited her to have** dinner with us.

BE CAREFUL! Do not forget the object after these verbs.

Marta **persuaded us to go** dancing.
NOT Marta ~~persuaded to go~~ dancing.

4 Verb + (Object) + Infinitive

An **infinitive** or an **object + infinitive** can follow some verbs.				
ask	help	prefer	teach	
choose	need	promise	want	
expect	pay	remind	would like	

VERB + INFINITIVE
She **wanted** **to take** dance lessons.

VERB + OBJECT + INFINITIVE
She **wanted Tomás** **to take** dance lessons.

USAGE NOTE After the verb **help**, you can use **the base form** of the verb **or the infinitive**.	He **helped** me **meet** new people. He **helped** me **to meet** new people.

PRONUNCIATION NOTE

▶ 24|02 **Pronunciation of *Want to***

In **informal conversation**, we often pronounce **want to** "wanna."	A: Do you **want to** go dancing Friday night? *(wanna)* B: Sure. Where do you **want to** go? *(wanna)*
IN WRITING Sometimes people use *wanna* in **informal notes**, **text messages**, and **email** to friends.	Hi, Lyn. I **wanna** ask you a question. *(email)*
BE CAREFUL! Do not use *wanna* when you write to people you have a formal relationship with. Also, do not use *wanna* in formal writing.	Professor, I **want to** ask you a question. *(email)* NOT Professor, I ~~wanna~~ ask you a question. Studies show that people **want to** be happy. *(paper)* NOT Studies show that people ~~wanna~~ be happy.

REFERENCE NOTES

For a list of **verbs followed by infinitives**, see Appendix 14 on page 459.

For a list of **verbs** followed by **object + infinitive**, see Appendix 16 on page 459.

EXERCISE 1   DISCOVER THE GRAMMAR

Ⓐ GRAMMAR NOTES 1–4   **Read Alissa's journal entry. Underline all the verb + infinitive and the verb + object + infinitive combinations. Circle the objects.**

I have been unhappy since I moved here. Dara advised (me) to join a club. I didn't know

anyone, and I wanted to make new friends. So, I finally did it! I decided to join the

school's Outdoor Adventure Club, and I went to my first meeting last night. I'm really

excited about this. The club is planning a hiking trip next weekend. I can't wait to go.

I hope it won't be too hard for my first adventure. Last night, they also decided to go

rafting in the spring. At first, I didn't want to sign up, but the leader was so nice.

He urged me not to miss this trip, so I put my name on the list. After the meeting,

a group of people asked me to go out with them. We went to a coffee shop and talked

for hours. Well, I hoped to make some new friends when I joined this club, but I didn't

expect everyone to be so friendly. I'm glad Dara persuaded me not to give up.

Ⓑ **Read what people said to Alissa. Then find the words in her journal entry that describe the situation.**

1. "We're going out for coffee. Why don't you come?" _A group of people asked me to go out with them._

2. "We're all going rafting in the spring." _____

3. "Don't miss this trip!" _____

4. "I'm happy that I listened to Dara. I didn't quit." _____

5. "You really should join a club." _____

6. "I'm really looking forward to going!" _____

7. "I'm going to join!" _____

8. "I'm surprised everyone is so friendly." _____

9. "I don't think I'll sign up." _____

10. "I'd like to make some new friends." _____

EXERCISE 2 VERB + INFINITIVE

GRAMMAR NOTES 1–2 Psychologist Martin Seligman advises people to make a list of things that went well during the day. Complete Lucas's list. Use the verbs in parentheses. Choose between affirmative and negative.

1. I've been feeling tired, so I _____*refused to work*_____ late today. I needed the rest.
   (refuse / work)

2. I _____ on my problem with my co-worker. Instead, I
   (decide / focus)
   thought about her good qualities.

3. I _____ my aunt. Yesterday, I forgot.
   (remember / call)

4. I _____ to my friends so much. It's really not appropriate.
   (try / complain)

5. I _____ to Miguel's party. I need to have some fun.
   (agree / go)

6. Jon and I _____ to work today. It's better to walk.
   (choose / drive)

7. I _____ at the health fair. I think it's an important event.
   (volunteer / help)

EXERCISE 3 VERB + OBJECT + INFINITIVE

GRAMMAR NOTES 1, 3–4 Read these tips from Helen's Happiness Workshop. Rewrite each tip using an object + infinitive. Choose between affirmative and negative.

1. "Go outside every day. But don't stay out in the sun too long."

   Helen advised _us to go outside every day_____.

   But she warned _us not to stay out in the sun too long_____.

2. "Get enough sleep. Aim for at least six hours."

   She urged _____.

   She told _____.

3. "Stay healthy. Don't eat junk food."

   She told _____.

   She urged _____.

4. "Do something fun every day."

   She encouraged _____.

5. "Don't spend too much time alone."

   She persuaded _____.

6. "Don't give up! Be patient!"

   She urged _____.

   and reminded _____.

7. "Come to the next happiness workshop!"

   She invited _____.

EXERCISE 4 OBJECT OR NO OBJECT

GRAMMAR NOTES 1–4 Write a summary sentence for each conversation. Use the correct form of a verb from the box followed by an infinitive or an object + infinitive.

advise	ask	decide	encourage	forget	~~invite~~	remind

1. **JASON:** You look a little down, Meghan. We're going out. Would you like to join us?
   MEGHAN: I'd love to.

   Summary: Jason _invited Meghan to join them_ _____.

2. **INA:** This math problem is too hard. I can't do it.
   TIM: Come on, Ina. I'm sure you can do it. Don't give up. Just keep trying!

   Summary: Tim _____.

3. **SALLY:** Stop focusing on your problems. You'll only feel worse.
   DIEGO: You're probably right, but it's easier said than done.

   Summary: Sally _____.

4. **ROBERTO:** Don't forget to go to the happiness workshop. It's tomorrow night.
   EMILIA: Oh, OK. Thanks! I'll be there.

   Summary: Roberto _____.

5. **LYNN:** Can you help me plan a birthday party for Bill?
   LARRY: Sure. I'd be happy to. When's his birthday?

   Summary: Lynn _____.

6. **LISA:** I'm finally going take a photography class.
   KYLE: Great. You need to have more fun.

   Summary: Lisa _____.

7. **RITA:** So, did you go to the workshop?
   EMILIA: Oh, no! When was it?

   Summary: Emilia _____.

EXERCISE 5 *WANT TO* OR *WANNA*

▶24|03 PRONUNCIATION NOTE Listen to the sentences. Check (✓) *More Formal* if you hear *want to*. Check (✓) *Less Formal* if you hear *wanna*.

	More Formal	Less Formal
1. Most people want to be happy.	☑	☐
2. Do you want to go to a movie tonight?	☐	☐
3. I don't want to stay home.	☐	☐
4. We want to make more friends.	☐	☐
5. They want to focus on their goals.	☐	☐
6. Do you want to read this book on happiness?	☐	☐
7. I really want to learn how to be happier.	☐	☐

GRAMMAR NOTES 1–4 Read this article on friendship and happiness. There are ten mistakes in the use of infinitives. The first mistake is already corrected. Find and correct nine more.

How to Make New Friends and Increase Your Happiness

Studies show that happy people tend ~~having~~ *to have* more friends. You know from experience that friends are important for your happiness, and you'd like to make some new ones. Maybe you're at a new school or job, or, possibly, you have changed and the "new you" wants meet new people.

To begin with, psychologist Timothy Johnson strongly advises to turn off your computers. He says that "friending" people on Facebook just isn't the same as making real friends. You need go out and interact with real people. He says, "Decide right now to don't refuse invitations. When a classmate or co-worker invites you for coffee, just say *yes*." Join a club and volunteer to doing something. That responsibility will force you to attend the meetings. By doing these things, you will manage meeting a lot of new people. Dr. Johnson warns us, however, don't rush to become close friends with someone right away. Relationships take time. You have to learn to listen. It is important to encourage your new friend to talks by asking him or her questions. Allow each relationship develops naturally, and soon you'll have a group of people you are really comfortable interacting with. These types of friendships are important to happiness because they help you to feel connected, and feeling connected leads to increased happiness.

EXERCISE 7   LISTENING

▶24|04   Ⓐ Two friends are having a conversation after work. Listen to parts of their conversation. Read the pairs of sentences below. Then listen again to each part and choose the sentence you hear.

1. **a.** I expected to be on time. ⓐ
   b. I expected him to be on time.

2. **a.** He wanted to work on Saturday.
   b. He wanted me to work on Saturday.

3. **a.** She tends to be happy most of the time.
   b. She tends not to be happy most of the time.

4. **a.** My cousin wants to make dinner.
   b. My cousin wants me to make dinner.

5. **a.** I decided to go to the workshop.
   b. I decided not to go to the workshop.

6. **a.** She asked me to get dessert.
   b. She asked me not to get dessert.

▶24|04   Ⓑ Listen again. Work with a partner and compare your answers in A. Decide if Ana is happy or unhappy about each situation. Give reasons.

EXAMPLE: A: Ana said, "I expected to be on time."
   B: That's right. But she wasn't on time because she missed her bus.
   A: I think she felt bad because her boss was annoyed with her. He expected her to be on time, too.

EXERCISE 8   WHAT ABOUT YOU?

Ⓐ CONVERSATION   Complete these personal statements before you talk about them with a partner. Make sure you use infinitives.

1. When I'm happy, I tend _____ .

2. I like _____ . I always feel better afterwards.

3. Every day I try _____ .

4. I seem _____ when I spend time with my friends.

5. When I feel down, I don't want _____ .

6. I prefer _____ .

Ⓑ Now talk about your statements with a partner.

EXAMPLE: A: When I'm happy, I tend to want to be with other people. What about you?
   B: Me too. Sometimes when I'm feeling down, I prefer to spend time alone.

EXERCISE 9 QUOTABLE QUOTES

DISCUSSION Work with a partner. Read these quotes about happiness. Choose three quotes and discuss them. What do they mean? Do you agree with them? Why or why not?

1. The best way to cheer yourself is to try to cheer someone else up.
   —*Mark Twain (1835–1910, U.S. author)*

   EXAMPLE: A: Mark Twain said, "The best way to cheer yourself is to try to cheer someone else up." I agree with that. If you try to cheer another person up, you think less about your own problems.
   B: It's true. When I want to feel better fast, I always try to help another person.

2. If you want others to be happy, practice compassion. If you want to be happy, practice compassion.
   —*Dalai Lama (1935– , Tibetan religious leader)*

3. You will never be happy if you continue to search for what happiness consists of. You will never live if you are looking for the meaning of life.
   —*Albert Camus (1913–1960, French philosopher and author)*

4. We tend to forget that happiness doesn't come as a result of getting something we don't have, but rather of recognizing and appreciating what we have.
   —*Frederick Koenig (1774–1833, German inventor)*

5. When what we are is what we want to be, that's happiness.
   —*Malcolm Forbes (1919–1990, U.S. magazine publisher)*

6. Happiness is a choice. You can choose to be happy. There's going to be stress in life, but it's your choice whether you let it affect you or not.
   —*Valerie Bertinelli (1960– , U.S. actor)*

EXERCISE 10 RECIPE FOR HAPPINESS

DISCUSSION Work in a group. What is important for happiness? Consider the issues in the list below.

EXAMPLE: A: I don't think you have to be rich, but it helps to have enough money for the things you need.
B: I agree. Money can make a significant difference in your life. You don't want to struggle to pay the rent or to put food on the table.
C: Yes, but I'd like to . . .

- money
- health
- age
- friends
- family
- education
- work
- hobbies and interests

- *Other:* _____

FROM GRAMMAR TO WRITING

A BEFORE YOU WRITE Think about a time that you were unhappy about something in your life. What was the problem? What steps did you take to try to change the situation? How did you feel afterwards? Complete this outline.

The problem: _____

Steps I took to change the situation:

1. _____

2. _____

3. _____

How I felt after: _____

B WRITE Use your outline to write a paragraph about how you tried to improve a situation you were unhappy about. Use *First*, *Then*, and *Finally* to introduce the steps you took. Try to avoid the common mistakes in the chart.

EXAMPLE: I was unhappy with my apartment. I couldn't afford to move, so I decided to improve the situation. First, I asked my friends to help me paint. Then, I . . . Finally, I . . . Afterwards, I felt . . .

Common Mistakes in Using Infinitives

Use an **infinitive** after **certain verbs**. Do not use the base form of the verb or verb + *-ing*.	I *want* **to be** happy. NOT I ~~want be~~ happy. NOT I ~~want being~~ happy.
Put *not* before the infinitive to form the **negative**. Do not put *not* before the base form of the verb.	I chose *not* **to go** to the party. NOT I chose ~~to not go~~ to the party.
Use *want to*. Do not use *wanna*.	They **want to** be friends with me. NOT They ~~wanna~~ be friends with me.

C CHECK YOUR WORK Read your paragraph. Underline all the verb + infinitive and the verb + object + infinitive combinations. Circle the objects. Use the Editing Checklist to check your work.

Editing Checklist

Did you use . . . ?

- [ ] infinitives after the correct verbs
- [ ] the correct form of the negative (*not* + infinitive)
- [ ] verb + object + infinitive correctly

D REVISE YOUR WORK Read your paragraph again. Can you improve your writing? Make changes if necessary. Give your paragraph a title.

UNIT 24 REVIEW

Test yourself on the grammar of the unit.

A Complete each sentence with the infinitive form of the correct verb from the box.

call	finish	go	meet	play	read

1. Would you like _____ this book about happiness? It's really good.

2. I've heard so much about you. I can't wait _____ you!

3. Did you manage _____ your paper on time?

4. Where did you decide _____ on your next vacation?

5. I love the piano. I want to learn _____.

6. Remember _____ when you get home.

B Unscramble the words to complete the sentences.

1. I _____.
   (visit / Mary / invited / us / to)

2. She _____.
   (come / to / agreed)

3. She _____.
   (to / wants / new friends / make)

4. I _____.
   (early / her / to / told / come)

5. I _____.
   (Tom / not / decided / invite / to)

6. He _____.
   (his project / to / needs / finish)

C Find and correct eight mistakes.

1. A: I want invite you to my party.

   B: Thanks. I'd love coming.

2. A: I plan to not get there before 8:00.

   B: Remember getting the soda. Don't forget!

3. A: Sara asked I to help her.

   B: I agreed helping her, too.

4. A: I promised pick up some ice cream.

   B: OK. But let's do it early. I prefer don't arrive late.

Now check your answers on page 480.

UNIT 25

More Uses of Infinitives

SMART DEVICES

OUTCOMES
- Express purpose with an infinitive or *in order to*
- Use adjectives/adverbs + infinitives
- Identify important details and opinions in a short text with quotes
- Identify key details in a TV ad
- Discuss the pros and cons of new technologies
- Write a paragraph describing the pros and cons of a smart device

---

STEP 1	GRAMMAR IN CONTEXT

BEFORE YOU READ

Look at the photo and at the title of the article. Discuss the questions.

1. Why is the article called "The World in Your Hand—or on Your Wrist"?

2. What can you use a smartphone or smartwatch for?

3. Do you have a smartphone or a smartwatch? How do you use it?

READD

▶25|01 Read this article about smart devices.

The World in Your Hand—or on Your Wrist

No device has changed people's lives as much as the smartphone. When smartphones first came out, people used them for just three major purposes: to make calls, to check email, and to connect to the Internet. Today, people of all ages and walks of life[1] are using them for a lot more. In order to find out how people are using them, we conducted a survey. Here's what some happy users report:

"I use my smartphone to play games, listen to music, and watch videos. It's awesome!"—*Todd Miller, 16, high school student* ● "I use it to translate words I don't understand."—*Lia Chang, 21, nurse* ● "When I'm considering buying something in a store, I use it to look up reviews."—*Rosa Ortiz, 56, accountant* ● "When I'm on the road, I use it to avoid traffic jams. And if I get lost, I use it to get directions."—*Brad King, 32, reporter*

It's easy to see why these multipurpose devices are so popular. They combine the functions of a phone, GPS,[2] camera,

---

1 *walks of life:* occupations
2 *GPS:* Global Positioning System, a device that tells you where you are and gives you directions

computer, calculator, organizer, and much more. They have also become cheap enough for more people to afford.

And then came the smartwatch. At first, some people thought it was too big and unattractive to wear, but in time, it became smaller and more fashionable. It also has some benefits that the smartphone doesn't have. You can use it to check quickly for emails and text messages, without anyone noticing. Just a glance³ at your wrist alerts⁴ you to important information. (And, of course, you can check the time, too.)

What will come next? It's hard to predict. By the time you read this article, the smartwatch may be a thing of the past, or it may be so common that everyone is "wearing the world" on their wrists.

---

3 *glance:* a quick look
4 *alerts:* makes you notice something important

AFTER YOU READ

Ⓐ VOCABULARY **Choose the word or phrase that best completes each sentence.**

1. An **old-fashioned** idea is not _____.
   a. good   **b.** modern   **c.** interesting

2. A **device** is a small _____.
   a. phone   **b.** machine   **c.** video

3. If something is **multipurpose**, it has many _____.
   a. uses   **b.** pieces   **c.** meanings

4. If you **combine** several things, you _____.
   a. separate them   **b.** clean them   **c.** bring them together

5. Another word for **function** is _____.
   a. information   **b.** purpose   **c.** computer

6. A **benefit** is a _____ result.
   a. positive   **b.** surprising   **c.** negative

Ⓑ COMPREHENSION **Read the statements. Check (✓) *True* or *False*.**

	True	False
1. People mostly use smartphones to make calls.	☐	☐
2. Todd Miller uses one to have fun.	☐	☐
3. Rosa Ortiz uses one to write reviews.	☐	☐
4. It's surprising that smartphones are so popular.	☐	☐
5. They have become cheaper.	☐	☐
6. You can't check for emails with a smartwatch.	☐	☐
7. We can easily predict what the next device will be.	☐	☐

Ⓒ DISCUSSION **Work with a partner. Compare your answers in B. Why did you check *True* or *False*?**

INFINITIVES

Infinitives of Purpose

Affirmative
I use it **to call** my friends.
People use it **in order to perform** better.

Negative
I left at 9:00 **in order not to be** late.
Charge it daily **in order not to lose** power.

Infinitives After Adjectives and Adverbs

With *Too*				
	(Too)	Adjective/ Adverb	*(For* + Noun/ Object Pronoun)	Infinitive
It's	(too)	**hard**		**to use.**
It's not		**expensive**	for Todd	**to buy.**
She spoke	too	**quickly**	for him	**to understand.**
They worked		**slowly**		**to finish.**

With *Enough*				
	Adjective/ Adverb	*(Enough)*	*(For* + Noun/ Object Pronoun)	Infinitive
It's	**easy**	(enough)		**to use.**
It's	**cheap**		for Todd	**to buy.**
She spoke	**slowly**	enough	for him	**to understand.**
They didn't work	**quickly**			**to finish.**

GRAMMAR NOTES

1 **Infinitives of Purpose**

You can use an infinitive to explain the **purpose of an action**.

An infinitive (*to* + **base form** of the verb) can explain the purpose of an action. It often answers the question *Why?*	A: **Why** did you go to the mall? B: I went there **to buy** a new phone.
USAGE NOTE In **conversation**, you can answer the question *Why?* with an incomplete sentence beginning with *to*.	A: **Why** did you go to the mall? B: **To buy** a new phone.
USAGE NOTE We usually **do not repeat** *to* when we give more than one purpose.	I went to the mall **to buy** a phone, **eat** lunch, and **see** a movie. *(more common)* I went to the mall **to buy** a phone, **to eat** lunch, and **to see** a movie. *(less common)*

2 Infinitives of Purpose with *In order (not) to*

You can also use *in order (not) to* + **base form** of the verb to explain the **purpose of an action**.

In order to is quite **formal** and we use it mostly in **formal speech** and **formal writing**.	People use their devices **in order to perform** many everyday functions. *(magazine article)*
USAGE NOTE In everyday **conversation** and **informal writing**, we usually don't use *in order to* to explain a purpose. We just use the **infinitive**.	I use my smartphone **to check** email. *(blog)*
We use *in order not to* + **base form** of the verb to explain a **negative purpose**. Again, we use it mostly in **formal speech** and **formal writing**.	Users should back up all their files daily **in order not to lose** information. *(newspaper)*
USAGE NOTE In everyday **conversation** and **informal writing**, we usually express a **negative purpose** with *because* + a **reason** or *so that* + a **reason**.	I back up my files every day *because* **I don't want to lose information.** *(conversation)* I back up my files every day *so that* **I don't lose information.** *(email)*

3 Infinitives After Adjectives and Adverbs

You can use an infinitive after an adjective or an adverb.

• **adjective + infinitive** • **adverb + infinitive**	ADJECTIVE It's *difficult* **to use.** ADVERB We worked *hard* **to finish** on time.
Sometimes we use *for* + **noun/pronoun** before the infinitive.	It's **easy** *for Todd* **to use.** It's **easy** *for him* **to use.**
Use *too* before the adjective or adverb to show the reason something is **not possible**.	It was *too expensive* **to buy.** *(It was expensive, so I couldn't buy it.)*
Use *enough* after the adjective or adverb to show the reason something is **possible**.	It was *cheap enough* **to buy.** *(It was cheap, so I could buy it.)*
BE CAREFUL! *Enough* goes after the adjective or adverb.	It was **easy** *enough* to use. NOT It was ~~enough easy~~ to use.
Notice the word order in sentences with: • *too* + adj. + *for* + noun/pro. + infinitive • adj. + *enough* + *for* + noun/pro. + infinitive	It's **too hard** *for my son* **to understand.** It's **easy enough** *for Jana* **to use.**
USAGE NOTE We don't need the infinitive when the meaning is clear.	A: Did you buy a smartwatch? B: Yes. It's finally **cheap enough** *for me*. *(It's cheap enough for me to buy.)*

EXERCISE 1
DISCOVER THE GRAMMAR

GRAMMAR NOTES 1–3
Read about changes in the telephone. Underline once all the infinitives of purpose. Underline twice all the adjective + infinitive or adverb + infinitive combinations. Circle *too* and *enough*.

PHONE TALK The telephone has really changed a lot in less than a century. From the 1920s through the 1950s, there was the good old-fashioned rotary phone. It had just one function, but it wasn't that convenient to use. Callers had to turn a dial to make a call. And it was too big and heavy to move from place to place. (Besides, there was that annoying cord connecting it to the wall!) The 1960s introduced the touch-tone phone. It was much faster to place a call with it. You just pushed buttons in order to dial. With cordless phones, introduced in the 1970s, callers were free to move around their homes or offices while talking. Then came a really major change—hand-held cell phones. These were small enough to carry with you, and you didn't even have to be inside to talk to your friends. But it wasn't until the invention of the camera phone that people began to use the phone to do more than just talk. And that was nothing compared to today's multipurpose smartphones. People use them to do almost everything. What will the newest technology bring to the phone? It's hard to predict. But one thing is certain: It will be faster and cheaper. And, as always, people will find uses for it that are difficult to imagine today.

EXERCISE 2 AFFIRMATIVE AND NEGATIVE PURPOSES

Ⓐ GRAMMAR NOTES 1–2 Match the actions with their purposes.

Action		Purpose	
_b_	**1.** She bought a smartphone because she	**a.**	didn't want to get calls.
___	**2.** He took the bus because he	~~**b.**~~	wanted to check email.
___	**3.** We turned our phone off because we	**c.**	wanted to buy a new phone.
___	**4.** She recorded her favorite TV show because she	**d.**	didn't want to be late.
___	**5.** He went to Eli's Electronics because he	**e.**	didn't want to miss it.

Ⓑ Now combine the sentences. Use infinitives of purpose.

1. _She bought a smartphone (in order) to check email._

2. _____

3. _____

4. _____

5. _____

EXERCISE 3 AFFIRMATIVE STATEMENTS

GRAMMAR NOTE 1 Look at these postings to a social media site. Complete the sentences with the correct phrases from the box. Use infinitives of purpose.

buy fruits and vegetables	drive to Montreal	get more gas	pass it
communicate with her	exchange money	have coffee	~~take a selfie~~[1]

My Trip to Montreal

1. That's me! I used my phone _to take a selfie_ _____ .

2. We rented this car _____ .

3. This truck was in front of us. We had to drive fast _____ .

4. We stopped here _____ .

5. We went to the bank _____ .

6. We came here _____ .

7. We stopped here _____ .

8. This is Léa. We had to speak French _____ .

1 _selfie:_ a picture someone takes of himself or herself, usually with a camera phone, to share on a social network site such as Facebook or Instagram

EXERCISE 4 INFINITIVES AFTER ADJECTIVES

GRAMMAR NOTE 3 Complete the responses to an online survey. Use the infinitive form of the verbs from the box.

find out	~~have~~	own	remember	spend	use	watch

○ ○ ●

2-10-2017   **SURVEY** Are you going to buy the latest and greatest smartwatch?

2-10-2017   **BobG:** Yes. I think it's important _____*to have*_____ the latest technology. And
             1.
             it's cool!

2-10-2017   **Finefone:** I don't know. I'm always a little nervous about buying a new device. I hope it
             isn't too difficult for me _____ .
             2.

2-10-2017   **YIKES:** No. I'm just not ready _____ the money on another new
             3.
             device. Besides, I'm happy with my current smartwatch. It does everything I want.

2-11-2017   **LilaX:** Definitely! I love the fact that it's not necessary _____ to take it
             4.
             with you when you go out or even go into another room. You can always wear it—even
             when you sleep. It sure beats having to carry a phone everywhere you go! And you don't
             have to search for it in your handbag or briefcase! Just look at your wrist!

2-11-2017   **Cat2:** Actually, I'm not sure. I really want a smart device for videos. But the screen on a
             smartwatch is too small _____ them on. I think, for me, a tablet is still
             5.
             the better choice.

2-11-2017   **TimeOut:** Not yet. I think I'll wait until the next one comes out. It'll be interesting
             _____ what new features it'll have—and how much it'll cost.
             6.

2-12-2017   **Rosy:** No thanks! Call me old-fashioned, but I really don't think it's necessary
             _____ all these multipurpose devices. Give me a cell phone, a digital
             7.
             watch, a laptop computer, a paperback book, a radio—and I'll be happy.

EXERCISE 5 INFINITIVES AFTER ADJECTIVES AND ADVERBS

A GRAMMAR NOTE 3 Complete the conversations. Use the words in parentheses with *too* or *enough* and the infinitive.

1. A: Did you buy the new smartwatch?

   B: No. Right now it's still _____*too expensive for me to buy*_____ .
                                      (expensive / for me)

2. A: Can we call Alicia now?

   B: Sure. It's _____ her.
                        (early)

3. A: What did Mrs. Johnson just say? I didn't understand her.

B: Me neither. She always speaks _____ her.
   (quickly / for me)

4. A: Did you see Dan last night?

B: No. Unfortunately, we got there _____ him.
   (late)

5. A: Does he have enough money to get that new device that he wants?

B: It's only $150. I think it's _____ .
   (cheap / for him)

6. A: Do you want to go to the movies tonight?

B: Sorry. I'm _____ tonight.
   (busy)

25|02 **B** LISTEN AND CHECK Listen to the conversations and check your answers in A.

EXERCISE 6 EDITING

GRAMMAR NOTES 1–3 Read this online bulletin board about smart devices. There are thirteen mistakes in the use of infinitives of purpose and infinitives after adjectives or adverbs. The first mistake is already corrected. Find and correct twelve more.

● ● ●

Click here ~~for telling~~ *to tell* us how you've used your smartphone or smartwatch recently.

I was riding my bike when I saw an accident. A car hit a truck, but it didn't stop. I used my smartphone take a picture of the car and the license plate number. Then I used it to call the police. It was so fast and convenient to using!   **Jason Harvey, England**

I was at a great concert in Mexico City. I wanted to share the experience with my best friend back home. I picked up my smartphone and used it to make a video and sending it to my friend. Instantly my friend was "there" with me. Awesome!   **Emilia Leale, Italy**

I was at the mall and used my smartwatch for paying for my purchases. It's quick, easy, and safe. I didn't have to take my wallet out of my pocket or hand my credit card to the store assistant. I just held my watch near the store's "reader" and double clicked. Done!   **Bruno Neves, Brazil**

I'm really into health and fitness. In order monitor my health, I use my smartwatch to check my heart rate when I run. I also use it to count my steps when I'm out and about. It's always on my wrist, so I don't have to remember to take it with me.   **Clarisa Flores, Mexico**

I sell houses. I always use my smartphone in order no waste my customers' time. When I see an interesting house, I immediately send a photo. Then, if they are interested, I make an appointment for them. That way, they can see the house enough fast to make an offer before other people. Without a smartphone, my job would be to hard to do.   **Andrea Cook, U.S.**

Last night, I used my phone to helping me make dinner. First, I searched online for a recipe. It was in ounces, so I used an app to converts it to grams. Then I used another app to create a shopping list. When I returned home from shopping, I set the phone's timer to reminded me when to take the food out of the oven. While dinner was baking, I used the phone to listen to my favorite songs. I love this thing! It combines functions for work and play, and it's enough smart to do almost everything. Too bad it can't do the dishes, too!   **Kim Soo-Min, South Korea**

STEP 4   COMMUNICATION PRACTICE

EXERCISE 7 LISTENING

25|03 **A** Listen to a TV ad for a new watch. Read the list. Then listen again and check (✓) the things the ad says you can do with the EZ-watch.

- ☐ **1.** bank online
- ☑ **2.** search for a restaurant
- ☐ **3.** find a recipe
- ☐ **4.** create a shopping list
- ☐ **5.** use a calculator
- ☐ **6.** pay for things in a store
- ☐ **7.** get driving directions
- ☐ **8.** find information in encyclopedias and dictionaries
- ☐ **9.** create a "To Do" list
- ☐ **10.** tell time
- ☐ **11.** look at newspaper headlines from around the world
- ☐ **12.** put together a clothing outfit

25|03 **B** Listen to the ad again. Work with a partner. Discuss these questions.

1. What uses does the ad mention that are or are not important to you? Why?

EXAMPLE: **A:** The ad says you can use the watch to search for a restaurant. This isn't an important feature for me. I get recommendations from friends to find out about good restaurants.

B: Yes. But you can use it to search for recipes. That's a nice feature.

A: True. But you can do that with a smartphone, too!

2. What uses doesn't the ad mention that *are* important to you? Why?

EXAMPLE: A: The ad doesn't mention online banking. I like to do that, so that I don't have to go to the bank and stand in line.

B: You're right. The ad doesn't mention it, but I know you can use a smartwatch to do online banking.

EXERCISE 8 WHAT DO *YOU* THINK?

SURVEY Work in a group. Complete the sentences with infinitives to give your opinion about new technology. Compare your opinions. Give reasons or examples.

1. Most smart devices are (not) easy . . .

EXAMPLE: A: I think most smart devices are easy to use. Smartphones, for example, are very easy to use.

B: I don't agree. They're not easy enough for *me* to use yet!

C: I only use mine to make calls!

D: Yes, but it's easy enough to learn the new features. The more you use it, the easier it becomes.

2. The price is (not) low enough . . .

3. New technology is important . . .

4. People over age eighty are (not) too old . . .

5. Teens are responsible enough . . .

EXERCISE 9 FOR OR AGAINST?

A DISCUSSION Work in a group. Look at the cartoon. Do you feel the same as the woman? If *yes*, which features don't you like? Why? Discuss the pros and cons of new technology.

EXAMPLE: A: I agree with the woman. Phones with a lot of features are too difficult for some people to use. But everyone needs a cell phone for emergencies.

B: I think people spend too much time with their phones. They're too involved with their apps to communicate with other people.

C: I don't agree with the woman . . .

B Imagine that you've just gotten a new smart device. What will you use it for? What won't you use it for? Discuss your answers with a partner. Give reasons for your answers.

EXAMPLE: A: I just got a new smartphone. I'll use it to send emails with photos or to watch videos . . .

B: I won't use it to watch videos! The screen isn't big enough.

A: I disagree. I think . . .

"Do you have a phone that doesn't do too much?"

EXERCISE 10 NEW USES FOR OLD THINGS

A BRAINSTORMING Work in a group. Brainstorm uses for these everyday objects. Use infinitives of purpose and your imagination! Share your ideas with other groups.

EXAMPLE: A: You can use a shell to hold coins.
        B: Right. You can also use it to keep soap in.
        C: You can even use it to eat with—like a spoon.

a pad of stickies

a toothbrush

a binder clip

a shell

a ziplock bag

a glass jar

a rubber band

a cork

B Which item is the most useful? Why?

EXAMPLE: A: I think the binder clip is the most useful.
        B: I agree. You can use it to do many things. For example, you can use it to . . .

EXERCISE 11 GET SMART!

A DISCUSSION Read the ad for a new smart device.

B Work in a group. Imagine that your smart device will control everything in your house—not only electronic equipment. What will you use it for?

EXAMPLE: A: I'll use it to turn on the shower.
        B: I'll use it to open and close the windows.
        C: I think I'll use it to . . .

SMART KEY 1000

Home
Messages
Lights
Appliances
Sound System
Basement
Outdoor
Security

Use the Smart Key 1000 to operate systems in your Smart House. Turn lights on and off, control appliances, and get text messages from your house about what's going on. It's easy and convenient to use. So, get smart. Get the Smart Key 1000.

FROM GRAMMAR TO WRITING

A BEFORE YOU WRITE Think about positive and negative ways smart devices have changed our lives. Complete the outline.

Positive	Negative
_____	_____
_____	_____
_____	_____

B WRITE Use your outline to write a paragraph about how smart devices have changed our lives in good and in bad ways. Remember to use infinitives. Try to avoid the common mistakes in the chart.

EXAMPLE: Smart devices, such as smartphones, have changed our lives in many ways. Most of the changes have been positive. For example, we can use them to . . . We can also use them to . . . Not all changes, however, have been positive. For example, people, . . .

Common Mistakes in Using Infinitives

Use an **infinitive** to express a **purpose**. Do not use the base form of the verb or a gerund. Do not use *for* before the infinitive.	I use it **to take** pictures. NOT I use it ~~take~~ pictures. NOT I use it ~~for~~ to take pictures.
Use *in order to* + **base form of the verb** to express an **affirmative purpose** and *in order not to* + **base form of the verb** to express a **negative purpose**. Do not leave out *in order*.	Many people use smartwatches **in order not to attract** attention when checking messages. NOT Many people use smartwatches ~~not to attract~~ attention . . .
Put *enough* after an adjective or adverb. Do not put *enough* before an adjective or adverb.	It's **easy *enough*** to program. NOT It's ~~enough easy~~ to program.

C CHECK YOUR WORK Read your paragraph. Underline once all the infinitives of purpose. Underline twice all the adjective + infinitive or adverb + infinitive combinations. Circle *too* and *enough*. Use the Editing Checklist to check your work.

Editing Checklist

Did you use . . . ?

☐ an infinitive or *in order to* + base form of the verb to express an affirmative purpose

☐ *in order not to* + base form of the verb to express a negative purpose

☐ adjective or adverb + infinitive

☐ *too* + adjective or adverb + infinitive

☐ adjective or adverb + *enough* + infinitive

D REVISE YOUR WORK Read your paragraph again. Can you improve your writing? Make changes if necessary. Give your paragraph a title.

UNIT 25 REVIEW

Test yourself on the grammar of the unit.

Ⓐ Circle the correct words to complete the sentences.

1. Todd uses his smartphone to <u>get / gets</u> directions when he travels.

2. Users should recharge their phones <u>in order not / not in order</u> to run out of power.

3. In order <u>to use / for using</u> this feature, you must download the software.

4. It's <u>too / enough</u> dark to read in here. Could you turn on a light?

5. It was raining hard. We couldn't see <u>clearly enough / too clearly</u> to drive.

Ⓑ Unscramble the words to complete the conversation. Use the infinitive form of the verbs.

A: How do you like your new watch? Was it _____?
           1. (enough / easy / program)

B: Yes. Luckily, this one isn't _____.
          2. (hard / too / use / for me)

A: Where's Kim's place? She was talking _____.
        3. (fast / too / understand / for me)

B: It's about 20 blocks from here. Is that _____?
        4. (too / for us / far / walk)

A: If you're worried, we could take the bus _____.
        5. (there / by 6:30 / get)

B: Well, it's only 6:00 now. I think it's _____.
        6. (for us / enough / early / walk)

A: Let's cross at the light. The traffic is _____ safely here.
        7. (heavy / cross / too / for us)

B: I think we're lost. Let's use _____.
        8. (get / directions / my phone)

A: You didn't speak _____. Let me try.
        9. (clearly / for it / enough / work)

B: We're pretty far away. Let's take _____.
        10. (save / a taxi / time)

Ⓒ Find and correct five mistakes.

    Is sixteen too young for drive? It's really hard to saying. Some kids are mature enough to drive at sixteen, but some aren't. I think most sixteen-year-olds are still too immature drive with friends in the car, though. It's for them easy to forget to pay attention with a lot of kids in the car. In order preventing accidents, some families have a "no friends" rule for the first year. I think that's a reasonable idea. And I think there should be a "no cell phone" rule, too—for talking or texting.

Now check your answers on page 481.

26

Gerunds and Infinitives

PROCRASTINATION

OUTCOMES
- Use verbs that can be followed by gerunds or infinitives
- Use prepositions/phrasal verbs + gerunds
- Identify key points in an article and in an interview
- Discuss solutions to common problems
- Give an opinion in response to a literary quote
- Write several paragraphs about how to achieve one's goals

STEP 1   GRAMMAR IN CONTEXT

BEFORE YOU READ

Look at the cartoon and at the title of the article. Discuss the questions.

1. What is procrastination?
2. What types of things do you put off doing?
3. Why do people procrastinate?

READ

▷ 26|01   Read this excerpt from a magazine article about procrastinating.

Stop Procrastinating—Now!

It's a beautiful day. Eva doesn't feel like studying for her test. She goes to the park instead. She keeps telling herself she'll work better the next day.

Todd planned to make an appointment with the dentist, but he decided to wait another week, or maybe two.

Procrastinating—putting off until tomorrow things you need to do today—is a universal problem. College students are famous for procrastinating, but we all do it sometimes. Why do people put off important tasks? Read what the experts say.

Unpleasant Tasks It's not always fun to do a lot of the things on our "To Do" lists. Most people prefer to do enjoyable things.

Poor Time Management[1] Having too little time for a task is discouraging. It's hard to get started on a project when you feel that you can't finish it.

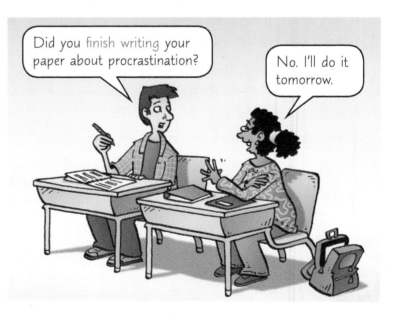

Did you finish writing your paper about procrastination?

No. I'll do it tomorrow.

---

1 *time management:* the skills for using your time well when you are trying to reach a goal

Fear An important test can make you feel so anxious that you put off studying.

Perfectionism The belief that you must do a perfect job can prevent you from starting or finishing a task.

As you can see, people often procrastinate because they want to avoid bad feelings. This tactic, however, usually fails because procrastinators end up feeling even worse as a result of their procrastination. It's a vicious cycle.[2] The only solution to the problem is to stop procrastinating—now!

---

2 *vicious cycle:* a situation where one problem causes another problem that then causes the first problem again

AFTER YOU READ

Ⓐ VOCABULARY Complete the sentences with the words from the box.

anxious	discouraging	project	tactic	task	universal

1. Have you finished your class _____ yet?

2. Procrastination is a _____ problem. People all over the world do it.

3. I get very _____ before a test.

4. Shopping for dinner is my least favorite _____ on my "To Do" list.

5. The problem is _____, but I won't give up hope!

6. Do you know a good _____ for solving this problem?

Ⓑ COMPREHENSION Check (✓) the reasons the article gives for procrastination.

☐ 1. being lazy

☐ 2. not enjoying the task

☐ 3. not understanding something

☐ 4. not having enough time

☐ 5. feeling anxious about the task

☐ 6. not getting enough sleep

☐ 7. feeling depressed

☐ 8. thinking your work has to be perfect

Ⓒ DISCUSSION Work with a partner. Compare your answers in B. Why did you or didn't you check each item?

GERUNDS AND INFINITIVES

Gerunds
Eva **enjoys going** to the park.
She **prefers taking** long breaks.
She **stopped studying**.
Starting a project is hard.
She's worried **about finishing** her paper.

Infinitives
Eva **wants to go** to the park.
She **prefers to take** long breaks.
She **stopped to study**.
It's hard **to start** a project.

GRAMMAR NOTES

1 Verb + Gerund

Some verbs are followed by a **gerund** (base form + **-ing**).

These are some common verbs followed by a gerund:

avoid	*deny*	*keep*
consider	*enjoy*	*postpone*
delay	*finish*	*quit*

Eva *avoids* **doing** her work.
She *doesn't enjoy* **studying**.
She *delays* **getting** to work.

2 Verb + Infinitive

Some verbs are followed by an **infinitive** (**to** + base form).

These are some common verbs followed by an infinitive:

agree	*decide*	*need**	*promise**
arrange	*expect**	*offer*	*want**
*choose**	*fail*	*plan*	*would like**

*These verbs can also be followed by:
object + infinitive

Todd *decided* **not to work** late.
He *arranged* **to leave** early.
He *plans* **to meet** some friends.

We *expect* **to start** the project soon.
We *expect* **them to start** the project soon.

USAGE NOTE We usually do not repeat *to* when there is more than one infinitive.

He plans **to watch** TV, **read** the paper, and **call** his friends. *(more common)*
He plans **to watch** TV, **to read** the paper, and **to call** his friends. *(less common)*

3 Verb + Gerund or Infinitive

Some verbs are followed by **a gerund or an infinitive**. They have the same meaning.

These are some common verbs that are followed by a gerund or an infinitive:

begin	*hate*	*prefer*
can't stand	*like*	*start*
continue	*love*	*try*

Jeff *hates* **studying**. or Jeff *hates* **to study**.
He *likes* **reading**. or He *likes* **to read**.
He *loves* **dancing**. or He *loves* **to dance**.

USAGE NOTE When two or more verbs follow another verb, we use the same form of the verb. (In writing, this is called *parallel structure*.)

He *hates* **studying** and **doing** homework.
NOT He hates studying and ~~to do~~ homework.
He *hates* **to study** and **do** homework.
NOT He hates to study and ~~doing~~ homework.

BE CAREFUL! Some **verbs**, such as the ones below, can be **followed by a gerund or an infinitive**, but they have a very different meaning:

stop   *remember*   *forget*

Eva *stopped* **taking** breaks.
(She doesn't take breaks anymore.)
Eva *stopped* **to take** a break.
(She stopped an activity in order to take a break.)

Todd *remembered* **reading** the story.
(First he read the story. Then he remembered that he did it.)
Todd *remembered* **to read** the story.
(First he remembered. Then he read the story. He didn't forget.)

Jeff *forgot* **meeting** Dana.
(Jeff met Dana, but afterwards he didn't remember the event.)
Jeff *forgot* **to meet** Dana.
(Jeff had plans to meet Dana, but he didn't meet her because he forgot about the plans.)

4 Preposition or Phrasal Verb + Gerund

A **gerund** is the only verb form that can **follow a preposition or a phrasal verb**.

- **preposition + gerund**

PREPOSITION
He's worried *about* **writing** it.
PREPOSITION
He's looking forward *to* **finishing** it.
PREPOSITION
Jeff doesn't feel *like* **working** on his paper.

- **phrasal verb + gerund**

PHRASAL VERB
He won't *put off* **starting** it anymore.

5 For General Statements

To make **general statements**, you can use either:

- **gerund as subject**

- ***it* + infinitive**

They have the **same meaning**.

Writing a paper is hard.
or
It's hard **to write** a paper.

REFERENCE NOTES

For a list of **verbs followed by a gerund**, see Appendix 13 on page 459.

For a list of **verbs followed by an infinitive**, see Appendix 14 on page 459.

For a list of **verbs followed by a gerund or an infinitive**, see Appendix 15 on page 459.

For more information on **gerunds after prepositions**, see Unit 23 on page 320, and Appendices 17 and 18 on pages 459 and 460.

STEP 3   FOCUSED PRACTICE

EXERCISE 1
DISCOVER THE GRAMMAR

Ⓐ GRAMMAR NOTES 1–5

Read this paragraph. Underline the gerunds. Circle the infinitives.

Like many students, Eva is a procrastinator. She keeps putting off her schoolwork. When she studies, she often stops to go for a walk in the park. She wants to improve her study habits, but she isn't sure how. Eva decided to make a list every day of tasks she needs to do. She always remembers to make her list, but she often forgets to read it. It's very discouraging, and Eva is worried about getting bad grades. Last night, Eva remembered reading an article in the school newspaper about a support group for procrastinators. She thinks being in a group is a good idea. It's difficult to try to change on your own. She likes sharing ideas with other students. Maybe it will help.

Ⓑ Now read the statements. Check (✓) *True* or *False*. Correct the false statements.

		True	False
1.	*puts off doing* Eva ~~never does~~ her schoolwork.	☐	☑
2.	She quit going for walks in the park.	☐	☐
3.	She'd like to be a better student.	☐	☐
4.	Eva makes a list every day.	☐	☐
5.	She always reads her list.	☐	☐
6.	She read about a support group.	☐	☐
7.	She thinks it's good to be in a group.	☐	☐
8.	She doesn't like to share ideas with others.	☐	☐

GRAMMAR NOTES 1–4
Read the quiz. Circle
the correct form of
the verbs. In some
cases, both forms
are correct.

Are You a Procrastinator?

☐ When I don't feel like to do / (doing) something, I often put off to start / starting it.
           1.   **2.**

☐ I sometimes start to study / studying the night before a test.
                                  3.

☐ I sometimes start a job but then postpone to finish / finishing it.
                                                       4.

☐ I often delay to make / making difficult decisions.
                          5.

☐ I find excuses for not to do / doing things I dislike.
                                6.

☐ When a task seems too difficult, I often avoid to work / working on it.
                                                    7.

☐ I prefer to do / doing easy tasks first.
        8.

☐ I often promise myself to work / working on a project but then fail to do / doing it.
                                9.   **10.**

☐ I worry about to make / making mistakes or about not to be / being perfect.
                              11.   **12.**

☐ I often choose to do / doing other tasks instead of the most important one.
                              13.

☐ I want to improve / improving, but I keep to put / putting it off.
                14.   **15.**

EXERCISE 3 GERUND OR INFINITIVE

GRAMMAR NOTES 1–4 Complete these tips from a website. Use the correct form of the
verbs in parentheses.

● ● ●

Some Tips for _____Stopping_____ Procrastination
                        1. (stop)

■ If you have a large project to work on, break it into small tasks. Finish _____
                                                                  2. (do)

one small task before _____ the next.
                        3. (start)

■ Choose _____ the hardest task first. You'll get it out of the way, and you'll feel
                      4. (do)

better about yourself.

■ Promise yourself _____ at least fifteen minutes on a task even if you don't really
                            5. (spend)

feel like _____ it. You'll be surprised. You can get a lot done in fifteen minutes—
                6. (do)

and you'll often keep _____ even longer.
                          7. (work)

■ Stop _____ short breaks—but for no longer than ten minutes at a time.
             8. (take)

■ Arrange _____ yourself a reward when you succeed in _____ a
              9. (give)   **10. (finish)**

task. Do something you enjoy _____.
                                  11. (do)

■ Consider _____ a support group for procrastinators.
               12. (join)

EXERCISE 4 GENERAL STATEMENTS

Ⓐ GRAMMAR NOTE 5 Complete these conversations. The people talking agree on everything. Read one person's opinion and write the other's. If the first person uses a gerund, use an infinitive. If the first person uses an infinitive, use a gerund.

1. EVA: It's hard to start a new project.

   TODD: I agree. *Starting a new project is hard.*

2. PAT: Taking short breaks is helpful.

   LEE: You're right. *It's helpful to take short breaks.*

3. UTA: It's difficult to work on a long project.

   KAY: That's true. _____

4. LEV: Completing a job on time feels great.

   JEFF: You're right. _____

5. PAT: Rewarding yourself for finishing a project is a good idea.

   LEE: I agree. _____

6. UTA: Being in a support group is very helpful.

   KAY: Yes. _____

7. EVA: It's good to meet people with the same problem.

   TODD: I feel the same way. _____

▶26|02 Ⓑ LISTEN AND CHECK Listen to the conversations and check your answers in A.

EXERCISE 5 GERUND OR INFINITIVE

GRAMMAR NOTES 1–3 Read these conversations that took place at a procrastinators' support group meeting. Complete the summary statements. Use a gerund or an infinitive.

1. SARA: Hi, Todd. Did you bring the soda?
   TODD: Yes. Here it is.

   Summary: Todd remembered *to bring the soda* _____ .

2. CHO: Eva, do you remember Todd?
   EVA: Oh, yes. We met last year.

   Summary: Eva remembers _____ .

3. EVA: Todd, will Miriam be here tonight? I haven't seen her in ages!
   TODD: Yes, she's coming later.

   Summary: Todd expects Miriam _____ .

4. SARA: You take too many breaks.
   TODD: No, I don't!

   Summary: Todd denied _____ .

5. EVA: What do you do in your free time, Aki?
   AKI: I listen to music a lot.

   Summary: Aki likes _____ .

6. UTA: I'm tired. Let's go home.
   AKI: OK. Just five more minutes.

   Summary: Uta wants _____ .

7. UTA: Eva, can we give you a ride home?
   EVA: Thanks, but I think I'll stay a little longer.

   Summary: Uta offered _____ .

   Eva decided _____ .

8. DAN: Good night. Please drive carefully.
   UTA: Don't worry. I will.

   Summary: Uta promised Dan _____ .

EXERCISE 6 EDITING

GRAMMAR NOTES 1–5 **Read Eva's blog entry. There are eight mistakes in the use of gerunds and infinitives. The first mistake is already corrected. Find and correct seven more.**

The Test of Time

For months I was thinking about ~~to go~~ *going* to a support group for procrastinators, but I kept putting it off! Last night, I finally decided going, and I'm glad I did. I'm not alone! There were a lot of people there with the same problem as me. I expected them being boring, but they were really quite interesting—and helpful. I even knew some of the other students there. I remembered to meet a few of them at a school party last year. I really enjoyed to talk to Todd, and before I left I promised coming again.

I have a math test tomorrow, so I really should stop to write now and start studying. See, I've already learned some helpful tactics from to be in this group! I have to stop making excuses and start my work! NOW!

EXERCISE 7 LISTENING

▶26|03 **A** The school newspaper is interviewing Eva about her study habits. Listen to the interview. Then read the list of activities. Listen again and check (✓) the things Eva *Does* or *Doesn't Do* now when she is studying for a test.

	Things Eva Does	Things Eva Doesn't Do
1. clean her work area	✓	☐
2. start studying the night before the test	☐	☐
3. study the hardest thing first	☐	☐
4. make a "To Do" list	☐	☐
5. take long breaks	☐	☐
6. do relaxation exercises	☐	☐
7. reward herself for finishing	☐	☐

▶26|03 **B** Listen to the interview again. Then work with a partner. Compare your answers to the questions in A. For each answer, give the reason why Eva does or doesn't do the activity.

EXAMPLE: **A:** So Eva cleans her work area.
   B: Yes. She says it's distracting to work at a messy desk. What about number 2?

EXERCISE 8 TAKE A BREAK!

A BRAINSTORMING Taking short breaks can help you work more effectively. Work in a group. Brainstorm ideas for ten-minute work breaks.

EXAMPLE: **A:** I enjoy . . .
   B: It's relaxing . . .
   C: You could consider . . .
   A: I prefer . . .

B Share your ideas with the rest of your classmates.

EXAMPLE: **A:** We all think it's relaxing to go for a short walk every few hours.
   B: A few of us think it's a good idea to . . .

EXERCISE 9 THE UPSIDE OF PROCRASTINATION?

CONVERSATION Work in a group. Is there a positive side to procrastination? Talk about it.

EXAMPLE: **A:** I think there can sometimes be an advantage to procrastinating.
   B: Really? Can you give an example?
   A: Yes. I once wanted to buy a leather jacket, but I couldn't decide which one to buy. I kept putting off the decision. When I finally went back online to buy the jacket, I discovered it was on sale! Because of my procrastination, I was able to buy it for half price.
   C: Something similar once happened to me. I wanted to . . .

EXERCISE 10 QUOTABLE QUOTES

DISCUSSION Work with a partner. Read the quotes about procrastination. Choose three quotes and discuss them. What do they mean? Do you agree with them? Why or why not?

1. Never put off till tomorrow what you can do today.
   —*Lord Chesterfield (British politician, 1694–1773)*

   EXAMPLE: A: Lord Chesterfield advises doing things right away.
   B: I think that's not always possible because . . .

2. Procrastination is the art of keeping up with yesterday.
   —*Don Marquis (U.S. author, 1878–1937)*

3. Procrastination is the thief of time.
   —*Edward Young (British poet, 1683–1765)*

4. When there is a hill to climb, don't think that waiting will make it smaller.
   —*Anonymous[1]*

5. Putting off an easy thing makes it hard, and putting off a hard one makes it impossible.
   —*George H. Lorimer (U.S. magazine editor, 1868–1937)*

6. Procrastination is like a credit card: It's a lot of fun until you get the bill.
   —*Christopher Parker (British actor, 1983–)*

---

1 *anonymous:* The writer's name is not known.

EXERCISE 11 IT'S A PROBLEM!

PROBLEM SOLVING Look at the picture. Like procrastination, clutter is a universal problem. What are some solutions to the problem? Work in a group. Think of ways of stopping clutter. You can use the verbs from the box.

| avoid | decide | don't forget | keep | need | plan | remember | start | stop |

EXAMPLE: A: You need to put away your things every night. You really can't put it off.
B: Plan on . . .
C: Remember to . . .

EXERCISE 12 AT THE SUPPORT GROUP

A INFORMATION GAP Work with a partner. Student A will follow the instructions below. Student B will follow the instructions on page 488.

> **STUDENT A**
>
> - Look at the picture. Ask your partner questions to complete what people said at the support group meeting.
>
>   EXAMPLE: A: What does Eva remember doing?
>   B: She remembers meeting Todd.
>
> - Answer your partner's questions.
>
>   EXAMPLE: B: What does Todd hope to do?
>   A: He hopes to see Eva again.

B Now compare pictures with your partner. Are they the same?

Ⓐ BEFORE YOU WRITE Writing a goals worksheet is a good way to help prevent procrastination. First, complete the worksheet. List three goals for this month in order of importance (1 = the most important goal). Include a complete-by date for each goal.

This Month's Goals

Goal 1: _____ Complete by: _____

Goal 2: _____ Complete by: _____

Goal 3: _____ Complete by: _____

Ⓑ WRITE Use your worksheet to write three paragraphs (one for each goal) on how you plan to accomplish your goals. Try to avoid the common mistakes in the chart.

EXAMPLE: My first goal is to finish writing my English paper by March 28. First, I plan to . . .
Then I . . . Next, I . . . Finally, I . . .
My second goal is to . . .
My third goal is to . . .

Common Mistakes in Using Gerunds and Infinitives

Use the **correct verb form**, gerund or infinitive, after another verb or after a preposition.	I *need* **to get** a part-time job. NOT I need ~~getting~~ a part time job. I *enjoy* **working**. NOT I enjoy ~~to work~~. I'm worried *about* **finding** a good job. NOT I'm worried about ~~to find~~ a good job.
When two or more verbs follow another verb, use the **same form of the verb** for parallel structure. Do not use different verb forms.	I hate **sitting** and **working** at a messy desk. NOT I hate sitting and ~~to work~~ at a messy desk. I hate **to sit** and **work** at a messy desk. NOT I hate to sit and ~~working~~ at a messy desk.

Ⓒ CHECK YOUR WORK Read your paragraphs. Underline the gerunds and circle the infinitives. Use the Editing Checklist to check your work.

Editing Checklist

Did you use . . . ?

☐ correct verbs + gerunds

☐ correct verbs + infinitives

☐ prepositions + gerunds

☐ parallel structure

Ⓓ REVISE YOUR WORK Read your paragraphs again. Can you improve your writing? Make changes if necessary.

UNIT 26 REVIEW

Test yourself on the grammar of the unit.

A Circle the correct words to complete the sentences.

1. Don't put off to start / starting your project.

2. I expect you to finish / finishing on time.

3. I keep to try / trying to improve my study habits.

4. Did you decide to join / joining our study group?

5. I look forward to see / seeing you there.

6. Don't forget to call / calling me the night before.

7. To study / Studying together can help.

B Complete the conversation with the correct form of the verbs in parentheses.

A: Have you finished _____ your homework?
      1. (do)

B: No, not yet. I decided _____ a break.
                          2. (take)

A: Already? You just started _____.
                                3. (work)

B: I know. But I'm tired of _____ at my desk.
                              4. (sit)

A: Well, _____ a short break is OK, I guess.
          5. (take)

B: Don't worry. I promise _____ it done before dinner.
                            6. (get)

A: OK. I know you hate _____, but it's important.
                          7. (study)

B: I agree.

C Find and correct six mistakes.

I hate clutter. But before now, I wasn't able to prevent it from to happen. I even put off going home because seeing the mess made me feel bad. Then I remembered recently to read an interesting magazine article about clutter. I decided trying one of the recommended tactics. I learned that I need cleaning up every night before I go to bed. Just ten minutes can make a big difference. I've stopped to avoid going home now, and I enjoy being in my nice, neat apartment. To clean up every night isn't always easy, but it's really worth it!

Now check your answers on page 481.

Pronouns and Phrasal Verbs

PART **8**

OUTCOMES

- Use *each other*, *one another*, and reflexive pronouns
- Identify the subject of a description in an article
- Identify important information in a conversation
- Complete a questionnaire and discuss the results
- Write an email or letter, giving advice

OUTCOMES

- Use a range of phrasal verbs
- Use phrasal verbs with separated objects
- Identify key details in an article and a conversation
- Discuss illustrations, using phrasal verbs
- Conduct an online search and share results with the class
- Write a paragraph about animal intelligence

Reflexive and Reciprocal Pronouns

SELF-TALK

OUTCOMES
• Use *each other*, *one another*, and reflexive pronouns
• Identify the subject of a description in an article
• Identify important information in a conversation
• Complete a questionnaire and discuss the results
• Write an email or letter, giving advice

STEP 1   GRAMMAR IN CONTEXT

BEFORE YOU READ

Look at the photos and at the examples of self-talk. Discuss the questions.

1. What do you think *self-talk* is?

2. Is the man's self-talk positive or negative?

3. What about the woman's self-talk? Is it positive or negative?

READ

▶27|01   Read this article from a psychology magazine.

Self-Talk

SELF-TALK is the way we explain a problem to ourselves. It can impact how we feel and how we act. Take the case of Tom and Sara. They both got laid off[1] from their jobs at the same company, but their reactions were totally different. Sara maintained her normal life. She frequently talked on the phone with her friends, continued her usual activities, and kept herself fit.

Tom, on the other hand, spent all of his time at home by himself, didn't allow himself to have a good time, and gained 10 pounds (4.5 kilograms).

Why were their reactions so very different from one another? They both lost their jobs, so the situation itself can't explain

It was all my fault.

I'll never find another job.

---

1 *got laid off*: lost their jobs because their employer didn't have enough money to keep them or because there wasn't enough work

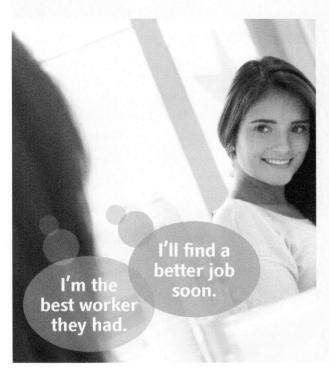

I'll find a better job soon.

I'm the best worker they had.

Tom's problems. The main difference was the way Tom and Sara explained the problem to themselves.

Sara told herself that the problem was temporary and that she herself could change it. Tom saw himself as completely helpless and likely[2] to be unemployed forever.

Tom and Sara both got their jobs back. Their reactions when they talked to each other were, again, very different. For his part, Tom grumbled,[3] "Oh, I guess they were really desperate." Sara, on the other hand, smiled and said, "Well! They finally realized that they need me!"

---

2 *likely:* probably
3 *grumbled:* complained in a quiet but slightly angry way

AFTER YOU READ

A VOCABULARY **Complete the sentences with the words from the box.**

| fault | impact | maintain | reaction | realize | temporary |

1. What was Tom's _____ when he heard the news? Was he surprised?

2. At first, they didn't _____ that the problem at work was so serious.

3. It wasn't the workers' _____. They didn't do anything wrong.

4. Sara believed that the problem was just _____. She expected to find another job.

5. The layoffs didn't _____ their boss's job. She's still at the company.

6. Sara exercised and saw friends in order to _____ her health and positive attitude.

B COMPREHENSION **Read the questions. Check (✓) *Tom*, *Sara*, or *Tom and Sara*.**

	Tom	Sara	Tom and Sara
1. Who stayed in good physical condition?	☐	☐	☐
2. Who spent a lot of time alone?	☐	☐	☐
3. Who thought the problem was temporary?	☐	☐	☐
4. Who felt helpless?	☐	☐	☐
5. Who had a conversation back at work?	☐	☐	☐

C DISCUSSION **Work with a partner. Compare your answers in B. Why did you check *Tom*, *Sara*, or *Tom and Sara*?**

REFLEXIVE AND RECIPROCAL PRONOUNS

Reflexive Pronouns			
Subject Pronoun		**Reflexive Pronoun**	
I		**myself**	
You		**yourself**	
He		**himself**	
She	looked at	**herself**	in the mirror.
It		**itself**	
We		**ourselves**	
You		**yourselves**	
They		**themselves**	

Reciprocal Pronouns		
Subject Pronoun		**Reciprocal Pronoun**
We You They	looked at	**each other.** **one another.**

GRAMMAR NOTES

1   Reflexive Pronouns

Use a **reflexive pronoun** when the **subject and object** refer to the **same people or things**.

- **same people**

      SUBJECT   =   OBJECT
  Sara looked at **herself** in the mirror.
  (Sara looked at her own face.)

- **same things**

      SUBJECT   =   OBJECT
  My **office light** turns **itself** off.
  (It turns off automatically.)

2   Reflexive Pronouns for Emphasis

You can also use a reflexive pronoun to **emphasize a noun** or **a pronoun**.

The reflexive pronoun usually **follows** the noun or pronoun **directly**.	Tom was upset when he lost his job. The **job itself** wasn't important to him, but he needed the money. Tom believed that **he himself** was at fault for losing his job.
USAGE NOTE When we use a reflexive pronoun for emphasis, we often stress the identity of the person or thing the pronoun is referring to in **comparison to other people or things**.	**Sara herself** didn't get depressed, but her co-workers felt terrible. *(This compares Sara to her co-workers.)*

3 Reflexive Pronouns in Imperative Sentences

Imperative sentences can have reflexive pronouns.

• *yourself* when the subject is singular	"Don't push **yourself** so hard, **Tom**," Sara said. *(talking to one person)*
• *yourselves* when the subject is plural	"Don't push **yourselves** so hard, **guys**," Sara said. *(talking to several people)*

4 Reflexive Pronouns in Common Expressions

Some **common expressions** use reflexive pronouns.

• *by* + **reflexive pronoun** *(alone or without help)*	Sara lives **by herself.** *(Sara lives alone.)* We finished the job **by ourselves.** *(No one helped us.)*
• *be* + **reflexive pronoun** *(act in the usual way)*	Just **be yourself** at your interview. *(Act like you usually act.)*

5 Reciprocal Pronouns

Use a **reciprocal pronoun** when the **subject and object** of a sentence refer to the **same people**, and these people have a **two-way relationship**.

• *each other* for two people	SUBJECT = OBJECT **Tom and Sara** met **each other** at work. *(Tom met Sara, and Sara met Tom.)*
• *one another* for more than two people	SUBJECT = OBJECT **We all** told **one another** about our jobs. *(Each person exchanged news with every other person.)*
USAGE NOTE In conversation, many people use *each other* and *one another* in the **same way**.	**Sara and Tom** saw **each other.** or **Sara and Tom** saw **one another.** **All six men** knew **each other.** or **All six men** knew **one another.**
BE CAREFUL! Reciprocal pronouns and **plural reflexive pronouns** have different meanings.	Fred and Jane blamed **each other.** *(Fred blamed Jane, and Jane blamed Fred.)* Fred and Jane blamed **themselves.** *(Fred blamed himself, and Jane blamed herself.)*
Reciprocal pronouns have **possessive forms:** *each other's, one another's.*	Tom and Sara took **each other's** numbers. *(Tom took Sara's number, and Sara took Tom's.)*

REFERENCE NOTE

For a list of **verbs and expressions that often take reflexive pronouns**, see Appendix 3 on page 454.

EXERCISE 1 DISCOVER THE GRAMMAR

GRAMMAR NOTES 1–3, 5 Read this article about positive self-talk. Underline the reflexive pronouns once and the reciprocal pronouns twice. Draw an arrow to the words that the pronouns refer to.

Positive Self-Talk and Athletes

POSITIVE SELF-TALK can affect our thoughts, feelings, and actions. It can even make the difference between winning and losing. Top athletes not only compete against one another, they also compete against themselves when they try to improve their performances. Many athletes use self-talk to maintain their self-confidence and help themselves reach new goals. If you've asked yourself how Korean Olympic gold and silver winner Yuna Kim can do those perfect jumps under so much stress, now you know it's probably because she's telling herself, "Yuna! You can! You will! You are!"

One sports psychologist believes that Olympic athletes are not very different from one another—they are all the best in their sports. When two top athletes compete against each other, the winner is the one with the most powerful positive "mental movies." According to many psychologists, ordinary people themselves can use these techniques, too. (And they can do it by themselves, without getting professional help.) They can create "mental movies" to help themselves succeed in difficult situations. So, when you are feeling discouraged about something, picture yourself succeeding and tell yourself, "You can do it!"

EXERCISE 2 REFLEXIVE OR RECIPROCAL PRONOUNS

A GRAMMAR NOTES 1–5 Tom and Sara's company had an office party. Circle the correct pronouns to complete the conversations.

1. A: Listen, guys! The food and drinks are over here. Don't be shy. Please come and help

   (yourselves) / themselves.

   B: Thanks. We will.

2. A: Isn't that the new head of the accounting department over there?

   B: I think so. Let's go over and introduce himself / ourselves.

3. A: I'm really nervous about my date with Nicole after the party. I actually cut

   herself / myself twice while shaving, and then I lost my car keys.

   B: Come on. This is a party, Tom. Just relax and be yourself / yourselves. You'll do just fine.

4. A: What are you giving your boss for the holidays this year?

   B: We always give ourselves / each other the same holiday gifts. Every year, I give him a

   book, and he gives me a box of candy. I realize that this doesn't sound very exciting, but I

   myself / ourselves am quite happy with the arrangement. It makes things easy that way.

5. A: What's your department's reaction to the new computer program?

   B: I'm not sure. We're still teaching ourselves / themselves how to use it.

6. A: Jessica looks upset. Didn't she get a promotion?

   B: No, and she keeps blaming herself / himself. She thinks it's all her fault. Of course it isn't.

7. A: The Aguayos are finally going to Japan on vacation this year.

   B: That's wonderful. They really need one. Are they going by each other / themselves or

   with a tour group?

8. A: This was a great party.

   B: Yeah. We really enjoyed ourselves / myself.

▶27|02 **B** LISTEN AND CHECK Listen to the conversations and check your answers in A.

EXERCISE 3 REFLEXIVE OR RECIPROCAL PRONOUNS

GRAMMAR NOTES 1–5 Read the interview with George Prudeau, a high school French teacher. Complete the interview. Use the correct reflexive or reciprocal pronouns.

INTERVIEWER: How did you become a teacher?

GEORGE: When I got laid off from my sales job, I told _____*myself*_____, "Here's your
                                                          1.

chance to finally do what you really want." One of the great things about teaching is

the freedom I have. I run the class by _____—just the way I want to.
                                          2.

Reflexive and Reciprocal Pronouns **375**

I also like the way my students and I learn from _____. My teaching
3.
impacts my students' lives, but they teach me a lot, too.

INTERVIEWER: What about maintaining discipline? Is that a problem?

GEORGE: We have just a few rules. I tell my students, "Keep _____ busy.
4.
Discuss the lessons, but don't interfere with _____'s work."
5.

INTERVIEWER: What do you like to teach best?

GEORGE: I love French, but the subject _____ really isn't all that important. A
6.
good teacher helps students learn by _____ and encourages them
7.
not to give up when they have problems. For instance, John, one of my students, just
taught _____ how to bake French bread. The first few loaves were
8.
failures. His first reaction was to give up, but I encouraged him to use positive self-
talk, and in the end he succeeded.

INTERVIEWER: What teaching materials do you use?

GEORGE: Very simple ones. I pride _____ on the fact that I can teach
9.
anywhere, even on a street corner.

INTERVIEWER: What do you like least about your job?

GEORGE: The salary. I teach French culture, but I can't afford to travel to France. I have to
satisfy _____ with trips to French restaurants!
10.

EXERCISE 4 VERBS WITH REFLEXIVE OR RECIPROCAL PRONOUNS

GRAMMAR NOTES 1, 4–5 Sara and Tom went to an office party. Look at each picture and
write a sentence describing what happened. Use the correct form of a verb from the box
with a reflexive or reciprocal pronoun. You will use one verb more than once.

| buy | cut | drive | greet | introduce | smile at | talk to |

1. _Sara bought herself a new dress._   2. _____

3. _____

4. _____

5. _____

6. _____

7. _____

8. _____

EXERCISE 5 EDITING

GRAMMAR NOTES 1–5 Read this woman's diary. There are seven mistakes in the use of reflexive and reciprocal pronouns. The first mistake is already corrected. Find and correct six more.

Jan's birthday was Wednesday, and I forgot to call him. I reminded ~~me~~ *myself* all day, and then I forgot anyway! I felt terrible. My sister Anna said, "Don't be so hard on yourselves." But I myself didn't believe her. She prides herself on remembering everything. Then I finally remembered the article on self-talk. It said that people can change the way they explain problems to theirselves. Well, I listened to the way I talked to me, and I realized it sounded really insulting—like the way our high school math teacher used to talk to us. I thought, Jan and I are good friends, and we treat each other's well. One mistake shouldn't impact our friendship that much. In fact, he forgave myself for my mistake right away. And I forgave him for forgetting our dinner date two weeks ago. Friends can forgive themselves, so I guess I can forgive myself.

STEP 4 COMMUNICATION PRACTICE

EXERCISE 6 LISTENING

27|03 **A** Employees are at an office party. Read the sentences. Then listen to the conversations. Then listen again and circle the pronouns that you hear.

1. They should be really proud of (themselves) / each other.

2. You know Ed blames him / himself for everything.

3. Are you going by yourself / yourselves or with a tour?

4. The doctor herself / himself called me this morning.

5. Megan keeps asking herself / her if Jennifer can do the job.

6. They're talking to themselves / each other.

7. In our department, we're still teaching each other / ourselves how to use it.

8. I'm glad you enjoyed yourself / yourselves.

B Work with a partner. Then listen to each conversation again. Discuss these questions.

1. Why should the workers be proud of themselves?

    EXAMPLE: A: They should be proud of themselves because they did a great job this year.
    B: Right. They had the best sales in the company.

2. Why does the man think Ed shouldn't blame himself?

3. Does the woman plan to travel alone? Why or why not?

4. Who called the patient? Was it the doctor's assistant?

5. Why hasn't Megan given Jennifer the promotion yet?

6. What is the woman surprised about? Why?

7. Is someone teaching the man how to use the new computer?

8. Did the woman go to the party alone or with other people? How do you know?

EXERCISE 7 OPTIMIST OR PESSIMIST?

A QUESTIONNAIRE Test yourself by completing the questionnaire.

Are you an optimist or a pessimist?

Optimists see bad situations as temporary or limited. Pessimists see them as permanent. What's your reaction when things go wrong? What do you tell yourself? Check (✔) your most likely self-talk for each situation below. Then find out if you're an optimist or a pessimist.

1. Your boss doesn't say good morning to you.
    ☐ **a.** She isn't herself today.
    ☐ **b.** She doesn't like me.

2. Your family forgets your birthday.
    ☐ **a.** Next year, we should keep in touch with one another more.
    ☐ **b.** They only think about themselves.

3. You gain 10 pounds (4.5 kilograms).
    ☐ **a.** I promise myself to eat properly from now on.
    ☐ **b.** Diets never work for me. I'll never maintain a healthy weight.

4. Your boyfriend or girlfriend decides to go out with other people.
    ☐ **a.** We didn't spend enough time with each other.
    ☐ **b.** We're wrong for each other.

5. You're feeling tired lately.
    ☐ **a.** I pushed myself too hard this week.
    ☐ **b.** I never take care of myself.

6. Your friend forgets an appointment with you.
    ☐ **a.** He sometimes forgets to read his appointment book.
    ☐ **b.** He never reminds himself about important things.

Score Your Questionnaire

All the **a** answers are optimistic, and all the **b** answers are pessimistic. Give yourself **0** for every **a** answer and **1** for every **b** answer.

If You Scored	You Are
0–2	very optimistic
3–4	somewhat optimistic
5–6	pessimistic

B Discuss your questionnaire with a partner. Which is more useful—optimistic or pessimistic self-talk? Why?

C Now interview five classmates and find out how they answered the questions. Report the results to another group.

EXAMPLE: For Question 1, three people checked "She isn't herself today."
Two people checked "She doesn't like me."

EXERCISE 8 WHO REMEMBERS MORE?

A GAME Work with a partner. First, look at the picture carefully for thirty seconds. Then shut your books and follow the steps below.

1. Write down as many things as you can remember about what the people are doing.

2. Then compare your notes. Use reflexive and reciprocal pronouns in your description.

EXAMPLE: A: Two men are waving at each other.
B: No, I think two women are waving at each other.

B When you are finished, open your books and check your answers. Who remembered the most? What did you leave out?

EXERCISE 9 PARTY TALK

PICTURE DISCUSSION **Look again at the picture in Exercise 8. With your partner, imagine the self-talk of some of the people at the party. Try to use reflexive and reciprocal pronouns.**

EXAMPLE: A: What do you think the man at the mirror is saying to himself?
B: Maybe something like: "I'll never give myself a haircut again!"
A: I think you're right!
B: OK. Your turn . . . What do you think the woman on the couch . . . ?

EXERCISE 10 HELP YOURSELF!

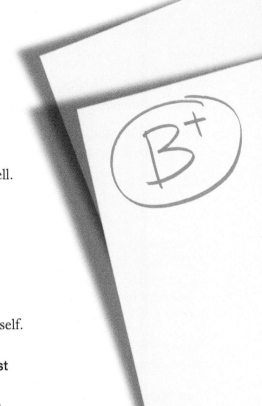

Ⓐ PROBLEM SOLVING **Work in a group. Discuss two or three of the situations in the list below. How do you make yourself feel better?**

EXAMPLE: A: When I'm going to take a big test, I tell myself that I usually get a good grade.
B: Me too. I tell myself that I've studied enough to do well.
C: I remind myself that . . .

- You're going to take a big test.
- You're stuck in traffic.
- You have a roommate you don't like.
- You're going to compete in a sports event.
- You're having an argument with a friend or relative.
- You forgot something important, and you're very angry at yourself.

Ⓑ **Report to the class. Then make a class list of some of the best self-talk for each situation.**

EXAMPLE: A: When they're going to take a big test, Donna and Yuri remind themselves that they usually get very good grades.
B: When she's having an argument with a friend or a relative, Jana tells herself that . . .
C: When Javier is upset with his roommate . . .

FROM GRAMMAR TO WRITING

A BEFORE YOU WRITE Imagine that you write an Internet advice column called "Help Yourself with Self-Talk." A reader writes that he or she is not doing well at school and is having problems with a friend. Complete the outline with positive and negative examples of self-talk.

	Positive	Negative
1. Problem at school	_____	_____
	_____	_____
2. Problem with a friend	_____	_____
	_____	_____

B WRITE Use your outline and some of the phrases below to complete the advice column. Try to avoid the common mistakes in the chart.

- Some people tell themselves . . .
- One person I know tells herself . . .
- Friends can remind each other that . . .
- Tell yourself . . .

EXAMPLE: I'm sorry you're having trouble at school. The best advice I can give you is to change your self-talk! What positive things can you say to yourself in this situation? What negative self-talk can you avoid? For example, some people tell themselves . . .

Common Mistakes in Using Reflexive and Reciprocal Pronouns

Use a **reflexive pronoun** when the subject and object refer to the **same people or things**. Do not use a reciprocal pronoun.	We asked **ourselves**, "What happened?" NOT We asked ~~each other~~, "What happened?"
Use the plural *yourselves* for more than one person. Do not use the singular *yourself*.	**You and Li** should believe in **yourselves**. NOT You and Li should believe in ~~yourself~~.
Use a **reciprocal pronoun** when the subject and object have a **two-way relationship**. Do not use a reflexive pronoun.	We help **each other**. I help him, and he helps me. NOT We help ~~ourselves~~.

C CHECK YOUR WORK Read your advice column. Underline the reflexive pronouns and circle the reciprocal pronouns. Use the Editing Checklist to check your work.

Editing Checklist

Did you use . . . ?

☐ correct reflexive pronouns when the subject and object refer to the same people or things

☐ reciprocal pronouns to show a two-way relationship

☐ *yourself* when the subject is singular; *yourselves* when the subject is plural

D REVISE YOUR WORK Read your advice column again. Can you improve your writing? Make changes if necessary.

UNIT 27 **REVIEW**

Test yourself on the grammar of the unit.

A Circle the correct pronouns to complete the sentences.

1. Jana asked <u>me / myself</u> to pick her up at 8:00.

2. I reminded <u>me / myself</u> to set my smartphone alarm for 7:00.

3. Jana and I often help <u>ourselves / each other</u> with our schoolwork. She's a great friend.

4. Jana <u>himself / herself</u> likes to get up without an alarm. She hates the sound of the alarm.

5. My mother told both of us, "You're pushing <u>yourself / yourselves</u> too hard. Relax."

6. The class <u>himself / itself</u> isn't too difficult.

7. The students all know <u>themselves / one another</u>. We were together last semester.

8. Before my last test, I told <u>myself / herself</u>, "You're going to get an A." An example of positive self-talk!

B Complete the sentences with the correct form of the verbs in parentheses and the correct pronouns.

1. Karl and Ana are good friends. They _____ every day.
   (talk to)

2. Ina and Eva always _____ with a kiss.
   (greet)

3. Lee, please _____ to some more cake.
   (help)

4. Rita and Tom are at the beach. They're really _____.
   (enjoy)

5. Tania couldn't get a ride, so she _____ to the party.
   (drive)

C Find and correct seven mistakes.

When I first met Nicole, I told myself, "I'm not going to like working with herself."

Negative self-talk! I was really wrong. Nicole has helped myself out with so many things.

When she oneself didn't know something, she always found out for me. That way, both of

ourselves learned something. After I learned the job better, we helped each other's out. The

job themselves isn't that challenging, but I'm really enjoying myself. All of us in the office

have become good friends. We all like each another. That makes it a great place to work. I

feel lucky to be here.

Now check your answers on page 481.

Phrasal Verbs

SCIENCE

OUTCOMES
• Use a range of phrasal verbs
• Use phrasal verbs with separated objects
• Identify key details in an article and a conversation
• Discuss illustrations, using phrasal verbs
• Conduct an online search and share results with the class
• Write a paragraph about animal intelligence

STEP 1 GRAMMAR IN CONTEXT

BEFORE YOU READ

Look at the photos. Discuss the questions.

1. What kind of work do you think Dr. Eloy Rodriguez does?

2. Where do you think he is in the photo below?

3. What is he doing?

READ

▶ 28|01 Read this article about Dr. Eloy Rodriguez.

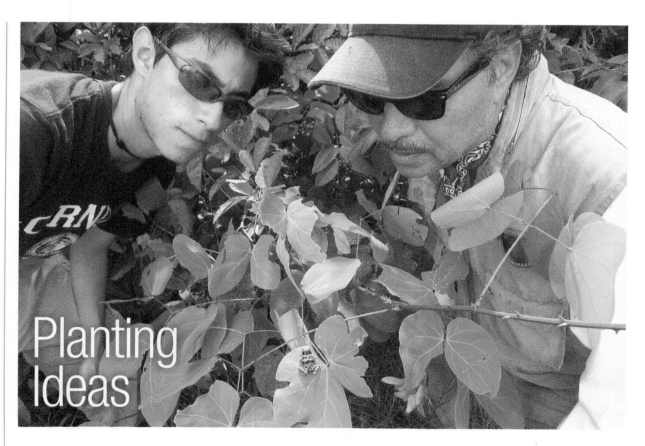

Planting Ideas

As a child, Eloy Rodriguez picked cotton to help support his family. He also picked up an interest in plants. Dr. Rodriguez is now a famous scientist, but he is still interested in plants. Every summer, he takes off his lab coat, puts on his mosquito repellent,[1] and travels to the Amazon region of Venezuela with his students. There, they search for medicinal plants.

Dr. Rodriguez grew up in Texas. The adults in his very large family (sixty-seven cousins lived nearby) brought their children up to be honest, fair, and *vivo*, or quick-thinking. Rodriguez did well in high school, especially in chemistry, and he went on to college. He took a job there cleaning a laboratory. He became a science major and then went on to graduate school. Soon he was managing the lab.

Eloy Rodriguez and anthropologist[2] Richard Wrangham once noticed that sick animals often pick out certain plants to eat. They turned their observations into a new area of science—zoopharmacognosy (the study of how animals use plants as medicine). Today, Rodriguez is one of the most brilliant scientists in the United States. Rodriguez thanks his family. He points out that sixty-four of his cousins graduated from college, eleven with advanced degrees. "Although poverty was there, family was what helped us get by in life."

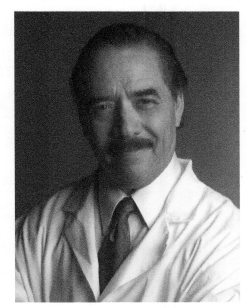

Dr. Eloy Rodriguez

---

1 *mosquito repellent:* a chemical that keeps mosquitoes (small flying insects that bite) away from people
2 *anthropologist:* a scientist who studies people and their societies

AFTER YOU READ

A VOCABULARY **Match the phrasal verbs with their meanings.**

_____ **1. take off**   **a.** to continue

_____ **2. grow up**   **b.** to choose

_____ **3. go on**   **c.** to get

_____ **4. pick out**   **d.** to remove

_____ **5. get by**   **e.** to become an adult

_____ **6. pick up**   **f.** to survive

B COMPREHENSION **Read the statements. Check (✓) *True* or *False*.**

	True	False
1. Dr. Rodriguez became interested in plants when he was a child.	☐	☐
2. Rodriguez's family helped him survive.	☐	☐
3. After high school, Rodriguez quit school.	☐	☐
4. He doesn't wear his lab coat in the Amazon.	☐	☐
5. He doesn't do anything to prevent mosquito bites in the Amazon.	☐	☐
6. Sick animals often choose special plants to eat.	☐	☐

C DISCUSSION **Work with a partner. Compare your answers in B. Why did you check *True* or *False*?**

PHRASAL VERBS: TRANSITIVE AND INTRANSITIVE

Transitive Phrasal Verbs

Subject	Verb	Particle	Object (Noun)
He	**put**	**on**	his lab coat.
	helped	**out**	his students.

Subject	Verb	Object (Noun/Pronoun)	Particle
He	**put**	his lab coat	**on.**
		it	
	helped	his students	**out.**
		them	

Intransitive Phrasal Verbs

Subject	Verb	Particle	
She	**started**	**over.**	
He	**grew**	**up**	in Texas.
They	**got**	**back**	early.

GRAMMAR NOTES

1 **Form of Phrasal Verbs**

Phrasal verbs (also called *two-word verbs*) are made up of a **verb + particle**.

- **phrasal verb = verb + particle**

VERB + PARTICLE
He **put on** his lab coat.

These are some **common particles** that combine with verbs to form a phrasal verb:

- *on* (go on, put on, turn on)
- *off* (call off, take off, turn off)
- *up* (bring up, grow up, look up)
- *down* (sit down, turn down, write down)
- *out* (help out, pick out, point out)

She **turned on** the light.
He **turned off** the TV.
They **looked up** the word.
She **wrote down** the address.
He **helps out** a lot.

Prepositions and **particles** look the same. However, **particles** are part of the verb phrase, and they often **change the meaning** of the verb.

VERB + PREPOSITION
She's **looking up** at the sky.
   (She's looking in the direction of the sky.)
VERB + PARTICLE
She's **looking up** the word.
   (She's searching for the word in the dictionary.)

2 Meaning of Phrasal Verbs

Many **phrasal verbs** and **one-word verbs** have **similar meanings**.

To the right are some **common phrasal verbs** and one-word verbs with similar meanings.

USAGE NOTE Phrasal verbs are often **less formal** than one-word verbs.

PHRASAL VERB	ONE-WORD VERB
(less formal)	*(more formal)*
figure out	solve
give up	quit
hand in	submit
help out	assist
keep on	continue

3 Transitive and Intransitive Phrasal Verbs

Phrasal verbs can be **transitive** or **intransitive**.

Transitive phrasal verbs have **objects**.

VERB + OBJECT
He **took off** *his lab coat*.

Most transitive phrasal verbs are **separable**. This means that the **object** can come:

- **after** the verb + particle

- **between** the verb + particle

VERB + PARTICLE + OBJECT
He **helped out** *the students*.
or
VERB + OBJECT + PARTICLE
He **helped** *the students* **out**.

BE CAREFUL! When the **object is a pronoun**, it must come **between** the verb and the particle.

He **helped** *them* **out**.
NOT He ~~helped out them~~.

A few phrasal verbs can have a **gerund** (verb + *-ing*) as an **object**. The gerund always comes **after** the particle.

She **kept on** *learning*.
He **didn't put off** *applying* to school.

Intransitive phrasal verbs do not have objects.

Eloy Rodriguez **grew up** in Texas.
He never **gives up**.

USAGE NOTE Intransitive phrasal verbs are often action verbs and they occur frequently in the **imperative**.

Please, **sit down**.
Don't get up.

IN WRITING Transitive phrasal verbs are common in conversation and formal writing. **Intransitive phrasal verbs** are very common in conversation, but they are rare in formal writing.

They **carried out** *experiments*. *(conversation and formal report)*
He **went on** with his studies. *(conversation)*
He **continued** with his studies. *(formal report)*

REFERENCE NOTES

For a list of **transitive phrasal verbs** and their meanings, see Appendix 4 on page 455.
For a list of **intransitive phrasal verbs** and their meanings, see Appendix 5 on page 456.

EXERCISE 1 DISCOVER THE GRAMMAR

A GRAMMAR NOTES 1–3 **Read this article. Underline the phrasal verbs. Circle the objects of the transitive phrasal verbs.**

Eloy Rodriguez grew up in Edinburg, Texas, where his elementary school teachers passed (Chicano[1] students) over for special honors classes. They also punished them for speaking Spanish. Before Rodriguez went on to become the first U.S.-born Chicano biology instructor at his university, he worked eighteen hours a day and slept in his lab, getting by on very little sleep. "I was very aware that I was the first this, and the first that, and I knew that some people were waiting for me to slip up." Rodriguez didn't slip up. However, he knows that when students feel teachers don't treat them fairly, it turns them off education. Many of them just give up.

Today, Dr. Rodriguez is passing his own success on. When he became a professor at Cornell University, he set out to find Latino[2] graduate students. He takes these students with him on many of his trips and works hard to turn them into top scientists. In 1990, he set up KIDS (Kids Investigating and Discovering Science)—a science program for minority elementary school children. They put on white lab coats and investigate science with university teachers who treat them like research scientists. They observe nature and figure out problems. In interviews, Rodriguez always brings up role models. "I saw my first snowflake before I saw my first Chicano scientist," he says. Because of Rodriguez's efforts, many students will not face the same problem.

1 *Chicano:* Mexican-American
2 *Latino:* from a Spanish-speaking country in Central or South America

B **Read the statements. Check (✓) *True* or *False*.**

	True	False
1. In Eloy Rodriguez's elementary school, teachers chose Chicano students for honors classes.	☐	☑
2. When Rodriguez became a biology instructor, some people expected him to fail.	☐	☐
3. Unfair treatment makes students less interested in education.	☐	☐
4. Today, Dr. Rodriguez wants to forget his own success.	☐	☐

	True	False
5. He searches for Latino graduate students for his program at Cornell.	☐	☐
6. In 1990, Rodriguez visited a program called KIDS.	☐	☐
7. Children in KIDS wear the same lab clothes as the scientists.	☐	☐
8. Rodriguez rarely mentions role models.	☐	☐

EXERCISE 2 MEANING

GRAMMAR NOTE 2 Complete this advertisement for a field trip to the Amazon. Choose the phrasal verb from the box that is closest in meaning to the verb in parentheses. Use the correct form of the phrasal verb. See Appendices 4 and 5 on pages 455 and 456 for help.

fill out	get up	keep on	pick up	sign up	try out
find out	hand in	pass up	~~set up~~	talk over	work out

Two Weeks in the Amazon! Sign Up Now!

The Biology Department is now _____setting up_____ its summer field trip to the Amazonian
                                    1. (prepare)

rain forest in Venezuela. If you want to _____, _____ your
                                            2. (register)   **3. (get)**

application from the Department Office (Room 215), and _____ it

_____ right away. _____ it _____ by May 1.
4. (complete)   **5. (submit)**

Last summer, we collected plants and identified them. This summer, we plan to talk to

local people and _____ how they use plants in traditional medicine. This trip is
                    6. (learn)

extremely challenging. We travel to our camp by canoe. When there are problems, we

_____ them _____ by ourselves. We _____ very
                7. (solve)   **8. (get out of bed)**

early, and we _____ working until dark. There is
                9. (continue)

also some danger, so please _____ the trip

_____ with your families before you decide.
10. (discuss)

This is a wonderful chance to _____ your
                                    11. (use)

research skills and make a real contribution. We really

hope you won't _____ this
                12. (decide not to use)

opportunity to do important

"hands-on" science.

EXERCISE 3 PARTICLES

GRAMMAR NOTES 1-2 Circle the correct particle to complete each phrasal verb. See Appendices 4 and 5 on pages 455 and 456 for help.

Eat Some Leaves and Call Me in the Morning

In 1972, Richard Wrangham of Harvard University set (out)/ up to study
                                                    1.
chimpanzees in Tanzania. He observed that these chimps get by / up
                                                          2.
at dawn to eat the leaves of *Aspilia*. They clearly hate the taste. This

brought back / up a question: Why do chimpanzees pick out / over this
        3.   **4.**
plant but pass out / up delicious fruit nearby? Wrangham thought this
              5.
question over / up for several years. He then asked Eloy Rodriguez to
        6.
help him in / out with the analysis. Together, they worked over / out the
          7.   **8.**
puzzle: *Aspilia* contains an antibiotic. Zoopharmacognosy—the study of

how animals "doctor" themselves with plants—was born.

EXERCISE 4 SEPARABLE PHRASAL VERBS AND PRONOUNS

Ⓐ GRAMMAR NOTE 3 Complete the conversations. Use phrasal verbs and pronouns.

1. A: Don't forget to put on your mosquito repellent!

   B: Don't worry! I _____ *put it on* _____ as soon as we got here.

2. A: Can we take off our hats? It's really hot.

   B: Don't _____. They protect you from the sun.

3. A: How do you turn on the generator?

   B: It's easy. You _____ with this switch.

4. A: Did you cover up the leftover food? We don't want the ants to get at it.

   B: Don't worry. We'll _____.

5. A: Is Dr. Rodriguez going to call off the field trip tomorrow?

   B: He'll only _____ if someone gets sick.

6. A: Good night. Oh, can someone wake Mike up tomorrow morning?

   B: No problem. I'll _____.

⊙28|02 Ⓑ LISTEN AND CHECK Listen to the conversations and check your answers in A.

EXERCISE 5 WORD ORDER

GRAMMAR NOTE 3 Unscramble the words to make sentences. If more than one answer is possible, give both.

1. on / put / your lab coats _Put on your lab coats._ or _Put your lab coats on._

2. the experiment / set / up _____

3. out / it / carry _____

4. down / sit / when you're done _____

5. to page 26 / on / go _____

6. up / your reports / write _____

7. in / them / hand _____

8. off / take / your lab coats _____

9. them / put / away _____

10. the lab / clean / up _____

EXERCISE 6 EDITING

GRAMMAR NOTES 1–3 Read these notes from a student's journal. There are nine mistakes in the use of phrasal verbs. The first mistake is already corrected. Find and correct eight more.

                     got back

I just ~~got~~ from Venezuela ~~back~~! I spent two weeks in the Amazon rain forest with Dr. Rodriguez. We carried out research there on plants that the Piaroa people use as medicine. We made down a list of these plants, and we're going to analyze them when we get back to school next week.

We set down camp near the Orinoco River, hundreds of miles from any major city. Life there is hard. You get very early up every morning. You must always watch up and never touch a new insect or plant. If you pick up it, you can get a bad skin rash. But plants can also cure. One day, I felt sick. One of the Piaroa gave me the stem of a certain plant to chew. It worked! Later, I found up that the same plant helps cure insect bites. And believe me, insects are a big problem in the rain forest. I used up many bottles of repellent. But even when I put on it, it didn't totally keep the insects away.

This trip changed my life! I'm now thinking about switching my major to pharmacology. I want to find over more about how people can use the same plants that animals use as medicine.

EXERCISE 7 LISTENING

▶28|03 **A** Some college students are taking a science class. Listen to their conversations. Read the statements. Then listen again and check (✓) *True* or *False*.

		True	False
1.	Dr. Rodriguez brought in a DVD.	☐	☑
2.	Terry is giving some reports to the teacher.	☐	☐
3.	Rea is going to look for some information in a reference book.	☐	☐
4.	They're going to make the music lower.	☐	☐
5.	Jason feels that the class is going too fast for him.	☐	☐
6.	Lila visited the class yesterday.	☐	☐
7.	It's time to return the lab coats.	☐	☐
8.	He needs to choose a book for his report.	☐	☐

B Work with a partner. Discuss your answers in A. Why did you check *True* or *False*?

EXAMPLE: A: The answer to number 1 is *False*.
          B: Right. Dr. Rodriguez didn't bring *in* a DVD. He brought *up* a DVD. That means he talked about it. What's your answer to number 2?

EXERCISE 8 CLASS TRIP

ROLE PLAY Work in a group. Imagine that you are going to take a class field trip. Decide where to go—for example, the zoo, a museum, a park. Then assign tasks and make a list. Try to include some of the phrasal verbs from the box. You can also use Appendices 4 and 5 on pages 455 and 456 for help.

EXAMPLE: A: I'll write down the "To Do" list.
          B: Good idea. I'll call up to find out the hours.
          C: I can pick up a bus schedule.

call up	figure out	look over	make up	pick out	talk over
clean up	hand out	look up	pass out	pick up	write down

EXERCISE 9 A NEW LEAF

PICTURE DISCUSSION Work with a partner. Discuss these pictures. Who are the people and what are they doing in each picture? Use phrasal verbs from the box. Make up a story about the pictures and write a number under each one to show the time order. Compare your story to those of your classmates. There's more than one way to tell a story!

bring back	figure out	hand in	look up	put on	talk over
carry out	find out	lie down	point out	shut off	turn on

EXAMPLE: A: So, what do you think about picture **a**?
B: I think the man on the left is a teacher or maybe a guide. He's holding a leaf and pointing something out.
A: I think the other two people are students. The young man is looking something up. Maybe information about the leaf. The young woman . . .

a. _____

b. _____

c. _____

d. _____

e. _____

f. _____

EXERCISE 10 SAFETY FIRST!

A GROUP PROJECT Work in a group. Do an Internet search on "science lab safety rules." Find rules that use phrasal verbs. Write them down.

Always clean up spills immediately.

B Share the rules with the rest of the class. Create one list to put on the board.

A BEFORE YOU WRITE Think about an animal you know or that you've read about or observed in a zoo or on a TV show. Make a list of things the animal can or can't do.

_____
(the animal)

Things it can do   **Things it can't do**

_____   _____

_____   _____

_____   _____

_____   _____

B WRITE How intelligent are animals? Use your list to write a paragraph about the animal you chose. Use phrasal verbs. Try to avoid the common mistakes in the chart.

EXAMPLE: I think animals have a lot of intelligence. Chimpanzees, for example, are very
smart animals. Even though they don't like the taste of the Aspilia plant, they pick it
out among many other plants to eat. Somehow the chimps have figured out that the
plant has important health benefits . . .

Common Mistakes in Using Phrasal Verbs

Use the **correct particle**. The wrong particle changes the meaning of the verb.	The chimp **picked _out_** a plant to eat. _(The chimp chose a plant.)_ The chimp **picked _up_** a plant to eat. _(The chimp lifted the plant.)_
Put **pronoun objects** between the verb and the particle in transitive separable phrasal verbs. Do not put pronoun objects after the verb.	He **picked _it_ up**. NOT He picked up it.

C CHECK YOUR WORK Read your paragraph. Underline the phrasal verbs and circle the objects. Use the Editing Checklist to check your work.

Editing Checklist

Did you use . . . ?

☐ the correct phrasal verbs

☐ the correct particles

☐ the correct word order for object pronouns

D REVISE YOUR WORK Read your paragraph again. Can you improve your writing? Make changes if necessary. Give your paragraph a title.

UNIT 28 REVIEW

Test yourself on the grammar of the unit.

Ⓐ Circle the correct words to complete the sentences.

1. Have you figured <u>in</u> / <u>out</u> the homework problem yet?

2. Not yet, but I won't give <u>up</u> / <u>back</u>.

3. I'm going to keep <u>away</u> / <u>on</u> trying.

4. Let me know if I can help you <u>out</u> / <u>over</u>.

5. I need to look <u>down</u> / <u>up</u> some information online.

6. Maybe you can look <u>out</u> / <u>over</u> my answers when I'm finished.

Ⓑ Unscramble the words to make sentences. Give two answers when possible.

1. _____
(early / Joe / up / gets)

2. _____
(on / the TV / turns / he)

3. _____
(he / down / with Ana / sits)

4. _____
(get / well / they / along)

5. _____
(his schedule / over / they / look)

6. _____
(talk / over / they / it)

7. _____
(they / put / away / it)

8. _____
(put / on / their coats / they)

Ⓒ Find and correct six mistakes.

As soon as Ina wakes out, she quickly gets dressed, puts off her mosquito repellent, and goes out with her classmates into the rain forest. They keep up walking until they find what they are looking for—chimpanzees. They've been studying the chimps for weeks. The chimps are really intelligent. They know which plants have medicinal qualities and which plants don't. Somehow these amazing animals have figured out it!

At the end of each day, Ina and her classmates go back to their camp. It's late, and they're tired. But, before they turn on the lights to go to bed, they talk up their plans for the next day. Everyone is tired but excited to be doing such interesting work.

Now check your answers on page 482.

More Modals and Similar Expressions

OUTCOMES
- Express necessity or absence of necessity
- Identify key ideas in an article about travel rules
- Identify details in a conversation about driving regulations
- Recognize and discuss the meaning of common signs
- Discuss rules, regulations, and future plans
- Write a paragraph explaining procedures for obtaining an official document

OUTCOMES
- Express expectations with *be supposed to*
- Identify key points in an article about manners
- Identify details in a conversation about manners
- Discuss customs and life events from one's culture
- Describe an illustration, discussing polite and impolite behavior
- Write a paragraph about a life event in a specific culture

OUTCOMES
- Express likelihood of future events
- Distinguish between possibility and certainty of a future event
- Identify key details in a transcript
- Identify the probability of a situation in a report
- Describe future plans and intentions in detail, giving degrees of probability
- Write an email or short letter that expresses the probability of future plans

OUTCOMES
- Come to conclusions about present situations
- Express varying degrees of certainty about the present
- Identify main ideas in a short story
- Identify the certainty of speakers about events
- Draw conclusions about everyday objects and situations
- Write a paragraph about a short story, drawing possible conclusions

Necessity: *Have (got) to, Must, Can't*
RULES AND REGULATIONS

OUTCOMES
- Express necessity or absence of necessity
- Identify key ideas in an article about travel rules
- Identify details in a conversation about driving regulations
- Recognize and discuss the meaning of common signs
- Discuss rules, regulations, and future plans
- Write a paragraph explaining procedures for obtaining an official document

STEP 1	GRAMMAR IN CONTEXT

BEFORE YOU READ

Look at the title and the photo. Discuss the questions.

1. Have you ever traveled to a different country?

2. How did you prepare for your trip?

3. What did you need to know before you went?

READ

29|01   Read this article about some rules for international travel.

Know Before You Go

What do international travelers have to know before they go? This week's column answers some questions from our readers.

Q My passport is going to expire in three months. Can I use it for a short trip to Asia next month?

A For many countries, your passport must be valid for at least six months after you enter the country. Renew your passport before you leave, or you'll have to check the rules of each country you plan to visit.

Q I'm a French citizen. Last month, I visited the United States, and I brought some gifts for friends. Why did U.S. Customs agents take the cheese?

A You can't bring most types of soft cheese into the U.S. Many governments have strict rules about bringing food into their countries. To avoid problems, don't bring gifts of fresh food, and eat your snacks on the plane.

Q Do I have to put my laptop computer through the X-ray machine at airport security?[1] I'm worried that the machine will damage it.

A You don't have to put your laptop through the X-ray machine as long as it is in a "checkpoint-friendly" bag.[2] If it isn't, then you must remove it for X-ray inspection. But don't worry. This particular X-ray won't hurt your equipment.

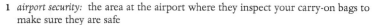

1 *airport security:* the area at the airport where they inspect your carry-on bags to make sure they are safe

2 *checkpoint-friendly bag:* a special bag without zippers or pockets that allows you to keep your laptop in it while you go through airport security

Q I'm from Australia. My family and I are planning a trip to Europe and North America. We'd like to rent cars in a few places. Do I have to get an International Driver's Permit (IDP)?

A Regulations differ: In Italy, for example, you must not drive without an IDP (unless you have a European Union driving license); in Canada, you don't have to have one for a short trip, but it's recommended. For a world tour, you really should get an IDP to avoid problems and disappointment. And remember, you still have to carry a valid driver's license from home in addition to the IDP.

Q I'm planning a trip from Toronto to Hong Kong. There's a new nonstop flight, but it's more expensive, and it's more than fifteen hours long! What do you recommend?

A Several airlines are now offering super-long flights. They provide more comfortable seats, Wi-Fi, and lots of entertainment. They cost a bit more, but you won't have to make as many connecting flights. That saves you time and hassles. But remember: To stay healthy on long flights, you've got to get up and move around. You also must drink plenty of water. On a long flight, these are "musts," not "shoulds"!

AFTER YOU READ

A VOCABULARY Cross out the one word that does not belong in each category.

1. They must be **valid**:   passports   licenses   computers
2. Agents **inspect** them at airports: rules   luggage   tickets
3. They can be **hassles**:   cars   flights   movies
4. There are **regulations** for them: sleeping   driving   traveling
5. They can be **strict**:   books   laws   agents
6. They are **equipment**:   cameras   X-ray machines   bags

B COMPREHENSION Read the statements. Check (✓) *True* or *False*.

	True	False
1. Passengers must put computers through security X-ray equipment.	☐	☐
2. A passport is always valid.	☐	☐
3. Travelers are not allowed to bring some types of cheese into the United States.	☐	☐
4. You can't eat cheese on the plane.	☐	☐
5. Non-European Union visitors need an IDP to drive in Italy.	☐	☐
6. It isn't necessary to have an IDP to drive in Canada.	☐	☐
7. To stay healthy on long flights, passengers must stay in their seats.	☐	☐

C DISCUSSION Work with a partner. Compare your answers in B. Why did you check *True* or *False*?

NECESSITY: *HAVE (GOT) TO, NOT HAVE TO*

Affirmative Statements

Subject	Have to/ Have got to	Base Form of Verb	
I You We They	**have to** **have got to**	**leave**	now.
He She It	**has to** **has got to**		

Negative Statements*

Subject	Do not	Have to	Base Form of Verb	
I You We They	**don't**	**have to**	**leave**	now.
He She It	**doesn't**			

*There is no negative form for *have got to*.

Contractions*

have got to	=	**'ve got to**
has got to	=	**'s got to**

*There are no contractions for *have to* and *has to*.

Yes/No Questions

Do	Subject	Have to	Base Form of Verb
Do	I you we they	**have to**	**leave?**
Does	he she it		

Short Answers

Affirmative			Negative		
Yes,	you I/we you they	**do.**	**No,**	you I/we you they	**don't.**
	he she it	**does.**		he she it	**doesn't.**

Wh- Questions

Wh- Word	Do	Subject	Have to	Base Form of Verb
When	**do**	I you we they	**have to**	**leave?**
	does	he she it		

NECESSITY: *MUST, MUST NOT, CAN'T*

Must*			
Subject	*Must (not)*	Base Form of Verb	
I You He She It We They	**must**	**leave**	very early.
	must not	**arrive**	too late.

Contraction
must not = **mustn't**

Can't*			
Subject	*Can't*	Base Form of Verb	
You He They	**can't**	**sit**	over there.

* *Must* and *can't* are modals. Modals have only one form.
They do not have *-s* in the third-person singular.

GRAMMAR NOTES

1 *Have to, Have got to, Must*

Use *have to*, *have got to*, or the modal *must* to show that something is **necessary**.

• *have to*	You **have to carry** your passport when you travel to most countries.
• *have got to*	I**'ve got to apply** for a new passport right away!
• *must*	All passengers **must show** their passports when they check in.

USAGE NOTE *Have to* is the **most common** expression in conversation and writing. You can also use *have got to* in conversation and **informal** writing.

A: We **have to check in** now.
B: OK. But I**'ve got to make** a quick call first.

USAGE NOTE *Must* is much **stronger** than *have to* and *have got to* and is not very common in conversation. Usually only people with power use it (government leaders, police officers, customs agents, teachers, parents).

A: You **must put on** your seat belt.
B: Yes, Officer.

A: Lia, honey. You really **must pack** tonight.
B: OK, Mom.

IN WRITING You will see *must* in **formal writing** and in official forms, signs, and notices that describe **rules and regulations**.

Passengers **must have** their passports out and ready to show the agent before boarding the plane. (*sign*)

2 For Present, Future, and Past Necessity

Use a form of *have (got) to* or *must* to express a **present or future** necessity.	
• **present necessity**	He **has (got) to travel** a lot for his job. You **must turn off** your phone now.
• **future necessity**	We **have (got) to leave** tomorrow. We**'re going to have to leave** at 2:00. We**'ll have to visit** them soon. We **must meet** the new clients tomorrow.
Use a past form of *have to* to express a **past** necessity.	
• **past necessity**	He **had to travel** a lot last year.
BE CAREFUL! *Have got to* and *must* have no past forms. Use only *have to* for the past.	We **had to** work last night. NOT We ~~had got to~~ work last night. NOT We ~~must~~ work last night.

3 Questions

Use *have to* for most questions. Again, it can refer to a **present**, **future**, or **past** necessity.	
• **present necessity**	**Do** you **have to check** your bags?
• **future necessity**	When **do** we **have to get** to the airport? **Are** we **going to have to check** this bag? When **will** we **have to show** our passports?
• **past necessity**	**Did** you **have to renew** your passport?
USAGE NOTE We almost never use *must* in questions.	**Must** I leave right now? *(not common)*
BE CAREFUL! Do not use *have got to* in questions.	**Do** I **have to** leave right now? NOT ~~Have I got to~~ leave right now?

4 Negative Statements

Use a form of *not have to* to show that something is **not necessary**. There is a **choice**.	
• **no present necessity**	Tourists **don't have to have** an IDP in Canada.
• **no future necessity**	We **don't have to get** there before 7:00 p.m. You **won't have to go** through customs.
• **no past necessity**	We **didn't have to show** our passport.
BE CAREFUL! There is no negative form of *have got to*. Use *don't have to*.	Tourists **don't have to** have an IDP in Canada. NOT Tourists ~~haven't got to~~ have an IDP in Canada.

CONTINUED ▶

Use *must not* to express **prohibition** (to say something is **against the rules**). There is **no choice**.	You **must not drive** without a license. It's against the law.
Must not can refer to the **present** or the **future**.	You **must not smoke** on the plane. *(present)* You **must not get up** until the "fasten your seat belt" sign is turned off. *(future)*
The contraction *mustn't* is less formal than *must not*.	You **mustn't forget** to renew your license, Tommy!

BE CAREFUL! In the affirmative, *have (got) to* and *must* have similar meanings. However, *not have to* and *must not* have very **different meanings**.	Passengers **don't have to board** now.
	  (They can board now, but it isn't necessary.)
	Passengers **must not board** now.
	  (They can't board now. It's against the rules.)

USAGE NOTE In **conversation**, we often use *can't* instead of *must not* to express prohibition.	You **can't drive** without a license. *(very common)*

PRONUNCIATION NOTE

▶29|02

Pronunciation of *Have to, Has to, Have got to,* and *Mustn't*	

In **informal conversation**, we often pronounce *have to* "hafta" and *has to* "hasta."	A: What time do we **have to** be at the airport?
	  (hafta)
	B: Eight o'clock. But John still **has to** pack.
	  (hasta)

For *have got to*, we often pronounce *got to* "gotta," and we sometimes leave out *have*.	We**'ve got to** leave now. *('ve gotta)* **or** *(gotta)*
We always pronounce the contraction for *must not* "musnt." We never pronounce the first -t in *mustn't*.	You **mustn't** forget to take your passport. *(musnt)*
IN WRITING Sometimes people use *hafta, hasta,* and *gotta* in **informal notes**, **text messages**, and **emails** to friends.	I **gotta** go now. See you later. *(text to friend)*
BE CAREFUL! Do not use *hafta, hasta,* and *gotta* when you write to people you have a formal relationship with.	Dear Professor Chin, I **have to** take my parents to the airport today, so I'll be late for class. *(email)* NOT Dear Professor Chin, I ~~hafta~~ take . . .

REFERENCE NOTES

For general information on **modals**, see Unit 13, Grammar Notes 1–2, on page 177.

For *have (got) to, must,* and *can't* for **present conclusions**, see Unit 32 on page 440.

For *can't* for **ability and possibility** (see Unit 13), for **permission** (see Unit 14), or for **requests** (see Unit 15).

For a list of **modals and their functions**, see Appendix 19 on page 460.

EXERCISE 1 DISCOVER THE GRAMMAR

(A) GRAMMAR NOTES 1–4 Read Ben Leonard's telephone conversation with a clerk from the Italian consulate. Underline the words that show that something is *necessary*, *not necessary*, or *against the rules*.

BEN: Hello. I'm Australian, and I'm planning to spend several weeks in Europe with my family. I have some questions. First, <u>do we have to get</u> visas to visit Italy?

CLERK: No. Australians don't have to have a visa to enter Italy, but you can't stay for longer than ninety days without one. And, of course, you must have a valid passport to enter the country.

BEN: Can my wife and I use our Australian driver's licenses in Italy?

CLERK: You have to carry your Australian license, but you must also have a valid International Driver's Permit. And you've got to be at least eighteen years old.

BEN: When do we have to get the IDPs? Is it possible to apply for them when we get to Europe?

CLERK: No, you must apply before you leave. The Australian Automobile Association can help you. You'll also have to purchase accident insurance, but you can do this at the car rental agency in Italy.

BEN: We'll be in Italy in January. We don't have a set schedule, so we haven't made any reservations. Is that going to be a problem?

CLERK: Yes. You've really got to have reservations, even in January—especially in major cities like Rome, Florence, or Venice.

BEN: One more question. What about travel insurance? Is it necessary?

CLERK: You don't have to get travel insurance, but we strongly recommend it. That way, if something goes wrong, you can save yourselves a lot of money and hassles.

BEN: You're right. Better safe than sorry! Thanks a lot. You've been very helpful.

B Read the instructions. Check (✓) *Necessary*, *Not Necessary*, or *Against the Rules*.

	Necessary	Not Necessary	Against the Rules
1. Get a visa for a two-week visit.	☐	☑	☐
2. Have a valid passport to enter Italy.	☐	☐	☐
3. Use only an Australian driver's license.	☐	☐	☐
4. Be at least eighteen years old to rent a car.	☐	☐	☐
5. Apply for an IDP in Italy.	☐	☐	☐
6. Buy accident insurance.	☐	☐	☐
7. Buy travel insurance.	☐	☐	☐
8. Make hotel reservations.	☐	☐	☐

EXERCISE 2 AFFIRMATIVE AND NEGATIVE STATEMENTS WITH *HAVE TO*

GRAMMAR NOTES 1, 4 The Leonards have checked off the things they've already done to get ready for their trip. Read the lists and write sentences about what the Leonards still *have to do* and what they *don't have to do*.

BEN
✓ make copies of passports and IDPs

buy euros

give the house keys to Nora

ANN
buy phone cards online

✓ call Pet Care

buy batteries for the camera

✓ stop the mail for two weeks

SEAN AND MAYA
✓ pack clothes

download music for the trip

say good-bye to friends

Ben doesn't have to make copies of passports and IDPs.

He has to buy euros, and he . . .

Ann . . .

_____

_____

_____

_____

_____

_____

EXERCISE 3 QUESTIONS AND STATEMENTS WITH
HAVE (GOT) TO AND CAN'T

GRAMMAR NOTES 1–4 Ben's family is traveling from Australia to Italy. Complete the conversations. Use the correct form of *have to*, *have got to*, or *can't* and the verbs in parentheses. Use short answers.

1. BEN: What time _____*do*_____ we _____*have to leave*_____ tomorrow?

a. (leave)

   ANN: We _____ later than 5:30. We _____ with

b. (leave)   **c.** (check in)

the airline by 7:00.

   SEAN: Our flight leaves at 10:00. We've got plenty of time before then. _____ we really

_____ there so early?

d. (get)

   ANN: Yes, _____. It takes a long time to check in and get through

e.

airport security these days. They're very strict, and they inspect everything. It's a hassle,

but they _____ it!

f. (do)

   MAYA: And Mom _____ the car. That takes some time, too!

g. (park)

2. BEN: Maya, this bag _____ over 50 pounds (23 kilograms), or we

a. (weigh)

_____ extra. _____ you _____ so

b. (pay)   **c.** (bring)

many clothes?

   MAYA: Yes, _____. I _____ all my stuff! We'll be

d.   **e.** (have)

gone for weeks.

   ANN: Put some in my bag. And hurry. We _____!

f. (go)

3. BEN: I'm tired. Why _____ we _____ so long to check in?

a. (wait)

   ANN: Relax. We _____ much longer. We're next.

b. (not wait)

4. SEAN: This is exciting! I _____ Randy when we take off. I promised him!

a. (call)

   BEN: We _____ our phone on this plane. Sorry.

b. (use)

5. ANN: We _____ around again. Come on, everybody, let's go.

a. (walk)

   SEAN: Why _____ we _____ all the time?

b. (get up)

   BEN: Remember our rules? We _____ for more than three hours.

c. (sit)

It's unhealthy.

6. MAYA: Are we there yet? This flight is endless!

   ANN: We _____ in here much longer. We're landing in an hour.

a. (not be)

EXERCISE 4 *MUST* OR *MUST NOT*

GRAMMAR NOTES 1, 4 **Complete the rules for airline travel. Use *must* or *must not*.**

1. Passengers _____*must arrive*_____ three hours before an international flight.
   (arrive)

2. They _____ their bags with them at all times.
   (keep)

3. Carry-on bags _____ bigger than 45 inches (115 centimeters).
   (be)

4. They _____ under the seat or in the overhead compartment
   (fit)
   of the airplane.

5. They _____ knives, scissors, or other dangerous items.
   (contain)

6. Checked bags _____ labels with the passenger's name.
   (have)

7. They _____ more than 50 pounds (23 kilograms), or there will be
   (weigh)
   additional charges.

8. Travelers _____ identification when they check in with the airline.
   (show)

9. Everyone _____ a ticket in order to go through security.
   (have)

10. On board, passengers _____ when the seat belt sign is on.
    (get up)

11. On many flights, passengers _____ cell phones when the plane is
    (use)
    in the air.

EXERCISE 5
MUST NOT OR *DON'T HAVE TO*

GRAMMAR NOTE 4

Read the sign at the Casa Luciani swimming pool. Complete each statement. Use *must not* or *don't have to*.

Swimming Pool Rules and Regulations

Pool Hours 10:00 a.m.–10:00 p.m.

Children under twelve years NOT ALLOWED in pool without an adult.

Towels available at front desk.

- NO radio
- NO diving
- NO ball playing
- NO glass bottles
- NO alcoholic beverages

1. Children under age twelve ____*must not (or mustn't) swim*____ without an adult.
   (swim)

2. You _____ your own towel.
   (bring)

3. You _____ ball in or around the pool.
   (play)

4. You _____ into the pool.
   (dive)

5. Teenagers _____ with an adult.
   (swim)

6. You _____ the pool before 10:00 a.m.
   (enter)

7. You _____ the swimming pool at 8:00 p.m.
   (leave)

8. You _____ in the pool past 10:00 p.m.
   (stay)

EXERCISE 6 *HAVE TO* OR *HAFTA*, *GOT TO* OR *GOTTA*

29|03 PRONUNCIATION NOTE **Listen to the conversations. Check (✓) *More Formal* if you hear *have to*, *got to*, or *must not*. Check (✓) *Less Formal* if you hear *hafta*, *hasta*, *gotta*, or *mustn't*.**

		More Formal	Less Formal
1.	A: John has to renew his passport. What about you? B: I don't have to renew mine yet. It's valid for another year.	✓	☐
2.	A: My passport expires next May. B: Oh. You must not forget to renew it. You'll need it when we go to Italy.	☐	☐
3.	A: When does he have to be at the airport? B: He has to be there by 8:00.	☐	☐
4.	A: He's got to leave now. Is he ready? B: Almost. He's got to bring his bags downstairs, that's all.	☐	☐
5.	A: Will we have to show our tickets before we board? B: Yes. And you'll have to show your passports, too.	☐	☐
6.	A: We've got to hurry. B: Relax. We still have plenty of time.	☐	☐
7.	A: Sir, you must not use your phone during take off. B: Oh, sorry. I forgot. I'll turn it off right away.	☐	☐
8.	A: You've got to turn right here. B: No. I have to turn left. Look at the sign.	☐	☐
9.	A: It's 9:00. I've got to go. B: OK. See you later.	☐	☐

EXERCISE 7 EDITING

GRAMMAR NOTES 1–4 **Read Sean's email to his friend. There are six mistakes in expressing necessity. The first mistake is already corrected. Find and correct five more.**

● ● ●

Hi Randy,

We're on our way back to Australia. We ~~have~~ *had* to leave the hotel at 5:30 this morning, and

then we had got to wait in line at the airport for hours. What a hassle! This flight is great,

though. There are TVs at every seat and hundreds of movies to watch. But Mom says

we can't sit for more than three hours at a time because it's unhealthy, and we must to

drink water every hour when we're not sleeping. This flight is fourteen hours long, so we

---

have to taking care of ourselves. Thanks for the camping knife. I used it a lot in Italy, but

before we left, I has to put it in my checked suitcase because of the safety regulations.

You don't have to bring knives in carry-on bags. Well, I've got to get up and walk around

again. Email me. We'll be on this plane for ten more hours!   —Sean

EXERCISE 8 LISTENING

▶29|04 Ⓐ Two tourists are driving in Italy. Listen to their conversations. Read the statements. Then listen again and check (✓) *True* or *False*.

		True	False
1.	The young man has to turn right.	☐	☑
2.	The young woman must drive slower.	☐	☐
3.	The man has to stop.	☐	☐
4.	The woman is driving too fast.	☐	☐
5.	The young man was not preparing to stop.	☐	☐
6.	The man has to pass.	☐	☐

▶29|04 Ⓑ Work with a partner. Listen again to the conversations. Write the number of each conversation next to the appropriate sign. Discuss your answers. What does each sign mean?

EXAMPLE: A: The woman in Conversation 1 says: "You have to turn left."
    B: The sign in "f" shows a left turn. That means you can turn left, but you can't turn right.
    A: I agree.

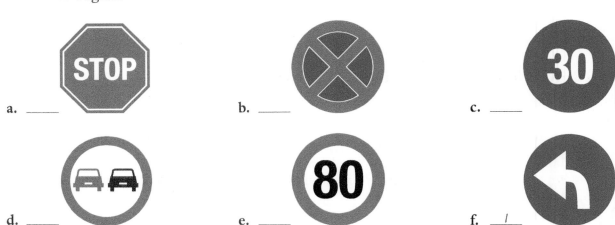

a. _____   b. _____   c. _____

d. _____   e. _____   f. _/_

EXERCISE 9 IT'S A SIGN!

PICTURE DISCUSSION Work with a partner. Where can you find these signs? What do they mean? What do you have to do when you see each one? What can't you do? What do you think of the rules?

EXAMPLE: A: You can find this sign at a crossing over railroad tracks in the United States.
B: Right. It means drivers have to slow down and look both ways before they drive across the tracks.
A: Well, that's definitely a necessary rule!

EXERCISE 10 INVENT A SIGN

GAME Work with a partner. Together, draw your own sign to illustrate something people *have to do* or *must not do*. Show it to your classmates. Can they guess the meaning? Decide where the sign belongs.

EXAMPLE: A: I think that means you have to wear shoes.
B: Right! And where can you find a sign like this?
A: Near some poolside restaurants.
C: You can also find it . . .

EXERCISE 11 WHAT ABOUT YOU?

CONVERSATION Work with a partner. Make a list of your most important tasks for this week. Check (✓) the things you've already done. Talk about what you still *have to do* and what you *don't have to do*.

EXAMPLE: A: What's on your "To Do" list for this week?
B: Well, I don't have to renew my driver's license. I've already done it, but I still have to... What about you?

EXERCISE 12 RULES AND REGULATIONS

A DISCUSSION Work in a group. Discuss your school's rules and regulations about the topics below. What do you have to do? What don't you have to do? What can't you do?

EXAMPLE: A: Our cars have to have a sticker for the student parking lot.
B: But we don't have to pay for parking.
C: We can't leave our cars in the parking lot overnight.

- student cars and parking
- clothing
- phones

- calculators
- class hours
- homework

- cigarettes
- food
- music

B Compare answers with your classmates. Complete a chart on the board like the one below.

Things we have to do	Things we don't have to do	Things we can't do
have a parking sticker	pay for parking	leave cars in the parking lot overnight

FROM GRAMMAR TO WRITING

A BEFORE YOU WRITE Think about the application procedure for getting a driver's license, a passport, a travel visa, a work permit, school admission, or a new job. What do you have to do? What don't you have to do? What can't you do? Complete the outline.

Application for _____ in _____
(city, state, or country)

Things you have to do	Things you don't have to do	Things you can't do
_____	_____	_____
_____	_____	_____
_____	_____	_____

B WRITE Use your outline to write a paragraph about the application procedure. Use *have to, must, don't have to, must not,* or *can't.* Try to avoid the common mistakes in the chart.

EXAMPLE: To get a driver's license in my state, you must be at least fifteen and a half years old. Drivers under the age of seventeen and a half also have to take a driver's education course. You usually don't have to take the road test if you already have a license from another state. However, you can't use a license from another country. If you . . .

Common Mistakes in Using *Have to, Must, Not have to, Must not,* and *Can't*

Use *must not* or *can't* for things that are **against the rules**. Do not use *don't have to*.	You **must not** drive without a license. NOT You ~~don't have to~~ drive without a licence.
Use *don't have to* for things that are **not necessary**. Do not use *must not* or *can't*.	I'm nineteen. I **don't have to** take that course. NOT I'm nineteen. I ~~must not~~ take that course. NOT I'm nineteen. I ~~can't~~ take that course.
Use *have to* or *must* in **formal writing**. Do not use *hafta* or *gotta*.	You **must** bring a valid ID to the test. NOT You ~~hafta~~ bring a valid ID to the test. NOT You ~~gotta~~ bring a valid ID to the test.

C CHECK YOUR WORK Read your paragraph. Underline once the words for things that are necessary. Underline twice the words for things that are against the rules. Circle the words for things that are not necessary. Use the Editing Checklist to check your work.

Editing Checklist

Did you use . . . ?

- [ ] *must* or *have to* to show that something is necessary
- [ ] *don't have to* to show that something is not necessary
- [ ] *must not* or *can't* to show that something is against the rules
- [ ] *have to* and *got to* instead of *hafta* and *gotta*

D REVISE YOUR WORK Read your paragraph again. Can you improve your writing? Make changes if necessary. Give your paragraph a title.

UNIT 29 REVIEW

Test yourself on the grammar of the unit.

A Circle the correct words to complete the sentences.

1. You <u>don't have to</u> / must not buy euros for the trip. I've already done it.

2. <u>Do</u> / Does Ken have to leave already? It's still early.

3. They said we <u>can't</u> / don't have to carry scissors onto the airplane.

4. We've <u>got to</u> / can't arrive at the airport by 9:00, or we won't be able to board.

5. Jake <u>has</u> / had to renew his passport before he left for Italy.

6. Tomorrow, Tara will <u>have</u> / got to take her driving test again. She failed the last time.

B Complete the sentences with *can't* or the correct form of *have to* and the verbs in parentheses.

1. I've downloaded several movies, so I _____ it now.
   (do)

2. We forgot to get a gift for Uncle Fred. We _____ something at the airport.
   (pick up)

3. I _____ never _____ in line this long in my entire life.
   (stand)

4. Relax. We're next. We _____ much longer.
   (wait)

5. Sir, you _____ on any part of the plane.
   (smoke)

6. The passenger in 23B _____. She's in the wrong seat.
   (move)

7. Sorry. You _____ here. May I see the seat number on your boarding pass?
   (sit)

8. We _____ some French cheese at dinner tonight. I can't wait to try it.
   (have)

9. We _____ the cheese before landing last night.
   (eat)

C Find and correct five mistakes.

1. He can't boards the plane yet.

2. Passengers must not stay in their seats when the seat belt light is off.

3. Passengers: Please note that you gotta pay extra for luggage over 50 pounds (23 kg).

4. You don't have got to show your passport right now, but please have it ready.

5. Paul will has to unpack some of his stuff. His suitcase is much too heavy.

Now check your answers on page 482.

Expectations:
Be supposed to
MANNERS

OUTCOMES
• Express expectations with *be supposed to*
• Identify key points in an article about manners
• Identify details in a conversation about manners
• Discuss customs and life events from one's culture
• Describe an illustration, discussing polite and impolite behavior
• Write a paragraph about a life event in a specific culture

STEP 1 **GRAMMAR IN CONTEXT**

BEFORE YOU READ

Look at the cartoon. Discuss the questions.

1. Who are the people? What is their relationship?

2. Are they having a nice evening? How are they feeling?

3. What is the problem?

READ

▶ 30|01 Read this article about manners.

It Was Supposed to Be a Nice Evening

Last week, my friend (let's call her Anna) invited her new boyfriend (we'll call him Andy) home to meet her family for the very first time. It was supposed to be a nice evening, but it didn't exactly turn out as expected. To begin with, Andy came late. He was supposed to arrive at 7:00, but didn't get there until 7:20. Anna was upset. In her family, people always arrive exactly on time. Being even ten minutes late is considered rude. Then, when Anna introduced Andy to her mother, he tried to give her a kiss on the cheek. Her mother was shocked. In her culture, men aren't supposed to kiss women they don't know.

The evening went from bad to worse. When they sat down to eat, Andy put his elbows on the table—a definite no-no[1] in Anna's house, but the norm in Andy's more relaxed home. Andy thought the food was delicious, but when he helped himself to a second serving of potatoes, Anna kicked him under the table. He was supposed to wait until someone offered him more food. Andy sensed there was something wrong, but he didn't know what it was. He tried to break the ice[2] by asking some questions. He asked Anna's father about the nice, new car he saw in the driveway and got a polite answer. But when he asked about the price, there was a very uncomfortable silence around the table. Andy didn't realize that in many families, you aren't supposed to discuss money issues with strangers.

---

1 *no-no:* something people are not supposed to do because it is wrong or dangerous
2 *break the ice:* to say something to make someone you just met feel more comfortable

The details can vary, but the general story probably sounds familiar. Different cultures and even different families often have different rules of behavior. What are good manners for one group may be impolite for another group. For example, in some cultures you're not supposed to make any noise while eating, but in other cultures, such as Japan, slurping[3] is a way of showing that you like the food.

If good manners vary from place to place, how is a person supposed to know what to do? The Internet can provide a lot of helpful information about manners. Even better, you should try to discuss these issues with someone familiar with the situation you are going to be in. Andy needed to talk to Anna about her and her family's expectations before showing up at Anna's home. The evening was a disaster, and Andy and Anna are not seeing each other anymore. Andy feels bad, but he won't make the same mistakes twice. Sometimes experience is the best teacher.

---

3 *slurping:* making noise while you are eating or drinking something like noodles or soup

AFTER YOU READ

A VOCABULARY Choose the word or phrase that best completes each sentence.

1. Our plans are **definite**. We won't _____ them.
   a. change   b. enjoy   c. explain

2. A **rude** person is not _____.
   a. right   b. polite   c. late

3. The **norm** is the _____ way of doing something.
   a. wrong   b. new   c. usual

4. Andy **sensed** there was a problem, but he wasn't completely _____ about it.
   a. certain   b. unhappy   c. comfortable

5. An **issue** is a _____ or problem that people discuss.
   a. magazine   b. story   c. topic

6. If you are **familiar** with a custom, you _____ something about it.
   a. like   b. know   c. ask

B COMPREHENSION Read the statements. Check (✓) *True* or *False*. If there isn't enough information in the reading to answer, check *Don't Know*.

	True	False	Don't Know
1. Andy and Anna expected to have a nice evening.	☐	☐	☐
2. Andy arrived on time.	☐	☐	☐
3. He kissed Anna's mother.	☐	☐	☐
4. Anna's father wanted to discuss the price of the family car.	☐	☐	☐
5. Andy made noises while he was eating.	☐	☐	☐
6. It was OK for Andy to take more potatoes.	☐	☐	☐

C DISCUSSION Work with a partner. Compare your answers in B. Why did you check *True, False,* or *Don't Know*?

EXPECTATIONS: *BE SUPPOSED TO*

Statements

Subject	Be	(Not)	Supposed to	Base Form of Verb	
I	am was				
You We They	are were	(not)	supposed to	arrive	at 7:00.
He She It	is was				

Yes/No Questions

Be	Subject	Supposed to	Base Form of Verb
Am Was	I		
Are Were	you	supposed to	call?
Is Was	she		

Short Answers

Affirmative		
	you	are. were.
Yes,	I	am. was.
	she	is. was.

Negative		
	you	aren't. weren't.
No,	I	'm not. wasn't.
	she	isn't. wasn't.

Wh- Questions

Wh- Word	Be	Subject	Supposed to	Base Form of Verb
Where	am was	I	supposed to	sit?
	are were	you		
	is was	she		

GRAMMAR NOTES

1 *Be supposed to* for Different Kinds of Expectations

Use the expression *be supposed to* + **base form** of the verb to express different kinds of expectations.

• **rules**	You**'re supposed to turn** right here. You can't turn left.
• **customs** (usual ways of doing things)	You**'re supposed to bring** a small gift.
• **predictions**	The forecast says it**'s supposed to rain** tonight.
• **hearsay** (something you have heard from other people, but don't know to be true)	Anna **is supposed to be** very nice. Everyone says so.
• **plans** or **arrangements**	Let's hurry. We**'re supposed to be** there at 7:00. They're expecting us then.

IN WRITING *Be supposed to* is common in conversation, informal writing (emails, text messages), and in journalistic writing (newspapers, magazines). However, in formal writing, it is more common to use other expressions, such as: *It is customary to*.

You**'re supposed to bring** a gift. *(conversation)*
What time **are** we **supposed to get** there? *(email)*
In the past, people **were supposed to write** a thank-you note to their dinner host. *(magazine)*
It is customary to bring a gift. *(formal writing)*

2 *Be supposed to* for Present, Future, and Past Expectations

You can use a form of *be supposed to* to express a **present**, **future**, or **past** expectation.

• **present expectation**	You**'re supposed to wait** until someone offers you more food. *(simple present)*
• **future expectation**	It**'s supposed to be** nice tomorrow. *(simple present)*
• **past expectation**	They **were supposed to get** there by 6:00 p.m. yesterday, so they took a taxi. *(simple past)*

USAGE NOTE We often use *was/were supposed to* when something we expected to happen did not happen.

Andy **was supposed to arrive** at 7:00, but he came late.

BE CAREFUL! For future expectations, do not use *will* with *be supposed to*.

We**'re supposed to** help out tomorrow.
NOT We ~~will be~~ supposed to help out tomorrow.

3 Word Order in Negative Statements

Use this word order in negative statements: **subject** + *be not* + *supposed to* + **base form** of the verb

You**'re not supposed to arrive** late.

BE CAREFUL! *Not* goes directly **before** *supposed*. Do not use *not* after *supposed*.

You**'re not supposed to** kiss her mother.
NOT You're ~~supposed not to~~ kiss her mother.
NOT You're ~~supposed to not~~ kiss her mother.

EXERCISE 1 DISCOVER THE GRAMMAR

Ⓐ GRAMMAR NOTES 1–3 Read this article about manners. Underline the phrases that express expectations.

Manners
THE GOOD,
THE BAD,
AND THE CONFUSING

THE DICTIONARY defines *manners* as polite ways of behaving in social situations. Manners are governed by rules (called *etiquette*). They tell us what we <u>are supposed to do</u> and, just as important, what we are not supposed to do. Manners are like the oil in a machine. They are supposed to make things run more smoothly.

Some examples of "good" manners seem very logical and easy to understand. You are supposed to hold the door open for the person behind you. If you don't, the door can hit the person in the face. In some cultures, you are not supposed to keep your street shoes on when you enter someone's home. Leaving your shoes on is considered "bad" manners. It's rude because they bring dirt into the home. Again, the reason for the custom is clear. But why in many cultures are you supposed to shake hands when you meet someone for the first time? Many historians believe that in the past, the handshake was supposed to prove that people were not hiding weapons (knives, for example) up their sleeve.

Many customs, such as the handshake, have complicated rules connected to them. Who is supposed to offer their hand first? How firmly and for how long are you supposed to hold the other person's hand? If you are wearing gloves, are you supposed to remove your glove before shaking hands? The answers to these and other questions vary from culture to culture. It can be confusing, and it is not always easy to know the right thing to do.

B Read each sentence. Then write a sentence based on the information from A that has a similar meaning.

1. The rules of etiquette give us information about what is OK behavior.

They tell us what we are supposed to do.

2. The purpose of manners is to help make social interactions easier.

_____

3. Holding the door open for the person behind you is an example of good manners.

_____

4. Leaving your street shoes on when you enter someone's home is an example of bad manners.

_____

5. Shaking hands used to show that you didn't have a weapon up your sleeve.

_____

6. How long should you hold the other person's hand?

_____

EXERCISE 2 AFFIRMATIVE AND NEGATIVE STATEMENTS

GRAMMAR NOTES 1–3 Read about manners in different countries. Complete the sentences with the correct form of *be supposed to* and the words in parentheses. Choose between affirmative and negative.

In the United States You _____*'re supposed to stand up*_____ when you're introduced
                                        1. (stand up)
to an older person. It's rude to stay seated.

In China You _____ white or black to a wedding.
                              2. (wear)
These colors are connected to death.

In Turkey You _____ the bottom of your shoes when
                              3. (show)
you are sitting. It's impolite because they aren't clean.

In Argentina You _____ at a party thirty to sixty
                                4. (arrive)
minutes later than the "starting" time. It's the norm.

In Japan You _____ gifts in front of the gift giver. It's
                            5. (open)
not polite.

In Brazil You _____ gifts immediately. Don't wait
                             6. (open)
until later.

In Jordan You _____ a little food on your plate when
                             7. (leave)
you are finished eating. This shows your host that he or she gave you enough to eat.

EXERCISE 3 AFFIRMATIVE AND NEGATIVE STATEMENTS

GRAMMAR NOTES 1–3 Read about table manners in the United States. Rewrite the rules
with *be supposed to*. Choose between affirmative and negative.

1. Don't put your elbows on the table.

   You're not supposed to put your elbows on the table.

2. Chew with your mouth closed.

   _____

3. Don't reach across the table for food. Ask someone to pass it.

   _____

4. Eat quietly.

   _____

5. Use your napkin to clean your fingers and mouth.

   _____

6. Keep your napkin on your lap when you are not using it.

   _____

7. Do not start eating before your host.

   _____

8. Do not comb your hair at the table.

   _____

9. Don't put your napkin on the chair when you are finished eating.

   _____

10. Say "Excuse me" if you leave the table before the end of a meal.

    _____

EXERCISE 4 QUESTIONS AND STATEMENTS

(A) GRAMMAR NOTES 1–3 Complete the conversations. Use the verbs in parentheses and
the correct form of *be supposed to*. Choose between the simple present and simple past.

1. **A:** Carlos invited me to dinner at his parents' home tonight.

   B: Oh, that's nice. What time _____*are*_____ you _____*supposed to get*_____ there?

a. (get)

   A: He said 7:00. Tell me, _____ I _____ something? I'm

b. (bring)

   not familiar with the customs here.

   B: Why don't you bring flowers?

2. **A:** Last time I met Mia's mother, I shook her hand. I sensed that something was wrong. She

   seemed a little uncomfortable. _____ I _____ that?

a. (do)

B: I'm not sure. I think you _____ until the woman offers her
      b. (wait)

hand first.

3. A: It _____ tonight, so don't forget your umbrella.
      a. (rain)

B: I'm driving, so it won't be a problem. But I'm a little nervous about going to a formal dinner.

A: Don't worry. The Chandlers _____ very nice. Everyone
      b. (be)

likes them.

4. A: What _____ I _____ Miguel's mother?
      a. (call)

B: Call her *Mrs. Gomez*, unless she tells you to use her first name.

5. A: Are you going to the party alone?

B: Yes. I _____ with Teresa, but she's sick.
      a. (go)

6. A: What _____ I _____ when I meet Ina's parents?
      a. (say)

B: Just say, "It's nice to meet you." And try to relax. You'll meet a lot of nice people there. It's a

party. It _____ fun!
      b. (be)

▶30|02 **B** LISTEN AND CHECK **Listen to the conversations and check your answers in A.**

EXERCISE 5 EDITING

GRAMMAR NOTES 1–3 **Read this Q & A on etiquette and manners. Find and correct eight
mistakes in the use of *be supposed to*. The first mistake is already corrected. Find and
correct seven more.**

What's the Right Thing to Do?

Q: I had dinner at a friend's house last week. The first course was soup and it was already on the table. When

I sat down, I began to eat it. My friend's mother looked a little surprised. Did I do something wrong? ~~Am~~ I
                                                                                                   Was

supposed to wait before starting to eat?

A: Yes. In this country, you supposed to wait until your host begins or says "Please begin." You are supposed

not to start first.

Q: My friend is getting married, and he chose me to be his "best man." What does this mean? As the best

man, what I am supposed to do?

A: First of all, you should feel very good. It is an honor to be the best man. In general, the best man's job is

to help the groom. You can find online lists with all your tasks (and there are many!). Perhaps one of the

Expectations: *Be supposed to* **421**

most important ones is that you are supposed to keep the ring for your friend until he needs it during the ceremony. (Nervous grooms are famous for forgetting or losing the ring.)

Q: We supposed to get married, but we just decided to cancel the wedding. We've already received some wedding gifts. What do we do with them? Do we supposed to return them to our friends and relatives now that the wedding is canceled?

A: Yes, unfortunately you are supposed to return all the gifts you received—unless you have already used them.

Q: I was in line at the supermarket waiting to pay. It was the "express" line, but the woman in front of me had a shopping cart filled with food and beverages. I had just one item. I said to the woman, "Sorry, but you are supposed to not be on this line if you have more than ten items." She got very angry at me. Was I wrong to say something?

A: No, you weren't wrong, the woman was wrong. First, for being in the wrong line, and then for getting angry at you. People are supposing to follow the rules, and her behavior was a definite violation of the rules. You were right to say something—as long as you did it politely.

STEP 4   COMMUNICATION PRACTICE

EXERCISE 6 LISTENING

▶30|03 **A** People are calling *Ask Mr. Ed*, a radio show about etiquette and manners. Listen to the conversations. Read the statements. Listen again and circle the words to complete the information Mr. Ed gives to each caller.

1. In the United States, a dinner guest (is) / is not supposed to bring a small gift.

2. In the United States, party guests are / are not supposed to ask questions about religion or politics.

3. At a traditional Chinese wedding, a wedding guest is / is not supposed to wear white or black.

4. In Peru, you are / are not supposed to leave food on your plate when you are finished eating.

5. In Mexico, you are / are not supposed to shake hands when you meet someone for the first time.

30|03 **B** Work with a partner. Listen again to *Ask Mr. Ed*. Discuss Mr. Ed's answers to the five callers' questions. Is the answer the same in your country or culture?

EXAMPLE: **A:** Ed told the first caller that in the United States, dinner guests are supposed to bring a small gift.

B: Yes. He said that many guests bring flowers, wine, or chocolate. In my country, Egypt, you're supposed to bring a gift, too. But, you aren't supposed to bring flowers. Flowers are for weddings, funerals, and hospital visits. And you aren't supposed to bring wine. Most Muslims don't drink alcohol.

A: In my country, Russia, . . .

EXERCISE 7 MIND YOUR MANNERS

A GAME Work with a partner. Look at the picture. Find all the examples of bad table manners. You have five minutes.

EXAMPLE: **A:** The woman is reaching across the man to get the salt. You aren't supposed to do that. You're supposed to ask someone to pass anything that's not close to you.

B: The little boy . . .

B Who found the most answers in five minutes? Compare your answers with the rest of the class.

EXERCISE 8 WHAT ABOUT YOU?

CONVERSATION Work with a partner. Think about a time when you didn't know the correct way to act in a social situation. Describe the situation to your partner. Answer some of the questions below. Your partner will ask you for more information.

EXAMPLE: **A:** Five years ago, I went to a friend's wedding. I wasn't familiar with the customs here, and I made quite a few mistakes. First of all, I arrived late and missed some of the ceremony.

B: What time were you supposed to be there?

A: At 1:00, but I got there at 1:30. I felt terrible.

B: OK. What happened next?

- Where were you?
- What happened?
- What did (or didn't) you do?

- What were (or weren't) you supposed to do?
- When did you realize your mistake?
- How did you feel?

EXERCISE 9 IMPORTANT LIFE EVENTS

CROSS-CULTURAL COMPARISON Work in a group. Discuss some of the important life events in the list below. What are people in your culture supposed to do and say at these times? Is there a ceremony? Are people expected to give certain gifts? Wear special clothing? What roles do certain family members and friends play? Report to the class.

EXAMPLE: **A:** In traditional Japanese weddings, the bride and groom are supposed to wear kimonos.

B: Oh. What color are they supposed to be?

A: They're usually white or red. What about in your country, Salma? What color is a bride supposed to wear?

C: In Morocco, brides are supposed to wear a bright color like green or yellow. These colors are supposed to bring good luck.

- a wedding
- an important birthday
- a school graduation
- an engagement to be married
- an anniversary
- a birth
- a funeral

A BEFORE YOU WRITE Look at the list of events in Exercise 9. Choose one to write about. Complete the outline.

The event: _____   The culture: _____

Ceremony? _____

Role of friends? _____

Role of family members? _____

Special clothing? _____

Special food? _____

Gifts? _____

B WRITE Use your outline to write a paragraph about the event. Use *be supposed to* and *not be supposed to* to describe customs and rules. Try to avoid the common mistakes in the chart.

EXAMPLE: In the United States, high schools and colleges have graduation ceremonies. In many schools, the students line up in alphabetical order. Then, when their names are called, they are supposed to go to the stage to receive their diplomas. Friends and family . . .

Commons Mistakes in Using *Be supposed to*	
Use a form of *be* before *supposed to*. Do not leave out a form of *be*.	You're **supposed to** bring a present. NOT You supposed to bring a present.
Use only the **simple present or simple past** form of *be*. Do not use the future or the present perfect.	I'm supposed to arrive tomorrow. NOT I'll be supposed to arrive tomorrow.
For the negative, put *not* **before** *supposed*. Do not put *not* after *supposed*.	You're **not supposed to** come late. NOT You're supposed not to come late.

C CHECK YOUR WORK Read your paragraph. Underline all the forms of *be supposed to*. Circle *not* in the negative use of *be supposed to*. Use the Editing Checklist to check your work.

Editing Checklist
Did you use . . . ?
☐ *be supposed to* for customs and rules
☐ only the simple present or simple past of *be* in *be supposed to*
☐ the correct word order in the negative

D REVISE YOUR WORK Read your paragraph again. Can you improve your writing? Make changes if necessary. Give your paragraph a title.

UNIT 30 REVIEW

Test yourself on the grammar of the unit.

Ⓐ Choose the correct answer to complete each sentence.

1. Tomorrow is graduation, and we _____ supposed to be at school at 10:00.
   a. 're   **b.** 'll   **c.** do

2. The weather is _____ to be very nice.
   a. suppose   **b.** supposed   **c.** supposing

3. Jan and Stu _____ supposed to drive me, but they can't.
   a. are   **b.** weren't   **c.** were

4. The ceremony was _____ supposed to be outside, but it's going to be in the park.
   a. not   **b.** no   **c.** didn't

5. What time are we supposed _____?
   a. leave   **b.** leaving   **c.** to leave

Ⓑ Complete the conversations with the correct form of *be supposed to* and the verbs in parentheses.

1. A: Hurry up! We _____ there in ten minutes.
                        a. (be)

   B: Don't worry. The ceremony _____ until 10:15.
                                    b. (not start)

2. A: Where _____ we _____?
                           a. (sit)

   B: I think we _____ over there, on the right side.
                     b. (go)

3. A: Oh, no. Most men are wearing ties. _____ I _____ one?
                                                        a. (wear)

   B: I think you _____ a jacket, but ties are optional. So, you're fine.
                      b. (wear)

4. A: It _____, but look at those clouds!
            a. (not rain)

   B: I know. It _____ a beautiful day.
                     b. (be)

Ⓒ Find and correct seven mistakes.

1. Dahlia was suppose to drive. She was supposed not to fly.

2. She is supposed to wear her blue dress, but she changed her mind.

3. What are we supposed to doing after the ceremony?

4. My parents will supposed to fly home tomorrow, but they're staying another day.

5. It was no supposed to be this cold, and it didn't suppose to rain.

Now check your answers on page 482.

Future Possibility:
May, Might, Could
WEATHER

OUTCOMES
- Express likelihood of future events
- Distinguish between possibility and certainty of a future event
- Identify key details in a transcript
- Identify the probability of a situation in a report
- Describe future plans and intentions in detail, giving degrees of probability
- Write an email or short letter that expresses the probability of future plans

STEP 1	GRAMMAR IN CONTEXT

BEFORE YOU READ

Look at the weather map for Europe. Discuss the questions.

1. Are the temperatures in Celsius or Fahrenheit?

2. What are the possible high and low temperatures for Ankara?

3. What's the weather forecast for Moscow? For London?

READD

▶31|01 Read this transcript of a weather report on British TV.

Weather Watch

CAROL: Good morning. I'm Carol Johnson, and here's the local forecast for tomorrow, Wednesday, January 10. The cold front that has been affecting much of northern Europe is moving quickly toward Great Britain. Temperatures may drop as much

World Weather Channel

FORECAST
Wednesday

Stockholm 1/-3

Moscow 3/-4

London 2/-4

Berlin 6/3

Warsaw 9/3

Paris 8/2

Budapest 15/1

Madrid 19/6

Rome 20/10

Ankara 16/4

Athens 22/18

as 11 degrees by late tomorrow afternoon. In London, expect a high of only 2 and a low of –4 degrees. We might even see some snow flurries[1] later on in the day. By evening, winds could exceed 40 miles per hour. So, bundle up;[2] it's going to be a cold one! And now it's time for our travelers' forecast with Ethan Harvey. Ethan?

ETHAN: Thank you, Carol. Take your umbrella if you're traveling to Paris. Stormy conditions may move into France by tomorrow morning. Rain could turn into snow by evening when temperatures fall to near or below freezing in the region. But look at the forecast for Italy! You may not need your coat at all if you plan to be in Rome, where we'll see partly cloudy skies with early morning temperatures around only 10 degrees on Wednesday. But later in the day, temperatures could climb to above 20 as skies clear up in the afternoon. The warming trend could reach the rest of western Europe by Thursday. But if not, it still looks like it will turn out to be a beautiful, sunny weekend in central Italy, Carol.

CAROL: Italy sounds great! Will you join me on a Roman holiday, Ethan?

ETHAN: I might!

---

1 *flurries:* small amounts of light snow that fall and blow around
2 *bundle up:* wear warm clothes

AFTER YOU READ

A VOCABULARY **Choose the word or phrase that best completes each sentence.**

1. A weather **forecast** tells you about _____ weather.
   a. foreign
   b. yesterday's
   c. tomorrow's

2. **Local** news gives you information about places that are _____ you.
   a. near
   b. far from
   c. interesting to

3. When the weather **affects** people, they always feel _____.
   a. better
   b. worse
   c. different

4. A **region** is a(n) _____.
   a. area
   b. ocean
   c. city

5. If winds **exceed** 30 miles per hour, they will be _____ 30 miles per hour.
   a. exactly
   b. less than
   c. more than

B COMPREHENSION **Read the statements. Check (✓) True or False.**

	True	False
1. Temperatures will definitely drop 11 degrees in Great Britain.	☐	☐
2. Snow is possible in London.	☐	☐
3. There will definitely be stormy weather in France.	☐	☐
4. Snow is possible in Paris.	☐	☐
5. Western Europe is going to get colder.	☐	☐
6. Temperatures will definitely be above 20 degrees Celsius in Rome.	☐	☐

C DISCUSSION **Work with a partner. Compare your answers in B. Why did you check** *True* **or** *False*?

FUTURE POSSIBILITY: *MAY, MIGHT, COULD*

Statements

Subject	Modal*	Base Form of Verb	
You It They	**may (not)** **might (not)** **could**	**get**	cold.

* *May*, *might*, and *could* are modals. Modals have only one form. They do not have *-s* in the third-person singular.

Yes/No Questions

Are you going to fly to Paris? Are you leaving on Monday?		
Are you going to Will you Is it possible you'll	**be**	there long?

Short Answers

	may (not).* might (not).* could.	
I	**may (not).*** **might (not).*** **could.**	
We	**may (not)*** **might (not)*** **could**	**(be).**

* *May not* and *might not* are not contracted.

Wh- Questions

When are you **going** to Paris?
How long are you going to **be** there?

Answers

I	**may**	**go**	next week.
We	**could**	**be**	there a week.

GRAMMAR NOTES

1 **Affirmative Statements**

Use the modals *may*, *might*, and *could* to express the **possibility** that something **will happen** in the future.

May, *might*, and *could* have very similar meanings. You can use any one to express **future possibility**.

- *may*   It **may rain** tonight. *(It's possible.)*
- *might*   It **might rain** tonight. *(It's possible.)*
- *could*   It **could rain** tonight. *(It's possible.)*

Remember that we use a **form of the future** (*be going to* or *will*) when we are **certain** that something **will happen**. (See Unit 6.)

It**'s going to rain** tonight. *(It's certain.)*

BE CAREFUL! *May be* and *maybe* both express possibility. Notice these differences:

May be is a modal + *be*. It is always two words.

Demetrios **may be** late today.

Maybe is an adverb. It is always one word, and it usually comes at the beginning of the sentence.

Maybe he'll take the train.

NOT He'll ~~maybe take~~ the train.

2 Negative Statements

Use *may not* and *might not* to express the **possibility** that something **will not happen** in the future.

• *may not*	There are a lot of clouds, but it **may not rain**.
• *might not*	There are a lot of clouds, but it **might not rain**.
	(It's possible that it won't rain, but we're not certain.)

Remember that we use a **form of the future** *(not be going to* or *won't)* when we are **certain** that something **will not happen**. (See Unit 6.)	You **won't need** a coat. *(I'm certain that you will not need a coat.)*

BE CAREFUL! We **never contract** *may not*, and we rarely contract *might not*.	You **may not** need a coat. NOT You ~~mayn't~~ need a coat.

3 Questions and Answers

Questions about future possibility do not usually use *may*, *might*, or *could*, but **answers** to these questions often **use** *may*, *might*, or *could*.

Questions about future possibility usually use *will*, *be going to*, the present progressive, or the simple present. They rarely use *may*, *might*, or *could*.	When **will** it **start** snowing? When **might** it **start** snowing? *(rare)*

Answers to questions about future possibility often use *may*, *might*, or *could*.	A: **Are** you **going to drive** to work? B: I don't know. I **may take** the bus. A: When **are** you **leaving**? B: I **might leave** in a few minutes. A: Do you think it**'ll snow** tomorrow? B: It **could stop** tonight.

In **short answers** to *yes/no* questions, we usually use *may*, *might*, or *could* alone. We do not repeat the main verb in the question.	A: **Will** your office **close** early? B: It **may**. or It **may not**. NOT It may not ~~close~~.

USAGE NOTE If *be* is the main verb, it is common to include *be* in the short answer.	A: **Will** our flight **be** on time? B: It **might** *be*. or It **might**. It **might not** *be*. or It **might not**.

REFERENCE NOTES

For general information on **modals**, see Unit 13, Grammar Notes 1–2, on page 177.

For *may* for **permission**, see Unit 14 on page 191.

For *might* for **present conclusions**, see Unit 32 on page 440.

For *could* for **ability and possibility** (see Unit 13), for **permission** (see Unit 14), for **requests** (see Unit 15), and for **present conclusions** (see Unit 32).

For a list of **modals and their functions**, see Appendix 19 on page 460.

EXERCISE 1   DISCOVER THE GRAMMAR

A GRAMMAR NOTES 1–3 **Anna is a college student who works part-time; Cody is her husband. Read their conversation. Underline the words that express future possibility.**

ANNA: Are you going to drive to work tomorrow?

CODY: I don't know. I might. Why?

ANNA: I just heard the local weather report. A cold front is moving into the region. It may snow tonight.

CODY: Oh, then I may have to shovel snow before I leave. You know, on second thought, I might just take the 7:30 train instead of driving. I have a 9:00 meeting, and I don't want to miss it. Do you have a class tomorrow morning?

ANNA: No, but I'm going to the library to work on my paper. Maybe I'll bundle up and take the train with you in the morning. And let's try to go home together, too. Maybe we could meet at the train station at 6:00, OK? I'm taking the 6:30 train home.

CODY: I might not be able to catch the 6:30 train. My boss said something about working late tomorrow. I may be stuck there until 8:00. I'll call you tomorrow afternoon and let you know what I'm doing.

ANNA: OK. I'll get some takeout on the way home. Do you mind eating late?

CODY: No. I definitely want to have dinner together.

ANNA: Me too. Definitely.

B **Read the conversation again. Check (✓) *Certain* or *Possible* for each activity that they discuss.**

CODY	Certain	Possible
1. drive to work		✓
2. shovel snow		
3. take 7:30 a.m. train		
4. 9:00 meeting		
5. work until 8:00 p.m.		
6. call Anna		
7. dinner with Anna		

ANNA	Certain	Possible
1. go to library	✓	
2. work on paper		
3. take train with Cody		
4. 6:00 p.m.—meet Cody		
5. take 6:30 train home		
6. buy takeout for dinner		
7. dinner with Cody		

EXERCISE 2 AFFIRMATIVE AND NEGATIVE STATEMENTS

GRAMMAR NOTES 1–2 Anna is graduating from college with a degree in meteorology.[1]
Circle the correct words to complete her journal entry.

I just got the notice from my school. I might not / (I'm going to) graduate in June, but I still
                      1.

don't know what I'm going to do after graduation. Some TV stations hire students to help

out their meteorologists, so I could / may not apply for a job next month. On the other hand,
                    2.

I might / might not apply to graduate school and get my master's degree in atmospheric
       3.

science. I'm just not sure, though—these past two years have been really hard, and I

may / may not be ready to study for two more years. At least I am sure about my career.
    4.

I'm going to / I might forecast the weather—that's certain. I made an appointment to discuss
      5.

my grades with my advisor, Mrs. Humphrey, tomorrow. I maybe / may talk about my plans
                         6.

with her. She won't / might have an idea about what I should do.
     7.

---

1 *meteorology:* the scientific study of weather

EXERCISE 3
STATEMENTS WITH *MAY, MIGHT, BE GOING TO*

GRAMMAR NOTE 1 Look at Anna's schedule for Monday. She put a question mark (?) next to each item she wasn't sure about. Write sentences about Anna's plans for Monday. Use *may* or *might* (for things that are possible) and *be going to* (for things that are certain).

MONDAY
1. call Cody at 9:00
2. buy some notebooks before class ?
3. go to the meeting with Mrs. Humphrey at 11:00
4. have coffee with Sue after class ?
5. go to work at 1:00
6. go shopping for snow boots after work ?
7. take the 7:00 train ?

1. Anna is going to call Cody at 9:00.

2. _____

3. _____

4. _____

5. _____

6. _____

7. _____

EXERCISE 4 SHORT ANSWERS

A GRAMMAR NOTE 3 **Complete the conversations with short answers. Use** *could* **(for things that are possible) or** *won't* **(for things that are certain). Use** *be* **when possible.**

1. **A:** Do you think the roads will be dangerous? It's snowing really hard.

   B: _They could be._____ It's a big storm.

2. **A:** Will the schools stay open?

   B: I'm sure _____. It's too dangerous for school buses.

3. **A:** Will it be very windy?

   B: _____ The winds are very strong already. They might even exceed 40 miles per hour. So, bundle up!

4. **A:** Will it get warmer later today?

   B: _____, unfortunately. The temperature in Centerville is already below zero.

5. **A:** Is it possible that the storm will be over by tomorrow?

   B: _____ It's moving pretty quickly across the region now.

6. **A:** Do you think it will be warmer on Tuesday?

   B: _____ There seems to be a warming trend. It's stopped snowing already.

▶31|02 **B** LISTEN AND CHECK **Listen to the conversations and check your answers in A.**

EXERCISE 5 EDITING

GRAMMAR NOTES 1–3 **Read this student's report about El Niño. There are seven mistakes in the use of** *may*, *might*, **and** *could*. **The first mistake is already corrected. Find and correct six more.**

Every few years, the ocean near Peru becomes warmer. This change is called El Niño. El Niño
~~maybe~~ *may* cause big weather changes all over the world. The west coasts of North and South America

might have very heavy rains. On the other side of the Pacific, New Guinea might becomes very

dry. Northern regions could have warmer, wetter winters, and southern areas maybe become

much colder. These weather changes affect plants and animals. Some fish mayn't survive in

warmer waters. They may die or swim to colder places. In addition, dry conditions could causing

crops to die. When that happens, food may get very expensive. El Niño does not happen regularly.

It may happen every two years, or it might not come for seven years. Will El Niño get worse in

the future? It could be. Pollution will increase the effects of El Niño, but no one is sure yet.

EXERCISE 6   LISTENING

31|03   Ⓐ   Look at the charts. Listen to the weather forecast and check (✓) *Certain* or *Possible* for each day.

FRIDAY	Certain	Possible
Dry	✓	
Sunny		
Low 50s		

SATURDAY	Certain	Possible
Sunny		
62°		
Windy		

SUNDAY	Certain	Possible
Cold		
Windy		
Snow flurries		

31|03   Ⓑ   Work with a partner. Listen again to the weather forecast. Compare answers. Why did you check *Certain* or *Possible*?

EXAMPLE: A: For Friday, the answer for "Dry" is *Certain*.
            B: Yes. The weather forecaster said, "Dry air from the south is moving into the region."
            A: Right. And he said it will be there by Friday. What did you check for "Sunny"?

EXERCISE 7   WHAT'S THE WEATHER FORECAST?

Ⓐ   ROLE PLAY   Work with a partner. You are both TV meteorologists. Give yourselves TV names.

EXAMPLE: A: I'm Sunny Sue.
            B: And I'm Steven Storm.

Ⓑ   Check the weather forecast for tomorrow and the next day for your city or region. Then, together, write up your weather report.

EXAMPLE: *Tomorrow is going to be cold again, and we might see . . .*

Ⓒ   Read your forecasts to the class.

EXAMPLE: A: Hello, this is Sunny Sue reporting for Channel 2. Tomorrow is going to be cold again, and we might see temperatures as low as . . .
            B: But cheer up. Friday will be more comfortable as warmer air moves into the region. You may finally be able to leave your jackets at home . . . This is Steven Storm for Channel 2 news.

EXERCISE 8 WEEKEND PLANS

CONVERSATION Work with a partner. Talk about your weekend plans. Use *be going to* or *will* for plans that are certain. Use *may, might,* or *could* for plans that are possible. Will the weather affect your plans? If so, how?

EXAMPLE: A: What are you doing this weekend?
B: I'm not sure. I might go to the park with some friends on Saturday.
A: The forecast says it may rain.
B: Well, in that case, I guess we could go to the movies instead. What about you?

EXERCISE 9 FUTURE PLANS

A PROBLEM SOLVING Work in a group. Look at these student profiles from a school newspaper. Talk about what the students might do in the future. Use the information from the box or your own ideas.

EXAMPLE: A: Marta is on the school newspaper. She might do creative writing as a hobby.
B: Nick dislikes crowded places. He might not be happy on the space shuttle.
C: I agree. He may . . .

About Your Classmates

Name:	Nick Vanek	Marta Rivera
Major:	TV broadcasting	Early Childhood Education
Activities:	Speakers Club, Sailing Club	Students' Association, school newspaper
Likes:	learning something new	adventure, meeting new people
Dislikes:	crowded places	snow, boring routines
Plans:	go to a four-year college	teach in a preschool
Dreams:	be a TV weather forecaster	travel around the world

	Occupations	Hobbies	Achievements
FUTURE POSSIBILITIES	• weather forecaster	• dancing	• fly on space shuttle
	• teacher	• skiing	• teach in Alaska
	• manager, day-care center	• creative writing	• develop a new weather satellite

B Now write your own profile. Use the profiles in A as a model.

C Work with a partner. Talk about your future possibilities.

EXAMPLE: A: I'm not sure what I'll do, but I might go back to school and study computer science. What about you?
B: I may learn another language. Then maybe I could get a job as a tour guide.

FROM GRAMMAR TO WRITING

A BEFORE YOU WRITE Think about your weekend plans. Make lists of things that you are going to do and things that you may do. Put question marks (?) next to the things you may do.

My Weekend Plans

Saturday	Sunday
_____	_____
_____	_____
_____	_____

B WRITE Use your lists to write an email to a friend about your weekend plans. What plans are you certain about? What plans do you think are possible? How will the weather affect your plans? Use *may*, *might*, *could*, and *be going to* or *will*. Try to avoid the common mistakes in the chart.

EXAMPLE:　　Hi, Erik. What are you doing this weekend? I'm afraid my plans aren't very exciting. I'm going to stay home and study for my science test. If the weather is nice, I might go for a bike ride. If I do that, maybe you could join me. In the evening, Marta and I are going to see that new movie *Snowstorm*. It's playing at CinemaWorld. Let me know soon if you want to go with us and I'll get tickets online. It's very popular and could get sold out.

Common Mistakes in Using *May*, *Might*, *Could* for Future Possibility

Use *may*, *might*, or *could* for things you are **not certain** about. Do not use *will* or *be going to*.	I'm not sure, but I **may** go for a bike ride. NOT I'm not sure, but I'll go for a bike ride.
Use the full forms *may not* and *might not*. Do not use contractions.	It **may not** be nice enough for the park. NOT It mayn't be nice enough for the park.
Use the **base form** of the verb after *may*, *might*, and *could*. Do not add *-s* to the main verb.	It **may rain** tomorrow. NOT It may rains tomorrow.

C CHECK YOUR WORK Read your email. Underline the words that express future certainty. Circle the words that express future possibility. Use the Editing Checklist to check your work.

Editing Checklist

Did you use . . . ?

☐ *will*, *be going to*, or the present progressive for things you are certain will happen in the future

☐ *may*, *might*, or *could* for things you think are possible in the future

☐ the full forms for *may not* and *might not*

☐ the base form of the verb after *may*, *might*, and *could*

D REVISE YOUR WORK Read your email again. Can you improve your writing? Make changes if necessary. Give your email a subject title.

UNIT 31 REVIEW

Test yourself on the grammar of the unit.

Ⓐ Circle the correct words to complete the sentences.

1. Does / Will it rain tomorrow?

2. It might / might be. I'm not sure.

3. When is Ileana might / going to leave for work?

4. She maybe / may not go to work today. She hasn't decided.

5. It could get / gets very cold tonight. Bundle up!

6. The train will / could be late because of bad weather. It's possible, but it doesn't happen often.

7. Maybe / May be I'll take the train with you this evening.

Ⓑ Complete the conversations with the correct form of *may*, *might*, *could*, or *be going to* and the verbs in parentheses. Choose between affirmative and negative. Use short answers.

1. A: _____ you _____ to the game with us on Sunday?
                                            a. (go)

   B: I _____. There's a good chance. I just have to finish this paper.
                      b.

2. A: _____ Marta _____ at Trish's wedding on Saturday?
                                            a. (be)

   B: She _____. She and Trish had a big argument about something.
                      b.

3. A: How late _____ you _____ this evening?
                                            a. (work)

   B: I _____ until 6:00. I'll call and let you know, OK?
             b. (stay)

4. A: Schools _____ tomorrow. They're predicting a lot of snow tonight.
                      a. (open)

   B: Or they _____ late. They do that sometimes.
                      b. (open)

Ⓒ Read this review of the movie *Day After Tomorrow*. Find and correct five mistakes.

Suddenly, weather forecasts all over the world are predicting terrible storms. Climatologist Jack Hall understands weather trends, and he thinks that a new ice age could to begin very quickly. His son Sam is in New York with his high school class. One student is sick and mayn't live without medicine. May those kids survive by themselves? They maybe not. Jack bundles up and starts walking to New York to save them. There might could be a happy ending. Or the world could end. You'll have to watch to find out!

Now check your answers on page 482.

Present Conclusions:
Must, Have (got) to, May, Might, Could, Can't
MYSTERIES

OUTCOMES
- Come to conclusions about present situations
- Express varying degrees of certainty about the present
- Identify main ideas in a short story
- Identify the certainty of speakers about events
- Draw conclusions about everyday objects and situations
- Write a paragraph about a short story, drawing possible conclusions

STEP 1   GRAMMAR IN CONTEXT

BEFORE YOU READ

Look at the photo. Discuss the questions.

1. Who is Sherlock Holmes?
2. Have you ever read or watched a Sherlock Holmes mystery?
3. Do you like mystery stories? Why?

READ

▶ 32|01   Read the first part of this Sherlock Holmes story.

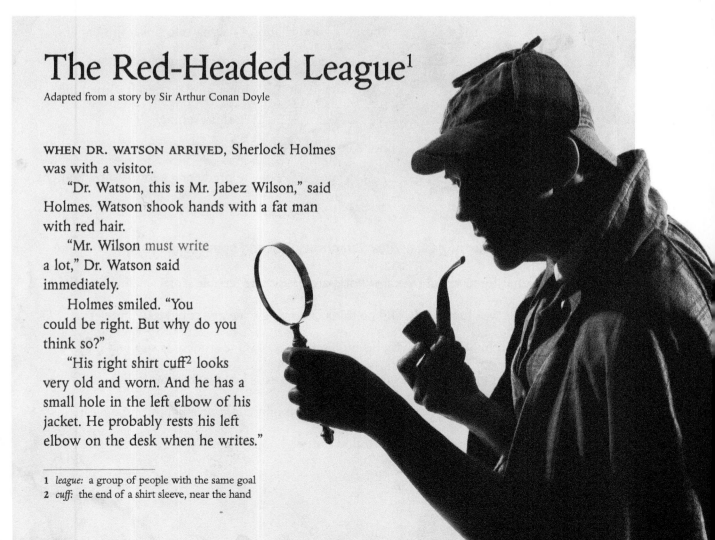

The Red-Headed League[1]

Adapted from a story by Sir Arthur Conan Doyle

WHEN DR. WATSON ARRIVED, Sherlock Holmes was with a visitor.

"Dr. Watson, this is Mr. Jabez Wilson," said Holmes. Watson shook hands with a fat man with red hair.

"Mr. Wilson must write a lot," Dr. Watson said immediately.

Holmes smiled. "You could be right. But why do you think so?"

"His right shirt cuff[2] looks very old and worn. And he has a small hole in the left elbow of his jacket. He probably rests his left elbow on the desk when he writes."

---

1 *league:* a group of people with the same goal
2 *cuff:* the end of a shirt sleeve, near the hand

Wilson looked amazed. "Dr. Watson is correct," he told Holmes. "Your methods may be useful after all."

"Please tell Dr. Watson your story," said Holmes. Dr. Watson looked very interested.

"I have a small shop," began the red-headed man.

"I don't have many customers, so I was very interested in this advertisement. My clerk, Vincent, showed it to me." He showed Watson a newspaper ad that said:

> An American millionaire started the Red-Headed League to help red-headed men. The League now has one position open. The salary is £4 per week for four hours of work every day. The job is to copy the encyclopedia in our offices.

"They couldn't pay someone just for having red hair and copying the encyclopedia," Watson laughed. "This has to be a joke."

"It might not be," said Holmes. "Listen to Wilson tell the rest of his story."

"I got the job, and I worked at the League for two months. Then this morning I found a note on the door." Wilson gave Holmes the note . . .

(to be continued)

AFTER YOU READ

A VOCABULARY **Complete the sentences with the words from the box.**

advertisement	amazed	method	position	salary

1. Dr. Watson read the newspaper _____.

2. It's strange. The job is very easy, but the _____ is high.

3. Dr. Watson uses a special _____ to solve mysteries.

4. Mr. Wilson took the _____ at the Red-Headed League.

5. Mr. Wilson was _____. How did Dr. Watson know that he writes a lot?

B COMPREHENSION **Circle the correct information to complete each statement.**

1. Dr. Watson is <u>very sure / thinks it is possible</u> that Mr. Wilson writes a lot.

2. Holmes thinks Watson is <u>definitely / possibly</u> right.

3. Wilson thinks Watson's methods will <u>definitely / possibly</u> work.

4. Watson <u>believes / doesn't believe</u> the League pays people just to copy the encyclopedia.

5. Watson thinks the ad <u>is / is not</u> a joke.

6. Holmes thinks the ad is <u>definitely / possibly</u> not a joke.

C DISCUSSION **Work with a partner. Compare your answers in B. Why did you choose each answer?**

PRESENT CONCLUSIONS: *MUST, HAVE (GOT) TO, MAY, MIGHT, COULD, CAN'T*

Affirmative Statements

Subject	Modal*	Base Form of Verb	
I You He It They	must may might could	be	wrong.

Negative Statements

Subject	Modal + *Not*	Base Form of Verb	
I You He It They	must not may not might not couldn't can't	be	right.

*Must, may, might, could, and *can't* are modals. Modals have only one form. They do not have *-s* in the third-person singular.

Affirmative Statements with *Have (got) to*

Subject	*Have (got) to*	Base Form	
I You They	have (got) to	be	right.
He It	has (got) to		

Yes/No Questions

Can/Could	Subject	Base Form	
Could Can	he	know	that?

Do	Subject	Base Form	
Does	he	know	that?

Short Answers

Subject	Modal
He	must (not). may (not). might (not). could(n't). has (got) to. can't.

Yes/No Questions with *Be*

Can/Could	Subject	*Be*	
Could Can	he	be	a detective?

Be	Subject	
Is	he	a detective?

Short Answers

Subject	Modal	*Be*
He	must (not) may (not) might (not) could(n't) has (got) to can't	be.

Wh- Questions with *Can* and *Could*

Wh- Word	Can/Could	Subject	Base Form
Who What	can could	it they	be? want?

GRAMMAR NOTES

1 Conclusions and Degrees of Certainty

We often make guesses and come to **conclusions** about present situations using the facts we have.

We use **modals** and similar expressions to show how **certain or uncertain** we are about our conclusions.

Affirmative		Negative	FACT	CONCLUSION
must	**VERY CERTAIN**	*can't, couldn't*	He has only one clerk.	His shop **must be** very small.
			I just saw him.	He **can't be** dead!
have (got) to		*must not*	The lights are on.	He **has to be** there.
			The shop is dark.	He **must not be** there.
may, might, could	**LESS CERTAIN**	*may not, might not*	His sleeve has a hole.	He **may write** a lot.
			He seems calm.	He **may not know** the news.

Use **the simple present** when you are **completely certain** about something.

He**'s** a detective. He **investigates** crimes.

2 Affirmative Conclusions About Present Situations

Use **affirmative modals** to show that you think something is **probable** or **possible** because of the facts you have.

Use *must*, *have to*, or *have got to* if you are **very certain** about your conclusion and you think something is **probable**.

- *must*

Wilson has only one clerk. His shop **must be** very small. *(His shop is probably very small.)*

- *have to*

Wilson applied for a position. He **has to need** money. *(He probably needs money.)*

- *have got to*

They pay men for having red hair. It**'s got to be** a joke. *(It's probably a joke.)*

Use *may*, *might*, or *could* if you are **less certain** about your conclusions and you think something is **possible**.

- *may*

Wilson has a hole in his sleeve. He **may write** a lot. *(It's possible that he writes a lot.)*

- *might*

Vincent knows a lot about cameras. He **might be** a photographer. *(It's possible he's a photographer.)*

- *could*

Holmes solves a lot of crimes. His method **could be** a good one. *(It's possible his method is a good one.)*

3 Negative Conclusions About Present Situations

Use **negative modals** to show that you think something is **impossible** because of the facts you have.

Use *can't* and *couldn't* when you are **almost 100 percent certain** that something is impossible. Use *must not* when you are **slightly less certain**.

- *can't*

  He **can't be** dead! I just saw him. *(It's impossible that he's dead.)*

- *couldn't*

  Vincent **couldn't be** dishonest. He works for half-pay. *(I'm almost certain that he is not dishonest.)*

- *must not*

  He **must not earn** a good salary. He always needs money. *(He probably doesn't earn a good salary.)*

| BE CAREFUL! | Do not use the contraction *mustn't* for a conclusion about a present situation. |
He **must not** be at work.

NOT He ~~mustn't~~ be at work.

Use *may not* and *might not* when you are **even less certain**.

- *may not*

  He **may not know** about the plan. He seems very calm. *(It's possible that he doesn't know about the plan.)*

- *might not*

  His boss **might not tell** him everything. She doesn't trust him. *(It's possible that his boss doesn't tell him everything.)*

| BE CAREFUL! | Do not use *have to* and *have got to* for negative conclusions. |
It **can't** be true!

NOT It ~~doesn't have to~~ be true!

4 Questions and Short Answers

Use *can* and *could* in **questions**.

Someone's coming. Who **can** it be?
Could Vincent **be** in the shop?

In **short answers**, use a modal alone.

A: **Does** she still **work** at Wilson's?
B: She **may not**. I saw a new clerk there.
  NOT She may not ~~work~~.

| BE CAREFUL! | Use *be* in short answers to questions with *be*. |
A: **Is** Ron still with City Bank?
B: I'm not sure. He **might not be**.

REFERENCE NOTES

For *may, can,* and *could* for **permission**, see Unit 14 on page 191.

For *must, have to,* and *have got to* for **necessity**, see Unit 29 on page 400.

For *may, might,* and *could* for **future possibility**, see Unit 31 on page 429.

For a list of **modals and their functions**, see Appendix 19 on page 460.

For the **pronunciation and usage** of *have to* and *have got to*, see Unit 29 on page 403.

EXERCISE 1 DISCOVER THE GRAMMAR

Ⓐ GRAMMAR NOTES 1–4 **Read the next part of "The Red-Headed League." Underline the verbs that express conclusions.**

The Red-Headed League *(continued)*

Sherlock Holmes studied the note: *The Red-Headed League does not exist anymore.*

"This <u>could be</u> serious," Holmes told Wilson. "What can you tell us about your clerk Vincent?"

"Vincent couldn't be dishonest," replied Wilson. "In fact, he took this job for half the usual salary because he wanted to learn the business. His only fault is photography."

"Photography?" Holmes and Watson asked together.

"Yes," replied Wilson. "He's always running down to the basement to work with his cameras."

Wilson left soon after that.

"Wilson's clerk might be the key to this mystery," Holmes told Watson. "Let's go see him." An hour later, Holmes and Watson walked into Wilson's shop. The clerk was a man of about thirty, with a scar on his forehead.

Holmes asked him for directions. Then he and Watson left the shop.

"My dear Watson," Holmes began. "It's very unusual for a thirty-year-old man to work for half-pay. This clerk has to have a very special reason for working here."

"Could it have something to do with the Red-Headed League?" Watson asked.

"Yes. Perhaps the clerk placed that ad in the newspaper. He may want to be alone in the shop. Did you look at his legs?"

"No, I didn't."

"He has holes in his trouser knees. He must spend his time digging a tunnel from Wilson's basement. But where is it?"

Holmes hit the ground sharply with his walking stick. "The ground isn't hollow, so the tunnel can't be here in front of the shop. Let's walk to the street in back of Wilson's shop."

B Read the second part of the story again. How certain is Sherlock Holmes about each of the statements? Check (✓) *Very Certain* or *Less Certain* for each statement.

	Very Certain	Less Certain
1. Something serious is happening.	☐	☑
2. The clerk is the key to the mystery.	☐	☐
3. The clerk has a special reason for working in Mr. Wilson's shop.	☐	☐
4. He wants to be alone in the shop.	☐	☐
5. He's digging a tunnel from Wilson's basement.	☐	☐
6. The tunnel isn't in front of the shop.	☐	☐

EXERCISE 2 AFFIRMATIVE AND NEGATIVE STATEMENTS

GRAMMAR NOTES 1–3 Read each statement and look at the illustration for the story "The Red-Headed League." Come to a conclusion and circle the appropriate modal.

1. It (must) / could be very late.

2. It <u>must</u> / <u>must not</u> be hot outside.

3. Number 27 <u>might</u> / <u>can't</u> be a bank.

4. The delivery <u>couldn't</u> / <u>might</u> be for the bank.

5. The box <u>could</u> / <u>must not</u> contain gold.

6. The two men on the sidewalk <u>must not</u> / <u>could</u> notice the delivery.

7. The manager <u>might not</u> / <u>must</u> want people to know about this delivery.

8. Robbers <u>may</u> / <u>can't</u> know about it.

EXERCISE 3 *MUST* AND *MUST NOT*

GRAMMAR NOTES 1–3 Look at the poster and the map of Mr. Wilson's neighborhood.
Read each statement of fact. Write a conclusion. Use the words in parentheses with
must and *must not*.

1. Wilson's clerk is the man on the poster.

   He must be a criminal.
   (he / be a criminal)

2. The man on the poster is named John Clay.

   _____
   (Vincent / be the clerk's real name)

3. Wilson trusts Vincent.

   _____
   (he / know about the poster)

4. Clay has committed a lot of crimes, but the police haven't caught him.

   _____
   (he / be very clever)

5. The address of the bank on the map and the address in the picture for Exercise 2 are the same.

   _____
   (number 27 Carlisle Street / be City Bank)

6. The hat shop and the drugstore don't make much money.

   _____
   (Vincent's tunnel / lead to those shops)

7. There's a lot of money in the bank, and it's very close to Wilson's shop.

   _____
   (Vincent's tunnel / lead to the bank)

8. The bank is expecting a shipment of gold.

   _____
   (the tunnel / be almost finished)

EXERCISE 4 *HAVE GOT TO* AND *CAN'T*

A GRAMMAR NOTES 1–3 Ann and Marie are buying hats in the shop on Carlisle Street. Read their conversation. Rewrite each underlined sentence. Use *have got to* or *can't* and the word in parentheses. Use contractions.

ANN: Look at this hat, Marie. What do you think?

MARIE: Oh, come on. <u>That's got to be a joke.</u>

You can't be serious.
$\overline{}$ **1.** (serious)

It's much too expensive. Look at the price tag. I mean, I'm not a millionaire!

ANN: It's $100! <u>That can't be right.</u>

$\overline{}$ **2.** (wrong)

MARIE: I know. <u>It can't cost more than $50.</u>

$\overline{}$ **3.** (less)

Anyway, let's talk about it over lunch. I'm getting hungry.

ANN: It's too early for lunch. <u>It has to be before 11:00.</u>

$\overline{}$ **4.** (after)

MARIE: Look at the time. I'm amazed! It's already 12:30.

ANN: Then let's go to the café on Jones Street. <u>It can't be far.</u>

$\overline{}$ **5.** (nearby)

MARIE: Let's go home after lunch. I need a nap.

ANN: Oh, come on. <u>You're fine.</u> You're just hungry.

$\overline{}$ **6.** (tired)

○32|02 **B** LISTEN AND CHECK Listen to the conversation and check your answers in A.

EXERCISE 5 SHORT ANSWERS WITH *MIGHT (NOT)* OR *MUST (NOT)*

A GRAMMAR NOTE 4 Sherlock Holmes and Dr. Watson have been discussing the mystery all evening. Complete their conversation. Write a short answer to each question. Use *might (not)* or *must (not)* and include *be* where necessary.

WATSON: You sound terrible, Holmes. Are you sick?

HOLMES: I _____ *must be* _____. I have a headache, and my throat is starting to hurt. I'm sure
 **1.**
I'm sick. There's no other explanation!

WATSON: Hmm. This bottle is empty. Do you have more cough syrup?

HOLMES: I _____. I think it's the last bottle.
 **2.**

446   Unit 32

WATSON: I'll have to go get some. My patients like Pure Drops Cough Medicine. Does that work

for you, Holmes?

HOLMES: It _____. It's worth a try.
         3.

WATSON: I forgot to go to the bank today. Do you have any money?

HOLMES: I _____. Look in my wallet. It's on the table downstairs.
         4.

WATSON: I found it. It's 6:45. Is Drake Drugstore still open?

HOLMES: It _____. Their advertisement says, "Open 'til 7."
         5.

WATSON: Do you think they sell chicken soup? Some drugstores carry food.

HOLMES: They _____. It's a very small store.
         6.

WATSON: What about the café on Jones Street? Do they have soup?

HOLMES: They _____. They've got everything.
         7.

▶ 32|03 Ⓑ LISTEN AND CHECK **Listen to the conversation and check your answers in A.**

EXERCISE 6 QUESTIONS AND STATEMENTS WITH *BE*

GRAMMAR NOTES 1–4 **Mr. and Mrs. Wilson are trying to get to sleep. Complete their conversation. Write questions and answers. Use *could be*, *couldn't be*, or *can't be*. Choose between affirmative and negative.**

MRS. WILSON: Shh! I hear someone at the door. It's 9:30. Who ____*could*____ it ___*be*___?
              1.

MR. WILSON: It _____ a late customer. Mrs. Simms said she was going to stop by
             2.

this evening.

MRS. WILSON: No, it _____ her. It's much too late. Maybe it's the cat.
              3.

MR. WILSON: It _____. The cat is sleeping in the living room.
             4.

MRS. WILSON: _____ it _____ Vincent? He's always down in the
                                    5.

basement with his camera.

MR. WILSON: No, Vincent went out an hour ago. He _____ back this early. Wait a
                                                  6.

minute. It _____ Sherlock Holmes and Dr. Watson. They said they
            7.

wanted to talk to me.

MRS. WILSON: _____ they really _____ here so late?
                                            8.

MR. WILSON: No. You're right. It _____ them.
                                 9.

MRS. WILSON: What _____ it _____ then?
                                      10.

MR. WILSON: That door rattles whenever the wind blows. It _____ the wind.
                                                           11.

MRS. WILSON: That must be it. Let's go to sleep.

EXERCISE 7 EDITING

GRAMMAR NOTES 1–4 Read this student's reading journal for a mystery novel. There are six mistakes in the use of *must*, *have (got) to*, *may*, *might*, *could*, and *can't*. The first mistake is already corrected. Find and correct five more.

The main character, Molly Smith, is a college ESL teacher. She is trying to find her dead grandparents'

first home in the United States. It may ~~being~~ be in a nearby town. The townspeople there seem scared.

They could be have a secret, or they must just hate strangers. Molly found some letters hidden in

an old encyclopedia that might lead her to the place. They got to be important because the author

mentions them right away. The letters might contain family secrets. I'm almost certain of it. Who is

the bad guy? It couldn't be the student because he wants to help. It must be the newspaper editor in

the town. That's a possibility.

STEP 4 COMMUNICATION PRACTICE

EXERCISE 8 LISTENING

▶32|04 **A** Sherlock Holmes, Dr. Watson, and a police captain are in the bank's basement, waiting for John Clay. Listen to their conversation. Read the statements. Then listen again to the conversation. How certain is each speaker? Check (✓) *Completely Certain*, *Very Certain*, or *Less Certain* for each statement.

	Completely Certain	Very Certain	Less Certain
1. It's 10:00.	☐	☑	☐
2. They are going to have a long wait.	☐	☐	☐
3. There are 2,000 gold coins in one of the boxes.	☐	☐	☐
4. John Clay knows about the gold.	☐	☐	☐
5. An American millionaire didn't start the Red-Headed League.	☐	☐	☐
6. Clay ended the Red-Headed League.	☐	☐	☐
7. Clay's tunnel is finished.	☐	☐	☐
8. The tunnel is under the bank floor.	☐	☐	☐
9. Clay is dangerous.	☐	☐	☐
10. Clay wants Wilson to be asleep before he comes.	☐	☐	☐
11. Clay is in the tunnel.	☐	☐	☐

B Work with a partner. Listen to the conversation again. Discuss your answers in A. Give reasons for your answers.

EXAMPLE: **A:** For number 1, I checked *Very Certain*.
        B: Me too. The police captain said, "It must be 10:00." That means he was very sure about the time.

EXERCISE 9 DETECTIVE WORK

PICTURE DISCUSSION **Work in a small group. Look at the picture of Sandra Diaz and some things that she and her family own. Make guesses about the Diaz family. Give reasons for your guesses.**

EXAMPLE: **A:** Sandra might be a construction worker. She's wearing a hard hat.
        B: Or she could be . . .
        C: She couldn't . . .

EXERCISE 10 WHAT'S GOING ON?

PROBLEM SOLVING **Work with a partner. Read the situations. Discuss possible explanations for each situation. Then come to a conclusion. Discuss your explanations with the rest of the class. Use your imagination!**

1. Yolanda lives alone, but she hears a noise in the house.

    EXAMPLE: **A:** It might be an open window. Maybe the wind is blowing.
            B: It couldn't be. She closed all the windows five minutes ago.
            A: Well, then, it could be the cat . . .

2. Stefan has been calling his sister on the phone for three days. She hasn't returned any of his messages.

3. Allan is on the street. He's asked a woman three times for the time. She hasn't answered.

4. Lili sees a neighbor with a ten-year-old. She's never seen the child before.

5. Julia and Claudio went on a picnic in the park. They ate strawberries and cheese. Now they are sneezing and their eyes are watering.

FROM GRAMMAR TO WRITING

Read a mystery writer's outline about one of the characters in her new mystery. Work in a group to make guesses and come to conclusions about the story and the characters. Answer the questions below.

March 1 – Murder Suspect's Activities on the Day of the Crime

9:30	calls Dr. Lorenzo
11:00–1:00	hair salon—changes hair color
2:00	bank—withdraws $10,000
3:00	Mr. Jordan
4:30	calls travel agency—vegetarian meal?

- Is the murder suspect a man or a woman?
- Why does the suspect call Dr. Lorenzo?
- Why does the suspect need $10,000?
- Who is Mr. Jordan?
- What is Mr. Jordan's relationship to the suspect?

EXAMPLE: A: The suspect must be a woman. She's going to a hair salon.
　　　　　 B: It could be a man. Men go to hair salons, too.

B WRITE   Use your guesses and conclusions to write a paragraph about the story and the characters. Try to avoid the common mistakes in the chart.

EXAMPLE: The suspect could be a man or a woman. Both men and women . . .

Common Mistakes in Using Modals for Present Conclusions

Use **must**, **have to**, or **have got to** for **affirmative conclusions** when you are **very certain** something is true. Do not use *may, might,* or *could*.	He **must be** away. His house is completely dark. NOT He ~~might~~ be away. His house is completely dark.
Use **may**, **might**, or **could** when you think something is possible but you are **less certain**. Do not use *must, have to,* or *have got to*.	He **might be** in Chicago. He sometimes goes there. NOT He ~~must~~ be in Chicago. He sometimes goes there.
Use **can't**, **couldn't**, **must not**, **may not**, or **might not** for **negative conclusions**. Do not use *don't have to* or *haven't got to*.	He **can't be** in Chicago. The airport is closed. NOT He ~~doesn't have to~~ be in Chicago. The airport is closed.

C CHECK YOUR WORK   Read your paragraph. Underline the words that express strong certainty. Circle the words that express less certainty. Use the Editing Checklist to check your work.

Editing Checklist

Did you use . . . ?

- [ ] modals that show how certain or uncertain you are of your conclusions
- [ ] *must, have (got) to, may, might,* and *could* for affirmative conclusions
- [ ] *can't, couldn't, must not, may not,* and *might not* for negative conclusions

D REVISE YOUR WORK   Read your paragraph again. Can you improve your writing? Make changes if necessary. Give your paragraph a title.

UNIT 32 REVIEW

Test yourself on the grammar of the unit.

Ⓐ Circle the correct words to complete the sentences.

1. Rosa got 100 on her test. She <u>may</u> / <u>must</u> be a good student.

2. It's a gold ring with a very large diamond. It <u>has got to</u> / <u>might</u> cost a lot of money.

3. I'm really not sure how old he is. He <u>has to</u> / <u>could</u> be 21.

4. Doug <u>can't</u> / <u>doesn't have to</u> be married. He's much too young!

5. <u>Could</u> / <u>May</u> Doug know Rosa?

6. The phone is ringing. It <u>must not</u> / <u>could</u> be Alexis. She sometimes calls at this time.

Ⓑ Complete the conversations with the verbs in parentheses. Choose between affirmative and negative.

1. A: That _____ George's brother. He looks nothing like George.
              a. (could / be)

   B: He _____. Sometimes brothers don't look at all alike.
            b. (could / be)

2. A: Someone's at the door. What _____ they _____ at this hour?
                                 a. (could / want)

   B: I don't know. _____ it _____ Leon?
                    b. (could / be)

   A: No. It _____ Leon. Leon's in Spain.
           c. (can / be)

3. A: _____ this road _____ to Greenville?
                    a. (could / lead)

   B: I'm not sure. Ask Talia. She _____.
                    b. (might / know)

Ⓒ Find and correct seven mistakes.

1. Jason has been coughing all morning. He might having a cold.

2. Diana must not likes fish. She left most of it on her plate.

3. May the package be from your parents?

4. That's impossible! It might not be true.

5. Is the bank still open? That's a good question. I don't know. It might.

6. She could be a thief! I trust her completely!

7. It's got be a joke. I don't believe it's serious.

Now check your answers on page 483.

Appendices

1 Irregular Verbs

BASE FORM	SIMPLE PAST	PAST PARTICIPLE
arise	arose	arisen
awake	awoke	awoken
be	was/were	been
beat	beat	beaten/beat
become	became	become
begin	began	begun
bend	bent	bent
bet	bet	bet
bite	bit	bitten
bleed	bled	bled
blow	blew	blown
break	broke	broken
bring	brought	brought
build	built	built
burn	burned/burnt	burnt/burned
burst	burst	burst
buy	bought	bought
catch	caught	caught
choose	chose	chosen
cling	clung	clung
come	came	come
cost	cost	cost
creep	crept	crept
cut	cut	cut
deal	dealt	dealt
dig	dug	dug
dive	dived/dove	dived
do	did	done
draw	drew	drawn
dream	dreamed/dreamt	dreamed/dreamt
drink	drank	drunk
drive	drove	driven
eat	ate	eaten
fall	fell	fallen
feed	fed	fed
feel	felt	felt
fight	fought	fought
find	found	found
fit	fit/fitted	fit
flee	fled	fled
fling	flung	flung
fly	flew	flown
forbid	forbade/forbid	forbidden
forget	forgot	forgotten
forgive	forgave	forgiven
freeze	froze	frozen
get	got	gotten/got
give	gave	given
go	went	gone
grind	ground	ground
grow	grew	grown
hang	hung	hung

BASE FORM	SIMPLE PAST	PAST PARTICIPLE
have	had	had
hear	heard	heard
hide	hid	hidden
hit	hit	hit
hold	held	held
hurt	hurt	hurt
keep	kept	kept
kneel	knelt/kneeled	knelt/kneeled
knit	knit/knitted	knit/knitted
know	knew	known
lay	laid	laid
lead	led	led
leap	leaped/leapt	leaped/leapt
leave	left	left
lend	lent	lent
let	let	let
lie (lie down)	lay	lain
light	lit/lighted	lit/lighted
lose	lost	lost
make	made	made
mean	meant	meant
meet	met	met
pay	paid	paid
prove	proved	proven/proved
put	put	put
quit	quit	quit
read /rid/	read /rɛd/	read /rɛd/
ride	rode	ridden
ring	rang	rung
rise	rose	risen
run	ran	run
say	said	said
see	saw	seen
seek	sought	sought
sell	sold	sold
send	sent	sent
set	set	set
sew	sewed	sewn/sewed
shake	shook	shaken
shave	shaved	shaved/shaven
shine (intransitive)	shone/shined	shone/shined
shoot	shot	shot
show	showed	shown
shrink	shrank/shrunk	shrunk/shrunken
shut	shut	shut
sing	sang	sung
sink	sank/sunk	sunk
sit	sat	sat
sleep	slept	slept
slide	slid	slid
speak	spoke	spoken
speed	sped/speeded	sped/speeded

BASE FORM	SIMPLE PAST	PAST PARTICIPLE	BASE FORM	SIMPLE PAST	PAST PARTICIPLE
spend	spent	spent	take	took	taken
spill	spilled/spilt	spilled/spilt	teach	taught	taught
spin	spun	spun	tear	tore	torn
spit	spit/spat	spat	tell	told	told
split	split	split	think	thought	thought
spread	spread	spread	throw	threw	thrown
spring	sprang	sprung	understand	understood	understood
stand	stood	stood	upset	upset	upset
steal	stole	stolen	wake	woke	woken
stick	stuck	stuck	wear	wore	worn
sting	stung	stung	weave	wove/weaved	woven/weaved
stink	stank/stunk	stunk	weep	wept	wept
strike	struck	struck/stricken	win	won	won
swear	swore	sworn	wind	wound	wound
sweep	swept	swept	withdraw	withdrew	withdrawn
swim	swam	swum	wring	wrung	wrung
swing	swung	swung	write	wrote	written

2 Non-Action Verbs

APPEARANCE	EMOTIONS	MENTAL STATES		POSSESSION AND RELATIONSHIP	SENSES AND PERCEPTIONS	WANTS AND PREFERENCES
appear	admire	agree	know	belong	feel	desire
be	adore	assume	mean	come from (origin)	hear	hope
look (seem)	appreciate	believe	mind	contain	notice	need
represent	care	consider	presume	have	observe	prefer
resemble	detest	disagree	realize	own	perceive	want
seem	dislike	disbelieve	recognize	possess	see	wish
signify	doubt	estimate	remember		smell	
	envy	expect	see (understand)		sound	
VALUE	fear	feel (believe)	suppose		taste	
cost	hate	find (believe)	suspect			
equal	like	guess	think (believe)			
weigh	love	hesitate	understand			
	miss	hope	wonder			
	regret	imagine				
	respect					
	trust					

3 Verbs and Expressions Used Reflexively

allow yourself	behave yourself	enjoy yourself	introduce yourself	see yourself
amuse yourself	believe in yourself	feel proud of yourself	kill yourself	take care of yourself
ask yourself	blame yourself	feel sorry for yourself	look at yourself	talk to yourself
avail yourself of	buy yourself	forgive yourself	prepare yourself	teach yourself
be hard on yourself	cut yourself	help yourself	pride yourself on	tell yourself
be pleased with yourself	deprive yourself of	hurt yourself	push yourself	treat yourself
be proud of yourself	dry yourself	imagine yourself	remind yourself	wash yourself
be yourself				

(s.o. = someone   s.t. = something)

PHRASAL VERB	MEANING
ask s.o. **over**	invite to one's home
blow s.t. **out**	stop burning by blowing air on it
blow s.t. **up**	make explode
bring s.o. or s.t. **back**	return
bring s.o. **up**	raise (a child)
bring s.t. **up**	bring attention to
burn s.t. **down**	burn completely
call s.o. **back**	return a phone call
call s.t. **off**	cancel
call s.o. **up**	contact by phone
calm s.o. **down**	make less excited
carry s.t. **out**	complete (a plan)
clean s.o. or s.t. **up**	clean completely
clear s.t. **up**	explain
close s.t. **down**	close by force
count on s.t. or s.o.	depend on
cover s.o. or s.t. **up**	cover completely
cross s.t. **out**	draw a line through
do s.t. **over**	do again
drink s.t. **up**	drink completely
drop s.o. or s.t. **off**	take someplace in a car and leave there
empty s.t. **out**	empty completely
end up doing s.t.	do something you didn't plan to do
figure s.o. **out**	understand (the behavior)
figure s.t. **out**	solve, understand after thinking about it
fill s.t. **in**	complete with information
fill s.t. **out**	complete (a form)
find s.t. **out**	learn information
get off s.t.	leave (a bus, a couch)
get over s.t.	recover from
give s.t. **back**	return
give s.t. **up**	quit, abandon
give up doing s.t.	quit, stop
go on doing s.t.	continue
hand s.t. **in**	give work (to a boss/teacher), submit
hand s.t. **out**	distribute
hand s.t. **over**	give
help s.o. **out**	assist
keep s.o. or s.t. **away**	cause to stay at a distance
keep s.t. **on**	not remove (a piece of clothing/ jewelry)
keep on doing s.t.	continue
keep s.o. or s.t. **out**	not allow to enter
lay s.o. **off**	end employment
leave s.t. **on**	1. not turn off (a light/radio) 2. not remove (a piece of clothing/ jewelry)
leave s.t. **out**	not include, omit
let s.o. **down**	disappoint
let s.o. or s.t. **in**	allow to enter
let s.o. **off**	allow to leave (from a bus/car)
light s.t. **up**	illuminate
look for s.o. or s.t.	try to find
look s.o. or s.t. **over**	examine

PHRASAL VERB	MEANING
look s.t. **up**	try to find (in a book/on the Internet)
make s.t. **up**	create
pass s.t. **on**	give to others
pass s.t. **out**	distribute
pass s.o. or s.t. **over**	decide not to use
pass s.o. or s.t. **up**	decide not to use, reject
pay s.o. or s.t. **back**	repay
pick s.o. or s.t. **out**	choose
pick s.o. or s.t. **up**	1. lift 2. go get someone or something
pick s.t. **up**	1. get (an idea/a new book) 2. answer the phone
point s.o. or s.t. **out**	indicate
put s.t. **away**	put in an appropriate place
put s.t. **back**	return to its original place
put s.o. or s.t. **down**	stop holding
put s.t. **off**	delay
put off doing s.t.	delay
put s.t. **on**	cover the body (with clothes/lotion)
put s.t. **together**	assemble
put s.t. **up**	erect
set s.t. **up**	1. prepare for use 2. establish (a business)
shut s.t. **off**	stop (a machine/light)
straighten s.o. **out**	change bad behavior
straighten s.t. **up**	make neat
switch s.t. **on**	start (a machine/light)
take s.o. or s.t. **back**	return
take s.t. **off/out**	remove
take over s.t.	get control of
talk s.o. **into**	persuade
talk s.t. **over**	discuss
tear s.t. **down**	destroy
tear s.t. **off**	remove by tearing
tear s.t. **up**	tear into small pieces
think about doing s.t.	consider
think s.t. **over**	consider
think s.t. **up**	invent
throw s.t. **away/out**	put in the trash, discard
try s.t. **on**	put clothing on to see if it fits
try s.t. **out**	use to see if it works
turn s.t. **around**	make it work well
turn s.o. or s.t. **down**	reject
turn s.t. **down**	lower the volume (a TV/radio)
turn s.t. **in**	give work (to a boss/teacher), submit
turn s.o. or s.t. **into**	change from one form to another
turn s.o. **off**	[slang] destroy interest in
turn s.t. **off**	stop (a machine/light), extinguish
turn s.t. **on**	start (a machine/light)
turn s.t. **up**	make louder (a TV/radio)
use s.t. **up**	use completely, consume
wake s.o. **up**	awaken
work s.t. **out**	solve, find a solution to a problem
write s.t. **down**	write on a piece of paper
write s.t. **up**	write in a finished form

5 Intransitive Phrasal Verbs

PHRASAL VERB	MEANING
blow up	explode
break down	stop working (a machine)
burn down	burn completely
call back	return a phone call
calm down	become less excited
catch on	1. begin to understand 2. become popular
clear up	become clear
close down	stop operating
come about	happen
come along	come with, accompany
come by	visit
come back	return
come in	enter
come off	become unattached
come on	1. do as I say 2. let's go
come out	appear
come up	arise
dress up	wear special clothes
drop in	visit by surprise
drop out	quit
eat out	eat in a restaurant
empty out	empty completely
find out	learn information

PHRASAL VERB	MEANING
fit in	be accepted in a group
follow through	complete
fool around	act playful
get ahead	make progress, succeed
get along	have a good relationship
get away	go on vacation
get back	return
get by	survive
get through	finish
get together	meet
get up	1. get out of bed 2. stand
give up	quit
go ahead	begin or continue to do something
go away	leave
go on	continue
grow up	become an adult
hang up	end a phone call
help out	assist
keep away	stay at a distance
keep on	continue
keep out	not enter
keep up	go as fast
lie down	recline

PHRASAL VERB	MEANING
light up	illuminate
look out	be careful
make up	end a disagreement, reconcile
pass away	die
play around	have fun
run out	not have enough
set out	begin an activity or a project
show up	appear
sign up	register
sit down	take a seat
slip up	make a mistake
stand up	rise
start over	start again
stay up	remain awake
straighten up	make neat
take off	depart (a plane)
tune in	1. watch or listen to (a show) 2. pay attention
turn up	appear
wake up	stop sleeping
watch out	be careful
work out	1. be resolved 2. exercise

6 Irregular Plural Nouns

SINGULAR	PLURAL
half	halves
knife	knives
leaf	leaves
life	lives
loaf	loaves
shelf	shelves
wife	wives

SINGULAR	PLURAL
man	men
woman	women
child	children
foot	feet
tooth	teeth
goose	geese
mouse	mice
person	people

SINGULAR	PLURAL
deer	deer
fish	fish
sheep	sheep

7 Non-Count Nouns

Non-count nouns are singular.

ACTIVITIES	COURSES OF STUDY	FOOD		IDEAS AND FEELINGS	LIQUIDS AND GASES	MATERIALS	VERY SMALL THINGS	WEATHER
baseball	archeology	bread	fruit	anger	air	ash	dust	fog
biking	art	broccoli	ice cream	beauty	blood	clay	pepper	ice
exploring	economics	butter	lettuce	fear	gasoline	cotton	rice	rain
farming	English	cake	meat	freedom	ink	glass	salt	snow
football	geography	cheese	pasta	friendship	milk	gold	sand	wind
golf	history	chicken	pizza	happiness	oil	leather	sugar	
hiking	mathematics	chocolate	salad	hate	oxygen	paper		
running	music	coffee	soup	hope	paint	silk		
sailing	photography	corn	spaghetti	loneliness	smoke	silver		
soccer	psychology	fat	spinach	love	soda	stone		
swimming	science	fish	tea	truth	water	wood		
tennis		flour	yogurt			wool		

NAMES OF CATEGORIES

clothing	(BUT: coats, hats, shoes ...)
equipment	(BUT: computers, phones, TVs ...)
food	(BUT: bananas, eggs, vegetables ...)
furniture	(BUT: beds, chairs, lamps, tables ...)
homework	(BUT: assignments, pages, problems ...)
jewelry	(BUT: bracelets, earrings, necklaces ...)
mail	(BUT: letters, packages, postcards ...)
money	(BUT: dinars, dollars, euros, pounds ...)
time	(BUT: minutes, months, years ...)
work	(BUT: jobs, projects, tasks ...)

OTHER

Some non-count nouns don't fit into any list. You must memorize these non-count nouns.

advice
garbage/trash
help
information
luggage
news
traffic

8 Proper Nouns

Write proper nouns with a capital letter. Notice that some proper nouns use the definite article *the*.

PEOPLE
- first names — Anne, Eduardo, Mehmet, Olga, Shao-fen
- family names — Chen, García, Haddad, Smith
- family groups — the Chens, the Garcias, the Haddads, the Smiths
- titles — Doctor, Grandma, President, Professor
- title + names — Mr. García, Professor Smith, Uncle Steve

PLACES
- continents — Africa, Asia, Australia, Europe, South America
- countries — Argentina, China, France, Nigeria, Turkey, the United States
- provinces/states — Brittany, Ontario, Szechwan, Texas
- cities — Beijing, Istanbul, Rio de Janeiro, Toronto
- streets — the Champs-Elysées, Fifth Avenue
- structures — Harrods, the Louvre, the Petronas Towers
- schools — Midwood High School, Oxford University
- parks — Central Park, the Tivoli Gardens
- mountains — the Andes, the Himalayas, the Pyrenees
- oceans — the Atlantic, the Indian Ocean, the Pacific
- rivers — the Amazon, the Ganges, the Seine
- lakes — Baikal, Erie, Tanganyika, Titicaca
- canals — the Suez Canal, the Panama Canal
- deserts — the Gobi, the Kalahari, the Sahara

DOCUMENTS
the Bible, the Koran, the Constitution

LANGUAGES
Arabic, Chinese, Portuguese, Russian, Spanish

NATIONALITIES
Brazilian, Japanese, Mexican, Saudi, Turkish

RELIGIONS
Buddhism, Christianity, Hinduism, Islam, Judaism

COURSES
Introduction to Computer Sciences, Math 201

PRODUCT BRANDS
Adidas, Dell, Kleenex, Mercedes, Samsung

TIME
- months — January, March, December
- days — Monday, Wednesday, Saturday
- holidays — Bastille Day, Buddha Day, Christmas, Hanukah, New Year's Day, Ramadan

9 Adjectives That Form the Comparative and Superlative in Two Ways

ADJECTIVE	COMPARATIVE	SUPERLATIVE
cruel	crueler/more cruel	cruelest/most cruel
deadly	deadlier/more deadly	deadliest/most deadly
friendly	friendlier/more friendly	friendliest/most friendly
handsome	handsomer/more handsome	handsomest/most handsome
happy	happier/more happy	happiest/most happy
likely	likelier/more likely	likeliest/most likely
lively	livelier/more lively	liveliest/most lively
lonely	lonelier/more lonely	loneliest/most lonely
lovely	lovelier/more lovely	loveliest/most lovely
narrow	narrower/more narrow	narrowest/most narrow
pleasant	pleasanter/more pleasant	pleasantest/most pleasant
polite	politer/more polite	politest/most polite
quiet	quieter/more quiet	quietest/most quiet
shallow	shallower/more shallow	shallowest/most shallow
sincere	sincerer/more sincere	sincerest/most sincere
stupid	stupider/more stupid	stupidest/most stupid
true	truer/more true	truest/most true

10 Irregular Comparisons of Adjectives, Adverbs, and Quantifiers

ADJECTIVE	ADVERB	COMPARATIVE	SUPERLATIVE
bad	badly	worse	the worst
far	far	farther/further	the farthest/furthest
good	well	better	the best
little	little	less	the least
many/a lot of	—	more	the most
much*/a lot of	much*/a lot	more	the most

* *Much* is usually only used in questions and negative statements.

11 Participial Adjectives

-ED	-ING	-ED	-ING	-ED	-ING
alarmed	alarming	disturbed	disturbing	moved	moving
amazed	amazing	embarrassed	embarrassing	paralyzed	paralyzing
amused	amusing	entertained	entertaining	pleased	pleasing
annoyed	annoying	excited	exciting	relaxed	relaxing
astonished	astonishing	exhausted	exhausting	satisfied	satisfying
bored	boring	fascinated	fascinating	shocked	shocking
charmed	charming	frightened	frightening	surprised	surprising
confused	confusing	horrified	horrifying	terrified	terrifying
depressed	depressing	inspired	inspiring	tired	tiring
disappointed	disappointing	interested	interesting	touched	touching
disgusted	disgusting	irritated	irritating	troubled	troubling

12 Order of Adjectives Before a Noun

1 When **adjectives from different categories** are used before a noun, they usually go in the order as displayed in the chart below. Do not use a comma between these adjectives. Remember that we do not usually use more than three adjectives before a noun.

EXAMPLES: I bought an **antique Greek flower** vase.   NOT a ~~Greek antique~~ flower vase
She took some **easy college** courses.   NOT some ~~college easy~~ courses
We sat at an **enormous round wooden** table.   NOT a ~~wooden enormous round~~ table

OPINION	SIZE*	AGE	SHAPE	COLOR	ORIGIN	MATERIAL	NOUNS USED AS ADJECTIVES	
beautiful	enormous	antique	flat	blue	Asian	cotton	college	
comfortable	huge	modern	oval	gray	European	gold	flower	
cozy	little	new	rectangular	green	Greek	plastic	kitchen	+ NOUN
easy	tall	old	round	purple	Pacific	stone	mountain	
expensive	tiny	young	square	red	Southern	wooden	vacation	

*EXCEPTION: *Big* and *small* usually go first in a series of adjectives: *a small comfortable apartment.*

2 When **adjectives from the same category** are used before a noun, they do not follow a specific order. Use a comma between these adjectives.

EXAMPLES: We rented a **beautiful, comfortable, cozy** apartment. **or**
We rented a **cozy, comfortable, beautiful** apartment. **or**
We rented a **comfortable, cozy, beautiful** apartment.

13 Verbs Followed by Gerunds (Base Form of Verb + *-ing*)

acknowledge	consider	enjoy	go on*	permit	report
admit	delay	escape	imagine	postpone	resent
advise	deny	excuse	justify	practice	resist
allow	detest	explain	keep *(continue)*	prevent	risk
appreciate	discontinue	feel like	keep on*	prohibit	suggest
avoid	discuss	finish	limit	put off*	support
ban	dislike	forgive	mention	quit	think about*
can't help	end up*	give up*	mind *(object to)*	recall	tolerate
celebrate	endure	go	miss	recommend	understand

*A few phrasal verbs like these are followed by a gerund.

14 Verbs Followed by Infinitives (*To* + Base Form of Verb)

agree	can't wait	fail	manage	prepare	struggle
aim	claim	help*	mean *(intend)*	pretend	threaten
appear	choose	hesitate	need	promise	volunteer
arrange	consent	hope	neglect	refuse	wait
ask	decide	hurry	offer	request	want
attempt	deserve	intend	pay	rush	wish
can('t) afford	expect	learn	plan	seem	would like

* *Help* is often followed by the base form of the verb (example: *I helped paint the kitchen*).

15 Verbs Followed by Gerunds or Infinitives

begin	forget*	like	prefer	regret*	stop*
can't stand	hate	love	remember*	start	try
continue					

*These verbs can be followed by either a gerund or an infinitive, but there is a big difference in meaning *(see Unit 26)*.

16 Verbs Followed by Object + Infinitive

advise	encourage	help**	pay*	remind	urge
allow	expect*	hire	permit	request	want*
ask*	forbid	invite	persuade	require	warn
cause	force	need*	prefer*	teach	wish
choose*	get	order	promise*	tell	would like*
convince					

*These verbs can also be followed by an infinitive without an object (example: *ask to leave or ask someone to leave*).
** *Help* is often followed by the base form of the verb, with or without an object (example: *I helped (her) paint the kitchen*).

17 Adjective + Preposition Combinations

accustomed to	bad at	curious about	good at	responsible for	sorry for/about
afraid of	bored with/by	different from	happy about	sad about	surprised at/
amazed at/by	capable of	disappointed with	interested in	safe from	about/by
angry at	careful of	excited about	nervous about	satisfied with	terrible at
ashamed of	certain about	famous for	opposed to	shocked at/by	tired of
aware of	concerned about	fond of	pleased about	sick of	used to
awful at	content with	glad about	ready for	slow at/in	worried about

18 Verb + Preposition Combinations

admit to
advise against
apologize for
approve of

believe in
choose between
complain about
count on

deal with
dream about/of
feel like
insist on

look forward to
object to
pay for
plan on

rely on
resort to
succeed in
talk about

thank someone for
think about
wonder about
worry about

19 Modals and Their Functions

FUNCTION	MODAL OR EXPRESSION	TIME	EXAMPLES
Ability	can can't	Present	Sam **can swim**. He **can't skate**.
	could couldn't	Past	We **could swim** last year. We **couldn't skate**.
	be able to* not be able to*	All verb forms	Lea **is able to run** fast. She **wasn't able to run** fast last year.
Permission	can can't could may may not	Present or future	**Can** I **sit** here? **Can** I **call** tomorrow? Yes, you **can**. No, you **can't**. Sorry. **Could** he **leave** now? **May** I **borrow** your pen? Yes, you **may**. No, you **may not**. Sorry.
Requests	can can't could will would	Present or future	**Can** you **close** the door, please? Sure, I **can**. Sorry, I **can't**. **Could** you please **answer** the phone? **Will** you **wash** the dishes, please? **Would** you please **mail** this letter?
Advice	should shouldn't ought to had better** had better not**	Present or future	You **should study** more. You **shouldn't miss** class. We **ought to leave**. We**'d better go**. We**'d better not stay**.
Necessity	have to* not have to*	All verb forms	He **has to go** now. I **had to go** yesterday. I **will have to go** soon. He **doesn't have to go** yet.
	have got to* must	Present or future	He**'s got to leave**! You **must use** a pen for the test.
Prohibition	must not can't	Present or future	You **must not drive** without a license. You **can't drive** without a license.

*The meaning of this expression is similar to the meaning of a modal. Unlike a modal, it has *-s* for third-person singular.
**The meaning of this expression is similar to the meaning of a modal. Like a modal, it has no *-s* for third-person singular.

FUNCTION	MODAL OR EXPRESSION	TIME	EXAMPLES
Possibility	**must** **must not** **have to***	Present	This **must be** her house. Her name is on the door. She **must not be** home. I don't see her car. She **had to know** him. They went to school together.
	have got to* **may** **may not** **might** **might not** **could**	Present or future	He**'s got to be** guilty. We saw him do it. She **may be** home now. It **may not rain** tomorrow. Lee **might be sick** today. He **might not come** to class. They **could be** at the library. It **could rain** tomorrow.
Impossibility	**can't**	Present or future	That **can't be** Ana. She left for France yesterday. It **can't snow** tomorrow. It's going to be too warm.
	couldn't	Present	He **couldn't be** guilty. He was away . . .

*The meaning of this expression is similar to the meaning of a modal. Unlike a modal, it has *-s* for third-person singular.

20 Spelling Rules for the Simple Present: Third-Person Singular (*He, She, It*)

1 Add *-s* for most verbs.

work	work**s**
buy	buy**s**
ride	ride**s**
return	return**s**

2 Add *-es* for verbs that end in *-ch*, *-s*, *-sh*, *-x*, or *-z*.

watch	watch**es**
pass	pass**es**
rush	rush**es**
relax	relax**es**
buzz	buzz**es**

3 Change the *y* to *i* and add *-es* when the base form ends in **consonant + *y***.

study	stud**ies**
hurry	hurr**ies**
dry	dr**ies**

4 Do not change the *y* when the base form ends in **vowel + *y***. Add *-s*.

play	play**s**
enjoy	enjoy**s**

5 A few verbs have **irregular forms**.

be	**is**
do	**does**
go	**goes**
have	**has**

21 Spelling Rules for Base Form of Verb + -ing (Progressive and Gerund)

1 Add **-ing** to the base form of the verb.

read	read**ing**
stand	stand**ing**

2 If the verb ends in a **silent -e**, drop the final **-e** and add **-ing**.

leave	leav**ing**
take	tak**ing**

3 In **one-syllable** verbs, if the last three letters are a consonant-vowel-consonant combination (CVC), double the last consonant and add **-ing**.

```
C V C
↓ ↓ ↓
s i t      sit**ting**

C V C
↓ ↓ ↓
p l a n    plan**ning**
```

EXCEPTION: Do not double the last consonant in verbs that end in **-w**, **-x**, or **-y**.

sew	sew**ing**
fix	fix**ing**
play	play**ing**

4 In verbs of **two or more syllables** that end in a consonant-vowel-consonant combination, double the last consonant only if the last syllable is stressed.

admít	admit**ting**	*(The last syllable is stressed.)*
whísper	whisper**ing**	*(The last syllable is not stressed, so don't double the -r.)*

5 If the verb ends in **-ie**, change the **ie** to **y** before adding **-ing**.

die	d**ying**
lie	l**ying**

Stress
´ shows main stress.

---

22 Spelling Rules for Base Form of Verb + -ed (Simple Past and Past Participle of Regular Verbs)

1 If the verb ends in a **consonant**, add **-ed**.

return	return**ed**
help	help**ed**

2 If the verb ends in **-e**, add **-d**.

live	live**d**
create	create**d**
die	die**d**

3 In **one-syllable** verbs, if the last three letters are a consonant-vowel-consonant combination (CVC), double the last consonant and add **-ed**.

```
C V C
↓ ↓ ↓
h o p      hop**ped**

C V C
↓ ↓ ↓
g r a b    grab**bed**
```

EXCEPTION: Do not double the last consonant in **one-syllable** verbs that end in **-w**, **-x**, or **-y**.

bow	bow**ed**
mix	mix**ed**
play	play**ed**

4 In verbs of **two or more syllables** that end in a consonant-vowel-consonant combination, double the last consonant only if the last syllable is stressed.

prefér	prefer**red**	*(The last syllable is stressed.)*
vísit	visit**ed**	*(The last syllable is not stressed, so don't double the -t.)*

5 If the verb ends in **consonant + y**, change the **y** to **i** and add **-ed**.

worry	worr**ied**
carry	carr**ied**

6 If the verb ends in **vowel + y**, add **-ed**. (Do not change the **y** to **i**.)

play	play**ed**
annoy	annoy**ed**

EXCEPTIONS:

lay	la**id**
pay	pa**id**
say	sa**id**

23 Spelling Rules for the Comparative (-er) and Superlative (-est) of Adjectives

1 With **one-syllable** adjectives, add **-er** to form the comparative. Add **-est** to form the superlative.

cheap	cheap**er**	cheap**est**
bright	bright**er**	bright**est**

2 If the adjective ends in **-e**, add **-r** or **-st**.

nice	nice**r**	nice**st**

3 If the adjective ends in **consonant + y**, change **y** to **i** before you add **-er** or **-est**.

pretty	prett**ier**	prett**iest**

EXCEPTION:

shy	shy**er**	shy**est**

4 If a one-syllable adjective ends in a consonant-vowel-consonant combination (CVC), double the last consonant before adding **-er** or **-est**.

C V C
↓ ↓ ↓
b i g   big**ger**   big**gest**

EXCEPTION: Do not double the consonant in adjectives ending in **-w** or **-y**.

slow	slow**er**	slow**est**
gray	gray**er**	gray**est**

24 Spelling Rules for Adverbs Ending in -ly

1 Add **-ly** to the corresponding adjective.

nice	nice**ly**
quiet	quiet**ly**
beautiful	beautiful**ly**

EXCEPTION:

true	tru**ly**

2 If the adjective ends in **consonant + y**, change the **y** to **i** before adding **-ly**.

easy	eas**ily**

3 If the adjective ends in **-le**, drop the **e** and add **-y**.

possible	possibl**y**

4 If the adjective ends in **-ic**, add **-ally**.

basic	basic**ally**
fantastic	fantastic**ally**

25 Spelling Rules for Regular Plural Nouns

1 Add **-s** to most nouns.

book	book**s**
table	table**s**
cup	cup**s**

2 Add **-es** to nouns that end in **-ch**, **-s**, **-sh**, or **-x**.

watch	watch**es**
bus	bus**es**
dish	dish**es**
box	box**es**

3 Add **-s** to nouns that end in **vowel + y**.

day	day**s**
key	key**s**

4 Change the **y** to **i** and add **-es** to nouns that end in **consonant + y**.

baby	bab**ies**
city	cit**ies**
strawberry	strawberr**ies**

5 Add **-s** to nouns that end in **vowel + o**.

radio	radio**s**
video	video**s**
zoo	zoo**s**

6 Add **-es** to nouns that end in **consonant + o**.

potato	potato**es**
tomato	tomato**es**

EXCEPTIONS:

kilo	kilo**s**
photo	photo**s**
piano	piano**s**

26 Contractions with Verb Forms

1 SIMPLE PRESENT, PRESENT PROGRESSIVE, AND IMPERATIVE

Contractions with *Be*

I am	=	I'm
you are	=	you're
he is	=	he's
she is	=	she's
it is	=	it's
we are	=	we're
you are	=	you're
they are	=	they're

I am not	=	I'm not		
you are not	=	you're not	or	you aren't
he is not	=	he's not	or	he isn't
she is not	=	she's not	or	she isn't
it is not	=	it's not	or	it isn't
we are not	=	we're not	or	we aren't
you are not	=	you're not	or	you aren't
they are not	=	they're not	or	they aren't

Contractions with *Do*

do not	=	don't
does not	=	doesn't

Simple Present	Present Progressive
I'm a student.	I'm studying here.
He's my teacher.	He's teaching verbs.
We're from Canada.	We're living here.

Simple Present	Present Progressive
She's not sick.	She's not reading.
He isn't late.	He isn't coming.
We aren't twins.	We aren't leaving.
They're not here.	They're not playing.

Simple Present	Imperative
They don't live here.	Don't run!
It doesn't snow much.	

2 SIMPLE PAST AND PAST PROGRESSIVE

Contractions with *Be*

was not	=	wasn't
were not	=	weren't

Contractions with *Do*

did not	=	didn't

Simple Past	Past Progressive
He wasn't a poet.	He wasn't singing.
They weren't twins.	They weren't sleeping.
We didn't see her.	

3 FUTURE

Contractions with *Will*

I will	=	I'll
you will	=	you'll
he will	=	he'll
she will	=	she'll
it will	=	it'll
we will	=	we'll
you will	=	you'll
they will	=	they'll

will not	=	won't

Future with *Will*
I'll take the train.
It'll be faster that way.
We'll go together.
He won't come with us.
They won't miss the train.

Contractions with *Be going to*

I am going to	=	I'm going to
you are going to	=	you're going to
he is going to	=	he's going to
she is going to	=	she's going to
it is going to	=	it's going to
we are going to	=	we're going to
you are going to	=	you're going to
they are going to	=	they're going to

Future with *Be going to*
I'm going to buy tickets tomorrow.
She's going to call you.
It's going to rain soon.
We're going to drive to Boston.
They're going to crash!

4 PRESENT PERFECT AND PRESENT PERFECT PROGRESSIVE

Contractions with *Have*

I have	=	I**'ve**
you have	=	you**'ve**
he has	=	he**'s**
she has	=	she**'s**
it has	=	it**'s**
we have	=	we**'ve**
you have	=	you**'ve**
they have	=	they**'ve**
have not	=	**haven't**
has not	=	**hasn't**

> You**'ve** already **read** that page.
> We**'ve been writing** for an hour.
> She**'s been** to Africa three times.
> It**'s been raining** since yesterday.
> We **haven't seen** any elephants yet.
> They **haven't been living** here long.

5 MODALS AND SIMILAR EXPRESSIONS

cannot **or** can not	=	**can't**
could not	=	**couldn't**
should not	=	**shouldn't**
had better	=	**'d better**
would prefer	=	**'d prefer**
would rather	=	**'d rather**

> She **can't dance**.
> We **shouldn't go**.
> They**'d better decide**.
> I**'d prefer** coffee.
> I**'d rather take** the bus.

27 Capitalization and Punctuation Rules

	USE FOR . . .	EXAMPLES
capital letter	• the first-person pronoun *I*	Tomorrow **I** will be here at 2:00.
	• proper nouns	His name is **Karl**. He lives in **Germany**.
	• the first word of a sentence	**When** does the train leave? **At** 2:00.
apostrophe (')	• possessive nouns	Is that **Marta's** coat?
	• contractions	**That's** not hers. **It's** mine.
comma (,)	• after items in a list	He bought **apples, pears, oranges,** and **bananas**.
	• before sentence connectors *and*, *but*, *or*, and *so*	They watched TV**, and** she played video games.
	• after the first part of a sentence that begins with *because*	***Because*** it's raining**,** we're not walking to the office.
	• after the first part of a sentence that begins with a preposition	***Across from*** the post office**,** there's a good restaurant.
	• after the first part of a sentence that begins with a time clause or an *if* clause	***After*** he arrived**,** we ate dinner. ***If*** it rains**,** we won't go.
exclamation mark (!)	• at the end of a sentence to show surprise or a strong feeling	You're here**!** That's great**!** Stop**!** A car is coming**!**
period (.)	• at the end of a statement	Today is Wednesday**.**
question mark (?)	• at the end of a question	What day is today**?**

28 Pronunciation Table

A|01 These are the pronunciation symbols used in this text. Listen to the pronunciation of the key words.

	VOWELS				CONSONANTS		
SYMBOL	**KEY WORD**	**SYMBOL**	**KEY WORD**	**SYMBOL**	**KEY WORD**	**SYMBOL**	**KEY WORD**
i	beat, feed	ə	banana, among	p	**p**ack, ha**pp**y	z	**z**ip, plea**s**e, goe**s**
ɪ	bit, did	ɚ	shirt, murder	b	**b**ack, ru**bb**er	ʃ	**sh**ip, ma**ch**ine, sta**ti**on,
eɪ	date, paid	aɪ	bite, cry, buy, eye	t	**t**ie		spe**ci**al, discu**ss**ion
ɛ	bet, bed	aʊ	about, how	d	**d**ie	ʒ	mea**s**ure, vi**s**ion
æ	bat, bad	ɔɪ	voice, boy	k	**c**ame, **k**ey, **qu**ick	h	**h**ot, **wh**o
ɑ	box, odd, father	ɪr	beer	g	**g**ame, **g**uest	m	**m**en
ɔ	bought, dog	ɛr	bare	ʧ	**ch**urch, na**t**ure, wa**tch**	n	su**n**, **kn**ow, **pn**eumonia
oʊ	boat, road	ɑr	bar	ʤ	**j**udge, **g**eneral, ma**j**or	ŋ	su**ng**, ri**ng**ing
ʊ	book, good	ɔr	door	f	**f**an, **ph**otograph	w	**w**et, **wh**ite
u	boot, food, student	ʊr	tour	v	**v**an	l	**l**ight, **l**ong
ʌ	but, mud, mother			θ	**th**ing, brea**th**	r	**r**ight, **wr**ong
				ð	**th**en, brea**the**	y	**y**es, **u**se, m**u**sic
				s	**s**ip, **c**ity, p**s**ychology	t̬	bu**tt**er, bo**tt**le

29 Pronunciation Rules for the Simple Present: Third-Person Singular (*He, She, It*)

1 The third-person singular in the simple present always ends in the letter *-s*. There are, however, three different pronunciations for the final sound of the third-person singular.

/s/	/z/	/ɪz/
talk**s**	love**s**	danc**es**

2 The final sound is pronounced /s/ after the voiceless sounds /p/, /t/, /k/, and /f/.

top	top**s**
get	get**s**
take	take**s**
laugh	lau**ghs**

3 The final sound is pronounced /z/ after the voiced sounds /b/, /d/, /g/, /v/, /m/, /n/, /ŋ/, /l/, /r/, and /ð/.

describe	descri**bes**
spend	spen**ds**
hug	hu**gs**
live	live**s**
seem	seem**s**
remain	remain**s**
sing	sin**gs**
tell	tel**ls**
lower	lower**s**
bathe	bat**hes**

4 The final sound is pronounced /z/ after all **vowel sounds**.

agree	agr**ees**
try	tr**ies**
stay	sta**ys**
know	kn**ows**

5 The final sound is pronounced /ɪz/ after the sounds /s/, /z/, /ʃ/, /ʒ/, /ʧ/, and /ʤ/. /ɪz/ adds a syllable to the verb.

miss	mi**sses**
freeze	free**zes**
rush	ru**shes**
massage	massa**ges**
watch	wat**ches**
judge	ju**dges**

6 *Do* and *say* have a change in vowel sound.

do /du/	does /dʌz/
say /seɪ/	says /sɛz/

30 Pronunciation Rules for the Simple Past and Past Participle of Regular Verbs

1 The regular simple past and past participle always end in the letter *-d*. There are three different pronunciations for the final sound of the regular simple past and past participle.

/t/	/d/	/ɪd/
raced	lived	attended

2 The final sound is pronounced /t/ after the voiceless sounds /p/, /k/, /f/, /s/, /ʃ/, and /tʃ/.

hop	hop**ped**
work	wor**ked**
laugh	lau**ghed**
address	addre**ssed**
publish	publi**shed**
watch	wa**tched**

3 The final sound is pronounced /d/ after the voiced sounds /b/, /g/, /v/, /z/, /ʒ/, /dʒ/, /m/, /n/, /ŋ/, /l/, /r/, and /ð/.

rub	ru**bbed**
hug	hu**gged**
live	li**ved**
surprise	surpri**sed**
massage	massa**ged**
change	chan**ged**
rhyme	rhy**med**
return	retur**ned**
bang	ba**nged**
enroll	enro**lled**
appear	appea**red**
bathe	ba**thed**

4 The final sound is pronounced /d/ after all **vowel sounds**.

agree	agr**eed**
die	di**ed**
play	pla**yed**
enjoy	enj**oyed**
snow	sn**owed**

5 The final sound is pronounced /ɪd/ after /t/ and /d/. /ɪd/ adds a syllable to the verb.

start	star**ted**
decide	deci**ded**

Glossary of Grammar Terms

action verb A verb that describes an action.

> Alicia **ran** home.

adjective A word that describes a noun or pronoun.

> That's a **great** idea.
> It's **wonderful**.

adverb A word that describes a verb, an adjective, or another adverb.

> She drives **carefully**.
> She's a **very** good driver.
> She drives **really** well.

adverb of frequency An adverb that describes how often something happens.

> We **always** watch that program.

adverb of manner An adverb that describes how someone does something or how something happens. It usually ends in -*ly*.

> He sings **beautifully**.

adverb of time An adverb that describes when something happens.

> We'll see you **soon**.

affirmative A statement or answer meaning *Yes*.

> He **works**. *(affirmative statement)*
> **Yes**, he **does**. *(affirmative short answer)*

article A word that goes before a noun.
The indefinite articles are *a* and *an*.

> I ate **a** sandwich and **an** apple.

The definite article is *the*.

> I didn't like **the** sandwich. **The** apple was good.

auxiliary verb (also called **helping verb**) A verb used with a main verb. *Be*, *do*, and *have* are often auxiliary verbs. Modals (*can, should, may . . .*) are also auxiliary verbs.

> I **am** exercising right now.
> **Does** he exercise every day?
> She **should** exercise every day.
> They**'ve** learned how to swim.
> They **can** swim very well.
> We **may** go to the pool tomorrow.

base form The simple form of a verb without any endings (-*s*, -*ed*, -*ing*) or other changes.

> **be**, **have**, **go**, **drive**

capital letter The large form of a letter. The capital letters are: *A, B, C, D, . . .*

> **A**licia lives in the **U**nited **S**tates.

clause A group of words that has a subject and a verb. A sentence can have one or more clauses.

> **We are leaving now.** *(one clause)*
> **When he calls, we'll leave.** *(two clauses)*

common noun A word for a person, place, or thing (but not the name of the person, place, or thing).

> Teresa lives in a **house** near the **beach**.

comparative The form of an adjective or adverb that shows the difference between two people, places, or things.

> Alain is **shorter** than Brendan. *(adjective)*
> Brendan runs **faster** than Alain. *(adverb)*

comparison A statement that shows the difference between two people, places, or things. A comparison can use comparative adjectives and comparative adverbs. It can also use *as . . . as*.

> Alain is **shorter than** Brendan.
> Alain isn't **as tall as** Brendan.
> He runs **faster than** Brendan.

consonant A letter of the alphabet. The consonants are:

> **b, c, d, f, g, h, j, k, l, m, n, p, q, r, s, t, v, w, x, y, z**

continuous See **progressive**.

contraction A short form of a word or words. An apostrophe (') replaces the missing letter or letters.

> **she's** = she is
> **hasn't** = has not
> **can't** = cannot
> **won't** = will not

count noun A noun that you can count. It has a singular and a plural form.

> one **book**, two **books**

definite article *the*

This article goes before a noun that refers to a specific person, place, or thing.

> Please bring me **the book** on the table. I'm almost finished reading it.

dependent clause (also called **subordinate clause**) A clause that needs a main clause for its meaning.

> **When I get home**, I'll call you.

direct object A noun or pronoun that receives the action of a verb.

> Marta kicked **the ball**. I saw **her**.

formal Language used in business situations or with adults you do not know.

> Good afternoon, Mr. Rivera. Please have a seat.

gerund A noun formed with verb + *-ing*. It can be the subject or object of a sentence.

> **Swimming** is great exercise.
> I enjoy **swimming**.

helping verb See **auxiliary verb**.

imperative A sentence that gives a command or instructions.

> **Hurry!**
> **Don't touch that!**

indefinite article *a* or *an*

These articles go before a noun that does not refer to a specific person, place, or thing.

> Can you bring me **a book**? I'm looking for something to read.

indefinite past Past time, but not a specific time. It is often used with the present perfect.

> **I've** already **seen** that movie.

indefinite pronoun A pronoun such as *someone, something, anyone, anything, anywhere, no one, nothing, nowhere, everyone,* and *everything*. An indefinite pronoun does not refer to a specific person, place, or thing.

> **Someone** called you last night.
> Did **anything** happen?

indirect object A noun or pronoun (often a person) that receives something as the result of the action of the verb.

> I told **John** the story.
> He gave **me** some good advice.

infinitive *to* + base form of the verb

> I want **to leave** now.

infinitive of purpose *(in order) to* + base form

This form gives the reason for an action.

> I go to school **(in order) to learn** English.

informal Language used with family, friends, and children.

> Hi, Pete. Sit down.

information question See *wh-* **question**.

inseparable phrasal verb A phrasal verb whose parts must stay together.

> We **ran into** Tomás at the supermarket.

intransitive verb A verb that does not have an object.

> We **fell**.

irregular A word that does not change its form in the usual way.

> **good** → **well**
> **bad** → **worse**

irregular verb A verb that does not form its past with *-ed*.

> **leave** → **left**

main clause A clause that can stand alone as a sentence.

> When I get home, **I'll call you**.

main verb A verb that describes an action or state. It is often used with an auxiliary verb.

> She **calls** every day.
> Jared is **calling**.
> He'll **call** again later.
> Does he **call** every day?

modal A type of auxiliary verb. It goes before a main verb or stands alone as a short answer. It expresses ideas such as ability, advice, obligation, permission, and possibility. *Can, could, will, would, may, might, should, ought to,* and *must* are modals.

Can you swim?
Yes, I **can**.
You really **should** learn to swim.

negative A statement or answer meaning *No.*

He **doesn't** work. *(negative statement)*
No, he **doesn't**. *(negative short answer)*

non-action verb (also called **stative verb**) A verb that does not describe an action. It describes such things as thoughts, feelings, and senses.

I **remember** that word.
Chris **loves** ice cream.
It **tastes** great.

non-count noun A noun that you usually do not count (*air, water, rice, love, . . .*). It has only a singular form.

The **rice** is delicious.

noun A word for a person, place, or thing.

My **sister**, **Anne**, works in an **office**.
She uses a **computer**.

object A noun or pronoun that receives the action of a verb. Sometimes a verb has two objects.

She wrote **a letter to Tom**.
She wrote **him a letter**.

object pronoun A pronoun (*me, you, him, her, it, us, them*) that receives the action of a verb.

I gave **her** a book.
I gave **it** to **her**.

paragraph A group of sentences, usually about one topic.

participial adjective An adjective that ends in *-ing* or *-ed*. It comes from a verb.

That's an **interesting** book.
She's **interested** in the book.

particle A word that looks like a preposition and combines with a main verb to form a phrasal verb. It often changes the meaning of the main verb.

He looked the word **up**.
    (He looked for the meaning in the dictionary.)
I ran **into** my teacher.
    (I met my teacher accidentally.)

past participle A verb form (verb + *-ed*). It can also be irregular. It is used to form the present perfect. It can also be an adjective.

We've **lived** here since April.
She's **interested** in math.

phrasal verb (also called **two-word verb**) A verb that has two parts (verb + particle). The meaning is often different from the meaning of its separate parts.

He **grew up** in Texas. *(became an adult)*
His parents **brought** him **up** to be honest. *(raised)*

phrase A group of words that forms a unit but does not have a main verb. Many phrases give information about time or place.

Last year, we were living **in Canada**.

plural A form that means two or more.

There **are** three **people** in the restaurant.
They are eating dinner.
We saw **them**.

possessive Nouns, pronouns, or adjectives that show a relationship or show that someone owns something.

Zach is **Megan's** brother. *(possessive noun)*
Is that car **his**? *(possessive pronoun)*
That's **his** car. *(possessive adjective)*

predicate The part of a sentence that has the main verb. It tells what the subject is doing or describes the subject.

My sister **works for a travel agency**.

preposition A word that goes before a noun or a pronoun to show time, place, or direction.

I went **to** the bank **on** Monday. It's **next to** my office.
I told him **about** it.

Prepositions also go before nouns, pronouns, and gerunds in expressions with verbs and adjectives.

We rely **on** him.
She's accustomed **to** getting up early.

progressive (also called **continuous**) The verb form *be* + verb + *-ing*. It focuses on the continuation (not the completion) of an action.

> She**'s reading** the paper.
> We **were watching** TV when you called.

pronoun A word used in place of a noun.

> That's my brother. You met **him** at my party.

proper noun A noun that is the name of a person, place, or thing. It begins with a capital letter.

> **Maria** goes to **Central High School**.
> It's on **High Street**.

punctuation Marks used in writing (period, comma, . . .). They make the meaning clear. For example, a period (.) shows the end of a sentence. It also shows that the sentence is a statement, not a question.

quantifier A word or phrase that shows an amount (but not an exact amount). It often comes before a noun.

> Josh bought **a lot of** books last year, but he only read **a few**.
> He doesn't have **much** time.

question See *yes/no* **question** and *wh-* **question**.

question word See *wh-* **word**.

reciprocal pronoun A pronoun (*each other* or *one another*) that shows that the subject and object of a sentence refer to the same people and that these people have a two-way relationship.

> Megan and Jason have known **each other** since high school.
> All the students worked with **one another** on the project.

reflexive pronoun A pronoun (*myself, yourself, himself, herself, itself, ourselves, yourselves, themselves*) that shows that the subject and the object of the sentence refer to the same people or things.

> He looked at **himself** in the mirror.
> They enjoyed **themselves** at the party.

regular A word that changes its form in the usual way.

> **play** ➡ play**ed**
> **fast** ➡ fast**er**
> **quick** ➡ quick**ly**

sentence A group of words that has a subject and a main verb. It begins with a capital letter and ends with a period (.), question mark (?), or exclamation point (!).

> **Computers are** very useful.

EXCEPTION: In imperative sentences, the subject is *you*. We do not usually say or write the subject in imperative sentences.

> **Call** her now!

separable phrasal verb A phrasal verb whose parts can separate.

> Tom **looked** the word **up** in a dictionary.
> He **looked** it **up**.

short answer An answer to a *yes/no* question.

> A: Did you call me last night?
> B: **No, I didn't.** or **No.**

singular one

> They have **a sister**.
> **She** works in **a hospital**.

statement A sentence that gives information. In writing, it ends in a period.

> Today is Monday**.**

stative verb See **non-action verb**.

subject The person, place, or thing that the sentence is about.

> **Ms. Chen** teaches English.
> **Her class** is interesting.

subject pronoun A pronoun that shows the person or thing (*I, you, he, she, it, we, they*) that the sentence is about.

> **I** read a lot.
> **She** reads a lot too.

subordinate clause See **dependent clause**.

superlative The form of an adjective or adverb that is used to compare a person, place, or thing to a group of people, places, or things.

> Cindi is **the best** dancer in the group. *(adjective)*
> She dances **the most gracefully**. *(adverb)*

tense The form of a verb that shows the time of the action.

> **simple present:** Fabio **talks** to his friend every day.

> **simple past:** Fabio **talked** to his teacher yesterday.

third-person singular The pronouns *he*, *she*, and *it* or a singular noun. In the simple present, the third-person-singular verb ends in *-s*.

> **Tomás works** in an office. *(Tomás = he)*

time clause A clause that begins with a time word such as *when*, *before*, *after*, *while*, or *as soon as*.

> I'll call you **when I get home**.

time expression A phrase that describes when something happened or will happen.

> We saw Tomás **last week**.
> He'll graduate **next year**.

transitive verb A verb that has an object.

> She **paints** beautiful pictures.

two-word verb See **phrasal verb**.

verb A word that describes what the subject of the sentence does, thinks, feels, senses, or owns.

> They **run** two miles every day.
> I **agree** with you.
> She **loved** that movie.
> We **smell** smoke.
> He **has** a new camera.

vowel A letter of the alphabet. The vowels are:

> **a, e, i, o, u**

wh- question (also called **information question**) A question that begins with a *wh-* word. You answer a *wh-* question with information.

> A: **Where** are you going?
> B: To the store.

wh- word (also called **question word**) A word such as *who*, *what*, *when*, *where*, *which*, *why*, *how*, and *how much*. It often begins a *wh-* question.

> **Who** is that?
> **What** did you see?
> **When** does the movie usually start?
> **How** long is it?

yes/no question A question that begins with a form of *be* or an auxiliary verb. You can answer a *yes/no* question with *yes* or *no*.

> A: **Are** you a student?
> B: **Yes**, I am. **or No**, I'm not.
> A: **Do** you come here often?
> B: **Yes**, I do. **or No**, I don't.

Unit Review Answer Key

UNIT 1

A
1. are you taking
2. I don't
3. often speak
4. He's talking
5. Do

B
1. are...doing
2. 'm...playing
3. Do...want
4. don't eat
5. 'm feeling or feel
6. looks
7. doesn't taste
8. are...shouting
9. Are
10. talk

C

I live in Qatar, but right now I ~~stay~~ *'m staying* in Wisconsin. I'm studying English here. I ~~have~~ *'m having* a good time this summer, but in some ways it's a pretty strange experience. Summer in Wisconsin ~~feel~~ *feels* like winter in Qatar! Every weekend, I go to the beach with some classmates, but I ~~go never~~ *never go* into the water—it's too cold! I'm ~~enjoy~~ *enjoying* my time here though, and my culture shock is going away fast.

UNIT 2

A
1. b
2. c
3. a
4. c
5. a
6. c

B
1. called
2. didn't answer
3. Did...go
4. Yes...did
5. went
6. did...see
7. saw
8. didn't like

C

The poet Elizabeth Alexander was born in New York City, but she didn't ~~grew~~ *grow* up there. Her father ~~taked~~ *took* a job with the government, and her family moved to Washington, D.C. As a child, she ~~have~~ *had* a loving family. Her parents were active in the civil rights movement, and Alexander ~~gots~~ *got* interested in African-American history. In her first book, she wrote about important African leaders. She met Barack Obama at the University of Chicago. They both ~~teached~~ *taught* there in the 1990s. On January 20, 2009, she ~~reads~~ *read* a poem at President Obama's inauguration.

UNIT 3

A
1. Did...hear
2. saw
3. turned
4. Were...driving or Did...drive
5. was working
6. was raining
7. was finishing
8. was leaving or left
9. stopped
10. looked

B
1. ...Danielle was watching TV, I was studying
2. I closed my book...the show *Dr. Davis* came on
3. Dr. Davis was talking to his patient...the electricity went off
4. ...the electricity went off, we lit some candles
5. We were talking (or We talked) about a lot of things...we were waiting for the lights to come on

C

When I turned on the TV for the first episode of *Dr. Davis*, I ~~unpacked~~ *was unpacking* boxes in my freshman dorm room. I stopped and watched for an hour. After that, I ~~wasn't missing~~ *didn't miss* a single show while I was attending school. While I was solving math problems, Dr. Davis was solving medical mysteries. And *just* ~~while~~ *when* my dumb boyfriend broke up with me, the beautiful Dr. Grace left Davis for the third time. I even watched the show from the hospital when I ~~was breaking~~ *broke* my leg. The show just ended. I was sad when I ~~see~~ *saw* the last episode, but I think it's time for some real life!

UNIT 4

A
1. did
2. used to
3. Did
4. play
5. used to
6. used to

B
1. a. used to look
   b. used to have
   c. used to wear
   d. wouldn't get
2. a. used to play
   b. would practice
   c. Did...use(d) to go
   d. used to love

C
1. As a little girl, Yi Ling ~~would~~ *used to* live in Singapore.
2. In 1998, her family ~~used to move~~ *moved* to England.
3. Singapore used to ~~being~~ *be* a part of Malaysia. Today, it is a separate country.

4. The Singapore River used to ~~had~~ *have* hundreds of small

   boats on it.

5. The water ~~would~~ *used to* be very dirty.

6. In the past, flights from England to Singapore
   would ~~took~~ *take* several days. Planes used to make

   many stops to refuel.

UNIT 5

A 1. h   3. f   5. g   7. c
   2. d   4. a   6. e   8. b

B 1. work   5. start
   2. did she   6. is her boss
   3. told   7. does
   4. did she leave

C A: What did you ~~did~~ *do* with my law book? I can't find it.

   B: Nothing. Where ~~you saw~~ *did you see* it last?

   A: In the living room. I was watching *Judge Judy* on
      TV. ~~What~~ *What's* Zack's phone number?

   B: I'm not sure. ~~Why you~~ *Why do you* want to know?

   A: He took the class last year. I'll call him. Maybe he

      still has his book.

   B: Good idea. What time does he ~~gets~~ *get* out of work?

UNIT 6

A 1. We're going   4. is giving
   2. I'll meet   5. is going to fall
   3. It's going to rain

B 1. does…leave or will…leave or is…leaving
      or is…going to leave
   2. 're going to feel or you'll feel
   3. is going to land or will land or lands
   4. is going to get
   5. 'll pay or I'm paying or I'm going to pay
   6. 's going to rain
   7. does…start or will…start or is…starting
      or is…going to start
   8. Is…going to call or Will…call or Is…calling
   9. won't forget or isn't going to forget
   10. 'll speak

C 1. When will Dr. Starr ~~gets~~ *get* home tomorrow?
   2. His lecture starts at 7:00, so I think I ~~go~~. *'ll go* or *'m going to go*
   3. Do you want to go with me, or are you ~~study~~ *studying* or *going to study*

      tonight?

4. What ~~you are~~ *are you* going to do next weekend?
5. I'm ~~going~~ *going to* be home all day.

UNIT 7

A 1. graduate   5. learning
   2. finish   6. until
   3. When   7. Are you
   4. Will

B 1. works or 's working
   2. won't register or isn't going to register
   3. 'll spend or 's going to spend
   4. studies or is studying
   5. won't look or isn't going to look
   6. graduates
   7. 'll take or 's going to take

C A: Are you going to call Phil when ~~we'll finish~~ *we finish* dinner?

   B: No, I'm too tired. I'm just going to watch TV ~~after~~ *before*
      I go to sleep.

   A: Before I wash the dishes, I'm ~~going~~ *going to* answer some

      emails.

   B: I'll help you as soon as ~~I'll drink~~ *I drink* my coffee.

   A: No rush. I have a lot of emails. I won't be ready to
      clean up until ~~you'll finish~~ *you finish*.

UNIT 8

A 1. for   5. Since
   2. since   6. For
   3. for   7. Since
   4. for

B 1. 've been   4. 've competed
   2. haven't had   5. 's won
   3. has loved   6. haven't seen

C 1. Marta and Tomás ~~lived~~ *have lived* here since they got married

      in 2013.

   2. Tomás has been a professional tennis player since
      he ~~has come~~ *came* to this country.

   3. He has won several competitions ~~for~~ *since* then.

   4. Since I have known Tomás, he ~~had~~ *has had* three different

      coaches.

   5. I haven't ~~see~~ *seen* Marta for several weeks.

   6. She ~~have~~ *has* been in Brazil since April 1.

   7. I've wanted to visit Brazil ~~since~~ *for* years, but I haven't

      had any vacation time since I got this new job.

A
1. already
2. still
3. yet
4. Has
5. told
6. yet

B
1. a. has already graduated **or** has graduated already
   b. still haven't had
2. a. Have…delivered…yet
   b. still hasn't set
   c. 's already started **or** 's started already
3. a. still haven't arrived
   b. has arrived yet
   c. have…met…yet

C
A: I can't believe it's the 10th already. And we still
   haven't
   ~~didn't~~ finished planning.

B: We haven't checked the guest list for a while. Who
   replied
   hasn't ~~replies~~ yet?

A: Sally hasn't called about the invitation ~~already~~. I
   yet
   wonder if she's coming.

B: Maybe she just forgot. Have you called ~~yet her~~?
   her yet

A: I've already ~~call~~ her a couple of times. She hasn't
   called
   called back ~~still~~. **or** She hasn't called back ~~still~~.
   yet   *still*

A
1. ever
2. just
3. been
4. Has
5. lately
6. has

B
1. Have…seen
2. 've…been
3. has…read
4. 's given
5. 've…wanted
6. has taken
7. 's…shown

C
1. I've ~~lately~~ traveled a lot.
   lately
2. We've ~~returned just~~ from an African safari.
   just returned
3. I've never ~~have~~ so much fun before.
   had
4. Have you ~~been ever~~ on a safari?
   ever been
5. No, but I've recently ~~went~~ hot-air ballooning.
   gone **or** *been*
6. My wife and I ~~has~~ decided to go next summer.
   have
7. I've ~~saw~~ a lot of great photos on a hot-air
   seen
   ballooning website.

A
1. When did you move to Vancouver?
2. How long have you been an engineer?
3. Did you work in Vancouver for a long time?
4. When did you get married?
5. How many years have you lived in Singapore?
6. Has your wife lived in Singapore long?

B
1. 've been
2. saw
3. 've crossed
4. haven't seen
5. took
6. was
7. has learned
8. ordered
9. didn't learn

C Tina and Ken lived apart for a while, but then Tina
   moved
found a job in Singapore. She ~~has moved~~ there last

month. Here are some of their thoughts:

KEN: I'm so glad Tina is finally here. Last year
   was
   ~~has been~~ the hardest time of my life.

TINA: Before I got here, I didn't ~~understood~~ Ken's
   understand
   I've been
   experiences. But ~~I was~~ in culture shock since I
   arrived
   ~~arrive~~. Now I know what a difficult time Ken

   had at first. But he never gave up.

A
1. has written
2. has been writing
3. I've been reading
4. has read
5. I've had
6. I've been taking

B
1. a. have…lived (**or** been living)
   b. 've been
   c. 've been enjoying
2. a. Have…read
   b. has…written
3. a. 've been trying
   b. 've been studying
4. a. has…been
   b. Has…chosen

C
1. Janet hasn't ~~been writing~~ a word since she sat
   written

   down at her computer.
2. Since I've known Dan, he's ~~been having~~ five
   had

   different jobs.
3. I've ~~drunk~~ coffee all morning. I think I've
   been drinking
   ~~been having~~ at least 10 cups!
   had
4. We've ~~been lived~~ here for several years, but we're
   been living **or** *lived*

   moving next month.

UNIT 13

A 1. speak   4. can't
2. was able to   5. couldn't
3. will be able to

B 1. could speak **or** was able to speak
2. was able to win
3. can speak **or** is able to speak
4. can't write **or** isn't able to write
5. 'll be able to improve **or** can improve
6. can travel **or** will be able to travel
7. can't afford **or** isn't able to afford
8. will be able to make **or** can make
9. could communicate **or** was able to communicate
10. can visit **or** will be able to visit

C A: I can't ~~to see~~ *see* the board. The guy in front of me is
  very tall.
  B: Let's change seats. ~~You be~~ *You'll be* able to see from
  this seat.
  A: Thanks. I don't want to miss anything. I ~~no can~~ *can't*
  believe what a great teacher Ms. Acosta is.
  B: I know. My sister had her last semester. She ~~could~~ *was able to*
  get an A on her final exam!
  A: ~~Were~~ *Was* your sister able to speak any Spanish before
  taking that class?
  B: No. She couldn't speak a word!
  A: That's amazing!

UNIT 14

A 1. come   4. if
2. Do   5. please shut
3. borrow

B 1. I borrow a pen
2. my sister leave
3. I open a window
4. my friend and I (**or** we) come early
5. I ask a question

C 1. A: Do you mind if I ~~changed~~ *change* the date of our next
  meeting?
  B: ~~Yes, I do.~~ *Not at all.* **or** *No, I don't.* **or** *No problem.* When would you like to meet?
2. A: Could I ~~calling~~ *call* you tonight?
  B: Sorry, but you ~~couldn't~~ *can't*. I won't be home.

3. A: Mom, ~~I may~~ *may I* have some more ice cream?
  B: No, you ~~mayn't~~ *may not*. You've already had a lot. You'll
  get sick.
4. A: Do you mind if my son ~~turn~~ *turns* on the TV?
  B: ~~Not at all.~~ *Sorry, (but)* I can't study with the TV on.
5. A: Can my sister ~~borrows~~ *borrow* your bike?
  B: Could I ~~letting~~ *let* you know tomorrow?
  A: Sure. No problem.

UNIT 15

A 1. a. turning   3. a. pick
  b. I'm sorry, I can't.   b. I'd be glad to.
2. a. please text
  b. No problem.

B 1. lending me five dollars
2. you drive me to school
3. you (please) explain this sentence to me (please)
4. you carry this suitcase for me
5. you (please) distribute the report (please)
6. walking the dog tonight

C 1. JASON: Hi, Tessa. It's Jason. Could you ~~taking~~ *take* some
  photos of the game today?
  TESSA: Sorry, Jason, but I ~~couldn't~~ *can't*. My camera is
  broken. Maybe Jeri can help.
2. JASON: Hi, Jeri. Would you ~~came~~ *come* to the game
  today? I need someone to take photos.
  JERI: Jason, ~~can~~ *would* you mind calling me back in a
  few minutes? I'm busy right now.
  JASON: Sorry, Jeri, I can't, but I'll email you. Would
  you ~~give me please~~ *please give me* your email address?
  JERI: ~~Not at all.~~ *Sure.* **or** *No problem.* **or** *Of course.* **or** *Certainly.* It's Rainbows@local.net.
3. JERI: Hi, Jason, it's Jeri. I'm sending you those
  photos. ~~You could~~ *Could you* call me when you
  get them?
  JASON: Thanks, Jeri. The photos are great.
  Now, ~~will teach~~ *will you teach* me how to put them on
  Facebook?

UNIT 16

A 1. a 3. a 5. a
  2. c 4. b

B 1. **a.** Should…call 3. **a.** Should…ask
  b. 'd better do **b.** Yes…should
  2. **a.** should…contact 4. **a.** Should…do
  b. ought to call **b.** No…shouldn't
  c. 'd better wait

C 1. Vanessa should ~~gets~~ *get* a new computer. She
  ~~should no~~ *shouldn't* keep her old one.
  2. She'd better not ~~buying~~ *buy* the first one she sees.
  3. She ~~ought~~ *ought to* read reviews before she decides on one.
  4. ~~Ought~~ *Should* she get one online or should she ~~goes~~ *go* to
  a store?

UNIT 17

A 1. a 3. c 5. a
  2. b 4. c

B 1. Music is 4. Clothing shows
  2. photos show 5. Food goes
  3. Money makes

C One night in ~~june~~ *June*, 1,400 ~~Years~~ *years* ago, a volcano
erupted in today's El Salvador and buried a village
of the great Mayan civilization. Archaeologists have
already found many large ~~building~~ *buildings* from this time,
but only a ~~little~~ *few* homes of farmers and workers.
The village of El Ceren contains perfect examples
of ~~a great deal of~~ *many* **or** *a lot of* **or** *a great many* everyday objects. The
archaeologists have found some knives (with ~~foods~~ *food*
still on them), ~~much~~ *many* **or** *a lot of* pots, ~~a lot~~ *a lot of* garden tools, some
fabrics, and a book. On the wall of one room, they
found a few ~~word~~ *words* in an unknown language. There is
still a lot to learn from this time capsule, called "the
~~pompeii~~ *Pompeii* of Latin America."

UNIT 18

A 1. a 3. Ø 5. Some 7. the
  2. a 4. an 6. Ø 8. the

B 1. **a.** the 2. **a.** a
  b. the **b.** a
  c. an

C Yesterday, I downloaded two movies. One
was ~~~~ *a* comedy, the other was ~~a~~ *an* Argentinian thriller.
We watched ~~a~~ *the* comedy first. It was really funny. ~~A~~ *The*
thriller wasn't that good. There wasn't enough action
in it. Tonight, I think I'd rather read ~~the~~ *a* book than
watch a movie. I recently bought ~~the~~ *a* book of fables
and a mystery. I think I'll read ~~a~~ *the* mystery before I go
to sleep.

UNIT 19

A 1. annoying 4. hard
  2. late 5. surprisingly
  3. perfect

B 1. interesting old house
  2. big cheerful yellow kitchen **or** cheerful big
  yellow kitchen
  3. peaceful residential street
  4. nice young international students
  5. didn't seem friendly at all (**or** at all friendly)
  6. charming little Greek restaurant
  7. really beautiful garden
  8. wonderful old round wooden table
  9. decide pretty quickly
  10. rent awfully fast

C The conditions in Parker Dorm are pretty
~~shocked~~ *shocking*. The rooms are ~~terrible~~ *terribly* small, and the
furniture is incredibly ugly. The locks on the doors
don't work ~~good~~ *well*, so your stuff is never ~~safely~~ *safe*. The
dorm counselors are great—they're all really nice,
friendly people—but they can't make up for the
~~badly~~ *bad* conditions.

UNIT 20

A 1. as 4. less
  2. better 5. longer
  3. more 6. the more impatient

B 1. more expensive than 4. more convenient
  2. bigger 5. farther
  3. larger than

C Last night, I had dinner at the new Pasta Place
on the corner of Main Street and Grove. This new
Pasta Place is just as good ~~than~~ *as* the others, and it has
just as many sauces to choose from. No one makes a

better ~~more good~~ traditional tomato sauce ^*than* them. But there

are much ~~interestinger~~ *more interesting* choices. Their mushroom

cream sauce, for example, is as ~~better~~ *good* as I've ever had.

Try the mushroom and tomato sauce for a healthier

~~than~~ meal. It's just as delicious. The new branch is

already popular. The later it is, ~~longer~~ *the longer* the lines. My

recommendation: Go early for a ~~more short~~ *shorter* wait. And

go soon. This place will only get ~~more popular~~ *more* and

more popular!

A 1. the coldest 4. the rainiest
  2. the highest 5. the most expensive
  3. the driest 6. the cheapest

B 1. the worst 5. the most difficult
  2. the most fantastic 6. the best
  3. the most popular 7. the funniest
  4. the most crowded

C Small towns aren't ~~most~~ *the most* dynamic places to visit,

and that's just why we love to vacation on Tangier

Island. This tiny island is probably ~~the less~~ *the least* popular

vacation spot in the United States. Almost no one

comes here. But it's also one of ~~the most safest~~ *the safest*

places to visit. And you'll find some of ~~the goodest~~ *the best*

seafood and ~~the beautiful~~ *the most beautiful* beaches here. It's one of

~~the easy~~ *the easiest* places to get around (there are no cars on

the island). If you get bored, just hop on the ferry.

You're only a few hours from Washington, D.C., and

a few more hours from New York and ~~the excitingest~~ *the most exciting*

nightlife ever.

A 1. well 5. as well
  2. doesn't run 6. the more tired he gets
  3. more accurately 7. harder
  4. of 8. better

B 1. well 4. the hardest
  2. faster 5. the worst
  3. the most accurately

C Last night's game was a very exciting one. The

Globes played the best they've played all season. But

they still didn't play as ~~good~~ *well* as the Stars. The Stars

hit the ball more ~~frequent~~ *frequently* and ran ~~more fast~~ *faster* than the

Globes, and their pitcher, Kevin Rodriguez, threw

the ball more accurately. Their catcher, Scott Harris,

handled ~~better the ball~~ *the ball better* than the Globes' catcher. The

Globes are good, but they are ~~less good than~~ *not as good as* the Stars.

All in all, the Stars just keep playing ~~good~~ *better* and better.

And the better they play, the ~~hardest~~ *harder* it is for their

fans to get tickets! These games sell out quicker than

hotcakes, so go early if you want to get a chance to

see the Stars.

A 1. not liking 5. swimming
  2. smoking 6. not eating
  3. feeling 7. improving
  4. joining

B 1. Laughing is
  2. suggests **or** suggested watching
  3. Telling…helps **or** will help
  4. advises **or** advised against drinking
  5. enjoy taking
  6. think about smoking

C 1. You look great. Buying these bikes ~~were~~ *was* a

   good idea.

  2. I know. I'm happy about ~~lose~~ *losing* weight, too. ~~Didn't~~ *Not*

   exercising was a bad idea.

  3. It always is. Hey, I'm thinking of ~~rent~~ *renting* a movie.
   What do you suggest ~~to see~~ *seeing*?

  4. I've been looking forward to ~~see~~ *seeing* Grown Ups. Have

   you seen it yet?

  5. Not yet. Do you recommend it? You're so good at
   ~~choose~~ *choosing* movies.

A 1. to read 4. to go
  2. to meet 5. to play
  3. to finish 6. to call

B 1. invited Mary to visit us
2. agreed to come
3. wants to make new friends
4. told her to come early
5. decided not to invite Tom
6. needs to finish his project

C 1. **A:** I want ~~invite~~ *to invite* you to my party.
    B: Thanks. I'd love ~~coming~~ *to come*.
2. **A:** I plan ~~to not~~ *not to* get there before 8:00.
    B: Remember ~~getting~~ *to get* the soda. Don't forget!
3. **A:** Sara asked ~~I~~ *me* to help her.
    B: I agreed ~~helping~~ *to help* her, too.
4. **A:** I promised ~~pick up~~ *to pick up* some ice cream.
    B: OK. But let's do it early. I prefer ~~don't~~ *not to* arrive late.

UNIT 25

A 1. get
2. in order not
3. to use
4. too
5. clearly enough

B 1. easy enough to program
2. too hard for me to use
3. too fast for me to understand
4. too far for us to walk
5. to get there by 6:30
6. early enough for us to walk
7. too heavy for us to cross
8. my phone to get directions
9. clearly enough for it to work
10. a taxi to save time

C Is sixteen too young ~~for~~ *to* drive? It's really hard to ~~saying~~ *say*. Some kids are mature enough to drive at sixteen, but some aren't. I think most sixteen-year-olds are still too immature ~~drive~~ *to drive* with friends in the car, though. It's ~~for them easy~~ *easy for them* to forget to pay attention with a lot of kids in the car. In order ~~preventing~~ *to prevent* accidents, some families have a "no friends" rule for the first year. I think that's a reasonable idea. And I think there should be a "no cell phone" rule, too—for talking or texting.

UNIT 26

A 1. starting
2. to finish
3. trying
4. to join
5. seeing
6. to call
7. Studying

B 1. doing
2. to take
3. working **or** to work
4. sitting
5. taking
6. to get
7. studying **or** to study

C I hate clutter. But before now, I wasn't able to prevent it from ~~to happen~~ *happening*. I even put off going home because seeing the mess made me feel bad. Then I remembered recently ~~to read~~ *reading* an interesting magazine article about clutter. I decided ~~trying~~ *to try* one of the recommended tactics. I learned that I need ~~cleaning~~ *to clean* up every night before I go to bed. Just ten minutes can make a big difference. I've stopped ~~to avoid~~ *avoiding* going home now, and I enjoy being in my nice, neat apartment. ~~To clean~~ *Cleaning* up every night isn't always easy, but it's really worth it!

UNIT 27

A 1. me
2. myself
3. each other
4. herself
5. yourselves
6. itself
7. one another
8. myself

B 1. talk to each other
2. greet each other
3. help yourself
4. enjoying themselves
5. drove herself

C When I first met Nicole, I told myself, "I'm not going to like working with ~~herself~~ *her*." Negative self-talk! I was really wrong. Nicole has helped ~~myself~~ *me* out with so many things. When she ~~oneself~~ *herself* didn't know something, she always found out for me. That way, both of ~~ourselves~~ *us* learned something. After I learned the job better, we helped ~~each other's~~ *each other* **or** *one another* out. The job ~~themselves~~ *itself* isn't that challenging, but I'm really enjoying myself. All of us in the office have become good friends. We all like ~~each another~~ *each other* **or** *one another*. That makes it a great place to work. I feel lucky to be here.

A 1. out   4. out
2. up   5. up
3. on   6. over

B 1. Joe gets up early.
2. He turns on the TV. **or** He turns the TV on.
3. He sits down with Ana.
4. They get along well.
5. They look over his schedule. **or** They look his schedule over.
6. They talk it over.
7. They put it away.
8. They put on their coats. **or** They put their coats on.

C As soon as Ina ~~wakes out~~ *wakes up*, she quickly gets dressed, ~~puts off~~ *puts on* her mosquito repellent, and goes out with her classmates into the rain forest. They ~~keep up~~ *keep on* walking until they find what they are looking for—chimpanzees. They've been studying the chimps for weeks. The chimps are really intelligent. They know which plants have medicinal qualities, and which plants don't. Somehow these amazing animals have ~~figured out it~~ *figured it out*!

At the end of each day, Ina and her classmates go back to their camp. It's late, and they're tired. But, before they ~~turn on~~ *turn off* the lights to go to bed, they ~~talk up~~ *talk over* their plans for the next day. Everyone is tired but excited to be doing such interesting work.

A 1. don't have to   4. 've got to
2. Does   5. had
3. can't   6. have

B 1. don't have to do
2. have to pick up **or** 'll have to pick up **or** 're going to have to pick up
3. 've…had to stand
4. don't have to wait **or** won't have to wait **or** aren't going to have to wait
5. can't smoke
6. has to move **or** will have to move **or** is going to have to move
7. can't sit
8. have to have **or** 'll have to have
9. had to eat

C 1. He can't ~~boards~~ *board* the plane yet.
2. Passengers ~~must not~~ *don't have to* stay in their seats when the seat belt light is off.
3. Passengers: Please note that you ~~gotta~~ *have to or must* pay extra for luggage over 50 pounds (23 kg).
4. You don't ~~have got to~~ *have to* show your passport right now, but please have it ready.
5. Paul ~~will has~~ *will have or has* to unpack some of his stuff. His suitcase is much too heavy.

A 1. a   3. c   5. c
2. b   4. a

B 1. a. 're supposed to be
   b. isn't supposed to start
2. a. are…supposed to sit
   b. 're supposed to go
3. a. Was (**or** Am)…supposed to wear
   b. 're (**or** were) supposed to wear
4. a. isn't (**or** wasn't) supposed to rain
   b. was (**or** is) supposed to be

C 1. Dahlia was ~~suppose~~ *supposed* to drive. She was ~~supposed not~~ *not supposed* to fly.
2. She ~~is~~ *was* supposed to wear her blue dress, but she changed her mind.
3. What are we supposed to ~~doing~~ *do* after the ceremony?
4. My parents ~~will~~ *were* supposed to fly home tomorrow, but they're staying another day.
5. It was ~~no~~ *not* supposed to be this cold, and it ~~didn't suppose~~ *wasn't supposed* to rain.

A 1. Will   5. get
2. might   6. could
3. going to   7. Maybe
4. may

B 1. a. Are…going to go
   b. may **or** might **or** could
2. a. Is…going to be
   b. may not (be) **or** might not (be)

3. a. are...going to work

    b. may stay **or** might stay **or** could stay

4. a. may not open **or** might not open

    b. may open **or** might open **or** could open

C   Suddenly, weather forecasts all over the world are predicting terrible storms. Climatologist Jack Hall understands weather trends, and he thinks that a new ice age could ~~to~~ begin *(begin)* very quickly. His son Sam is in New York with his high school class. One student is sick and ~~mayn't~~ *(may not)* live without medicine. ~~May those kids~~ *(Will those kids* **or** *Are those kids going to)* survive by themselves? They ~~maybe~~ *(may* **or** *might)* not. Jack bundles up and starts walking to New York to save them. There ~~might could~~ *(may* **or** *might* **or** *could)* be a happy ending. Or the world could end. You'll have to watch to find out!

UNIT 32

A 1. must   **4.** can't

  2. has got to   **5.** Could

  3. could   **6.** could

B 1. a. couldn't be   **3. a.** Could...lead

    b. could be   **b.** might know

  2. a. could...want

    b. Could...be

    c. can't be

C 1. Jason has been coughing all morning. He might ~~having~~ *(have)* a cold.

  2. Diana must not ~~likes~~ *(like)* fish. She left most of it on her plate.

  3. ~~May~~ *(Could* **or** *Can)* the package be from your parents?

  4. That's impossible! It ~~might not~~ *(couldn't* **or** *can't)* be true.

  5. Is the bank still open? That's a good question. I don't know. It ~~might~~ *(might be)*.

  6. She ~~could~~ *(couldn't* **or** *can't)* be a thief! I trust her completely!

  7. ~~It's got~~ *(It's got to)* be a joke. I don't believe it's serious.

EXERCISE 12 CELEBRITY PROFILE

A INFORMATION GAP Work with a partner. Student B will follow the instructions below. Student A will follow the instructions on page 30.

STUDENT B

- Read the profile of an actor who is also a poet, painter, and musician. Ask your partner questions to complete the missing information.

  EXAMPLE: B: Where was Viggo born?
  A: He was born in New York.

- Answer your partner's questions.

  EXAMPLE: A: When was Viggo born?
  B: He was born on October 20, 1958.

- If you don't know how to spell something, ask your partner.

  EXAMPLE: B: How do you spell New York?
  A: Capital *N*, *e*, *w*, space, capital *Y*, *o*, *r*, *k*.

SCREEN-TIME PROFILE

Viggo Mortensen
actor, poet, painter, musician

Date of Birth: October 20, 1958

Place of Birth: New York

Mini Bio:
- lived in Argentina, Venezuela, and Denmark as a child

- attended school in _____

- learned to speak Spanish

- returned to the United States in 1969

- became a movie actor in 19_____

- first movie was _____

- played the part of Aragorn in *Lord of the Rings* (This movie made him famous.)

- finished his first book of poems in 1993 (The title was *Ten Last Night*.)

- created _____ for the movie *A Perfect Murder* (He played the part of the artist.)

- wrote _____ for *Lord of the Rings*

B When you are finished, compare the profiles. Are they the same?

EXERCISE 7 PARTY CHORES

A INFORMATION GAP Work with a partner. Student B will follow the instructions below. Student A will follow the instructions on page 126.

STUDENT B

- Look at Gisela's "To Do" list. Ask your partner questions to find out which chores Gisela has already done. Check (✓) those chores.

    EXAMPLE: B: Has Gisela vacuumed the carpet yet?
    A: No, she hasn't. **or** No, not yet.

- Look at the picture of the Stangers' kitchen and at Karl's "To Do" list. Check (✓) the chores that Karl has already done. Then answer your partner's questions about Karl's chores.

    EXAMPLE: A: Has Karl bought a memory card yet?
    B: Yes, he has. **or** Yes, he's already gotten one.

To Do: Karl

- ☑ buy memory card for camera
- ☐ bake the cake
- ☐ put the turkey in the oven
- ☐ mop the floor
- ☐ wash the dishes
- ☐ cut up the vegetables

To Do: Gisela

- ☐ vacuum the carpet
- ☑ buy flowers
- ☐ wash the windows
- ☐ set the table
- ☐ hang the balloons
- ☐ wrap the gift

B Now compare lists with your partner. Are they the same?

EXERCISE 10 STORY TIME

A INFORMATION GAP **Work with a partner. Student B will follow the instructions below. Student A will follow the instructions on page 255.**

STUDENT B

- Look at the picture. Answer your partner's questions.

  EXAMPLE: A: Who's the man in the black cape?

  B: He's the magician.

- Ask your partner for the information you need to finish labeling the picture.

  EXAMPLE: B: What's the magician holding?

  A: A magic wand.

- If you don't know how to spell something, ask your partner.

  EXAMPLE: B: How do you spell "wand"?

  A: w, a, n, d

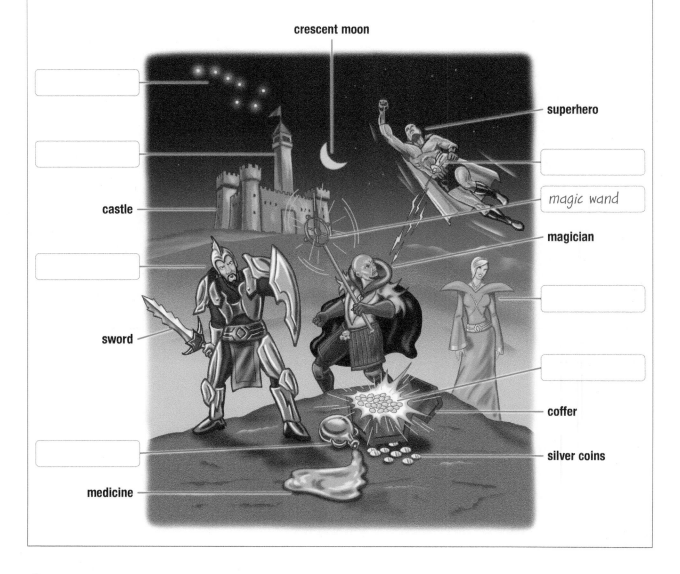

crescent moon

superhero

magic wand

castle

magician

sword

coffer

silver coins

medicine

B When you are finished, compare pictures. Are the labels the same?

EXERCISE 12 AT THE SUPPORT GROUP

A INFORMATION GAP Work with a partner. Student B will follow the instructions below. Student A will follow the instructions on page 365.

STUDENT B

- Look at the picture. Answer your partner's questions.

  EXAMPLE: **A:** What does Eva remember doing?
  B: She remembers meeting Todd.

- Ask your partner questions to complete what people said at the support group meeting.

  EXAMPLE: **B:** What does Todd hope to do?
  A: He hopes to see Eva again.

B Now compare pictures with your partner. Are they the same?

Index

This index is for the full and split editions. All entries are in the full book. Entries for Volume A of the split edition are in black. Entries for Volume B are in blue.